To
Rob
with regards
Ravi
1-6-95

THE STRUCTURED NOTE MARKET

•••••••••

THE DEFINITIVE
GUIDE FOR INVESTORS,
TRADERS & ISSUERS

•••••••••

SCOTT Y. PENG & RAVI E. DATTATREYA

PROBUS PUBLISHING

Chicago, Illinois
Cambridge, England

ISBN 1-55738-826-1

Printed in the United States of America

BB

1 2 3 4 5 6 7 8 9 0

PG

To my parents, Gary and Shirley, and to Julia

Scott Y. Peng

To Srivatsa

Ravi E. Dattatreya

Contents

About the Authors   ix

Acknowledgments   ix

1. INTRODUCTION   1

What Are Structured Notes?   2

Issuers of Structured Notes   4

Investors Who Purchase Structured Notes   9

Structured Note Termsheet   15

Considerations   18

Here We Go   19

2. STRUCTURED NOTE RISK AND PERFORMANCE MEASUREMENT   21

Introduction, Review, and Extension of Duration   22

Structured Note Risk Measurement: A Tale of Two Durations   23

Key Treasury Rate Duration (KTRD)   29

Volatility Risk   39

Structured Note Performance Measurement:
Internal Rate of Return and Present Value   41

Structured Note Purchasing Strategy
and Effect on Analysis Time Horizon   44

Comparison and Benchmarking Performance   44

Conclusion   46

3. **DETERMINISTIC ANALYSIS**   49

   Analysis I. Forward Analysis   50
   Analysis II. Expectation Analysis   59
   Analysis III. Historical Analysis   65
   Conclusion   74

4. **SIMULATION ANALYSIS**   77

   When Should Simulation Analysis Be Used?   78
   Monte Carlo Rate Simulation   79
   Simulation Analysis for a Range of Expectations   86
   Simulation versus Deterministic   93
   Simulation of Two or More Indices   97
   Volatility Duration   98
   Conclusion   99

5. **FIRST GENERATION STRUCTURES**   103

   Analysis of First Generation Structured Notes   104
   Structure I. Floating Rate Note (FRN)   107
   Structure II. Capped and Floored Floating Rate Note   119
   Structure III. Collared Floating Rate Note (CFRN)   145
   Structure IV. Inverse Floating Rate Note (IFRN)   153
   Structure V. Superfloater   162
   Conclusion   168

6. **SECOND GENERATION STRUCTURES**   171

   Analysis of Second Generation Structured Notes   173
   A. Index Maturity to Reset Frequency Mismatch   **174**
   Structure I. Constant Maturity Treasury (CMT) and
   Constant Maturity Swap (CMS) Floating Rate Notes   174
   Structure II. Deleveraged CMT FRN, or the SURF Note   181
   B. Multi-Index Notes   **192**
   Structure III. CMT-LIBOR Differential Notes   192
   Structure IV. Prime-LIBOR Differential Notes   203

C. Exotic Options   209

Structure V. Accrual Notes (Also Known as Range Notes)   210

Structure VI. One-Way Collared (OWC) Note
(Also Known as Ratchet, or Sticky Floater)   220

Structure VII. Index Amortizing Notes   226

D. Quanto Notes   238

Structure VIII. LIBOR Differential (Quanto) Notes   238

E. Unusual Leverage   245

Structure IX. Power Notes   247

Conclusion   254

7. CROSS-CATEGORY NOTES   255

Motivation for Purchasing Cross-Category Notes   255

Cross-Category Structure Classification   258

Structure I. Currency Indexed Note (CIN)   258

Structure II. Commodity Linked Note (CLN)   275

Structure III. Equity Linked Note (ELN)   290

Structure IV. Total Return Index Notes (TRIN)   293

Conclusion   296

8. CREATION AND CUSTOMIZATION
   OF STRUCTURED NOTES   297

I. Conceptual   298

II. Identification   299

III. Structuring or Construction   305

Conclusion   326

9. STRUCTURED NOTES AND PORTFOLIO
   MANAGEMENT   327

Portfolio Management: An Overview   327

Portfolio Risk and Asset/Liability Management (ALM)   333

Role of Structured Notes in Portfolio Management   338

Conclusion   351

10. STRUCTURED NOTES VERSUS CASH AND FUTURES **353**

Introduction 353
Overview of the Futures and Options Market 353
Investor Criteria for Exchange-Traded Products 358
Exchange-Traded Products versus Structured Notes 359
Replicability of Structured Notes via Exchange
and Cash Products 363
Conclusion 366

11. STRUCTURED NOTE VALUATION
IN THE SECONDARY MARKET **367**

Introduction 367
Asset Swap Pricing 367
Straight Pricing 371
Issuer Buyback Pricing 376
Straight Versus Asset Swap Pricing and Some Rules of Thumb 377
Other Secondary Pricing Considerations 378
Conclusion 381

12. LOOKING FORWARD **383**

Regulatory and Legislative Action 383
GAO Report of 1994 384
SEC 385
OCC 385
OTS 386
Federal Reserve 386
Accounting and Disclosure Requirements: FASB 387
Legislative 388
Structural Innovations 390
Looking Forward 393
Summary 393

Index **395**

About the Authors

Scott Y. Peng

Scott Y. Peng is a vice president at Sumitomo Bank Capital Markets, Inc. and head of the structured note desk at SBCM. He received his Ph.D. in Applied Plasma Physics from the Massachusetts Institute of Technology. Subsequent to obtaining his Ph.D., he joined the First Boston Corporation's financial engineering desk and later was a member of the structured products group at Lehman Brothers, Inc.

Ravi E. Dattatreya

Ravi E. Dattatreya is a senior vice president at Sumitomo Bank Capital Markets, Inc. He received his Ph.D. in Operations Research from the University of California at Berkeley, joined Goldman, Sachs & Co., and later became director of the financial strategies group at Prudential-Bache Securities. He is co-author of *Interest Rate and Currency Swaps* (Probus, 1994), *Active Total Return Management of Fixed Income Portfolios* (Probus, 1994), *The Handbook of Derivative Instruments* (Probus, 1991) and *Fixed Income Analytics* (Probus, 1991). He is a member of the editorial advisory board of the *Journal of Portfolio Management*.

Acknowledgments

We thank Akira Kondoh, Kenji Kita, and John Copenhaver of Sumitomo Bank Capital Markets, Inc., New York, and Atsuo Konishi of SBCM (UK) Ltd., London, for providing assistance and for their encouragement throughout this long project. We thank the following for reading early drafts of the book and for their useful comments: Alec Diacou, Miles Draycott, Joyce Frost, Patricia Murnane, and Tim Quinn, all of SBCM, New York.

We acknowledge the help of Tom Ho and Mark Abbott of Global Advanced Technology, Inc., for their candid discussions of linear path space and GAT's simulation technology.

Thanks are also due to Bob Lutey and Philippe Burke of Lehman Brothers, Inc., and Helaine Ayers of Deutsche Bank Financial Products for their insightful comments in the review of the book.

We also thank Leland E. Crabbe of Merrill Lynch Capital Markets for graciously permitting the use of the information on the structured note market he collected while at the Federal Reserve. Much of the structured note market statistics presented in Chapter 1 reflect his work.

Finally, we thank Frank Hsu, now at Chase Securities, and Joe Hanosek of SBCM. Frank performed an admirable job proofreading the manuscript and took on the often unglorious task of running the simulations. Joe was instrumental in every aspect of the preparation of the book from editing, graphics, analytics, simulations, to his many helpful and insightful comments.

Introduction

1

The structured note market has evolved rapidly over the last 10 years. The global volume of new issue structured notes has exploded from zero in 1983 to a notional amount of $100 billion in 1993. Including secondary structured notes, the structured notes market now amounts to over $200 billion (notional) and continues to grow with each new deal. This explosive growth has created a powerful new presence in the fixed income market.

Despite the large notional amount of newly issued and secondary structured notes, the structured note market itself is remarkably secretive. Only a fraction of new issue structured notes are displayed on publicly accessible sources such as Telerate Page 7869 or Reuters Page IIIA. The majority of new issue structured notes are sold to investors in relative obscurity with little or no fanfare. This sets the structured note market apart from the rest of the fixed income market, which heralds each new variant or deal with flashes on Telerate or Reuters, full-page advertisements in the *Wall Street Journal,* and an abundance of lucite tombstones.

This book will examine the most popular structures in recent years and the reasons for their appeal. The structures presented range in sophistication from the simplest floating rate note (FRN) to the most complicated cross-category structures. Investors may be surprised to discover that, in most instances, structured notes contain risks that are comparable to those of fixed rate notes.

Despite the recent bad press about derivatives and structured notes, the fact remains that structured notes offer some real and significant benefits to the investors who understand their behaviors and embedded risks. The primary purpose of this book is to shed some light on this complex and secretive market as well as to provide a standard set of analytic tools that investors can use in assessing the risk and reward associated with structured note investments.

WHAT ARE STRUCTURED NOTES?

Structured notes are fixed income debentures linked to derivatives. They can be issued by corporations, banks, financial institutions, municipals, U.S. Agencies, sovereigns, and supranationals. The maturity of structured notes range from as short as three months to as long as (or longer than) ten years.

A key feature of structured notes is that they are created by an underlying swap transaction. The issuer rarely retains any of the risks embedded in the structured note and is almost always hedged out of the risks of the note by performing a swap transaction with a swap counterparty. This feature permits issuers to produce notes of almost any specification, as long as they are satisfied that the hedging swap will perform for the life of the structured note. To the investor, this swap transaction is totally transparent since the only credit risk to which the investor is exposed is that of the issuer.

Structured notes can take the form of any of the following debentures: commercial paper, bank certificate of deposit, bank note, medium term note (MTN), corporate bond, and even private placements and 144A securities. The seniority of the structured note can be either senior or subordinated. Structured notes are very seldom secured by an underlying asset, relying instead on the underlying ratings of the issuer for its credit rating. The one exception to this statement is the structured repo market, in which securitization does occur. However, within the structured note market itself, few structured notes are credit enhanced as a result of asset securitization.

Growth of the Structured Note Market

The growth of the structured note market has been nothing less than explosive over the past five years. Since most of the structured notes created do not appear on public sources such as Telerate, only estimates of the growth of the market can be made. Recent Federal Reserve estimates of the structured note market are graphed below:

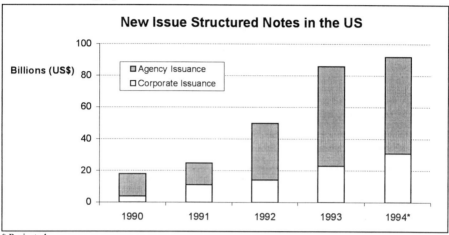

New Issue Structured Notes in the US

* Projected
[Source: Federal Reserve]

This estimate shows a four-fold increase in the volume of new issue structured notes from 1990 through 1994. This growth was unmatched by any other sector of the U.S. fixed income market during that period.

Why Do Investors Purchase Structured Notes?

Given the myriad of investment alternatives, why do investors purchase structured notes? The rapid and explosive growth of the structured note market indicates that structured notes can offer investors considerable benefits that cannot be obtained elsewhere. Some of these benefits are listed below:

1. **Customization.** Structured notes can be customized to fit the unique requirements of individual investors. This ability to provide customized solutions is unique among fixed income products and is one of the main driving forces behind investor purchase of structured notes.
2. **Yield enhancement.** Structured notes permit investors to obtain higher-than-market yields if certain scenarios were to come true.
3. **Exotic payoff.** Structured notes can provide a variety of customized and exotic-type payoffs that cannot be obtained in the fixed income arena.

4. **Risk allocation and diversification.** Structured notes permit investors to obtain exposure to different market sectors by purchasing only one packaged security. Investors can also reallocate capital currently deployed in one asset class into another asset class.

5. **Total return tracking.** Investors who track the total return of a certain index can purchase structured notes to eliminate the index tracking error and simplify portfolio management.

6. **Sole access.** Investors who have difficulty accessing certain market segments are able to access them via structured notes. Thus, an investor who seeks to perform a hedge in another market but who, for certain reasons, cannot transact in that market can purchase a structured note that contains the required hedge.

7. **Liquidity.** Although this has traditionally been the weak component of the structured note market, secondary market liquidity has improved dramatically within the past three years. As will be discussed in greater detail in Chapter 11, many investment and commercial banks have established desks dedicated to the trading of secondary structured notes. This fact, in conjunction with the large volume of outstanding secondary structured notes (currently estimated at over $200 billion and continuously growing with each new deal), have resulted in a greatly enhanced secondary market liquidity.

ISSUERS OF STRUCTURED NOTES

The rapid growth in the volume of new issue structured notes indicates that, in conjunction with the growth of investor interest, many issuers have made structured notes an integral component of their funding mix. The issuer is often able to achieve funding costs that are lower than levels achievable by issuing fixed rate notes. This additional savings is necessary for the issuer to cover extraneous costs associated with issuing structured notes. These include the bookkeeping cost of maintaining a swap with the counterparty, the required reserves against the swap counterparty's credit risk, the legal costs of setting up and maintaining a swap facility, and other costs such as daily positional monitoring and dynamic hedging. Nevertheless, the savings to issuer funding costs are sufficiently large such that many issuers find it advantageous to fund a significant portion of their debt via swapped structured note issuance.

Even though structured notes have been issued since as early as 1985, many investors continue to be uncomfortable taking both interest rate risk as well as credit risk. As a result, most investors prefer structured notes issued by sterling credits such as the supranationals like the World Bank, or U.S. government sponsored enterprises (GSEs, also known as U.S. Agencies) such as the Federal Home Loan Banks. In the United States, the GSEs' share of the structured note market (by notional amount of new issues) in the United States has consistently exceeded 70%.

The bull market of 1990–1994 brought about a rapid maturing of the structured note market. As investors attained a measure of comfort with some of the structures, their credit requirements were lowered in their quest for higher yield. More investors have begun to purchase structured notes issued by household names whose credit ratings may not be AAA, but whose name recognition renders them, in the eyes of the investor, relatively credit-worthy. In terms of the overall notional amount, however, corporate issued structured notes have remained at approximately 30% of the total structured note market. This is due to the fact that Agencies issue a large volume of generic products such as the multi-step-up callable notes.

U.S. Agency Issuers of Structured Notes

As mentioned earlier, U.S. Agencies have commanded the majority of the structured note market by issuing over 70% of all new issues. The five U.S. Agencies that are active issuers of structured notes are: Federal Home Loan Bank (FHLB), Federal National Mortgage Association (FNMA, or Fannie Mae), Student Loan Marketing Association (SLMA, or Sallie Mae), Federal Home Loan Mortgage Corporation (FHLMC, or Freddie Mac), and Federal Farm Credit Banks (FFCB). All five of the above GSEs have the *implicit* guarantee of the U.S. government, and hence all carry, if rated, AAA ratings. Their funding levels are typically more aggressive than comparable AAA corporations since investors willingly pay a premium to obtain the added confidence of the implicit government guarantee.

The U.S. Agency issuers and some of their characteristics are listed in Exhibit 1-1. Although the Agencies are all nominally GSEs, they vary in their sophistication level and funding philosophy. The most popular GSE issuer is the Federal Home Loan Bank, which not only has a low minimum size requirement for new issue structured notes but is willing and able to issue structured notes ranging in complexity from the very simple to the highly complex.

EXHIBIT 1-1 U.S. Agency Issuers of Structured Notes

Despite their status as GSEs, the Agencies are different in their levels of sophistication, funding requirements, and minimum issue size.

Issuer	Minimum Size of New Issue	Comments
FHLB	$15 to $25MM	Most frequent and largest issuer of structured notes. Able and willing to issue almost any structure. Small new issue minimum size requirement makes it a favorite of smaller investors. Minimum size requirement subject to funding requirements of 12 FHLB member banks.
SLMA	$20 to $25MM	Less aggressive in funding requirement versus other Agencies since Clinton Administration threatened to withhold future federal guarantee of SLMA's portfolio of student loans. SLMA's star with investors has dimmed considerably.
FFCB	$50MM	Structured notes issued on a consolidated basis as "Joint and Several Obligations" of entire FFCB System. Will not issue foreign interest rate denominated notes (as of 6/94).
FNMA	$50 to $100MM	Large new issue minimum size requirement makes it not as popular among investors wanting more non-generic structured notes.
FHLMC	$50MM	The last GSE to tap structured note market. Issues mostly step-up callable notes.

FHLB: Federal Home Loan Bank System
SLMA: Student Loan Marketing Association ("Sallie Mae")
FFCB: Federal Farm Credit Bank System
FNMA: Federal National Mortgage Association ("Fannie Mae")
FHLMC: Federal Home Loan Mortgage Corporation ("Freddie Mac")

As summarized in Exhibit 1-2, the tax implications of purchasing GSE debt are quite different for each GSE.[1] The two GSEs whose notes carry tax exemption status are the Federal Home Loan Banks and the Federal Farm Credit Banks. These two GSEs issue debt that is state and local tax exempt and are favored by many investors over other GSEs. None of the five GSEs described here can issue federal tax exempt structured notes.

1. See article by Goodman, Laurie, Judith Johnson, and Andrew Silver, "Federally Sponsored Agency Securities," in Frank J. Fabozzi (ed.), *The Handbook of Fixed Income Securities,* 3rd ed. Homewood, IL: Business One Irwin, 1991, pp. 208–222.

EXHIBIT 1-2 Tax Implications of U.S. Agency Paper

The only two U.S. Agencies whose debt carries state and local tax exempt status are the FHLB and the FFCB. These two GSEs are thus strongly favored as issuers by many investors.

Issuer	Federal	State	Local
FHLB	Not exempt	Exempt	Exempt
FFCB	Not exempt	Exempt	Exempt
FNMA	Not exempt	Not exempt	Not exempt
SLMA	Not exempt	Not exempt	Not exempt
FHLMC	Not exempt	Not exempt	Not exempt

Corporate Issuers of Structured Notes

Corporate issuance of structured notes has dramatically increased in the 1990s. The growth of the structured note market has significantly altered the traditional funding mix of large corporations. Whereas most issuers with medium term note programs previously only issued fixed rate notes off the shelf, many now use MTNs to access the structured note market to both issue debt at good funding levels as well as to reach a new class of investors. As seen below, structured notes' share of the funding mix of corporate MTNs has increased dramatically from 1990 to 1994.

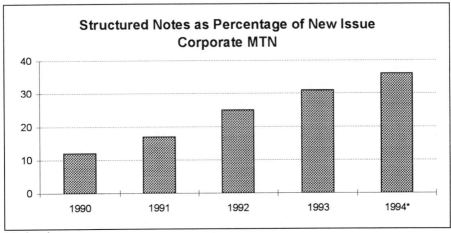

* Projected
[Source: Federal Reserve]

Although many investors have descended the ratings scale in search of higher yielding structured notes, the great majority of structured notes are still issued by highly rated entities. The Federal Reserve's estimate of structured note issuers' rating classification shows that over 97% of all structured notes were issued by corporates rated single-A or higher. The great majority of investors do not wish to complicate their interest rate risk with additional credit risk.

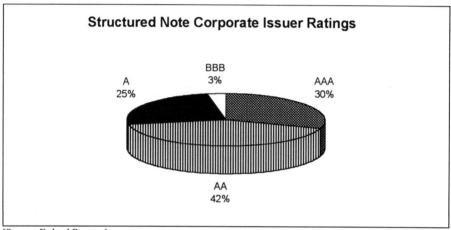

Structured Note Corporate Issuer Ratings

[Source: Federal Reserve]

Corporate Issuer Classification

The great majority of structured note corporate issuers are financial institutions. This has been true because historically, financial institutions were often the best equipped to handle the swap and derivative transactions that drive structured note creation. Since financial institutions have constant funding requirements, they can also be depended upon to issue structured notes on little or no notice. In contrast, industrial corporations' funding decisions are often strategically planned many months ahead of time and thus these non-financial corporations are not as likely to be as flexible to execute a structured note transaction on short notice.

Recently, however, as corporate treasury departments gained the swap and derivative expertise through liability management, the issuer base of new issue structured notes has become more diversified. Some of these non-financial corporations are now just as willing as their financial counterparts to utilize their MTN programs to obtain funding creatively via structured notes. Some can react just as quickly as financial institutions in response to investor inquiries.

A breakdown of the corporate issuers by business type shows a small but sizable fraction of structured note issuers that are non-financial in nature. This trend towards a more diversified base of issuers will continue as investors seek to diversify the issuers in their structured note portfolios and as more issuers seek out new sources of affordable funding.

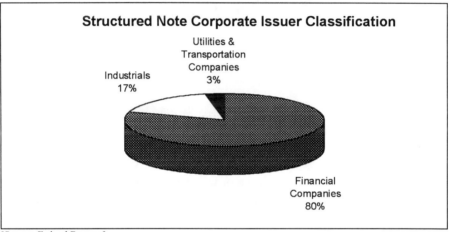

Structured Note Corporate Issuer Classification

Utilities & Transportation Companies 3%

Industrials 17%

Financial Companies 80%

[Source: Federal Reserve]

INVESTORS WHO PURCHASE STRUCTURED NOTES

From a small initial investor base of a few mutual funds, the investor base for structured notes has exploded over the last three years. Investors are as diverse as pension funds, money market funds, banks (trust departments), mutual funds, hedge funds, total return funds, and asset managers. They share one goal: to obtain performance that cannot be easily obtained from conventional fixed income instruments, and in return take on an acceptable level of risk.

The mix of investors of structured notes is illustrated on the next page. The largest purchasers of structured notes have been the funds (mutual and pension) and the banks and their trust departments. Insurance companies have only recently entered the structured note market, with most of their purchases used for the purpose of hedging or risk capital arbitrage.[2]

---

2. The issue of risk capital arbitrage will be discussed in Chapter 7.

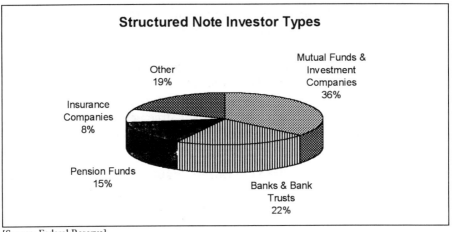

[Source: Federal Reserve]

Structured note investors can be broadly classified into four groups: the short-term/low risk investors, the enhanced yield investors, the high risk/high return investors, and the total return investors. Each class of investors has different investment philosophies and risk tolerances, which in turn drive the creation of structures that would be of interest to them. It is incumbent upon both the investor and structurer to ensure that the product that is being created for the investor is of the correct risk/return profile for the particular investor.

Short-Term Investors

The short-term structured note investors are primarily commercial paper (CP) investors, cash investors, and money market funds who invest in short-term money market instruments. They are among the most conservative of all investors because of their short maturity, strong issuer, and liquidity requirements. (See the table on page 11.)

Money market funds have special liquidity and price fluctuation restrictions since investors have come to regard money market funds as being akin to bank deposits. This has created a very strong impetus against "breaking the buck," i.e., losing principal. In fact, as of August 1994, no money market fund has yet broken the buck.[3] The money market fund man-

---

3. On July 1, 1994, the *Wall Street Journal* noted that " 'Breaking the Buck' . . . would roil the $600 billion money-fund industry, by causing a loss of principal to shareholders who have never seen such a thing."

Investor type:	Money market 2a-7 fund, cash investors, CP investors, government-only bond funds.
Issuer:	Mainly U.S. Agencies, some highly rated corporates for short maturities.
Maturity:	Up to 397 days (from initial trade date to maturity date) for highly rated corporates. Up to two years for U.S. Agency. Longer maturity possible with periodic (annually or more frequently) investor puts.
Coupon risk:	Some leverage possible. Generally non-zero minimum coupon.
Principal risk:	None.
Liquidity requirement:	Very high.
Special requirement:	Money market investors have to be fairly certain that the note will trade close to par for the life of the note. This severely limits their risk tolerance.

agers whose funds have lost money due to the fixed income market downturn in the first half of 1994 have opted to infuse the funds with cash or purchased back the instruments rather than declare a net asset value below $1 and breaking the buck.

Enhanced Yield Investors

The goal of enhanced yield investors is to obtain some measure of yield enhancement for minimal risk. Their maturity spectrum can extend out to 10 years if the credit is a good fit to the portfolio. A typical product that might appeal to this class of investors is one that floats off an index, but that has a high minimum coupon floor that limits the investor's maximum exposure.

Enhanced yield investors usually purchase structured notes for the duration of the note's life. Liquidity is thus not of the highest concern to these investors. Since the purchased structured notes are typically held to maturity, the selection of an appropriate issuer is an important issue to enhanced yield investors. A diverse collection of issuers is thus a key requirement of enhanced yield investors.

Investor type:	Pension, government and corporate funds, short-term bond funds.
Issuer:	BBB corporate to U.S. Agency.
Maturity:	2 to 10 years for corporate. 2 to 10 years for U.S. Agency.
Coupon risk:	Minimum coupon risk. Generally high minimum coupon.
Principal risk:	None.
Liquidity requirement:	Medium.
Special requirements:	High minimum coupon, diversity of issuers.

High Risk/High Return Investors

This investor class includes the mutual funds and hedge funds whose yield requirements are significantly higher than the other two investor classes discussed thus far. The structures that appeal to this class of investors are usually highly leveraged and redemption linked. The common feature of the structured note investments favored by this class of investors is that a large gain is returned if rates move in the investor's favor. These investors rarely hold the note to maturity and often trade when the rate movements are favorable.

Investor type:	Mutual, hedge funds. More speculative type investors.
Issuer:	BBB corporates to U.S. Agency.
Maturity:	1 to 5 years for corporate. 2 to 5 years for U.S. Agency.
Coupon risk:	Usually high leverage (if no principal risk). Zero minimum coupon.
Principal risk:	Yes (if no coupon risk). Highly leveraged principal return.
Liquidity requirement:	High.
Special requirements:	Highly leveraged structures that can provide rapid gains to the investor. Redemption linkage risk is usually acceptable, but a minimum principal at maturity in the 60–70% range is usually required.

Total Return Investors

These are investors who strive to produce a return as close to the total return of an existing market index as possible. They strive to replicate this total return at a minimum amount of risk. The investment philosophy of this class of investors will be discussed in greater detail in Chapter 9.

Investor type:	Total return fund, index funds, some pension funds.
Issuer:	BBB to AAA corporate.
Maturity:	Up to 10 years.
Coupon risk:	Linked to total return of index. Zero minimum coupon.
Principal risk:	Yes (if total return is negative on redemption date).
Liquidity requirement:	Low.
Special requirements:	Because the investor is receiving a total return on an index, the main risk is due to the issuer's credit. Thus, a set of highly rated and diverse issuers is required.

Evolution of the Structured Note Investor

As interest rates began to drop from the levels achieved in 1990, fixed income investors' goal of retaining or enhancing yield became an ever more difficult task. During this period of lowering rates, the structured note market likewise underwent a series of evolutionary phases. These six phases of structured note market evolution are:[4]

1. **The market risk period.** As short-term rates initially began to drop in 1990, investors started to take additional market risk to obtain enhanced yield. However, investors remained loyal to highly rated issuers since many do not wish to take both credit risk and market risk.
2. **The credit risk/non-domestic period.** As rates continued to decrease in 1991–92, investors began to reexamine their previous misgivings about taking both market and credit risk. As a result of

---

4. The authors are grateful to Philippe Burke for his comments regarding this topic.

investors lowering their credit requirements, lower rated issuers of
structured notes gained in popularity. At the same time, domestic
investors began to look to non-domestic markets to obtain enhanced
yield. These forays into the non-domestic markets were mostly limited to the indices of the largest economies in Europe (Germany and
France), as well as Japan.

3. **The leverage/alternative market period.** Shortly after structured note
   investors began to lower their credit requirements, the credit spread
   between AAA issuers and BBB issuers began to decrease. This lower
   credit spread greatly reduced investor incentive to purchase lower rated
   issuers and resulted in many investors pulling back from purchasing
   lower rated structured notes. Investors began to explore alternative
   methods of obtaining enhanced yield, settling on leverage as the means
   to achieve this goal. Many short-term investors began to purchase
   instruments with embedded leverage such as the leveraged capped
   floating rate notes (LCFRNs; discussed in Chapter 5). At the same
   time, investors who made forays into the non-domestic markets began
   to extend their reach into the indices of lesser developed economies,
   such as Italy, Portugal, and Spain, in the search for higher yield.

4. **The exotic option period.** As rates remained stable throughout most
   of 1993, even leverage was unable to provide some investors with
   their required enhanced yield. Thus was born the exotic options period. Structured notes with payoffs that do not fall under the traditional
   pattern of the FRN or interest rate options began to proliferate.
   Although these notes were able to provide investors with the required
   yield enhancement, they often introduced new and different types of
   risks that were more difficult to analyze and hedge.

5. **The principal linkage period.** In the final evolution of the market
   prior to the Federal Reserve's 1994 tightening action, investors
   extended the concept of leverage into principal linkage. By purchasing a note whose principal is linked to an index, the investor is potentially able to attain yield levels that cannot be achieved by coupon
   linkage. The downside is that the investor could lose just as much or
   more if the underlying index moved against the payoff formula.

6. **The quiescent period.** The period between the Federal Reserve's
   first interest rate hike in 1994 and the fourth quarter of 1994 marks
   the last and final period. Many investors who put on bullish leveraged transactions have sold their holdings and the great majority of
   structured note trading occurs in the secondary market.

STRUCTURED NOTE TERMSHEET

The investor's first glimpse of a new structure is often conveyed by a termsheet. The termsheet embodies the basic concepts of the trade and includes a myriad of interest rate setting specifications. A sample structured note termsheet is shown in Exhibit 1-3. The two basic sections of a structured note termsheet are the header/footer and the body.

The header/footer section usually contains information about the broker/dealer that is underwriting this structure, in this case ABC Underwriters, Inc. Structured notes are usually first shown to investors on an indicative basis, i.e., the bonds described are not actual bonds, but are, to the best knowledge of the underwriter, produceable upon investor request. Thus, an indication of whether this structure is an *actual* deal or an *indicative* termsheet is always provided. A brief description of the note and some selling points may also be present in this section. Finally, the regulatory disclaimer about non-solicitation of offers to buy the security is given. In the interest of brevity, this section will generally be excluded from the termsheets shown in this book, but readers should bear in mind that indicative termsheets shown by broker/dealers will include this section.

The body of the termsheet includes the essential information about the note. The essential facts to be gleaned from the termsheet are:

Issuer: The issuer name is usually not listed if the structured note is indicative in nature. For indicative structures, a general classification of the issuer is usually given. In Exhibit 1-3, the issuer is described as a single-A corporate, and the form of the note, if issued, would be an MTN.

Principal amount: This is the proposed new issue amount (if shown indicatively). Some issuers require a minimum new issue size of $25 million or more, while others may have only a $5 million minimum requirement.

Settlement date: Although five business days is the standard for corporate bond settlement in the United States, structured notes typically take longer to settle. The longer settlement also allows the underwriter and issuer to work out the appropriate language of the structured note's prospectus. Another reason for a longer settlement is to take advantage of the positively sloped curve. The extra week or two weeks in settlement can often mean an additional few basis points, which can be crucial in a tightly priced deal. The settlement date should be a valid business day.

Maturity date: This is one of three components that can float in a structured note (the other two being the coupon and the principal). In certain struc-

EXHIBIT 1-3   Sample Structured Note Termsheet

ABC Underwriter, Inc.	*Proprietary and Confidential*
Structured MTN	*Indicative Terms*

Fixed/CMT Note
09/21/94

Issue Terms

Issuer:	Single-A corporate
Principal amount:	US$25,000,000
Settlement date:	Jan. 15, 1994
Maturity date:	Jan. 15, 1996
Coupon paid in US$:	Year 1: 6.05% Year 2: (10-year CMT – 2-year CMT)
Rate reset and payment dates:	CMT rates reset and pay semiannually on May 15, Nov. 15. First coupon paid on May 15, 1994.
Day count:	30/360 with no adjustment for period end dates.
CMT determination:	The CMT rate shall be the daily constant maturity Treasury rate for the appropriate maturity applicable on the determination day of the Fed H.15(519) publication. Determination date is two New York and London business days prior to reset dates. Source: Telerate Page 7059.
Issue price:	100.00%

An investor who believes that the U.S. curve will continue to stay steep for the next two years should purchase this note. The investor receives an enhanced coupon for the first year, followed by a good coupon if the yield curve remains steep even 1 basis point from the spot curve.

Source: Sumitomo Bank Capital Markets.

tures, the maturity date may change depending on interest rate movements. The maturity date should be a valid business day.

Coupon: The structured note coupon is the component that usually contains the structuring elements. The coupon section describes the payoff formula to the investor. Structured notes are uniquely different from mortgage products in that all the contingent payments are fully specified. An absolute minimum coupon of zero is required since coupons cannot be negative (and result in the investor paying interest to the issuer). Some structured note coupons are subject to a coupon cap and these are likewise identified. If the index is a rate index that is not the native index, the coupon payment currency should also be specified, e.g., "Coupon is Yen LIBOR + 2%, paid in US$."

Day count basis: This describes the calculation of the actual cash flow paid out at the end of each period to the investor. Conventions are money-market yield, which accrues on an "Actual/360" basis, or bond equivalent yield, which accrues on a "30/360" basis. The coupons are paid on the day count basis, e.g., in the case of a quarterly Act/360 coupon, the actual cash flow received by the investor at the end of the quarter is:

$$\text{Coupon cash flow} = \text{(Notional amount)} * \text{(Nominal coupon rate)} \\ * \text{(Number of actual days in the period)}/360$$

Readers interested in additional details concerning the day count basis should consult Marcia Stigum's book.[5]

Adjustment for period end dates: This addresses the question, What if the coupon payment date falls on a weekend? If the note calls for adjusting for period end dates, the investor would continue to accrue interest through the actual period end date up until the next good business day, when the coupon payment would be made. If the note specifies no adjusting for period end dates, the investor would accrue interest up to the actual period end date (but not receive any interest past the actual period end date) and receive the coupon payment on the next good business day.

Index determination: The termsheet usually specifies the method of index determination. Typical sources of rates are information providers such as Telerate, Reuters, or Bloomberg Financial Markets. The Federal Reserve publication H.15(519), which is released by the Federal Reserve Board of

---

5. See Stigum, Marcia, *The Money Market.* Homewood, IL: Dow Jones-Irwin, 1983.

Governors every Monday afternoon, is also a favorite reference source for quoting Treasury bills, Treasury notes, Prime, and Fed fund rates. Non-U.S. rates are usually quoted off Reuters or Telerate listed broker screens. Some indices are determined based on an average of a number of dealer quotes.

Issue price: Typically, structured notes are issued and sold to the investor at par, but depending upon the situation, a note may be priced and sold to the investor at a premium or a discount. For these cases, the issue price will contain, instead of par, the following term: "Offered at Variable Prices."

For structured notes whose principals are linked to certain indices, the formula for the principal would be provided on the termsheet to specify the method of calculation.

Whenever possible, the terms of *actual* structured notes will be employed as examples to illustrate the various types and classes of structures. Unless otherwise specified, the information contained in the structured note termsheets described in this book are obtained from either or both of the following sources: Bloomberg Financial Markets, and issuers' prospectus/pricing supplements. The reader can obtain further information about these structured notes from the above sources by identifying the notes by the issuer, maturity date, and coupon structure.

With the sole exception of the gold linked note described in Chapter 7, all the examples and analyses described in this book will reflect, to the best knowledge of the authors, accurate market information as of the initial purchase date of the structures.

CONSIDERATIONS

Any new investor in the structured note market should first ascertain to his or her own satisfaction the suitability, tax, accounting, regulatory, and legal consequences of any purchase and subsequent sale. Certain structures (such as the bond index total-return notes) continue to receive a great deal of scrutiny from the SEC, and the investor should, to the best of his or her ability, ascertain the details of any relevant issues concerning the structure in question.

Because of the higher level of sophistication required of investors in the structured note market, certain large structured note issuers, such as the Federal Home Loan Banks, have begun to stipulate as part of all new issue terms that the end investors of structured notes be "sophisticated investors" as defined under Regulation D of the Securities Act of 1933. This is to ensure that the ultimate investor is at least technically able to understand the risks of these instruments.

An investor should always ask the questions: Is all this trouble worth it? Is the barrier to entry worth the potential payoff to be received from structured notes? The answers should be a qualified yes. Structured notes offer a tremendous amount of flexibility to an investor willing (and able) to put forth the effort to understand the note and the associated issues and risks. Instead of purchasing a piece of a large deal "because it is there," an investor can own an instrument that has been custom tailored to his or her views and risk profile.

HERE WE GO

This book is a practitioner's guide for (in order of relevance) investors, traders, and issuers. For too long, the structured note investor has had to struggle without much in the way of guidance or education in what is arguably the most complicated sector of the fixed income market. The main goal of this book is to address that need and to fill in some of the knowledge gaps that may exist in what is a closed and secretive field.

The organization of this book is as follows. Chapter 2 introduces the investor to the typical risk/return analyses that are performed on structured notes and the relevant measurements of risk in the structured note arena. Chapter 3 introduces the first of two classes of analysis, the deterministic analysis and the three types of deterministic analyses that are often employed to analyze structured notes. The second class of analysis, the simulation analysis, is introduced in Chapter 4. Chapters 5, 6, and 7 describe the various types of structures that have been created over the short lifetime of structured notes. Chapters 5, 6, and 7 describe the first generation of structured notes, the second generation, and the cross-category structured notes, respectively. Each type of structured note will be analyzed via the techniques discussed in Chapter 3 and 4. Chapter 8 introduces investors and traders to the creation of a structured note from the underlying derivative components. Chapter 9 demonstrates the concept of portfolio management using structured notes to combine enhanced performance with good risk management. Because some investors believe (rightly or wrongly) that they can duplicate any of the structured notes in the cash market, Chapter 10 is dedicated to a discussion of the merits of the cash/futures market versus structured notes. The large volume of outstanding structured notes has led to a healthy secondary market, and the issue of secondary market valuation and liquidity is addressed in Chapter 11. Finally, Chapter 12 provides a summary as well as a look forward to the new structures and regulatory issues that appear to be just around the corner.

The reader is assumed to possess an average understanding of the fixed income market and knowledge of some of the basic methods of risk and performance measurements in the fixed coupon note market. With the exception of portions of Chapters 2 and 4, calculus is avoided in favor of providing the reader with the maximum amount of insight and understanding of the behavior of these structures.

2

Structured Note Risk and Performance Measurement

The analysis of structured notes is of primary importance to investors, traders, and issuers. How does one assess the risk and return of such instruments? Will traditional techniques of risk analysis that apply in the fixed coupon bond market be applicable to structured notes? Is there a standard method of analysis or benchmark against which a particular structured note can be measured? In the structured note arena, the standard measurements of risk, such as duration, appear to lose the direct relevance that they possess in the fixed rate bond market. Upon closer examination, however, it will be evident that if applied correctly and interpreted properly, this traditional measurement of risk can be an extremely useful indicator of risk in the structured note arena.

This chapter will introduce the appropriate analysis techniques for the determination of structured note risk and performance characteristics. The chapter begins with a review of duration. This is useful in preparing the reader for the proper application and interpretation of structured note *risk* and *performance* measurements. Duration will then be extended to provide meaningful risk assessment in the structured note arena. The concept of key Treasury rate duration (KTRD) will be introduced. The volatility risk of structured notes will be discussed, followed by a short discussion of non-interest rate risk. The topic of structured note performance will subsequently be addressed, with the internal rate of return (IRR) introduced as the primary measurement of structured note performance. The issues of performance benchmarking and measurement time horizon conclude the chapter.

INTRODUCTION, REVIEW, AND EXTENSION OF DURATION

Before beginning our discussion of risk, a review and extension of the concept of duration is essential. Throughout each of the analyses, duration will be employed as the indicator of structured note risk, while the IRR will be employed as the indicators of structured note performance. However, it will be evident that the definition of duration from fixed income vernacular is insufficient to address the risks of structured notes.

The duration (modified duration) of fixed coupon notes is defined as

$$\text{DUR} = -\frac{1}{P}\left(\frac{dP}{dr}\right)$$

where P is the price of the note, and r the appropriate discounting rate for the maturity of the note. There is no ambiguity in this definition because the price of a fixed rate note depends solely upon the discounting curve.

In the case of a structured note, however, duration takes on an added level of ambiguity. The value of the note changes not only when the underlying discounting curve changes, but also when the coupon index changes. Take for example the following note:

Maturity: 3 years
Issuer: U.S. Agency
Coupon: 6-month Sterling LIBOR – 2.00% paid in US$

The value of the above note will change not only when the underlying U.S. Treasury rates changes, but also when Sterling rates change. In fact, the change in price of a structured note often depends more upon the movement of the coupon (or principal) index rather than the change in the underlying discount rate. Thus, the standard measure of duration defined as the percentage change in the value of the note divided by the change in the *underlying discounting rate* will not accurately reflect all the risks inherent in the above note. Indeed, that definition of duration is misleading because the overall risk of this particular note is associated with changes in both the coupon index of Sterling LIBOR as well as with the underlying U.S. discounting rate.

STRUCTURED NOTE RISK MEASUREMENT: A TALE OF TWO DURATIONS

As previously discussed, the value of a structured note not only changes with the underlying discounting yield curve, but also with the index upon which the coupon and/or principal is based. The conventional definition of duration as adopted from fixed income vernacular, then, is ambiguous because there are multiple factors that can affect the value of a structured note. In order to resolve this ambiguity, we will define an *index rate duration* (IRD, or $\text{DUR}_{\text{INDEX}}$) and a *discounting rate duration* (DRD, or DUR_{DISC}).

The index rate duration $\text{DUR}_{\text{INDEX}}$ is defined as the duration based upon a 1 basis point (bp) change in the index rate (IR) upon which the contingent cash flow (coupon and/or principal) is based, i.e.,

$$\text{DUR}_{\text{INDEX}} = -\frac{1}{P}\left(\frac{dP}{dr_{\text{index}}}\right)$$

The discounting rate duration DUR_{DISC} is the conventional duration based upon a basis point change in the discounting rate (DR), i.e.,

$$\text{DUR}_{\text{DISC}} = -\frac{1}{P}\left(\frac{dP}{dr_{\text{disc}}}\right)$$

The net duration of the note is thus a combination of both indices.

$$\text{DUR}_{\text{NET}} = \text{DUR}(r_{\text{disc}}, r_{\text{index}})$$

A non-trivial and important aspect of solving for the duration will be the identification of the index rate. The appropriate IR is most likely *not* equal to the underlying index, e.g., the appropriate IR of a LIBOR FRN is not 3-month LIBOR. Being able to correctly identify the IR will provide the investor with a clear view of the overall risk of structured notes.

Note that this process of splitting up of a note into its index and discounting components is an *approximation* that allows investors to easily grasp the components of the note's risk.

Discounting Rate Determination

The discounting rate (DR) is considerably easier to determine than the IR. The DR can be found by assuming that the note behaves in the same manner as a fixed rate note. Recall that for a fixed rate note, the only determinant of a note's value is the *to-maturity discounting rate*. In other words, if the contingent nature of the structured note were to be made non-contingent, the note would still have interest rate sensitivity, namely equal to that of a fixed coupon note. Thus, the discounting rate of a structured note is the to-maturity Treasury rate, and the note's interest rate sensitivity with respect to the DR constitutes the DRD. The DRD can, with some notable exceptions, be closely approximated by the duration of a comparable maturity fixed note. For example, a 3-year structured note has a DR equal to the 3-year Treasury rate, and a DRD equal to that of a 3-year fixed coupon note, or approximately 2.7.

The exception to the above estimate of the DR and the DRD are as follows:

1. **Note has maturity uncertainty.** If the note's maturity is indexed to a certain index, the DR and DRD can no longer be approximated by the to-maturity Treasury rate and the to-maturity duration of a fixed note. Rather, the maturity of the DR will be between the maturity date and the call date due to the maturity uncertainty, with the DRD changing in correspondence with the changing DR.
2. **Note is essentially a zero coupon.** If the note is an existing note with little possibility of regaining a non-zero coupon until maturity, the DRD of the note would be better approximated by that of a zero coupon note of the same maturity, i.e., the DR of the note would remain the to-maturity Treasury rate, but the DRD of the note would be equal to a comparable zero coupon note.

Index Rate Determination

As mentioned above, the IR is not simply the short-term index upon which a note's contingency payment is based. Rather, it is the resulting *aggregate* of the floating rate components of the note. A single index can result in either one IR, or a multitude of corresponding IRs. Take for example the following note:

Maturity: 3 years
Coupon: 3-month LIBOR paid quarterly

The floating rate component of the above note is the quarterly coupons, which reset off 3-month LIBOR. However, instead of a set of 12 IRs, a single IR can represent the entire cash flow. Since a stream of LIBOR coupons is equivalent to a fixed *swap* rate, one IR is sufficient to summarize the entire stream of 12 LIBOR cash flows.[1] Since the swap rate is quoted as a swap spread over the same maturity Treasury rate, which is assumed to be relatively constant (an adequate assumption based on historical data), the IR can be considered as equivalent to the 3-year maturity Treasury rate. The IRD is equal to the negative duration of that of a fixed coupon note, or –2.7. The sign is negative because the note gains in value from the rising LIBOR indices as the 3-year Treasury rate rises.

Combining the IRD of –2.7 with the DRD of +2.7 results in the net duration of a LIBOR FRN being zero.[2] The zero duration represents duration and interest rate neutrality and will be used in future risk analyses as representing the baseline risk of a floating rate note.

In many instances, the index component of the cash flow cannot be simply represented by a single IR as illustrated above, but rather is composed of a combination of IRs. This scenario will be addressed shortly in the context of KTRD.

Duration When Index Rate and Discounting Rate Are Identical

The above discussion represents a note whose index rate and discounting rate are identical. The discussion will now be expanded to illustrate the significance of this characteristic.

Returning to the previous example of the 3-year maturity LIBOR FRN. The index component of the cash flows is the stream of quarterly LIBORs

---

1. This is true when no optionality is involved. When optionality is involved, the floating rate cash flows can no longer be rigorously represented by a single IR since a dip in one portion of the yield curve can result in some of the short-term indices rising or falling, thus activating the option. The single IR representation of a series of short-term rates has the effect of combining all the shorter maturity key Treasury rate durations (KTRD) into one representative rate, the IR, and one representative duration, the IRD. This is a good approximation and serves the purposes of clarity and illustration. However, a more precise methodology to represent the risk of these short-term indices in the context of optionality would be either a zero rate based methodology (as outlined by Ho and Dattatreya in their respective papers) or one based on forward LIBORs as the underlying key rates.

2. The duration of the 3-month LIBOR FRN is zero here instead of the typical 0.25 that most fixed income practitioners associate with LIBOR FRNs. This difference is due to the duration of the example being calculated *prior* to the setting of the first coupon, resulting in total duration neutrality. Using a duration of zero for LIBOR FRNs has the effect of eliminating the 0.25 duration bias, establishing a LIBOR FRN as a riskless baseline case, thus providing a clearer view of the real underlying risks of the note.

for five years. The DR is the 3-year maturity Treasury rate. Since it was shown above that the IR is also the 3-year Treasury rate, the two rates are identical. The net duration would then be calculated as:

$$\text{DUR}_{\text{NET}} = \Delta P/(0.01\% * P)$$

where ΔP would now incorporate the change in the price as a result of the change in the index and discounting rate. Since the IR and the DR are both equal to the 3-year Treasury rate, the net duration DUR_{NET} would be calculated by shifting the 3-year Treasury rate by 1 basis point and observing the change in the value of the note. This situation is unique in that all the risk of the note is concentrated in one component of the yield curve. The result is that the note contains no yield curve risk. The risk of the note can be examined in full by looking at different interest rate scenarios of one key rate: the to-maturity Treasury rate.

What conditions would result in an IR being identical to the DR? From the swaps market, it is known that a series of short-term rates can be swapped into a fixed rate, which is quoted as a spread over the underlying Treasury rate. As long as this spread can be reasonably expected to be relatively stable, the IR of the stream of short-term rates can be represented by the to-maturity Treasury rate. Thus, an indication that a note possesses this type of risk profile is that the coupon index is a short-term index whose reset and payment frequency matches the period, e.g., 3-month LIBOR paid quarterly. The aggregate of these short-term cash flows is a rate (swap rate) that is of the same maturity as the term Treasury yield; hence the IR of the coupon index is the same as the DR, or the to-maturity Treasury rate. For example, a note whose quarterly paying coupon is reset daily based on the daily Fed Funds rate has identical IRs and DRs, provided the Fed Funds-to-fixed-rate swap spread does not vary much over time.

Calculation of Duration

How is duration calculated? For deterministic analysis, i.e., assuming the future cash flows are fully known based upon an assumed scenario, the answer is simple and straightforward. The future cash flow is determined by either some set of expectation or forward rates. A base cash flow case can then be constructed and the PV calculated by discounting this cash flow by the Treasury plus credit spread. A perturbed set of index rates can then be calculated by perturbing each rate by 1 basis point (bp). The present value of this new set of cash flows can then be calculated by discounting by the appropriately perturbed discounting rate. The duration can then be found through this price differential:

Duration = [PV(Original) – PV(New)]/PV(Original)/0.01%

The following example will illustrate this process.

Example 2-1

Calculate the duration of the following note given a set of forward LIBORs.

Issuer: AA (Credit spread = TSY + 0.20%)
Maturity: 3 years
Coupon: 6-month LIBOR + 0.50%. Maximum coupon 6%
Current 2-yr. TSY: 5.00%

Period	Scenario LIBOR (at Start of Period)
1	4.00%
2	4.85%
3	5.65%
4	6.15%
5	6.55%
6	7.05%

Solution

Given the above interest rate scenario, the following cash flows can be calculated.

Period	Original LIBOR (I)	Original Cash Flow (II)	Perturbed LIBOR (III)	Perturbed Cash Flow (IV)
1	4.00%	1.1406%	4.01%	1.1432%
2	4.85%	1.3561%	4.86%	1.3586%
3	5.65%	1.5208%	5.66%	1.5208%
4	6.15%	1.5208%	6.16%	1.5208%
5	6.55%	1.5208%	6.56%	1.5208%
6	7.05%	1.5208%	7.06%	1.5208%

Column II shows the coupon cash flows as calculated from the original forward LIBORs and the coupon formula of LIBOR + 0.50% (6% max coupon). The forward LIBORs are then each perturbed by 1 bp (column III) and the resulting coupon cash flows are shown in column IV. Since the result of perturbing each LIBOR by 1 bp is to increase the overall swap rate by 1 bp, this 1 bp increase in the swap rate is equivalent to a 1 bp increase in the to-maturity Treasury rate.

Next, the PVs of the note for each of the two scenarios can be calculated by discounting each cash flow by the appropriate to-maturity Treasury rate plus a credit spread. The original stream of cash flows (column II) would thus be discounted by 5.20% (5% Treasury + 0.2% credit spread), while the perturbed cash flow (column IV) should be discounted by 5.21% (5.01% Treasury + 0.2%). The perturbed cash flows are discounted by a higher Treasury yield because the IR and the DR are both equal to the 3-year Treasury rate, and therefore a 1 bp perturbation in the IR must result in a 1 bp perturbation in the DR.

The difference between the two PVs divided by the original PV is thus the duration of the bond.

$$PV(Original) = 93.5484\%$$
$$PV(New) = 93.5269\%$$

The duration is then calculated to be:

$$Duration = [PV(Original) - PV(New)]/PV(Original)/0.01\%$$
$$Duration = 2.30$$

This methodology will be used throughout the analysis section as the basis for calculating "deterministic duration," i.e., duration based upon deterministic cash flows.

Duration Calculation When Index Rate and Discounting Rate Are Not Identical: Key Treasury Rate Duration

How does one assess the risk of a structured note in the context of a non-parallel shift in the yield curve? As discussed above, notes whose IRs and DRs are identical have no yield curve risk and contain risk exposure to only one particular segment of the yield curve. What risk analysis can be performed that could portray the risk picture of notes containing yield curve risk?

Dattatreya[3] and Ho[4] were among the first to introduce the concept of analyzing interest rate risk with respect to sectors of the yield curve. KRD or the risk point measures the duration of a note with respect to one key portion of the yield curve, hence the term *key rate*. Ho uses the zero curve rates (also known as the spot rates) as the base or key rates for the risk measurement of fixed income instruments. In this book, we use Dattatreya's method and use the on-the-run Treasury rates as the base rates used in the calculation of structured note risk and reward, hence the term key *Treasury* rate duration.

KEY TREASURY RATE DURATION (KTRD)

KTRD calculates the change in price of a note with respect to a change in one specific segment of the Treasury curve.

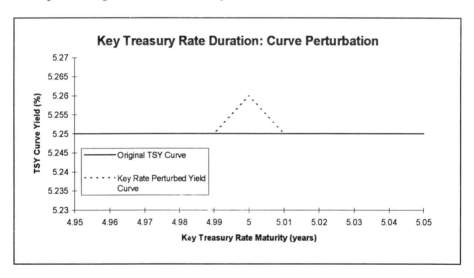

3. See discussion of risk point methodology in Dattatreya, Ravi E., "A Practical Approach to Asset/Liability Management," in Frank J. Fabozzi and Atsuo Konishi (eds.), *Asset/Liability Management*, Chicago, IL: Probus, 1991; Dattatreya, Ravi E., and Raj Pundarika, "Interest Rate Risk Management: The Risk Point Method," in Ravi E. Dattatreya and Kensuke Hotta (eds.), *Advanced Interest Rate and Currency Swaps*, Chicago, IL: Probus, 1994; Dattratreya, Ravi E., and Frank J. Fabozzi, *Active Total Return Management of Fixed Income Portfolios*, 2nd ed., Chicago, IL: Probus, 1994.
4. See Tom Ho's paper on key rate duration in Ho, Thomas S. Y. "Key Rate Durations: Measures of Interest Rate Risks," *Journal of Fixed Income* 2, September 1992, pp. 29–44.

This technique allows the full risk assessment of the note by calculating the change in the value of the note with a 1 bp change in any "key" segment of the Treasury yield curve. By making the perturbation small and local around the key rate, the 1 bp change in a specific segment of the yield curve can be made local and not affect any other segment. Thus, the real power of the KTRD analysis is that it provides the sensitivity of the note to a specific portion of the Treasury yield curve.

Recall from previous discussions that a structured note contains two components that can alter its value: discounting and index. The extension that will be made in this section will be to decompose the index component of risk into its elemental components, the KTRs. The net duration of the note will then be a composite of the durations with respect to each KTR.

Key Treasury Rate Durational Analysis Methodology

The risks of a structured note can be examined by calculating its KTRD. The methodology of a KTRD analysis is as follows:

1. Determine the basic components that will affect the performance of the note. Recall that these are the (a) discounting and (b) index components.
2. Determine the actual key Treasury rates that correspond to each component as they apply to the coupon. One index can correspond to multiple KTRs.
3. Calculate the effect of a 1 bp change in each KTR on the underlying PV of the note. This provides the KTRD of each sector of the Treasury yield curve.
4. Generate a spectrum of KTRD. This view provides a full assessment of the interest rate risk.
5. Update the KTRD spectrum as market conditions change and as time goes by.

The KTRD methodology will be employed to analyze notes with yield curve risk, i.e., notes whose IRs and DRs are not identical. As will be discussed in Chapter 5, the first generation structures do not have any yield curve risk. KTRD analysis will be applied to analyzing the risks of second generation and cross-category structures, which do contain embedded yield curve risks.

The following example will serve to illustrate the application of KTRD in analyzing the risk of a structured note.

Example 2-2

Analyze the risk of the following note using KTRD.

Issuer: U.S. Agency
Maturity: 3 years
Coupon: (10-year CMT – 12-month LIBOR) + 2.00%, paid annually

Analysis

Step 1.   Identify the components. The key components of this note are:

Discounting component: The DR is the to-maturity Treasury rate.
Index component: There are two floating rate indices that constitute the coupon.

    a. 10-year CMT
    b. LIBOR

Steps 2 and 3.   Identify the KTRs corresponding to each component and the KTRD corresponding to each key rate.

    a. **Discounting:** All structured notes have exposure to the DR, which is equal to the to-maturity Treasury rate. The DRD is equal to that of a comparable maturity fixed coupon note. For this example, the DR is the 3-year Treasury rate, and the DRD is 2.75.
    b. **10-year CMT:** The first index component is the 10-year CMT. The coupons are based on the then-current 10-year Treasury yield on each coupon reset date, i.e.,

$$\text{Coupon PV} = \frac{T_{10,0}}{(1+r_1)} + \frac{T_{10,1}}{(1+r_2)} + \frac{T_{10,2}}{(1+r_3)} + \cdots + \frac{T_{10,N}}{(1+r_n)}$$

where $T_{10,i}$ is the 10-year CMT rate for the ith annual period and r_i is the discount rate for the ith annual period. The forward 10-year rates can be calculated as follows:

$$(1 + 1/2T_{10,i})^{20} * (1 + 1/2T_i)^{2i} = (1 + 1/2T_{10+i})^{2(10+i)}$$

This is the bootstrap relationship linking the forward Treasury rate $T_{10,i}$ to the spot Treasury rates T_i and T_{10+i}. Solving for the forward rate:

$$T_{10,i} = 2 * \left\{ \left[\left(\left(1 + 1/2T_{10+i}\right)^{2(10+i)} \middle/ \left(1 + 1/2T_i\right)^{2i} \right)^{1/20} \right] - 1 \right\}$$

$$= 2 * \left\{ \left(1 + 1/2T_{10+i}\right) * \left[\left(\left(1 + 1/2T_{10+i}\right) \middle/ \left(1 + 1/2T_i\right) \right)^{i/10} \right] - 1 \right\} \quad (2\text{-}1)$$

where the item within the brackets [ ] of Equation 2-1 is approximately 1 for $i \ll 10$. For the purpose of illustration, it will assume here that [ ] is approximately 1. For a short note maturity where the maximum future period i is much less than the 10-year maturity of the index (10-year CMT), the forward rate $T_{10,i}$ is directly proportional to the Treasury rate whose maturity corresponds to the sum of the index maturity (i) and the note maturity (10), i.e., $T_{10,i} \approx T_{10+i}$. The rate T_{10+i} will be referred to as the sum maturity rate (SMR).

With this approximation, a 1 bp increase in the SMR T_{10+i} would correspond to a 1 bp increase in the forward 10-year Treasury rate $T_{10,i}$. Given this 1 bp increase in the forward rate $T_{10,i}$, the value of the note will increase by the present value of that 1 bp increase in the coupon for the ith period. These durations will be negative since the definition of duration is for PV to decrease as rates rise. Thus, for the annual coupons of this note, the KTRs and the corresponding KTRDs are as follows:

Key Rate	Duration of Note with Respect to Key Rate	Explanation
T_{10}	−0.96	PV of 1 bp yield for 1 year in 1 year
T_{11}	−0.91	PV of 1 bp yield for 1 year in 2 years
T_{12}	−0.85	PV of 1 bp yield for 1 year in 3 years

In summary, there are three IRs (T_{10}, T_{11}, T_{12}) corresponding to the 10-year CMT index component of the annual coupons, the longest of which is the 12-year Treasury rate since the CMT rate is determined at the beginning of the accrual year. The IRD with respect to each of the IRs is approximately –1.

c. **LIBOR:** From earlier discussions, it was determined that the IR corresponding to a stream of LIBOR coupons is the to-maturity Treasury rate, and the IRD is approximately the duration of a comparable maturity fixed rate note. The IR for the LIBOR index component of the coupon cash flows is the 3-year Treasury rate, and the IRD is approximately 2.75. The sign of the IRD is positive since the LIBOR component of the coupon appears in an inverse fashion, i.e., Coupon = CMT minus LIBOR. An increase in the term structure of LIBOR would thus result in a decrease in PV, hence a positive IRD for the LIBOR component.

The above KTRs and the corresponding durations can be summarized as follows:

Component	Index	Key Treasury Rate(s) for Index	Duration with Respect to Key Treasury Rate
Index rate	10-year CMT	T_{10}	–0.96
		T_{11}	–0.91
		T_{12}	–0.85
	12-month LIBOR	3-year Treasury rate: T_3	2.75
Discounting rate	To-maturity Treasury rate	3-year Treasury rate: T_3	2.75

Step 4. Plot the KTRD spectrum.

The net risk of the note can be seen by aggregating the component KTRDs in the above table and plotted in the KTRD spectrum on the next page. The KTRD spectrum provides the investor with the risk profile of the structured note in question. For a change in the interest rate of a particular sector of the Treasury yield curve, the change in the value of the note can then be found by simply multiplying the interest rate change of each sector by the KTRD of the corresponding maturity of the yield curve.

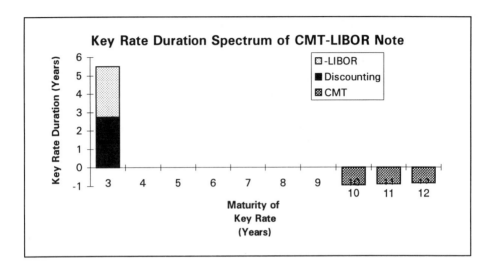

The KTRD spectrum above illustrates the risk of the note as a function of the KTRs whose changes will affect the value of the note. From the graph, it is seen that the (CMT-LIBOR) spread note has a duration of 5.5 with respect to the KTR of 3-year Treasury yield, and durations of –0.96, –0.91, and –0.85 with respect to the KTRs of T_{10}, T_{11}, and T_{12}, respectively. From a risk management perspective, this note is particularly vulnerable to a rise in the short-term rates and a drop in long-term rates, i.e., yield curve flattening will cause the note to lose value.

The net duration of the note for a parallel yield curve shift can also be calculated by summing up all the component KTRDs. The net duration of the CMT-LIBOR note for a parallel yield curve shift is found to be approximately 2.75, which is equal to that of a 3-year fixed rate note. This is an expected result since the CMT-LIBOR differential results in the note coupon being essentially fixed if future CMTs and LIBORs rise or fall by the same amount.

Step 5.   Update spectrum as required when rates and maturity change.

The KTRD approach illustrated above enables the investor to analyze the risk exposure of a note. However, just as a fixed coupon note changes in duration as time and rates change, the risk profile of structured notes will likewise be affected by changing time and interest rates. The investor must pay special attention to these changes because a structured note's properties can be very sensitive to, and thus change value drastically with, both market rate and maturity changes.

To illustrate this, examine the CMT-LIBOR spread note one year from the previous analysis date. The note now has two years of life remaining. The note not only has a reduced DRD (since the life is shorter), but also has a different KTRD spectrum as well.

The duration of the note has changed as follows:

a. **Discounting.** As the note currently has only two years of life remaining, the DR is the 2-year Treasury rate, and the DRD is now 1.9 , or that of a 2-year fixed coupon note.

b. **10-year CMT.** Since only two years of life remain, the 10-year CMT component of the two future annual coupon rates will depend upon the 10-year and 11-year Treasury rates. The 12-year TSY component is no longer present. The IRs for the 10-year CMT component are now only the 10- and 11-year Treasury rates, and the IRDs corresponding to the 10- and 11-year Treasury rates are respectively –0.96 and –0.91.

c. **LIBOR.** Again, since only two years of life remain, the IR corresponding to the LIBOR component of the coupon cash flow is now the 2-year Treasury rate, and the IRD is now 1.9.

The resulting KTRD spectrum of the CMT-LIBOR note after one year has passed is plotted below.

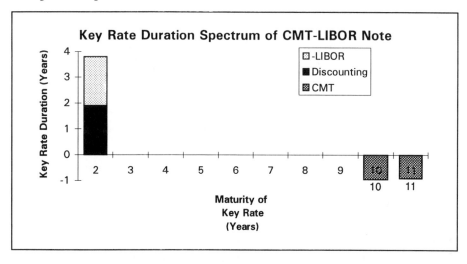

The power of KTRD is that it permits the examination of the performance of the note in the context of a portfolio of other securities. Notes of widely differing structures can now be combined together and treated as a portfolio with a combined KTRD spectrum. As will be discussed later in the portfolio management portion of the book, one of the advantages of structured notes lies in the ability of a manager to selectively fill in the durational gaps of the portfolio's KTRD spectrum while simultaneously achieving yield enhancement.

The assumption that was made in the above analysis was that the index maturity is much longer than the note maturity. This assumption permitted the ignoring of the term in the parenthesis in Equation (2-1):

$$\Gamma = [((1 + 1/2T_{10+i})/(1 + 1/2T_i))^{i/10}]$$

since in the sample case the index maturity (10 years) is significantly longer than the note maturity (3 years). However, in cases where the index maturity is close to the maturity of the note (e.g., 5-year note with coupons indexed to the 2-year CMT), the term Γ cannot be properly ignored. The result of not ignoring the term Γ is the appearance of a range of additional KTRDs corresponding to KTRs with maturities ranging from zero up to the maturity of the note. This effect will be illustrated in Chapter 6 when a CMT FRN with the coupon indexed to the 5-year CMT is analyzed.

The term *asymptotic duration* is defined in this book as the duration of the note in the limit of either very high or very low interest rate scenarios. It is a concept that will be useful in the interpretation of the durational characteristics of structured notes.

Common Misconception of Structured Note Duration

Many common misconceptions have been expressed by investors when attempting to assess the risks of a structured note. Some common misconceptions can be found by looking at the following note:

Coupon: (10-year CMT) – 1.60%
Payment frequency: Coupon resets and pays quarterly
Maturity: 3 years

The common misconceptions are:

1. The bond resets quarterly, and thus has a 3-month duration. As illustrated above in the discussion of non-parallel curve shift duration, it is obvious that assuming this note has a 3-month duration is incorrect.
2. The note depends on a 10-year maturity index; thus it should have a duration of a 10-year note, i.e., a 7.5-year duration. Likewise, KTRD showed that this concept is clearly wrong.

The important conclusion from the durational analysis demonstrated in this chapter is that one cannot make assumptions regarding the risk of a note based solely upon its reset frequency or its index maturity. A thorough durational analysis must be performed in order to fully determine the risk.

Duration for Notes with Embedded Optionality Components

The above discussion of duration dealt with deterministic scenarios, i.e., the duration for a definitive interest rate scenario. The durations are calculated based on the change in the price of the note with respect to a basis point change in some key rate(s). If a note should contain an optionality component, a deterministic analysis of the note will show that for each coupon reset, the embedded option will, depending upon the base case scenario, either be activated or not activated. In other words, only the intrinsic value of the option for the assumed scenario will be reflected. Thus, if a note contains embedded optionality, a deterministic analysis will reveal only the intrinsic value of the note for each scenario.

How good is the deterministic durational calculation in the context of notes containing optionality? Recall from option pricing theory that the value of a cap is as follows:

$$C = \exp(-rt)[FN(d_1) - KN(d_2)]$$

where $\quad d_1 = \ln (F/K)/\sigma(t)^{1/2} + 1/2\sigma(t)^{1/2}$
$\qquad\quad d_2 = \ln (F/K)/\sigma(t)^{1/2} - 1/2\sigma(t)^{1/2}$

This is the Black-76 Option Pricing Model,[5] which is used for pricing interest rate options. The price sensitivity of the option is expressed by δ, or the delta of

5. Black, Fischer. "The Pricing of Commodity Options," *Journal of Financial Economics* 3 (Jan.–March 1976), pp. 167–179.

the option. The δ measures the sensitivity of the option price as a function of the underlying interest rate F, and hence is directly related to the duration of a note containing optionality. By contrasting the true option delta with the deterministic delta of the note, the extent of over- or underestimation of the duration can be found. From option theory, it is a well known fact that the δ of an option lies between 0 and 1. On the other hand, deterministic delta would be either 0 or 1, depending upon whether the option is activated or not. Hence the deterministic durational calculations will, depending upon the rate scenario, either over- or underestimate the duration. This effect is clearly seen in the graph below.

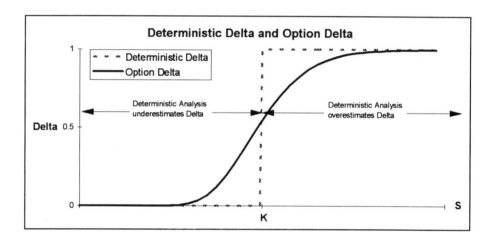

The above graph will be a useful guide in interpreting the deterministic durations of structured notes, specifically in understanding where deterministic duration will underestimate or overestimate the actual duration of a note.

Given the difficulty of deterministic analysis in providing an accurate view of the risks of structures with embedded options, what alternative risk analysis technique can assist investors in properly determining these risks? The solution is the simulation class of analysis. By properly and prudently employing simulations as outlined in Chapter 4, investors can, even without prior knowledge of the structure of the optionality, calculate the risk of structured notes with embedded optionality. As will be demonstrated in Chapter 4, simulation analysis provides an excellent approximation to the actual behavior of the note and should be used to compute the behavior of structured notes with skewed performance characteristics and embedded optionality components.

VOLATILITY RISK

As mentioned in the previous section, structured notes often include embedded options to provide certain performance characteristics. Changes in market volatility thus can have a significant impact on the value of the note. It will be demonstrated in Chapter 4 that only structures with embedded optionality or skewed performance characteristics will be affected by changes in volatility. Traditional floating rate notes such as Prime or LIBOR do not contain volatility risk.

The concept of *volatility duration* is introduced here as a measurement of volatility risk. In keeping with fixed income terminology, volatility duration is defined as follows:

$$ \mathrm{DUR}_{\mathrm{VOL}} = -\frac{1}{P}\left(\frac{dP}{d\sigma}\right) $$

where the volatility duration is expressed as a fractional change in the value of the note resulting from a change in volatility. The unit of volatility duration is defined in this book as +1 if the value of a note *declines* by 1 bp as the result of a 1% *increase* in term volatility.

Although the motivated investor can analyze the risk of a structure with respect to changing structure of volatility, the term structure of volatility has been assumed to be constant in the risk analyses performed in this book. The constant term volatility assumption will result in some departure from actual market conditions since very few indices trade on a flat volatility basis. However, this assumption permits investors to easily analyze volatility risk without requiring detailed information about the term structure of volatility.

Volatility risk is an integral component of the risk of structured notes. Unlike interest rate movements, which are readily observable, volatility risk is extremely difficult to quantify because of two reasons: first, unlike interest rates, volatility itself is not a directly observable quantity, and second, the volatility risk characteristics of structured notes are not intuitively obvious. Understanding the volatility duration of structured notes will thus enable investors to better quantify their overall risk.

Option Vega

For structured notes containing embedded optionality, it is logical to assume that the behavior of the note with respect to changing volatility would be cor-

related to the behavior of the underlying options. In other words, the volatility duration of a structured note is closely related to the *vega* of the option.
Understanding the behavior of an option with respect to changing volatility
will greatly enhance the understanding of volatility duration.

The vega of an option illustrates the change in the value of the option
with changing volatility. Recall from option pricing theory that vega is
defined as follows:[6]

$$\upsilon = \frac{dC}{d\sigma}$$

where C is the value of an option, in this case a call option, and σ is the
volatility. The graph below illustrates the behavior of the vega of a call
option with respect to changing levels of the underlying index.

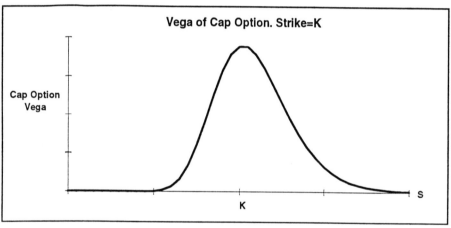

The above graph shows that vega is highest when the index is at the
strike level, in other words, the option gains the most value for an incremental rise in volatility when the index S is equal to the strike K. The vega of the
note decreases as the underlying index moves away from the strike level in
either direction. When the index is very far away from the strike, the vega
approaches zero. The behavior of the option vega can thus be summarized
as: largest vega as the index approaches the strike, lower vega the further
away from the strike.

---

6. See the classic options text by Cox, John, and Mark Rubinstein, *Options Markets.* Englewood Cliffs, NJ: Prentice-Hall, 1985. Vega is a term that is more often used on trading floors
than in textbooks. Zeta is a term more often seen in classic options texts as representing
volatility sensitivity.

This behavior will be helpful in the interpretation of the volatility duration of structured notes. In the simulation analyses of structured notes with embedded optionality and/or skewed performance behavior, the volatility duration of different structures will be calculated for a variety of base case scenarios. The volatility risks of these structures will then be interpreted with the help of option vega.

Other Index Risk

A structured note may be indexed to a non-interest rate index (such as the price of gold). The risk of a structure with respect to the spot movement of that index can also be calculated by defining a *non-interest rate duration* with respect to the price of the index, i.e.,

$$\text{DUR}_X = -\frac{1}{P}\left(\frac{dP}{dx}\right)$$

where x is the underlying index in question. The relationship of the future price of x can then be related to the spot price of x via an interest rate parity equation.

Like the volatility duration, the risk of notes with non-interest rate indices will include an analysis of this non-interest rate index duration for a variety of final base case scenarios.

STRUCTURED NOTE PERFORMANCE MEASUREMENT: INTERNAL RATE OF RETURN AND PRESENT VALUE

The second component of analyzing the risk/reward of a structured note is the performance analysis. One maxim that bears remembering is that higher return engenders higher risk. The performance of structured notes should be reflective of the risks inherent in the structure.

The analysis of performance is as follows: once the future indices and discounting rates are determined (using one of the three deterministic analyses discussed in Chapter 3), the IRR and the PV can be calculated deterministically. This is illustrated in the following example.

Example 2-3

Analyze the performance of the following note if the future cash flows and discounting rates are known. The current 2-year Treasury rate is 5.00%, and the issuer's corporate spread to Treasury is 0.20%. The specifications are as follows:

Issuer: AA
Maturity: 2 years
Coupon: 3-month LIBOR + 0.25%, paid quarterly Act/360

The future LIBORs are known and given in the table below.

Period	LIBOR at Beginning of Period
0 (Spot)	4.00%
1	4.25%
2	4.45%
3	4.65%
4	5.00%
5	5.25%
6	5.55%
7	5.75%
8	6.00%

Solution

Given the above set of LIBORs, the cash flow of the note can then be constructed at each period.

Period	LIBOR at Beginning of Period	Coupon: LIBOR + 0.25%	Cash Flow*
0 (spot)	4.00%	4.25%	−100%
1	4.25%	4.50%	1.08%
2	4.45%	4.70%	1.14%
3	4.65%	4.90%	1.19%
4	5.00%	5.25%	1.24%
5	5.25%	5.50%	1.33%
6	5.55%	5.80%	1.39%
7	5.75%	6.00%	1.47%
8	6.00%	6.25%	101.52%

*Cash flow: Investor pays 100% at beginning and receives 100% plus interest at the end of the last period. Coupon cash flows accrue on an Act/360 basis based on LIBOR set at beginning of period.

Based upon the above cash flow, the IRR and the PV can be simply calculated. The IRR is simply the rate of return as defined by the above cash flow stream. In this example, the IRR is calculated to be 5.096% (quarterly [Act/360]). The PV calculation requires the knowledge of a term discounting rate. The 2-year Treasury yield is given to be 5.00%. Since the corporate spread is 0.20%, the term DR is 5.20% (semiannual [30/360]). The PV can thus be calculated by discounting each of the cash flows by the appropriate discounting rate, adjusted back to quarterly [Act/360]. The appropriate quarterly DR r_{disc} is:

$$r_{disc} = \{[(1 + 5.20\%/2)^2]^{0.25} - 1\} * 4 * 360/365$$
$$= 5.096\% \text{ quarterly [Act/360]}$$

Each period discounting rate:

$$r_{per} = r_{disc} / 4 * (365/360)$$
$$= 1.292\%$$

$$PV = \frac{1.08\%}{(1.01292)} + \frac{1.14\%}{(1.01292)^2} + \cdots + \frac{101.52\%}{(1.01292)^8}$$
$$PV = 100.00$$

For this example, it is seen that the interest rate scenario chosen is such that, when combined with the to-maturity discounting rate, the PV is calculated to be par. This is obvious because the calculated IRR of 5.096% (quarterly Act/360) is equal to that of the DR used.

The PV as calculated above should not be construed as representing the real value of the note. It is what the note would be worth *if* the interest rate scenario given in the first table should come true, combined with the term DR being true. In short, the PV as calculated above should be used as a tool to illustrate the interest rate scenarios where the note would perform well and where it would underperform.

The PV of the note as calculated above thus depends upon both the interest rate scenario as well as the term discounting rate, and is often plotted as a 3-D graph as a function of both. Using the graph of the PV, an investor can quickly determine the interest rate scenarios that would result in the note performing well. Since the IRR depends only upon the coupon cash flows and hence the interest rate scenario, the IRR is typically plotted against a range of rate scenarios.

STRUCTURED NOTE PURCHASING STRATEGY AND EFFECT ON ANALYSIS TIME HORIZON

Depending upon the investor's purpose in purchasing the note, the time horizon over which the analysis should be performed would be different. There are two types of basic strategies: *buy-and-hold,* and *trading.* Not only are the structuring philosophies behind each strategy different, but the risk and performance analysis are different as well.

The buy-and-hold strategy assumes that the investor will purchase and then hold the structured note to maturity. Given such a strategy, any analysis should be performed to *maturity date.* The trading strategy assumes that the investor is purchasing the structured note with a view to trade out and take a profit within the near future. Thus, any analysis performed should be done to an *intermediate "horizon date"*[7] rather than the maturity date.

The issues of structuring for the above two investment strategies will be addressed in greater detail in Chapter 8.

COMPARISON AND BENCHMARKING PERFORMANCE

The performance of a structured note should be compared to a benchmark non-structured note of similar maturity and issued by the same or similar issuer. A fixed or a LIBOR floating rate note issued by the same issuer serves as a good benchmark for comparison because these two instruments are readily available investment alternatives that can be easily purchased by a prospective structured note investor.

Comparison to Fixed Rate Note

The comparison of the performance of a structured note to a fixed rate note is relatively straightforward. The fixed rate note yields a fixed IRR regardless of rate scenarios. The structured note would yield different IRR depending upon the rate scenarios used in the analysis.

To perform a benchmark analysis against a fixed rate note, the investor should produce the following table. The comparison is made using the linear smooth expectation analysis, which will be discussed in Chapter 3.

---

7. Dattatreya, Ravi E., and Frank J. Fabozzi. *Active Total Return Management of Fixed Income Portfolios.* Chicago, IL: Probus, 1989.

		IRR of Fixed Note: 4.50%
Final SN Index at Maturity	*IRR of Structured Note*	*Advantage of SN over Fixed Note*
3.00%	3.50%	−1.00%
4.00%	4.50%	0.00%
5.00%	5.50%	1.00%
6.00%	5.50%	1.00%

In the above table, the IRR of a fixed note issued by the same issuer of similar maturity as the structured note has a fixed yield of 4.50%. Using the first shaded line as an example and reading from left to right: for the rate scenario in which the structured note index at maturity is 3.00%, the IRR of the structured note is calculated to be 3.50%. The resulting yield advantage (disadvantage) of the structured note IRR as compared to the fixed note, which yields 4.50%, is −1.00%. This means that the structured note would underperform the fixed rate note by 100 bps of yield for this interest rate scenario.

A table such as the above illustrates the performance of a structured note relative to that of a fixed target. It allows the investor to see which rate scenarios would result in the structured note outperforming the fixed note.

Comparison to Floating Rate Note

A comparison of structured notes to floating rate notes is slightly more complicated than the comparison to fixed rate notes. Two scenarios, one for the structured note, and another for the floating rate benchmark note, have to be developed in order to make yield comparisons.

Example 2-4

Analyze the return of the following note for a range of final expectation rates. Compare the performance of the note to a benchmark floating rate note of the same issuer.

Issuer:	U.S. Agency
Maturity:	3 years
Coupon:	Year 1: 4.35%
	Years 2–3: 5.35% when 3-year Lira CMS ≤ 7.5%
	0.00% when 3-year Lira CMS > 7.5%
Benchmark FRN:	LIBOR − 0.20%

Solution

Two interest rate scenarios have to be generated and compared. The following yield table summarizes the analysis.

3-year ITL CMS at Last Reset	IRR of SN	LIBOR at Maturity →	3.375	4.000	5.000	6.000
		IRR of FRN* →	3.175	3.481	3.969	4.454
8.50	1.471		−1.704	−2.010	−2.498	−2.982
7.88**	1.471		−1.704	−2.010	−2.498	−2.982
7.00	4.103		0.928	0.622	0.134	−0.351
6.00	5.000		1.825	1.519	1.031	0.546
5.00	5.000		1.825	1.519	1.031	0.546

* Comparable note of issuer currently trades at US$ LIBOR minus 0.20%.
** Spot 3-year Lira CMS is 7.88%.

The comparison analysis is explained using the highlighted cell in the table as an example: If 3-month LIBOR at maturity remains at the current level of 3.375%, the IRR of a comparable maturity U.S. Agency FRN yielding LIBOR − 0.20% is 3.175%. The IRR of the Italian Bull Range Note when 3-year Lira CMS at maturity is 5.00% is 5.000%, which is 1.825% higher than the comparable FRN. Thus, this particular combination of rate scenarios results in the structured note outperforming the floating rate note by a yield margin of 1.825%.

These two methods of performance benchmarking provide investors with some grounds for comparing the scenario performance of the structured note to another comparable investment vehicle. The benchmarks will thus assist investors in making a more informed investment decision by bringing to light the interest rate scenarios that would result in the structured note underperforming another potential investment.

CONCLUSION

This chapter illustrates the necessity of modifying the concept of duration as a measurement of risk in the structured note market. Structured notes whose index and discounting rates are identical contain no yield curve risk and can be analyzed by employing scenarios of a single key rate: the to-maturity Treasury rate. However, this zero yield curve risk condition does not apply to a large class of structured notes. In order to adequately handle the complexity of such structures in a clear and consistent manner that preserves the simplicity and power of duration, the concept of KTRD was introduced as the logical extension of risk analysis.

In addition to interest rate risks, structured notes can contain volatility risk and non-interest rate risk. The concepts of *volatility duration* and *non-interest-rate-duration* that were introduced in this chapter will enable investors to gain a complete view of the various dimensions of risk surrounding structured notes.

Other tools are introduced for the analysis of the performance of the note. These measures of performance are the IRR and, to a lesser extent, the PV. The PV calculates the present value of the cash flows under different interest rate certainty scenarios and discounting rate scenarios, while the IRR calculates the net return to the investor under different scenarios. These two properties provide measurements of the performance of a structured note for a variety of different interest rate scenarios and compliements the risk analysis provided by KTRD to provide a complete risk/reward view of a structure.

In all future analyses, the performance of a structure will be measured by the IRR, and risk will be examined via the duration results.

Many investors require that the performance of a structured note be analyzed in the context of a benchmark. A methodology for comparing structured note performance with respect to benchmark non-structured securities was also provided.

3

Deterministic Analysis

Structured note analysis can be broadly classified into one of two classes: deterministic or simulation. The deterministic class of analysis performs scenario analysis based on the assumption that all scenarios will occur with equal probability. The analyzer is responsible for selecting a range of scenarios which can best quantify the range of risks that the note will likely face. This class of analysis is well suited for analyzing a wide range of "what-if" scenarios and permits investors to observe the performance of a structured note under a wide range of possible scenarios, including remote and low probability "meltdown" scenarios. This chapter will present and discuss the deterministic class of analysis, while the next chapter will complete the picture by describing the simulation class of analysis.

This chapter introduces investors to the first of two classes of analysis methodologies which, if properly applied, will enable investors to assess the risks and rewards of structured notes under various interest rate scenarios. The application of deterministic analysis in combination with the simulation analysis in Chapter 4 will provide the investor with a complement of analysis tools with which to analyze the risk and return of the majority of past, present, and future structures.

The three types of deterministic analyses which are commonly used in assessing structured note risk are forward analysis, expectation analysis, and historical analysis. Each analysis will be employed in this chapter to examine the rate sensitivities of the performance of a structured note as represented by the internal rate of return (IRR), and the risk as represented by the duration. Each analysis will be conducted within the context of the trading strategy and the associated time horizon. The performance and risk of structured notes will also be compared to that of comparable benchmark investments to assist investors in the purchasing decision.

ANALYSIS I. FORWARD ANALYSIS

The forward analysis is considered a "default" scenario analysis because it examines the performance of the structured note in the fulfillment of market expectation. Where the forward rates are known, the forward analysis uses the level of forward rates at each future coupon and/or principal reset date to evaluate the IRR, the present value (PV), and the duration of the note given that the forwards will come true.

The evaluation of the risk and return characteristics can, depending upon the investor's strategy, be calculated to either the maturity date or an intermediate horizon date. As mentioned in Chapter 2, a buy-and-hold strategy would entail an analysis to the maturity date, while a trading strategy would require an analysis to an intermediate horizon date. The IRR, PV, and durational characteristics of the note would be computed to the date which is appropriate for the investor's chosen strategy.

Forward Analysis Methodology

The forward analysis is applied in the following steps.

1. Determine the forward predicted rates from available market sources.
2. The floating rate indices for the coupon periods between the settlement and maturity dates are calculated by interpolating between the available forward rates.
3. The intermediate coupon cash flow can then be calculated from the corresponding floating rate indices.

Forward Analysis to Maturity Date

4. For the coupon cash flows calculated in Step 3, the IRR can be calculated by taking the resulting yield of all the cash flows to the maturity date.

5. The PV to maturity date is calculated by valuing the coupon cash flows at the applicable term discounting rate.
6. The duration of the note can then be found using the durational techniques described earlier in Chapter 2. For some notes, the index rate (IR) and discounting rate (DR) are identical and should be accounted for in the durational calculations. Other structures with inherent yield curve risk will require the use of the key Treasury rate duration (KTRD).

Forward Analysis to an Intermediate Horizon Date

The horizon date analysis examines the return to the investor if the structured note were to be sold on a future date prior to the maturity date. On the horizon date, the investor will receive a future value for the note plus the accrued coupon up to the horizon date. The future value (FV) of the note is calculated by valuing the coupon cash flows from the horizon date to the maturity date at the appropriate discounting rate between those two dates.

7. Calculate the FV by valuing the forward predicted cash flows at a forward term discounting rate.
8. Calculate the IRR that is implied from the FVs.

The mechanics of the forward analysis are outlined via the following example.

Example 3-1

An investor has purchased the following floating rate note. Using forward analysis, calculate the risk and performance of the note to:

1. the maturity date, and
2. an intermediate horizon date of 1 year

Issuer:	AA Bank
Coupon:	6-month LIBOR + 0.20%
Maturity:	3 years
Current 1-year Treasury:	3.535%
Current 3-year Treasury:	4.582%
Issuer credit spread to Treasury:	+0.40%

Period	Forward LIBOR	Period	Forward LIBOR
0	3.50%	4	5.50%
1	4.00%	5	6.00%
2	4.50%	6	6.50%
3	5.00%		

Solution

The forward analysis will be used to calculate the performance and risk of the note for the given set of forward rates.

Combining the first three steps of the forward analysis:

Steps 1, 2, and 3. Given the forward levels of LIBOR, the following coupon and cash flow table can be created:

Period (a)	Forward Implied LIBOR (b)	Coupon Based on Forward LIBOR (c)	Cash Flow* (d)
0			−100
1	3.50%	3.70%	1.8757
2	4.00%	4.20%	2.1292
3	4.50%	4.70%	2.3826
4	5.00%	5.20%	2.6361
5	5.50%	5.70%	2.8896
6	6.00%	6.20%	103.1431

* LIBOR coupon cash flows calculated on an Act/360 basis. Principal of 100% is paid by the investor on settlement date and received by investor with accrued interest of last period on maturity date.

For each period, the forward LIBORs (column b) are used to calculate the corresponding coupon flows (column c), which in this example is LIBOR + 0.20%. Finally, the cash flows (column d) can be computed from the coupons.

Note that the coupon cash flows are calculated on an Actual/360 day count basis. For example, if the LIBOR based coupon is calculated to be 3.70%, the actual cash flow paid out at the end of a 182-day period would be calculated as follows:

$$\text{Cash flow} = 3.70\% * (\text{No. of days in period})/360$$
$$= 3.70\% * (182/360)$$
$$= 1.8706\%$$

Since no exact dates are provided, the cash flow of the above table is calculated by approximating the Actual/360 day count convention by the following method:

$$\text{Cash flow} = 3.70\% * (1/N) * (365/360) \tag{3-1}$$
$$= 3.70\% * 0.5069$$
$$= 1.8757\%$$

where N is the number of payment periods per year.

The above approximation will be used throughout the book to calculate coupon cash flows based on Actual/360 (money market) day count basis.

Forward Analysis to Maturity Date

Step 4: IRR Calculation.   Since the cash flows are known, the IRR of the note can be determined. In this case, the IRR is calculated to be 4.982% (semiannual 30/360 yield).

Step 5: PV Calculation.   Given that the stream of future cash flows is known from the forward rates, finding the PV is simply a matter of discounting those cash flows by the proper discounting rate. The PV calculated to maturity is computed by present valuing all the future cash flows from settlement date at the appropriate term discounting rate:

$$\text{PV (to maturity)} = \frac{C_1}{\left(1+r_\text{disc}\right)} + \frac{C_2}{\left(1+r_\text{disc}\right)^2} + \frac{C_3}{\left(1+r_\text{disc}\right)^3} + \cdots + \frac{\left(C_n + P_0\right)}{\left(1+r_\text{disc}\right)^n}$$

where r_disc is the term discounting rate for the period, C_i is the ith period coupon, and P_0 is the principal returned at maturity. For this example, the term discounting rate is the sum of the to-maturity Treasury rate plus the appropriate issuer credit spread to Treasury, or 4.982% (4.582% + 0.40%). Discounting the coupon cash flows from column d with this discounting rate results in the present value of the note calculated to be 100.00%.

Step 6: Duration.   Recall that the duration of a note can be decomposed into two components: discounting and index.

Discounting: The DR of the note is the to-maturity Treasury rate, or the 3-year Treasury rate. The DR duration is approximately 2.75.

Index: The IR of the note must represent the aggregate result of the stream of LIBOR based cash flows. This aggregate IR is equivalent to the 3-year swap rate, which is equal to the 3-year Treasury rate plus a swap spread. Assuming the swap spread remains relatively constant, the IR can be represented by the 3-year Treasury rate. The IR duration of the note with respect to this IR is equal to –2.75.

The net duration of the note is obtained by combining the DRD and IRD. The result shows that this LIBOR FRN possesses a duration of zero, which is exactly as expected. Note that if the first LIBOR coupon has been set, the note would have a non-zero duration of approximately 0.25, which corresponds to the fixed stub.

Forward Analysis to Horizon Date

Step 7: Future Value on Horizon Date. The above calculation is applied in the same manner when analyzing to a horizon date, except that the PV-to-horizon-date is calculated by present valuing the cash flows from the horizon date to the maturity date, i.e.,

$$\text{FV (Horizon date)} = \frac{C_i}{(1+r_i)} + \frac{C_{i+1}}{(1+r_{i+1})^2} + \frac{C_{i+2}}{(1+r_{i+2})^3} + \cdots + \frac{(C_n + P_0)}{(1+r_n)^n}$$

where i is the first period after the horizon date, which is 3 in this example. The appropriate discounting rate is found by adding the forward Treasury rate to the credit spread. The in-1-year-for-2-year Treasury rate is calculated by bootstrapping the 1- and 3-year Treasury rates and is seen to be 5.108%. Discounting the cash flows from period 2 to period 6 (column c) using the sum of the forward Treasury rate plus the credit spread to Treasury produces a future value (FV) on horizon date of 100.00%. Again, this is an expected result since LIBOR FRNs should always be resettable back to par.

Step 8: IRR to Horizon Date. The IRR of the note to the horizon date is found by calculating the IRR of the note given the coupon cash flows to the horizon date and the future value which the investor is expected to receive on the horizon date. The net IRR to the 1-year horizon date is equal to 4.003%.

Example 3-2

The investor intends to purchase and hold the following structured note to maturity. Perform a forward analysis on this note and compare the note's performance against a benchmark LIBOR FRN.

Note Specification

Issuer:	Single-A U.S. corporate
Coupon:	3-month LIBOR + 0.10% subject to coupon floor
Coupon floor:	4.50%
Maturity:	3 years
Credit spread to Treasury:	+0.60%

Current Market Conditions

Current 3-year Treasury rate:	6.00%
Current 6-month T-bill rate:	4.00% (semiannual bond equivalent yield)
Benchmark FRN:	LIBOR + 0.40% (by same issuer)

The forward LIBORs for each period are as follows:

Period	LIBOR	Period	LIBOR	Period	LIBOR
0	3.75%	5	4.75%	10	5.25%
1	4.00%	6	4.85%	11	5.33%
2	4.25%	7	5.00%	12	5.40%
3	4.45%	8	5.10%		
4	4.60%	9	5.20%		

Solution

This structure is a floored FRN, which will be discussed in greater detail in Chapter 5. Since the investor intends to hold the note to maturity, the forward analysis will be performed to the maturity date.

Steps 1, 2, and 3. Using the forward rates as provided, the corresponding coupon and cash flow are calculated in the following table:

Period (a)	Forward Implied LIBOR (b)	Coupon Based on Forward LIBOR (c)	Cash Flow* (d)
0			−100
1	3.75%	4.50%	1.141
2	4.00%	4.50%	1.141
3	4.25%	4.50%	1.141
4	4.45%	4.55%	1.153
5	4.60%	4.70%	1.191
6	4.75%	4.85%	1.229
7	4.85%	4.95%	1.255
8	5.00%	5.10%	1.293
9	5.10%	5.20%	1.318
10	5.20%	5.30%	1.343
11	5.25%	5.35%	1.356
12	5.33%	5.43%	101.376

* LIBOR cash flows calculated on a quarterly Act/360 basis.

The coupon of column c is calculated using the coupon formula provided. Note that the minimum coupon is now floored at a level of 4.50%. The cash flow in column d is calculated on an Actual/360 day count basis.

Step 4: IRR.   The overall IRR is calculated from the cash flow (column d) to be 4.896% (quarterly Act/360).

Step 5: Present Value.   The present value of the note can be found by discounting the future cash flows by an appropriate discounting rate (Treasury + credit spread). The single-A credit in the example trades at Treasury + 0.60%, resulting in a DR of 6.60% (6.00% Treasury + 0.60% credit spread), which is equivalent to a quarterly rate of 6.546%. Discounting the cash flows (column d) by this quarterly rate yields a PV of 95.71%.

Step 6: Duration.   Once the PV is calculated, the duration of the note can also be found by examining the effect of 1 bp change in the discounting Treasury rate on the PV of the note. Since the IR and DR are identical in this example, the net duration can be found by perturbing the term LIBORs by 1 bp and at the same time perturbing the 3-year Treasury rate by 1 bp. Due to the presence of the coupon floor, this note is not expected to be duration neutral.

PV (Current) = 95.710%

PV (+1 bp term LIBORs, +1 bp 3-year Treasury) = 95.704%

Duration $= -1/P * (dP/dr)$

$= -1/(95.71\%) * (-0.006\%/0.01\%)$

Duration = 0.62

Using the above calculation, the duration of the note with respect to the IR/DR (which is the 3-year Treasury rate) is calculated to be 0.62. This means that the floored LIBOR FRN non-zero duration is *not duration neutral* and, unlike the LIBOR FRN, has exposure to interest rate movements.

Benchmarking

The benchmark of comparison is the issuer's floating rate note yielding LIBOR + 0.40%. The cash flow of the LIBOR FRN for the LIBOR scenario is calculated as follows.

Period (a)	Forward Implied LIBOR (b)	Benchmark Coupon Based on Forwards (c)	Cash Flow* (d)
0			−100
1	3.75%	4.15%	1.052
2	4.00%	4.40%	1.115
3	4.25%	4.65%	1.179
4	4.45%	4.95%	1.229
5	4.60%	5.00%	1.267
6	4.75%	5.15%	1.305
7	4.85%	5.25%	1.331
8	5.00%	5.40%	1.369
9	5.10%	5.50%	1.394
10	5.20%	5.60%	1.419
11	5.25%	5.65%	1.432
12	5.33%	5.73%	101.452

* LIBOR cash flows calculated on a quarterly Act/360 basis.

IRR of Benchmark FRN.   Given the above cash flows, the IRR of the benchmark LIBOR FRN is calculated to be 5.089%. This is a yield advantage of 0.193% over the floored FRNs IRR of 4.896%.

Duration of Benchmark FRN. A LIBOR FRN has been demonstrated earlier as having zero duration. Compared to the floored FRN's duration of 0.62, the benchmark LIBOR FRN thus contains much lower (in fact, zero) interest rate risk.

The conclusion that an investor should draw from this benchmark calculation is that, if the investor believes the forwards will come true, the benchmark LIBOR FRN provides better performance than the floored FRN in the example. Thus, an investor believing in the forward predicted rates should purchase the LIBOR FRN instead of the floored FRN. The advantage of the floored FRN is that it provides the investor with yield protection if rates drop, i.e., investors who purchase this note may believe in the forward rates but want to obtain yield protection in case the forwards do not come true.

In summary, the performance and risk of the note are as follows:

Note	Performance (IRR)	Risk (Interest Rate Duration)
Floored FRN	4.896%	0.62
LIBOR FRN (benchmark)	5.089%	0.00

Failure of the Forward Analysis

The forward analysis is the most theoretically rigorous of the three deterministic analyses because the assumptions of future rates are based upon market expectations (as opposed to the investor's own expectations) and therefore would be easiest to justify. However, the forward analysis does have certain drawbacks and is inappropriate in certain cases.

1. Forwards are notoriously bad predictors of future rates. The accompanying graph compares the forward predicted 3-month LIBOR using Eurodollar futures data from December 1990 to the actual historical 3-month LIBOR. The forward predictions of LIBOR far overestimated the future rates. Thus, one needs to be careful about using forwards as predictors of future values.

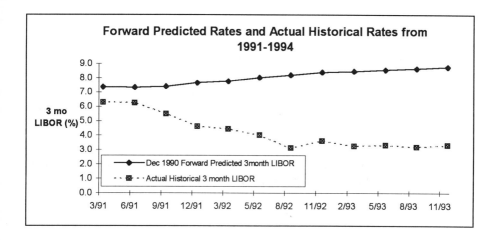

2. Lack of a publicly available forward market. Where forward rates are either not traded on an exchange or publicly available, the investor would be unable to directly infer the forward rates.
3. The structure can be a bet against the prediction of the forward rates becoming true. A structured note is often purchased to permit the investor to profit when forward rates predicted by the current yield curve fail to materialize. For these investors, analyzing the performance of the note in the context of the forward rates being realized is self-contradictory.
4. The structured note is purchased as a traded instrument. The investor purchased the note as a capital gains instrument with the goal of capitalizing quickly on momentary market movements. To accomplish that necessitates the instrument be cashed out when rates move in the investor's favor. For these investors, a forward analysis would also not be helpful.

ANALYSIS II. EXPECTATION ANALYSIS

An investor with a strong market and rate view can purchase a structured note in order to obtain a greatly enhanced yield if that view were to come true. Since that view may not coincide with the predicted forward rates, the forward analysis may not always be the appropriate analysis to use. The expectation analysis provides an alternative analysis which is favored by investors whose views do not necessarily coincide with the predictions of the forward rates. The basic assumption of the expectation analysis is the investor's expectations of the index behavior between the trade date and maturity date. A range of final expectation values are used to calculate a range of intermediate rates and the performance of the note can be computed for each scenario.

The performance of a structured note depends not only on the value of the index at maturity, but also upon its value on each intermediate coupon reset date. Thus, the assumption about the path taken by the index is an important factor in the determination of its performance. The most popular and straightforward path assumption is the linear smooth expectation (LSE).

Linear Smooth Expectation (LSE) Analysis

The basic assumption of the LSE analysis is that the underlying index (indices) will take a linear interest rate path between the initial level(s) and the final expected index level(s) at maturity. Although a smooth linear path is a simple approach to projecting a path, it has certain merits, the chief of which is that the linear path permits comparison of different structures in a consistent framework. Although readers are free to contort the path of future indices in any desired manner, great care should be exercised so that an overly optimistic path will not be used to represent the complete risk picture. The ultimate goal of LSE analysis is to enable the investor to determine the note's performance and risk across a wide variety of interest rate scenarios.

Linear Smooth Expectation Analysis Methodology

LSE analysis is applied in the following stepwise manner:

1. Determine a range of final expectation values for the index of interest. The final expectation level can either be specified to be at maturity, on final reset date, or on an intermediate date. The distinction between setting the final rate level at maturity and on the final reset date is important. Many structured note coupons reset based on the level of the index at the start of the period (but are paid at the end of the period). For these structures, the final coupon would be based on the level of the index on the last reset date and not the index-at-maturity. This is a subtle but definitive difference.
2. For each final expectation index value, the intermediate indices between the present date and maturity date can be calculated by lin-

early interpolating between the current index value and the final expectation index value.
3. The intermediate coupon cash flows can then be calculated from the corresponding intermediate index values.

LSE Analysis to Maturity: Indicators of Performance and Risk

Given the coupon cash flows, the indicators of performance and risk can be calculated to the maturity date.

4. The IRR to the maturity date is the first indicator of note performance. The investor is able to observe the return of the note under various scenarios.
5. The PV to the maturity date is calculated by valuing the coupon cash flows for each final expectation index value at the appropriate term discounting rate.
6. The risk of the note can be determined by examining the behavior of the duration of the note under different interest rate scenarios with the durational calculations described in Chapter 2. There are two components of risk: the index component, and the discounting component. Each component has a duration associated with it: DUR_{INDEX} and DUR_{DISC}. The resulting net duration of the note can then be plotted as a function of the final expectation rates.

LSE Analysis to Horizon Date

For investors with a trading strategy, LSE analysis can be performed to an intermediate horizon date. The horizon date analysis analyzes the return to the investor if the structured note were to be sold on the horizon date. On the horizon date, the investor receives a future value for the note and also the accrued coupons up to the horizon date. The FV of the note is calculated by valuing the coupon cash flows from the horizon date to the maturity date at the various term discounting rates.

7. The FV as a function of the final expectation index value and the term discounting rate can be calculated. This is the value that the investor can expect to receive on the horizon date if the selected scenario were to come true.

8. The IRR to the horizon date can be calculated for various final expectation scenarios. The return to the investor on the horizon date would be based upon the coupon accrued to the horizon date and the FV calculated above.

The LSE analysis is illustrated by the following example.

Example 3-3

The investor is considering purchasing the following note on a held-to-maturity basis. Analyze the IRR of the note using LSE analysis. Current 6-month LIBOR is 3.50%.

Issuer: U.S. Agency
Maturity: 3 years
Coupon: 6-month LIBOR plus 0.25%, subject to coupon cap
Coupon cap: 5.50%

Solution

The above note is a Capped FRN (CapFRN; discussed in detail in Chapter 5). The example will be analyzed using the LSE analysis outlined above. Since the note may be purchased on a held-to-maturity basis, the analysis will be performed to the maturity date.

Step 1.   Select a final expectation value of LIBOR. A level of 6.00% will be selected as the expectation LIBOR *on final reset date.*

Steps 2 and 3.   Calculate the interpolated index rates and the corresponding coupons. The following cash flow table can be set up.

Period (I)	LIBOR (%) (II)	Coupon (%) (III)	Cash Flow* (IV)
0	3.50		−100
1	4.00	3.75	1.90
2	4.50	4.25	2.16
3	5.00	4.75	2.41
4	5.50	5.25	2.66
5	6.00	5.50	2.79
6	6.50 (not used)	5.50	102.79

*LIBOR coupons are calculated based upon LIBOR at the start of the period on an Act/360 basis.

The expected LIBORs (column II) for the intermediate periods between settlement and maturity can be found by linearly interpolating between the spot LIBOR of 3.50% and the LIBOR of 6.00% on final coupon reset date. The corresponding LIBOR based coupon (column III) is LIBOR + 0.25%. If the coupon exceeds the cap of 5.50%, the coupon is set to the cap. Finally, the corresponding cash flows from the expectation coupons are calculated using the Actual/360 day count approximation of Equation (3-1).

Step 4: IRR. The IRR of the note can be calculated for a range of final expectation scenarios by repeating Steps 1 to 3.

A range of final expected LIBOR scenarios can be used for each analysis, and the IRR resulting from each expectation is calculated.

Expectation of Index on Final Reset Date of Note	IRR of Note
3.50	3.75%
4.25	4.06%
5.00	4.36%
5.75	4.64%
6.50	4.81%

The IRR of the CapFRN for a range of final expectation LIBORs is plotted in Exhibit 3-1. The performance of the note is compared to a benchmark LIBOR FRN for the same set of interest rate scenarios. From Exhibit 3-1, it is evident that the CapFRN analyzed above will outperform the benchmark LIBOR FRN in low interest rate scenarios. For higher interest rate scenarios, the CapFRN in the example will underperform a LIBOR FRN since many of the CapFRN's coupons will have reached the coupon cap level.

Step 5: PV. The PV of the note can be calculated for the set of above final expectation rates.

The present value of the CapFRN can be calculated by discounting the future cash flows in column IV of the first table for a range of term discounting rates. The PV is calculated using the following formula:

$$PV \text{ (to maturity)} = \frac{C_1}{(1+r_1)} + \frac{C_2}{(1+r_2)^2} + \frac{C_3}{(1+r_3)^3} + \cdots + \frac{(C_n + P_0)}{(1+r_n)^n}$$

where r_i is the discounting rate over 1 period for the ith period, C_i is the ith period coupon, and P_0 is the principal returned at maturity. For a given term

EXHIBIT 3-1 Performance of a Capped LIBOR FRN

The CapFRN is analyzed using LSE to construct a range of final interest rates. Each final rate is used to construct a series of intermediate rates which are employed in the cash flow calculations. From these cash flows, the rate of return can be calculated. This example shows that the capped LIBOR FRN will outperform a comparable maturity benchmark LIBOR FRN in low interest rate scenarios. The breakeven point at which the CapFRN and the benchmark LIBOR FRN produce identical results is the LIBOR at maturity = 7.5% scenario.

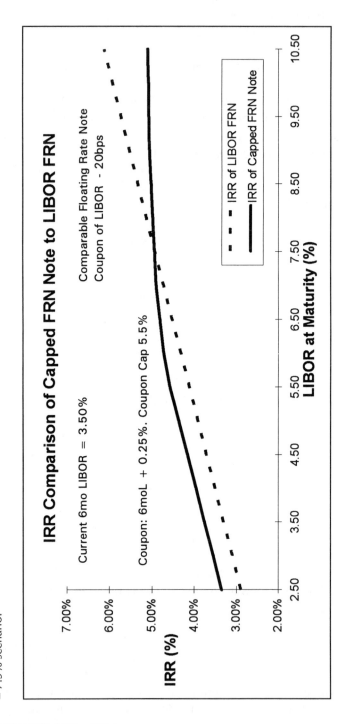

IRR Comparison of Capped FRN Note to LIBOR FRN

Current 6mo LIBOR = 3.50%

Comparable Floating Rate Note
Coupon of LIBOR - 20bps

Coupon: 6moL + 0.25%. Coupon Cap 5.5%

- - - IRR of LIBOR FRN
—— IRR of Capped FRN Note

IRR (%)

LIBOR at Maturity (%)

discounting rate r_{disc}, the discounting rates for each of the individual periods are then equal: $r_1 = r_2 = r_3 = r_n = r_{disc}$.

The appropriate term discounting rate r_{disc} is used to calculate the PV for each interest rate scenario. Like the interest rate scenarios, this term discounting rate must be adjusted as well. Higher interest rate scenarios will require a higher discounting rate r_{disc}. The appropriate r_{disc} is found by calculating the cumulative result of the intermediate interest rates for the particular scenario. Combining this cumulative rate with an appropriate spread will produce a discounting rate.

Step 6: Duration. Once the note's PV for the selected scenario has been calculated, the duration of the CapFRN can likewise be found. Since the CapFRN's floating index is 3-month LIBOR, which resets quarterly, the IR and DR are identical. The duration of the note can then be found by perturbing both the term LIBORs and the 3-year Treasury rate by 1 bp. The duration can be calculated for the different final interest rate scenarios and is plotted in Exhibit 3-2. The results will be discussed in greater detail in the CapFRN section of Chapter 5. However, what is evident is that the risk of the note is not constant, but changes with different interest rate scenarios. This characteristic distinguishes structured notes from non-callable fixed rate notes whose risk characteristics change very little over a wide range of interest rate environments.

Other Expectation Scenarios

As mentioned earlier, readers are free to create various interest rate paths to analyze structured notes. However, analyzers should ensure that the discounting rate used for calculating the PV and duration is consistent with the interest rate scenario chosen. Readers should try to use a consistent set of interest rate paths so that a reasonable comparison to a benchmark security as well as to other structures can be made.

ANALYSIS III. HISTORICAL ANALYSIS

The third and final deterministic analysis to be discussed is the historical analysis. Often, examining the performance of a structure on a historical basis yields further insight into the true risk properties of the note. Historical analy-

EXHIBIT 3-2 Deterministic Duration of CapFRN

LSE is used to calculate the intermediate LIBOR coupon cash flows. The index rate and the discounting rate are the same; hence, the note has rate risk with respect to the same rate, which is the 3-year Treasury rate. Deterministic duration shows that the note would perform like an FRN for low interest rate scenarios, which is reflected by the zero duration. For higher interest rate scenarios, more coupons will be capped, resulting in decreasing value for higher rates. This can be seen in the rising duration.

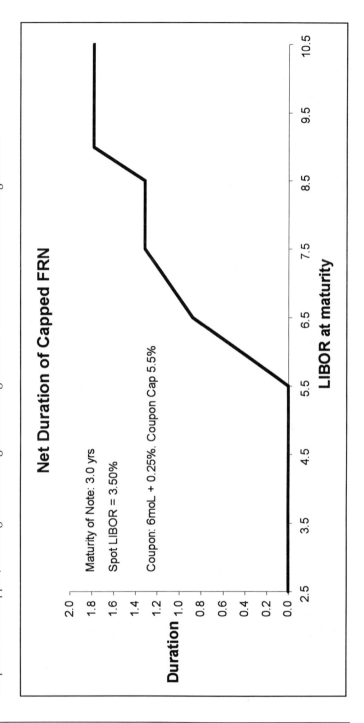

Net Duration of Capped FRN

Maturity of Note: 3.0 yrs

Spot LIBOR = 3.50%

Coupon: 6moL + 0.25%. Coupon Cap 5.5%

Duration

LIBOR at maturity

sis is used in conjunction with either the forward or expectation analysis to analyze the expected performance of a note.

Historical analysis provides the investor with insight into the behavior of the index using past historical data as a guide. This tool allows an investor who originally may not have any expectations about the index rate in question to formulate expectations based upon the historical performance of the index. Historical analysis is best applied to indices which are not traded on any futures and options exchange and which are difficult for one to have expectations.

The main goal of the historical analysis is to uncover from the historical data some relationship between the index (or combination of indices) in question and another set of relevant rates. The historical analysis examines the historical relationship between the coupon index and a *relevant index*. Statistical linear regression is then employed to determine the relationship between the two sets of historical data. This relationship would then be applied to the LSE analysis using the investor's expectations about the relevant index in combination with the historical relationship between the two data sets.

The basic premise of the historical analysis is that the past historical correlation between two indices will be relevant in the future. Since past history is by no means a guarantee of the future, the selection of the relevant index should be made carefully. In addition to a historical correlation, the investor should strive to find a rational explanation for this correlation. If the cause of this correlation is definitive, one can retain some measure of confidence that the correlated behavior would be continued into the future.

An ideal candidate for the historical analysis is the Prime-LIBOR spread. There are no traded futures contracts on the Prime rate, and while the Prime rate is often regarded as being closely correlated to LIBOR, the behavior of the differential between the two indices is not well understood. The historical analysis provides a means of uncovering the relationship of the Prime-LIBOR spread to a relevant index (or indices).

Exhibit 3-3 shows the historical behavior of both the Prime rate and LIBOR from 1986 to 1994. Exhibit 3-3 shows that the correlation between the Prime rate and 3-month LIBOR is extremely high (approximately 97%). However, since the coupon is based on the difference between the two indices, one needs to examine the historical behavior of the *spread* between the two indices. A relevant index should be selected against which the Prime-LIBOR spread can be measured. The 10-year CMT–3-month LIBOR spread is selected here as the relevant index. The graph of the historical

EXHIBIT 3-3 Historical Behavior of Prime- and 3-month LIBOR

Based on the historical data from 1986 to 1994, the correlation of 96.9% between Prime- and 3-month LIBOR has been extremely high.

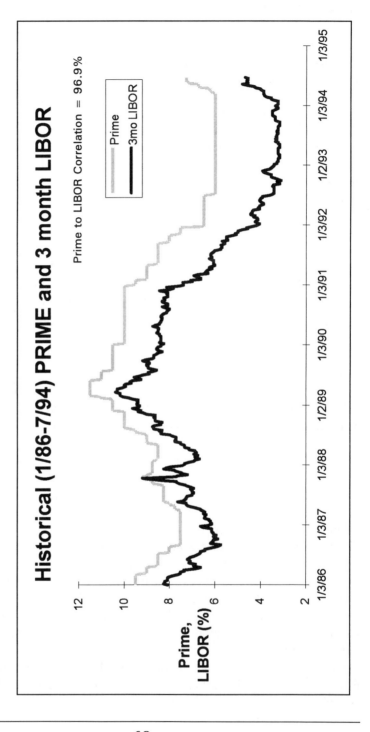

Historical (1/86-7/94) PRIME and 3 month LIBOR

Prime to LIBOR Correlation = 96.9%

Prime-LIBOR spread versus the yield curve spread (defined as the 10-year Treasury yield minus 3-month LIBOR) in Exhibit 3-4 appears to show some correlation between the two spreads. Upon further analysis, the correlation between the two spreads is calculated to be approximately 63%. This means that, on a historical basis, as the yield curve becomes flatter, the Prime-LIBOR spread becomes narrower as well.

The investor should search for a relevant index which provides a good correlation to the index in question. Since the correlation of 63% between the relevant index (CMT-LIBOR) spread and the Prime-LIBOR spread is fairly high (over 50%), it can be considered an adequate relevant index.

Historical Analysis Methodology

The historical analysis is applied in the following manner:

0. Select an appropriate relevant index. The selection process should be carefully conducted. Care must be taken not to select a relevant index which, contrary to its name, has little relevance to the index of interest.
1. Obtain the historical behavior of the index of interest R_{int} and the relevent index R_{RI} about which the investor has an active view.
2. Find the correlation between R_{int} and R_{RI} from the historical data:

$$R_{int} = m * R_{RI} + b$$

where m is the slope, and b is the intercept.

3. Employ LSE analysis to project a set of forward LSE rates for R_{RI}.
4. Use the linear regression analysis results to calculate a set of forward index rates of interest R_{int} corresponding to each R_{RI} rate.
5. Examine the performance of the note in this context.

A Prime-LIBOR spread note will serve to illustrate the implementation of the historical analysis.

Example 3-4

Analyze the following Prime-LIBOR differential note using historical analysis. Assume the investor has the view that the yield curve (10-year Treasury minus 3-month LIBOR) will gradually flatten from today's level to zero on the maturity day of the note. Calculate the note's performance and risk.

EXHIBIT 3-4 Linear Regression Analysis of Historical Prime-LIBOR Spread and Yield Curve Slope

A linear regression analysis on the historical data from 1986 to 1994 shows the correlation of the two spreads as 63.7%, which is high enough that the CMT-LIBOR spread can be considered as a relevant index.

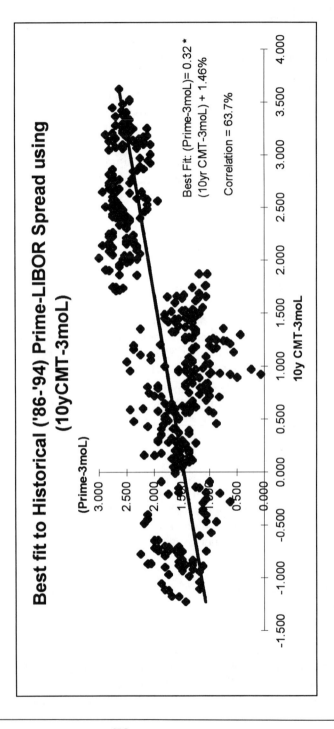

Best fit to Historical ('86-'94) Prime-LIBOR Spread using (10yCMT-3moL)

Best Fit: (Prime-3moL)= 0.32 * (10yr CMT-3moL) + 1.46%

Correlation = 63.7%

10y CMT-3moL

(Prime-3moL)

Note Specifications

Issuer:	U.S. Agency
Coupon:	Prime – 3-month LIBOR + 2.00%
Maturity:	3 years
Issuer credit	
spread to Treasury:	+0.10%

Current Market Conditions

3-year Treasury:	4.40%
Current yield curve:	2.80%
Yield curve:	10-year CMT – 3-month LIBOR

Solution

Step 0. Determine relevant index. The relevant index to be used here will be the 10-year CMT–3-month LIBOR spread, which has been shown to possess good correlation to the Prime-LIBOR index in question. One possible explanation for this correlation will be described in greater detail in Chapter 6.

Step 1. Gather historical data. The historical data of both the Prime-LIBOR spread and the 10-year CMT-LIBOR spread (the "relevant index") from 1986 to 1994 are plotted in Exhibit 3-4.

Step 2. Calculate correlation of index to relevant index. The correlation between Prime-LIBOR spread and the 10-year CMT-LIBOR spread is analyzed using linear regression analysis. The linear regression relationship between the two indices is shown in Exhibit 3-4 and is described by the following equation:

(Prime-LIBOR) = 0.32 * (CMT-LIBOR) + 1.46%

Step 3. Create a table of the LSE projected CMT-LIBOR ("yield curve") spread between the settlement and maturity dates. The current spread is 2.80%.

Period (Quarterly)	Yield Curve
0	2.80
1	2.57
2	2.33
3	2.10
4	1.87
5	1.63
6	1.40
7	1.17
8	0.93
9	0.70
10	0.47
11	0.23
12	0.00

Step 4. Using the scenario table above, the corresponding Prime-LIBOR spread can be calculated using the linear regression relationship found earlier.

Period (Quarterly)	Yield Curve (10-year Treasury – 3-month LIBOR)	Prime-LIBOR (0.32 * Yield Curve + 1.46%)
0	2.80	2.356
1	2.57	2.282
2	2.33	2.206
3	2.10	2.132
4	1.87	2.058
5	1.63	1.982
6	1.40	1.908
7	1.17	1.834
8	0.93	1.758
9	0.70	1.684
10	0.47	1.610
11	0.23	1.534
12	0.00	1.460

Step 5. The cash flows of the coupon can be calculated from the Prime-LIBOR spread calculated above.

Period (Quarterly)	Yield Curve	Prime-LIBOR	Coupon	Cash Flow*
0	2.80	2.356	4.356	–100
1	2.57	2.282	4.282	1.104
2	2.33	2.206	4.206	1.085
3	2.10	2.132	4.132	1.066
4	1.87	2.058	4.058	1.047
5	1.63	1.982	3.982	1.029
6	1.40	1.908	3.908	1.009
7	1.17	1.834	3.834	0.991
8	0.93	1.758	3.758	0.972
9	0.70	1.684	3.684	0.952
10	0.47	1.610	3.610	0.934
11	0.23	1.534	3.534	0.915
12	0.00	1.460	3.460	100.896

*Prime-LIBOR coupon cash flows are calculated on a quarterly Act/360 basis.

IRR. Given the expectation that the yield curve will flatten at maturity, the IRR of this note is 3.954% quarterly Act/360, or 4.029% semiannual bond equivalent yield (BEY). Comparing this to the 4.40% 3-year Treasury note, the IRR of this note is 37.1 bps *below* the Treasury yield. Thus, if the investor expects the yield curve to flatten by the end of the third year, historical analysis shows that this note would not be a good buy.

Duration. The duration of the note requires the use of KTRD since the IR(s) and the DR are not the same. Recall this linear regression relationship:

(Prime-LIBOR) = 0.32 * (CMT-LIBOR) + 1.46%

The risk of this note is thus similar to that of the CMT-LIBOR note analyzed in Chapter 2. The interest rate sensitivity of the Prime-LIBOR coupon, however, appears to be considerably less than that of the CMT-LIBOR note due to the deleveraging regression relationship described in the above equation.

The result of the KTRD analysis is plotted on the next page. The Prime-LIBOR differential note possesses higher duration in the 0- to 3-year sector of the Treasury yield curve than a 3-year fixed rate note, and has a duration in the 10- to 12.75-year sector of the curve which aggregate to approximately –1. Thus, the Prime-LIBOR note in this example would gain in value if the yield curve were to steepen. For scenarios in which the yield curve shifts in

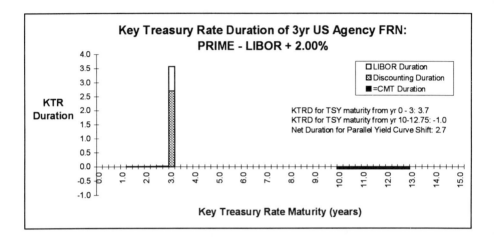

Key Treasury Rate Duration of 3yr US Agency FRN:
PRIME - LIBOR + 2.00%

KTR Duration

Key Treasury Rate Maturity (years)

parallel, the note would behave like a 3-year fixed rate note with a duration of approximately 2.7.

Historical analysis requires that extreme care be taken in the selection of a relevant index whose correlation to the index in question is non-trivial. If the correlation between the coupon index and the rate-of-view is low, i.e., below 50%, the investor would be better served by selecting an alternative relevant index with a higher correlation to the coupon index.

Historical analysis is essentially an analysis based upon mapping a complicated index to an uncomplicated index using historical correlation and regression. It is by no means a perfect and foolproof risk analysis tool since good historical correlation does not necessarily translate to good future correlation. However, it provides the investors with a means of analyzing extremely complicated indices whose risks are not transparent.

CONCLUSION

This chapter provided the basic framework for the examination of structured note risk and performance in a deterministic environment. Structured notes are considerably more complicated than and differ significantly from regular fixed income instruments and thus require more effort to analyze risk and return.

Three methods of deterministic scenario analyses were introduced in this chapter: expectation analysis, forward analysis, and historical analysis. Each analysis methodology has its strengths and weaknesses. The "correct" analysis for any investment is based upon both the investor's views and the type of embedded structured index. Each of these analyses is employed in the analysis of the risk and return profiles of structured notes. The performance and risk of these structured notes are also compared to benchmark alternative investments to assist investors in the purchasing decision process.

4

Simulation Analysis

The previous chapter discussed the deterministic class of analysis and its application to analyzing structured note risk. The main assumption of deterministic analysis is that all the rate scenarios will occur with certainty, and hence does not consider the probabilistic remoteness of the occurrence of any particular scenario. A potential investor in a structured note seeking to apply deterministic analysis would select a wide range of scenarios to assess the structure's performance and risk profiles. Some questions, however, cannot be answered by deterministic analysis: What is the probability of a note providing a yield that is higher than a target return? What is the probability of receiving an internal rate of return (IRR) between 1% and 1.50%? What is the "expected return" given a particular scenario? Deterministic analysis is unable to answer such questions because it does not probability weight the various scenarios. These questions, however, are perfectly appropriate for the simulation class of analysis.

Many investors tend to shy away when the term "simulation" is mentioned. Simulation analysis is used in this book to simply simulate a variety of different interest rate scenarios. From each of these interest rate scenarios, characteristics of the structured note being analyzed (duration, IRR) can be obtained. Given a sufficiently large number of simulations, the investor would be able to obtain a statistical picture of the risk and performance of a note.

Simulation in finance is not a new topic and has been ably addressed by many theoreticians. Hull presents a good summary of the various simulation techniques that are available.[1] Although many other good simulation techniques (such as Lattice and Finite Differencing) exist that can be employed to analyze structured notes, the focus of this chapter will be on simulation via Monte Carlo. Monte Carlo is the preferred technique in this book because it is the easiest for end users of all levels of sophistication to implement. However, investors seeking to apply other types of simulation techniques can readily find support via simulation platforms such as Global Advanced Technology's commercially available Simulation Interface Platform (SIP).[2]

This chapter will not introduce any new simulation techniques, but rather will apply a very useful simulation technique to the analysis of structured notes. A comparison of simulation and deterministic results to the actual option adjusted results will illustrate the accuracy of each analysis and a discussion of the applicability of each analysis is provided. Finally, simulation of multiple indices is briefly discussed and the methodology of extending the simulation technique to multiple indices is provided.

WHEN SHOULD SIMULATION ANALYSIS BE USED?

In theory, simulation can be applied to analyze any structured note. In practice, simulation analysis should only be employed to analyze structured notes with skewed performance characteristics. In other words, notes whose performance change differs significantly if rates deviate in one direction than in another direction should be analyzed via simulation analysis. The reason for this is that the base case scenario carries the implicit assumption that it is the *expected* scenario, i.e., 50% of the time rates would be higher, and 50% of the time they would be lower. If the performance of a structure is skewed in one direction over another, employing deterministic analysis would not properly reflect the performance and risk of the structure since deterministic result is calculated from only the base case scenario. Thus, notes with embedded optionality, skewed performance, and path dependent features should be analyzed using simulation analysis.

---

1. See Hull, John, *Options, Futures, and Other Derivatives Securities.* New York, NY: Prentice Hall, 1989, pp.214–245.
2. For a discussion of the methodology and theory behind GAT's SIP system, see Ho, T. S. Y., and S. B. Lee, "Term Structure Movements and Pricing of Interest Rate Contingent Claims," *Journal of Finance* 41 (1986), pp. 1011–1029; and Ho, T. S. Y., "Managing Illiquid Bonds and the Linear Path Space," *Journal of Fixed Income* (June 1992).

Simulation analysis is extremely useful in examining the behavior of notes with embedded optionality. Investors are often presented with a structured note containing embedded optionality without being informed about the pricing and structural details of the options embedded in the note since that information can be regarded as proprietary information. By employing simulation analysis, the investor is able to ascertain the risk and performance of the note without full knowledge of the composition and formulation of the underlying optionality components. This makes simulation analysis an extremely powerful analysis tool.

Simulation results should also be interpreted carefully. A simulation analysis of an FRN using forward rates as the base scenario should show only a 50% probability that the investor will obtain a return higher than predicted by the forward. This is, of course, expected since forward rates represent an equilibrium level between bullish and bearish sentiments. It would be illogical to expect Simulation to show any investment grade note (structured or unstructured) having a 97% probability of yielding 500 bps higher than the Treasury yield. The investor can, however, use simulation analysis to establish a good confidence level of obtaining an acceptable minimum return, e.g., 85% probability that the return will be above 4%.

MONTE CARLO RATE SIMULATION

Monte Carlo simulations were first used in physics to simulate random particle motion. Boyle[3] was one of the first to apply Monte Carlo Rate simulation to the field of finance to value options. Monte Carlo simulations, in short, employ random numbers to simulate future rates. However, these future rates are not totally governed by random numbers and rely on a set of predicted future rates as a guide. The Monte Carlo simulations discussed in this chapter are based on a set of "base case scenarios" generated from either the forward analysis or the linear smooth expectation (LSE) analysis.

The basic concept behind the Monte Carlo simulation is to allow the index rates to follow a random process, but to stipulate that the random walk be tied to a base rate scenario. The addition of the random walk to the analysis allows the investor to examine the various possible returns that would be obtained if the forward rates differ from the futures predicted levels. The

---

3. Boyle, Phelim P., "Options: A Monte Carlo Approach," *Journal of Financial Economics* 4 (May 1977), pp. 323–338.

Monte Carlo numerical simulation of the interest rate process has been ably
addressed by Hull[4] and Figlewski[5] and is briefly summarized here.

The Random Walk Model

The random walk process is described by:

$$dR = \mu R\, dt + \sigma R\, dz \tag{4-1}$$

This random walk model describes a random walk process with mean
growth rate μ, and a standard deviation σ. The dz term is the standard random walk component, i.e.,

$$dz = \varepsilon(dt)^{1/2}$$

where ε is a normal random number with mean of zero and standard deviation of one.

For simulating the rate R, the distribution is lognormal rather than normal. Hull[6] showed that Equation (4-1) becomes

$$R + \Delta R = R\,\exp[(\mu - 1/2\sigma^2)\Delta t + \sigma\varepsilon(\Delta t)^{1/2}]$$

The random walk calculation for the ith random rate $R_{\text{ran},i+1}$ as a function of the previous random rate $R_{\text{ran},i}$ is:

$$R_{\text{ran},i+1} = R_{\text{ran},i}\,\exp(\mu_i\,\Delta t_i + \sigma_i\,\varepsilon_i\,\Delta t_i^{0.5}) \tag{4-2}$$

This random walk model describes a random walk process with mean
growth rate μ_i, a standard deviation σ_i, and a normal random ε_i. The mean
growth rate μ_i is calculated as the volatility adjusted growth rate between the
future rate for the current period R_i and the next period R_{i+1}:

$$\mu_i = m_i - m_{i-1} \tag{4-3}$$
$$m_i = \{\ln(R_i/R_{\text{init}}) - 1/2\sigma_i^2\Delta t\}/\Delta t \tag{4-4}$$

4. Hull, John, *Options, Futures, and Other Derivative Securities*.
5. Figlewski, Silber, Subrahmanyam, *Financial Options from Theory to Practice*. Homewood, IL: Business One Irwin, 1990.
6. Hull, John, *Options, Futures, and Other Derivative Securities*.

where R_i is the base case scenario's future rate for period i, R_{init} is the initial index rate, and Δt is the period length in years.

The random rate R_{ran} is calculated for each period of the note, and the corresponding IRR and duration of that sequence of rates are calculated and recorded. The process is then repeated multiple times and the resulting distribution of IRR and duration is recorded. This distribution describes the statistical likelihood of obtaining a certain IRR, assuming that the base case scenario will occur.

Simulation Analysis Methodology

Equations (4-2), (4-3), and (4-4) constitute the basic framework for the implementation of the simulation analysis as described in this book. The steps to the implementation of a simulation analysis are as follows:

1. Construct a base case scenario. This can be implemented via either the forward analysis or the LSE.
2. For each base case scenario, generate the corresponding random indices on each coupon reset date.
3. Calculate the coupon cash flows corresponding to these randomized indices.
4. For each random scenario, the IRR and duration of the note can be calculated.
5. Repeat a multitude of random walks for each base case scenario.

The following example illustrates the simulation analysis methodology outlined above using future rates obtained from forward analysis.

Example 4-1

Analyze the following structured note using simulation analysis given future rates obtained from forward analysis. Calculate the probability that the note will yield an IRR of 4.00% or greater.

Note:	CapFRN
Issuer:	AA Bank
Maturity:	3 years
Coupon:	3-month LIBOR + 0.50% subject to coupon cap
Coupon cap:	6.00%

EXHIBIT 4-1 Sample Simulation Rate Scenario

The following four interest rate scenarios are shown below: the actual forward predicted rate R_{twd}, the random walk forward rate R_{ran}, the forward predicted rate plus one standard deviation, and the forward predicted rate minus one standard deviation.

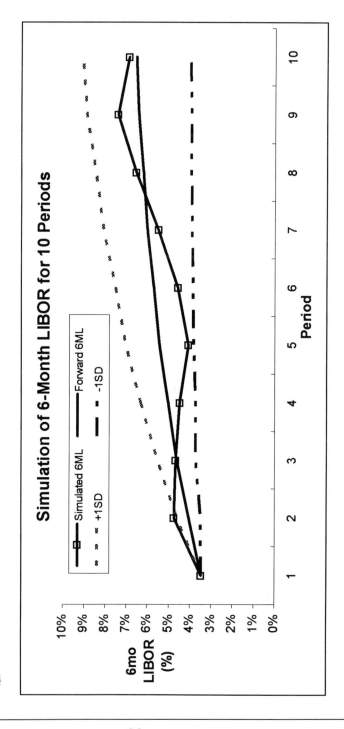

Simulation of 6-Month LIBOR for 10 Periods

The forward LIBORs are given as follows:

Period	LIBOR	Period	LIBOR	Period	LIBOR
0	3.50%	4	4.35%	8	5.20%
1	3.75%	5	4.55%	9	5.35%
2	4.05%	6	4.75%	10	5.60%
3	4.12%	7	4.95%	11	5.80%

Solution

Step 1.   Set up the base case forward rates and cash flows.

Period (I)	Forward LIBOR (II)	LIBOR + 0.50% (III)	Coupon (IV)	Cash Flow* (V)
0	3.50%	4.00 %	4.00%	−100
1	3.75%	4.25%	4.25%	0.99
2	4.05%	4.55%	4.55%	1.05
3	4.12%	4.62%	4.62%	1.12
4	4.35%	4.85%	4.85%	1.14
5	4.55%	5.05%	5.05%	1.20
6	4.75%	5.25%	5.25%	1.25
7	4.95%	5.45%	5.45%	1.30
8	5.20%	5.70%	5.70%	1.35
9	5.35%	5.85%	5.85%	1.41
10	5.60%	6.10%	6.00%	1.44
11	5.80%	6.30%	6.00%	1.48
12**	—	6.50%	6.00%	101.48

*LIBOR coupon cash flows are calculated on an Act/360 basis.
**LIBOR of last period is not used in calculation since LIBOR coupons are set at start of period.

From the given forward LIBOR rates in column II, the resultant LIBOR + 0.50% coupons are calculated in column III. If that coupon is greater than the cap level of 6.00%, the coupon (column IV) is set to the cap. Finally, the cash flows from the coupon are calculated in column V. The IRR of this base case scenario can then be calculated.

Steps 2, 3, and 4.   Set up the randomized LIBORs and the corresponding coupon cash flows.

Period (I)	Forward LIBOR (II)	Random LIBOR (III)	L(III) + 0.5% (IV)	Actual CPN (V)	Cash Flow* (VI)
0	3.50%	3.50%	4.00%	4.00%	−100
1	3.75%	3.75%	4.25%	4.25%	0.99
2	4.05%	3.77%	4.27%	4.27%	1.05
3	4.12%	3.49%	3.99%	3.99%	1.05
4	4.35%	4.64%	5.14%	5.14%	0.98
5	4.55%	5.16%	5.66%	5.66%	1.27
6	4.75%	5.17%	5.67%	5.67%	1.40
7	4.95%	5.29%	5.79%	5.79%	1.40
8	5.20%	5.43%	5.93%	5.93%	1.43
9	5.35%	4.59%	5.09%	5.09%	1.46
10	5.60%	5.45%	5.95%	5.95%	1.26
11	5.80%	6.14%	6.64%	6.00%	1.47
12**	6.00%	7.42%	7.92%	6.00%	101.48

*LIBOR coupon cash flows are calculated on an Act/360 basis.
**LIBOR of last period is not used in calculation since LIBOR coupons are set at start of period.

The forward LIBORs are calculated in the same fashion as before. This time, an additional column is present. Column III represents the stream of random indices calculated using Equation (4-2). An implied term volatility of 22% is used. The coupons of LIBOR + 0.50% from these random LIBORs are shown in column IV, and if LIBOR + 0.50% exceeds 6.00%, the coupon is set to 6.00%. Finally, the cash flow from this set of random LIBOR is calculated in column VI. Again, the IRR of this set of LIBORs can be calculated.

Step 5. Keeping the base case LIBORs (column II) the same, steps 2 through 4 are then repeated for a large number of rate simulations and the IRRs of each simulation run is recorded. For this example, 2000 simulation runs are performed.

Results

IRR. The IRR of the CapFRN is calculated using 2000 random scenarios for the base rate case. The first IRR result plotted in Exhibit 4-2 is the differential probability of attaining an IRR, representing the probabilities corresponding to different ranges of IRRs that can be attained by the note. Exhibit 4-2 shows that the IRR range from 5.10% to 5.55% is the performance sector that has the highest probability of being attained by the 3-year CapFRN.

EXHIBIT 4-2 Differential Probability of IRR

The differential probability shows the probability of the note attaining an IRR within a range. 2000 simulations were performed on the base case scenario. The note shows the highest probability of attaining a return in the 5.10% to 5.55% range.

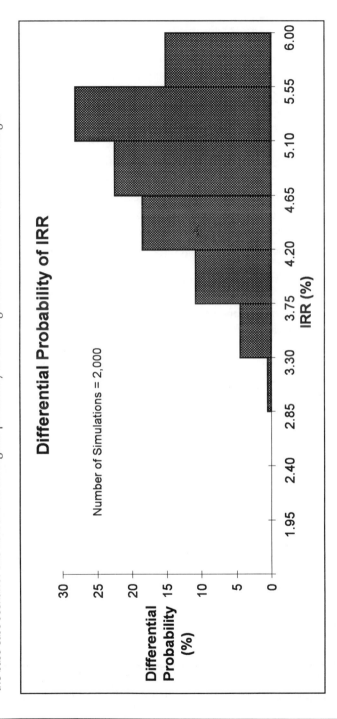

Differential Probability of IRR

Number of Simulations = 2,000

Exhibit 4-3 shows the cumulative IRR probability, i.e., the probability that the note will *exceed* a certain IRR level. The main features to glean from the analysis are the *expected IRR, maximum IRR,* and *minimum IRR.* The expected IRR is the probability weighted IRR of the note and is the figure of merit for performance in simulation analyses. The maximum IRR is the maximum attained IRR given the forward rates, the coupon cap, and the implied volatility of 22%. In this case, there is a definitive limit on the maximum IRR due to the presence of the coupon cap. Likewise, the minimum IRR is the lowest IRR for the 2000 simulation scenarios. Due to the lognormal interest rate process and the minimum coupon restriction of zero (no fixed income instruments can yield a negative coupon, otherwise the investor would have to make a payment to the issuer), the lowest IRR will always remain above zero.

Duration.   The duration of the CapFRN is calculated for each of the 2000 random scenarios. This note has identical IR and DR. The risk of the note is thus with respect to only one rate, the 3-year Treasury rate. As with the IRR, the differential probability of attaining a range of duration is plotted in Exhibit 4-4. The results clearly show that under the base case scenario, the duration that is most likely to be attained by the note is the 0 to 0.22 range of duration. Note that the highest duration achieved for this particular base case scenario is 2.25.

The cumulative durational results are plotted on Exhibit 4-5. This graph shows the probability of the note attaining a duration that is higher than the target. As with the IRR, the three features to note here are the *expected duration, maximum duration,* and *minimum duration.* The expected duration is the probability weighted duration of the note, which is 0.59. This means that based on forward rates being the base case scenario, the CapFRN is expected to have interest rate risk with respect to the 3-year Treasury rate. This risk level is low compared to the duration of a fixed rate note (2.7), but nevertheless shows the note to be sensitive to interest rate movement. The expected duration will be the figure of merit for interest rate risk in future simulation analyses. The maximum duration of the note is 2.25, while the minimum duration of the note is zero. This shows that for this base case interest rate scenario, the note's risk can range from that of a regular FRN (zero interest rate risk) up to approximately 81% of that of a 3-year fixed rate note.

SIMULATION ANALYSIS FOR A RANGE OF EXPECTATIONS

Although the above analysis illustrated the probabilistic performance of the note, only one indication of expected return (simulation average IRR) and

EXHIBIT 4-3 Simulation Analysis Using Forward Rates

The analysis calculates the probability of obtaining an IRR *greater* than a target. The target IRR is 4.00%. The results show that the CapFRN being analyzed has a 90% probability of producing a return exceeding the target IRR of 4.00%, and an expected IRR of 4.88%. The highest IRR is 5.87%, which is a result of the limitation imposed by the coupon cap.

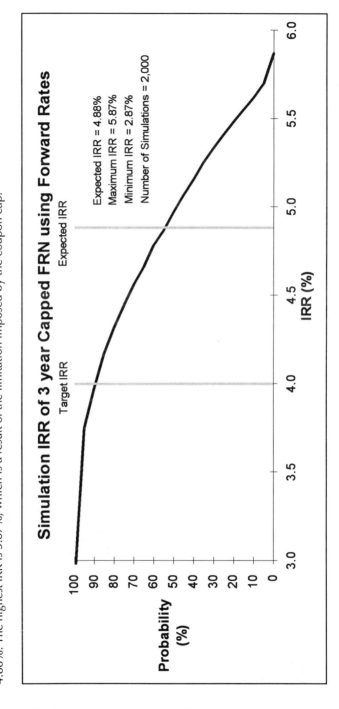

Simulation IRR of 3 year Capped FRN using Forward Rates

EXHIBIT 4-4 Differential Probability of Duration

The differential probability results show the probability of the note attaining a duration within a certain range. The duration that is most likely to be attained by the note under the base case scenario is the 0 to 0.23 duration range.

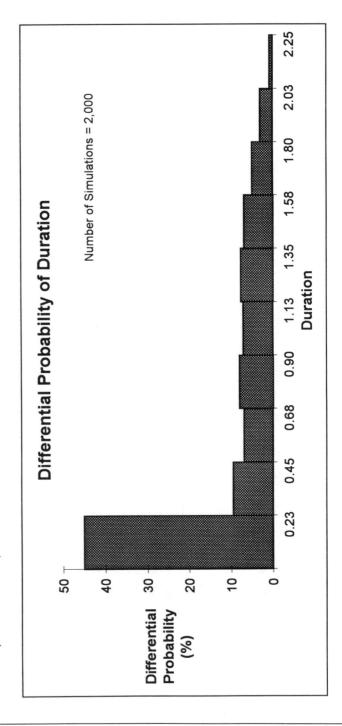

Differential Probability of Duration

Number of Simulations = 2,000

EXHIBIT 4-5   Simulation Duration of 3-Year CapFRN

The analysis calculates the probability of obtaining a duration *greater* than a target. The results show that the CapFRN being analyzed has an expected duration of 0.59, which is higher than that of a regular FRN. The highest duration is 2.25, which is approximately 81% of that of a 3-year fixed rate note. The lowest duration is zero.

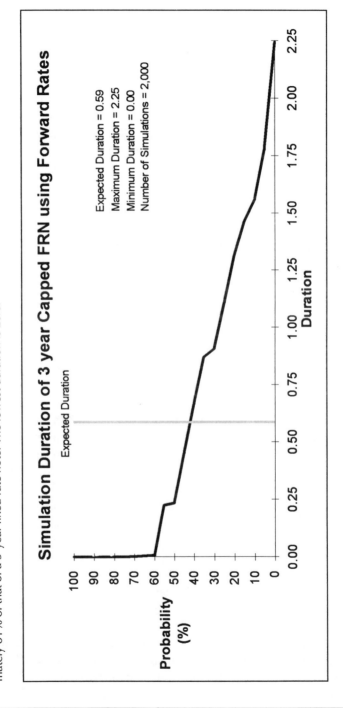

Simulation Duration of 3 year Capped FRN using Forward Rates

Expected Duration

Expected Duration = 0.59
Maximum Duration = 2.25
Minimum Duration = 0.00
Number of Simulations = 2,000

one indication of expected risk (simulation average duration) are generated since only one base interest rate scenario was used. To fully understand the risks of a note in a changing rate environment, an investor may wish to generate a range of final expectation values and perform simulation analysis on each of these expectation scenarios. By doing so, the investor is able to observe the performance and risk profiles for a variety of different scenarios. Simulation analysis for a range of base case scenarios thus combines the risk assessment ability of the deterministic LSE analysis with the probabilistic power of the simulation analysis.

Example 4-2

Analyze the performance and risk of the previous example for a variety of final expectation LIBOR scenarios.

Solution

Using LSE, a range of final expectation LIBORs can be generated, each with a series of intermediate rates. For each final expectation rate scenario, 2000 simulations are performed. The resulting expected simulation IRR and durations are plotted in the following exhibits and compared to the relevant deterministic IRR and durations.

IRR.   Both the simulation and deterministic IRRs are calculated for a variety of interest rate scenarios and plotted in Exhibit 4-6. The agreement between the two is quite good. Small deviations begin to appear at the time when the first coupon cap is hit. Since the deterministic IRR assumes that the coupon is definitively capped, the deterministic IRR of the note will be seen to start to be capped. The simulation IRR, on the other hand, will produce a spectrum of future rates, some of which will be capped, while others will not. This will skew the simulation IRR such that it will be lower than the deterministic duration for the base interest rate scenarios that bring the floating rate indices close to the coupon cap level. This discrepancy is relatively minor. In future analyses, the deterministic IRR will be used to analyze the performance of the note unless simulation IRR results differ significantly.

Duration.   The duration of the note as calculated from the simulation analysis and the deterministic analysis are both shown in Exhibit 4-7. Unlike the IRR results, the difference between the two durations is significant. In the deterministic calculations, the note is observed to perform like a regular

EXHIBIT 4-6 Simulation and Deterministic IRR Analysis Using Range of Final Expectation Rates

The maximum deviation between the two analyses occurs for scenarios close to where the first coupon will be capped (5.5% final LIBOR). For most other scenarios, the two IRRs agree well with each other.

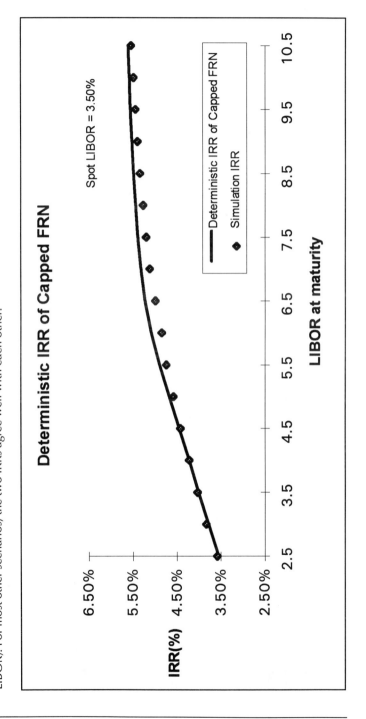

EXHIBIT 4-7   Simulation and Deterministic Duration Analysis Using Range of Final Expectation Rates

There is considerable difference between simulation duration and deterministic duration. When rates are low, deterministic duration is considerably lower than the simulation duration, while higher interest rate scenarios result in the deterministic duration over-estimating the simulation duration.

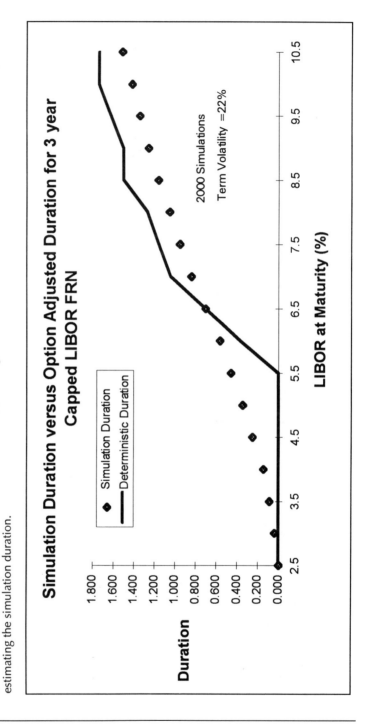

floating rate note (and have zero duration) until the first coupon cap has been reached. At that point the coupon in question is assumed to be capped at a fixed level for higher interest rate scenarios. In reality, however, the note will have a non-zero duration even prior to the index first attaining the coupon cap. Since CapFRNs are created by the investor effectively selling off the interest rate upside, i.e., a cap, the shorted cap will lose value for higher rates prior to the actual coupon cap level being reached. Thus, the note has interest rate risk even for low interest rate scenarios. This is reflected in the results of the simulation duration.

For extremely high interest rate scenarios, deterministic analysis will project cash flows that are all capped at the coupon cap level (except for the first coupon). The note will thus have a deterministic duration close to that of a fixed 3-year note in these scenarios. In reality, deep-in-the-money options have a delta that approaches but is never exactly one. In other words, the loss of the value from the option will be close to, but will never be exactly equal to, the deterministic loss. Thus, one would expect that the note would have a duration that is below (if only slightly) that of a comparable fixed note. This insight is again borne out in Exhibit 4-7.

SIMULATION VERSUS DETERMINISTIC

Now that the differences between the two types of simulation are evident, which one is correct? As mentioned before, simulation should be employed to analyze structured notes whose performance is skewed in one direction over another. Although it was shown in the previous section that deterministic duration results are quite different from simulation, it has not been demonstrated which analysis comes closer in approximating the actual behavior of a note.

Comparing the simulation and deterministic durations to a calculation that includes the correct formulation of the embedded option (option adjusted duration, or OAD) can serve to clarify this issue. A comparison between the deterministic duration and the OAD of the same CapFRN described in the previous section is calculated in Exhibit 4-8. The OAD employs the correct formulation of the interest rate cap option pricing (Black 76) in the valuation of the CapFRN.

Exhibit 4-8 shows the comparison between the deterministic duration and the OAD. For interest rate scenarios in which future LIBORs are low enough such that no cap is activated, the deterministic duration is zero, signi-

EXHIBIT 4-8   Comparison of LSE Deterministic Duration to OAD

The analysis is performed on a 3-year CapFRN whose coupon is LIBOR + 0.50% with a 6% coupon cap. Note that the deterministic duration underestimates the duration prior to activation of cap but overestimates the duration once the option is activated.

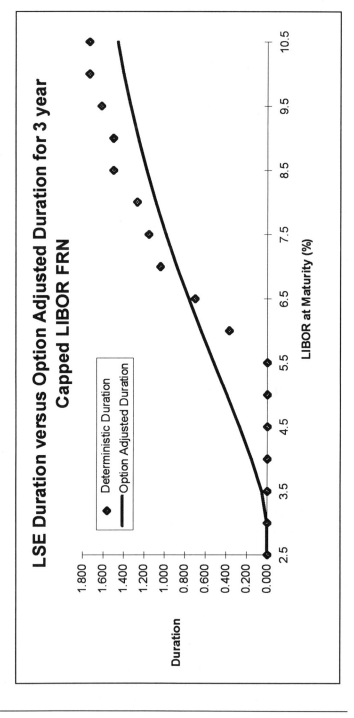

LSE Duration versus Option Adjusted Duration for 3 year Capped LIBOR FRN

fying that the note has a duration equivalent to a pure LIBOR FRN. The OAD, however, begins to gain duration prior to any coupon cap being activated, signifying that the shorted cap option is decreasing the value of the note as the cap level is approached. As the rate scenario changes to a rapidly rising scenario, more caps are activated. For each cap that is activated, the deterministic duration increases so as to accommodate the transformation of one coupon from floating rate to fixed rate. For each coupon that is fixed, the deterministic delta of the coupon changes from 0 to 1. This is exactly the behavior of the delta discussed earlier in Chapter 2. At some interest rate level, the deterministic duration will exceed the OAD. As noted in Chapter 2, deterministic duration tends to underestimate the duration when the rate scenario is such that many of the embedded options would be in-the-money. By the same token, deterministic duration will overestimate OAD when rates are such that few or none of the embedded options are in-the-money.

Comparing the OAD to the results of a 2000 interest rate simulation analysis in Exhibit 4-9 shows an extremely good match. Simulation analysis comes very close to matching the actual duration of the note. The rationale for this is simple: theoretical option pricing models are essentially the result of an aggregate of many different scenarios about a central base scenario, taken to the limit of an infinite number of scenarios. This is exactly what the simulation analysis seeks to accomplish, except with a finite (albeit large) number of scenarios. It is therefore expected that simulation duration should be a very close approximation of the actual duration. Thus, for notes with optionality components, simulation analysis will provide the closest and best approximation to the actual behavior of the note.

In the following chapters, all the risk analysis of structures involving optionality will include a discussion of both the deterministic and simulation durations. Although simulation is an excellent reflection of the actual behavior of the note, deterministic duration provides valuable intuitive insight into the behavior of a note. Once this insight into the behavior of the note has been interpreted using deterministic results, the simulation results can then be employed to further refine that understanding.

The power of simulation analysis is that it permits investors, *without knowledge of the underlying option structure and formulation* (which is often proprietary information), to easily understand and calculate the risks and returns of the structured note. An investor can employ a series of simulation analyses to gauge the performance and risk of the note without resorting to conjectures about the underlying optionality and/or forwards embedded in the note.

EXHIBIT 4-9   Comparison of LSE Simulation Duration to OAD

The analysis is performed on a 3-year CapFRN whose coupon is LIBOR + 0.50% with a 6% coupon cap. The simulation duration is an excellent methodology for calculating structured note risk. The actual duration of the note is the OAD, which as seen below is very closely approximated by the simulation duration. 2000 simulation runs were executed for each final duration computation.

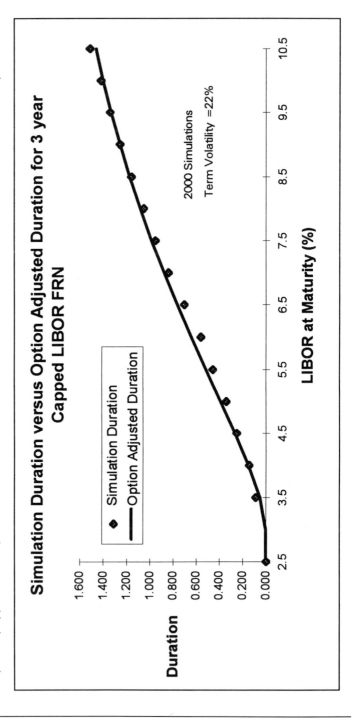

Simulation Duration versus Option Adjusted Duration for 3 year Capped LIBOR FRN

SIMULATION OF TWO OR MORE INDICES

The coupon index of a structure can be a combination of two or more rate indices. The simulation methodology as outlined above can be adapted to simulating multiple indices, although the process is more complicated due to the cross-correlation between the indices.

If the indices in question are totally independent rates, the randomization process outlined above would apply. In such situations, the calculation of the rate step ΔR (Equation 4-1) for each separate rate j would be modified as follows:

$$R_{j,i} = R_{j,i-1} \exp \{\mu_{j,i} \Delta t + \sigma_{j,i} \varepsilon_{j,i} (\Delta t)^{1/2}\}$$

where $\varepsilon_{j,i}$ is an independent normal random variable.

If the two indices were correlated in some manner, the individual $\varepsilon_{j,i}$'s would be linked, and the equation above would be slightly altered.

Assume two rates R_1 and R_2 are being simulated. The random but correlated variables for the two rates are ε_1 and ε_2 respectively. These two random correlated variables are calculated from two uncorrelated independent random variables x_1 and x_2, where

x_1 = Random normal variable 1 with mean of zero and variance of 1

x_2 = Random normal variable 2 uncorrelated with x_1 also with mean of
zero and variance of 1

The correlated random variables ε_1 and ε_2 can be calculated as:

$$\varepsilon_1 = x_1$$
$$\varepsilon_2 = (1 - \rho_{12}^2)^{1/2} x_2 + \rho_{12} x_1$$

where ρ_{12} is the correlation between the two rates R_1 and R_2.

This combination of ε_1 and ε_2 automatically results in the correlation between ε_1 and ε_2 as being ρ_{12}, the mean of each to be zero, and the variance of each to be 1.

The presence of the correlation factor ρ_{12} sets multi-index simulation apart from single index simulation. When performing multi-index simulations, investors should use a range of different correlations based on historical and current market data to observe the effect of different correlations on the risk profile of the note.

VOLATILITY DURATION

As mentioned in Chapter 2, changes in volatility can affect the value of structured notes. This effect can be envisioned by examining the same CapFRN example:

Note: CapFRN
Issuer: AA Bank
Maturity: 3 years
Coupon: 3-month LIBOR + 0.50% subject to coupon cap
Coupon cap: 6.00%

Examine a base case scenario that resets a coupon to 6.00%. If volatility were to rise, simulations about the base case scenarios would produce a wider distribution of rates than for a lower volatility. This wider distribution would result in scenarios in which more coupons would exceed the cap level. Since the coupon is capped and thus cannot exceed 6%, a higher level of volatility would produce a simulation averaged coupon that would be lower than lower volatility. This is illustrated in the following graph.

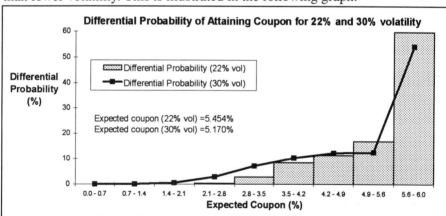

For higher volatility, the differential probability of attaining a range of coupons shows a broader distribution, resulting in a lower expected coupon given the cutoff introduced by the coupon cap. This lower expected coupon results in the CapFRN losing value for an increase in volatility. This behavior agrees with intuition since a CapFRN contains a shorted cap. For higher volatility, it is known from option pricing theory that a cap would gain in value. This gain results in a lower value for the CapFRN.

The graph further illustrates the point that volatility duration would only be present for notes with skewed performance or embedded optionality. Straight floating rate notes are unaffected by changing volatility since there is no cap or constraint on the distribution that can result in a changed expected value. For FRNs, higher volatility would only result in a broadening of the rate distribution but would not affect the performance or risk profiles.

The analysis of volatility risk involves examining the effect of an incremental rise in volatility on the value of the note. Simulations are performed using the same expectation base case scenarios as interest rate duration calculations. The resulting volatility duration can then be plotted as a function of the underlying final expectation rate. A volatility risk analysis of the above CapFRN is shown in Exhibit 4-10. To understand the volatility duration behavior, recall the discussion of option vega in Chapter 2. As the coupon indices approach the strike, the vega of the shorted coupon cap approaches a maximum. This accounts for the rise in volatility duration for rising interest rate scenarios. Beyond the maximum vega, higher interest rate scenarios would result in both the option vega and volatility duration decreasing as the coupon indices move further away from the strike.

A volatility duration calculation similar to the one performed in Exhibit 4-10 will be used as the basis for volatility risk analysis for all the option embedded and skewed performance structured notes described in this book. It will be evident that, depending upon the structure and maturity of the note, the volatility risk of structured notes can be quite considerable.

CONCLUSION

Simulation allows the investor to examine the risk and performance characteristics in a probabilistic environment. In a deterministic world, allowances for probabilistic weighting of scenarios are not made, hence the questions of certainty and probability cannot be addressed by the deterministic analysis. The simulation class of analysis is well suited to this task. However, simulation results should be carefully analyzed and interpreted in order for the investor to extract the correct and necessary information to make an informed purchasing decision.

Investors should be on guard against being lulled into a sense of false security of being fully immunized against risk if the simulation analysis shows a 95% probability that the note will perform phenomenally well, and a

EXHIBIT 4-10 Volatility Duration of CapFRN

The volatility duration is seen to rise for higher interest rate scenarios. This rise is attributable to the rise in vega as the option strike is approached. After a maximum level of duration is reached, the volatility duration begins to decrease as the coupon indices move further away from the strike. 2000 simulations were employed for each final LIBOR scenario to generate this volatility result.

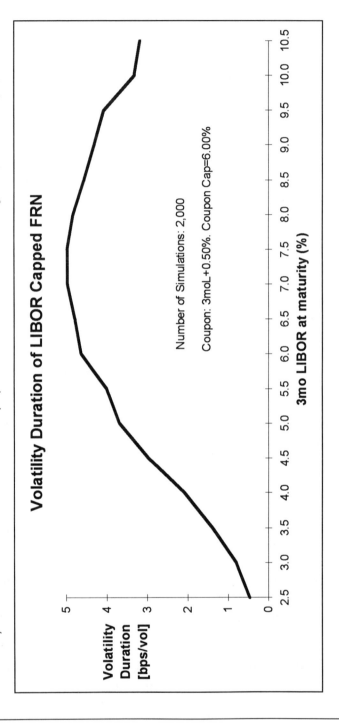

Volatility Duration of LIBOR Capped FRN

Number of Simulations: 2,000

Coupon: 3moL+0.50%. Coupon Cap=6.00%

3mo LIBOR at maturity (%)

Volatility Duration [bps/vol]

5% probability that the note will lose all value. The "3-sigma" or the "meltdown"—events that can wreak havoc with portfolios—are not given much weight in the simulation analysis, for the obvious reason that they are statistically remote events. The investor should, however, use deterministic analysis to ensure that the low-probability disaster events, if they do come true, do not result in the decimation of the portfolio.

Simulation analysis also permits the calculation of the volatility risk of structured notes in the same manner as the calculation of the interest rate risk. It was demonstrated that the volatility risk of a structure is not a constant, but is different for each base case scenario. The volatility risk of a structure is represented by the volatility duration.

The power of simulation analysis is that it enables investors to ascertain the risk and return of structured notes with embedded optionality whose formulation may not be available to the investor. Using simulation analysis, investors can examine the risk and reward of structured notes without being informed of the pricing and structural formulations of the exotic underlying option. This is the real strength of the simulation analysis.

5

First Generation Structures

The complexity and variety of structured notes in the market today have increased greatly since 1985 (when the first structured note was created), ranging in sophistication from the simple FRN to the highly complex cross-category notes. This chapter will describe the "first generation" structured notes and apply the analysis techniques developed in the previous chapters towards assessing the risk and performance of these notes.

The key characteristics of what constitutes a "first generation" structured note are as follows:

1. The structure contains only one floating rate index.
2. The maturity of the floating rate index must coincide with the reset and payment frequency, e.g., 3-month LIBOR coupons must be reset and paid quarterly. This is a key feature of first generation structures.
3. The floating rate index must be of the same country as the currency of denomination, e.g., if 3-month US$ LIBOR were the coupon index, the note and the associated cash flows must be denominated in U.S. dollars.
4. The structures may contain caps and/or floors on the underlying index but not unconventional or exotic options.

The implication of the above features is that the first generation structures' IR and DR are identical to each other and equal to the to-maturity Treasury rate.[1] This characteristic makes the analysis of first generation structures considerably more straightforward than second generation structures.

The notes that fit the above criteria of the first generation structures are not necessarily ordinary and uninteresting notes. Quite the contrary. In notional amount terms, the market for first generation structured notes is much larger than the sum of second generation and the cross-category notes. The reason for this is simple. Most investors prefer a note based on an index with which they are familiar (domestic rates) and whose structure does not impose a long familiarization time. Additional complications thus reduce the intended market audience of a note. But even within this constraint, the world of first generation notes is quite diverse and provides investors with a myriad of investment possibilities and views.

The first generation notes that will be examined in this chapter are:

1. **Floating rate notes (FRNs).** These are notes whose coupons are based on a single short-term floating index. The reset frequency is equal to the maturity of the index. No optionality is embedded.
2. **Capped and floored FRNs.** These are floating rate notes with embedded coupon caps or floors.
3. **Collared FRNs.** These are FRNs whose coupons can never drop below a floor nor rise above the cap. Extremely popular in Europe but did not catch on in the United States.
4. **Inverse FRNs.** These are bullish notes whose coupons are inversely linked to a floating rate index.
5. **Superfloaters.** These are bearish notes whose coupons are a multiple of the floating rate index.

The indices most often used in first generation notes are the short maturity indices that are familiar to short-term investors.[2] These indices are described in Exhibit 5-1.

ANALYSIS OF FIRST GENERATION STRUCTURED NOTES

Each of the first generation structures to be discussed in this chapter has its own distinct properties and characteristics. Certain analyses may be inappro-

---

1. Within the constraints of the approximation, as noted in Chapter 2.
2. For a description of money market instruments and indices, see Stigum, Marcia, *The Money Market.* Homewood, IL: Dow Jones-Irwin, 1983.

EXHIBIT 5-1   First Generation Structured Note Indices

The variety of short-term indices available to the investor is quite large. The most popular of all floating rate indices still is 3-month LIBOR.

Index	Maturity and Reset Frequency of Index	Comments
LIBOR	1-, 3-, 6-, 12-month	Most popular structured note floating rate index. 3-month LIBOR is the most popular LIBOR index.
Fed funds*	Daily	Fed funds is the overnight loan rate between banks and is one of the more volatile short-term indices. It is one of two indices that is directly controlled by the Federal Reserve (the other being the discount rate).
Cost of Funds Index (COFI)*	Monthly	Liked by investors familiar with mortgage products. COFI is an average cost of funds of a set of mortgage banks in the prescribed area. COFI is also a popular floating rate mortgage index. Most structured notes are based on 11th District (San Francisco area) COFI.
Prime**	Daily (implied)	Prime rate is a commercial loan rate. It is the preferred index of regional investors. Coupons based on Prime typically reset daily but pay quarterly.
Commercial paper (CP)	30, 60, 90, 180 days	The CP Index is not often seen in structured notes. Mostly used by issuers as a funding cost index.
Treasury bill	1-, 3-, 6-, 12-month	Most T-bill FRNs have been issued by U.S. Agencies. T-bill coupon rates usually reset weekly off the weekly bill auction rates. Most frequently used T-bill index is the 3-month T-bill rate.

* These are purely U.S. indices that are not available in other currencies.
** Prime rates exist in both the United States and Japan.

priate for certain structures, and each structure can also have more than one applicable analysis. The appropriate analyses for the various first generation structures are summarized below.

Structure	Appropriate Analysis	Why Is Analysis Appropriate?
Prime, Deleveraged Prime FRN	**Deterministic** (1) Historical (2) Expectation	Difficult to have view on Prime. Need historical data as point of reference. Since no optionality is involved, deterministic analysis is appropriate.
Capped (Levg) FRN Collared FRN Floored FRN Inverse FRN	**Simulation** (1) Expectation (2) Forward	Capped, floored, and collared FRNs are generally bets against the high predicted forward rates from occurring. All three produce higher coupons if rates rise. The inverse FRN is a very bullish structure which differs from the above three in that its coupon drops if rates rise. Since all the above notes contain optionality, simulation analysis is the appropriate analysis methodology.
Superfloater	**Simulation** (1) Expectation (2) Forward	The superfloater is a very bearish structure which provides high yield if forward rates rise rapidly. The embedded option is in the form of the zero coupon floor. Simulation analysis is thus required for a full analysis.

For example, the table shows that the analysis that is most relevant for the Prime FRN is the historical analysis. This is due to two reasons: first, it is difficult for investors to formulate forward views on Prime, and there is no publicly traded futures market for the investor to calculate forward Prime rates. The expectation analysis, though less applicable, can be used in conjunction with the historical analysis to provide a more complete risk assessment of the Prime FRN.

Chapter 4 demonstrated that the simulation class of analysis should be applied to the analysis of structured notes with embedded optionality or skewed performance characteristics. Notes that do not contain embedded optionality or skewed performance should be analyzed via the deterministic class of analysis.

The majority of the first generation structures contain views that run contrary to forward rate predictions, and thus it would be inappropriate to analyze these structures with the forward analysis. For these structures, the expectation analysis should be used to examine the range of risk and performance of the note. Likewise, historical analysis is inappropriate for analyzing structures if they contain indices for which investors have strong views, or if the index is actively traded on exchanges since the implied forward rates are readily available.

This chapter will introduce the various types of first generation structured notes and present them in the context of the appropriate analysis techniques. The note's behavior will be analyzed in the context of performance and risk and compared to that of alternative benchmark investments. Since first generation structures have identical IR and DR, the net risk of the notes is with respect to the IR/DR, which is the to-maturity Treasury rate of the notes.

STRUCTURE I. FLOATING RATE NOTE (FRN)

The first first generation structure is nothing more complicated than the FRN. FRNs are fixed income debentures whose coupons are not fixed, but "float" by resetting periodically off an index. The FRN is "structured" because the issuer can be swapped out of the floating rate index contained in the note into a funding index of choice. The most popular FRN index is LIBOR, or the London Inter-Bank Offered Rate. Other short-term indices whose popularity has waxed and waned are the Treasury bill, Prime, COFI, and Fed funds.

History

FRNs arose out of interest rate uncertainty. For environments in which interest rates threaten or are perceived to rise rapidly, investors who purchase fixed rate notes risk losing value quickly. The FRN enables investors to retain value in a rising rate environment with minimal interest rate exposure. Although railroad companies occasionally issued floating rate bonds as far back as the late 1800s, the modern era of FRNs did not begin until the popularization and acceptance of the Eurodollar futures contracts and the swap market in the early 1980s. The proliferation of these futures contracts enabled issuers who may not necessarily fund in LIBOR to issue a LIBOR FRN and be swapped back into their native funding targets.

Because of its simplicity, the FRN constitutes the largest structured note sector in terms of outstanding notional amount. It is tremendously popular with short-term money market investors who need a reset mechanism that would bring the value of the note back to par at each reset period (assuming the credit spread does not change). Another FRN investor is the bank sector. Since banks borrow money at LIBOR (plus or minus a yield spread), they could purchase a LIBOR FRN at a higher spread and retain the differential as gains (assuming the FRN issuer's credit rating is adequate). Banks are thus a natural buyer of FRNs in that they are able to offset liabilities via FRNs.

A representative FRN is the Prime FRN. As mentioned earlier, other FRNs are based on T-bills, Fed funds, and of course, LIBOR.

Prime FRN

Regional investors like Prime FRNs because many of them are familiar with the index, either as a Prime lender or borrower. Prime has an added appeal of being regarded as a "sticky" index when rates are descending, i.e., it generally lags LIBOR and stays at a certain level for a longer period before dropping. The historical Prime and LIBOR levels over the previous eight years are plotted in the chart below.

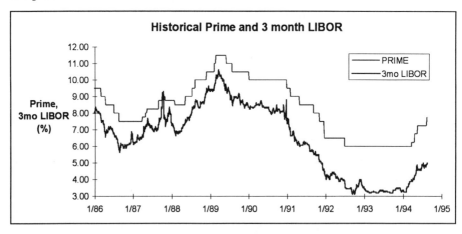

Unfortunately, the beneficial effect of the stickiness of Prime is more of a reputation than fact. It will be shortly demonstrated that, on a historical basis, the Prime rate and LIBOR are extremely well correlated. Thus, based on historical data, the perceived stickiness of the Prime rate does not appear to endow it with any significant yield advantage over LIBOR.

History

Investors purchase Prime FRNs for the high floating rate yield. In a falling rate environment such as the bull market of 1990–94, a Prime FRN provided yields that were higher than comparable maturity LIBOR FRNs. Certain investors purchased Prime FRNs and funded the purchase with either overnight or term funding. This allows the investor to retain the positive spread between the Prime floater and the financing cost over the financing period. In most cases, the funding cost is the overnight Fed funds rate. Since interest rate levels in late 1993 to early 1994 were extremely low by historical standards (Prime was 6% and Fed funds was 3%), these investors were able to earn large positive carry on the Prime FRNs.

Prime FRNs differ from most floating rate indices in that the market convention for Prime coupon accrual is for the Prime rate to be reset on a daily basis but paid out quarterly. This daily reset feature is one of the attractions of the Prime FRN in a rising rate environment because rising rates would be rapidly reflected in a higher coupon.

Analysis

The terms of a Prime FRN are shown in Exhibit 5-2. As indicated earlier, the Prime FRN should be analyzed with the historical analysis. The historical analysis provides investors with insight into the historical behavior of Prime with respect to a relevant index. The relevant index is chosen here to be 3-month LIBOR. Since LIBOR is regarded as a benchmark short-term rate, being able to relate Prime to LIBOR allows investors who have a view on short-term rates to take a view on the Prime rate as well. As seen in Exhibit 5-3, the correlation of Prime to 3-month LIBOR over the last 8 1/2 years has been excellent (96.9%). A regression analysis best-fitting Prime to 3-month LIBOR is shown in Exhibit 5-4 and produces the following regression relationship:

Prime = 3.33% + 0.78 * (3-month LIBOR)

EXHIBIT 5-2 Prime FRN

An investor could purchase this note, fund the purchase daily at the overnight Fed funds rate, and obtain a spot positive carry. (Interest rate levels on Jan. 26, 1994, are: 6.00% Prime, 3.00% Fed funds, resulting in a positive carry to the investor of 0.37%.) Even in a higher interest rate environment, this note produces a positive carry. (Rates on Aug. 19, 1994, are: 7.75% Prime, 4.625% Fed funds, resulting in a positive carry of 0.495%.)

Issue Terms (Actual)	
Issuer:	Federal National Mortgage Association ("Fannie Mae")
Principal amount:	US$300,000,000
Settlement date:	Jan. 26, 1994
Maturity date:	Jan. 26, 1996
Coupon paid in US$:	Prime – 2.63%
Day count basis:	Act/360 with no adjustment for period end dates.
Rate reset and payment dates:	Prime rate resets daily, paid quarterly. Payment dates are Jan. 26, Apr. 26, July 26, Oct. 26. First coupon paid on Apr. 26, 1994. Source: H.15(519). Standard two London and New York business day cutoff prior to period end dates.
Issue price:	100.00%

Using this regression relationship, one can calculate the performance of the note given a variety of expectation LIBORs.

Performance

The performance of the Prime FRN described in Exhibit 5-2 is analyzed via historical analysis. The regression result will be applied to analyzing the performance of the note.

IRR

The performance of the Prime FRN is calculated for a range of final LIBORs versus that of a comparable maturity LIBOR FRN. The Prime coupon cash flows are calculated from LIBOR via the regression relationship. Exhibit 5-4 shows that the Prime FRN's performance is close to the LIBOR FRN even though the historical regression relationship of Prime is only 0.78 times that of LIBOR. The reason for this is that Prime FRNs have the added advantage of a daily coupon reset, whereas LIBOR FRNs only reset at the start of each

EXHIBIT 5-3 Historical Prime-LIBOR Correlation

As noted previously in Chapter 2, the historical correlation between the two indices is extremely high at 96.9%. This demonstrates that the perceived "stickiness" of the Prime rate in decreasing interest rate environments does not endow it with any yield advantage over a "non-sticky" index such as LIBOR.

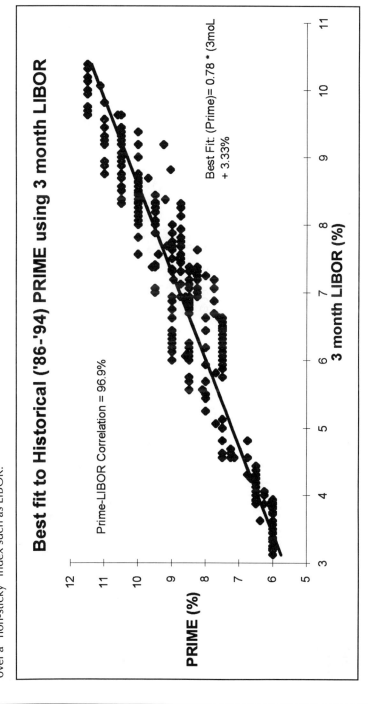

Best fit to Historical ('86-'94) PRIME using 3 month LIBOR

Prime-LIBOR Correlation = 96.9%

Best Fit: (Prime)= 0.78 * (3moL + 3.33%

EXHIBIT 5-4 Performance of Prime FRN

The Prime FRNs have the added advantage of a daily resetting coupon as opposed to a LIBOR FRN's quarterly resetting coupon. This helps the performance of Prime FRNs in a rising rate environment. The benchmark LIBOR FRN provides investors with a coupon of LIBOR − 0.20%, which is a typical benchmark level for Agency-type issuers.

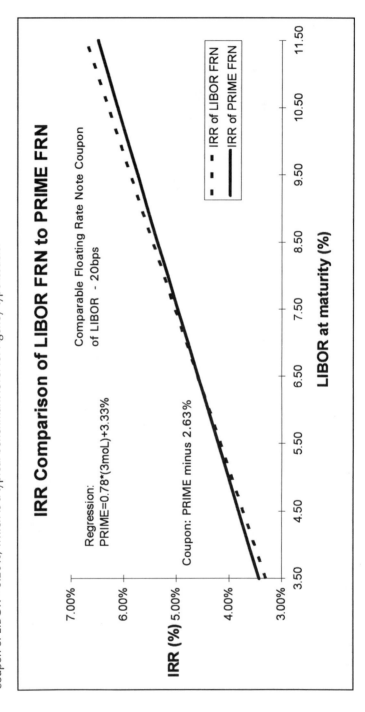

IRR Comparison of LIBOR FRN to PRIME FRN

Comparable Floating Rate Note Coupon
of LIBOR − 20bps

Regression:
PRIME=0.78*(3moL)+3.33%

Coupon: PRIME minus 2.63%

- - - IRR of LIBOR FRN
—— IRR of PRIME FRN

IRR (%)

LIBOR at maturity (%)

quarterly period. Thus, in a rising rate environment, the frequent reset of the Prime FRN boosts its performance relative to a LIBOR FRN.

Duration

The duration of the Prime FRN is equal to that of a LIBOR FRN, i.e., zero. This is a result of the Prime to LIBOR correlation being close to one. Thus, the IR of the 2-year Prime FRN is equal to the 2-year Treasury rate, and the IRD of the note is negative 1.9. Netting the IRD to the DRD of the Prime FRN, which is equal to positive 1.9, results in a net duration of zero. The Prime FRN is thus duration neutral and has no exposure to interest rate movement.

Deleveraged Prime FRN (DPF)

Investor purpose: To obtain a higher floating rate yield than is possible with Prime FRNs.

Risk: In an upwardly moving rate environment, investor will only receive part of the rate upside.

Equivalent investor position: Long half notional amount of fixed rate note, long half notional amount of Prime FRN.

A variant on the Prime FRN is the deleveraged Prime FRN. The term deleveraging refers to the fact that the coupon index is based on a fraction of Prime. By deleveraging, the investor is able to receive an upfront floating rate coupon that is higher than attainable (at the time of purchase) with either a Prime or a LIBOR FRN. The downside is that the investor is able to only partially participate in any upside if Prime rate should rise. The yield advantage of the deleveraged Prime floating rate note (DPF) over a Prime FRN would vanish rapidly in a rising rate environment.

History

As interest rates continued to drop in the 1990–94 bull market rally, floating rate note investors received yields that dropped with every coupon reset. In 1993, the benchmark short-term rate (3-month LIBOR) dropped to its lowest point since Eurodollar futures began trading. Given this backdrop of dismal yields, investors seeking higher yields sought the DPFs as a means of generating an above-market floating rate yield, yet retaining some upside if rates should rise. The graph on the next page illustrates the performance of an

Agency LIBOR note and an Agency DPF. A hypothetical DPF created in December 1992 would produce a yield advantage over the LIBOR FRN from December 1992 through January 1994, when LIBOR continued to drop but Prime remained at 6%. However, once rates began to rise in response to the Federal Reserve's raising of short-term Fed fund rates, the yield advantage of the DPF vanished rapidly.

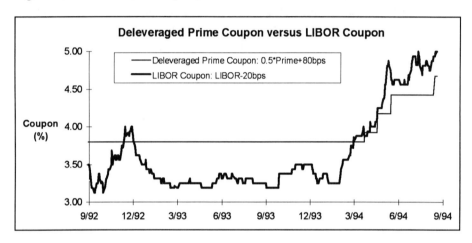

Analysis

The terms of a sample DPF are given in Exhibit 5-5 and can be summarized as follows:

Issuer: U.S. Agency
Maturity: 3 years
Coupon: 0.5 * (Prime) + 0.80%

This note contains the added twist that the Prime rate resets discretely at the start of each quarter (as opposed to a typical Prime FRN, which resets daily). The benchmark note of comparison will be a comparable maturity Prime FRN. The risk and performance of both notes will be analyzed with the LSE analysis for a range of final expected Primes.

The coupon of the DPF is plotted in Exhibit 5-6 versus a range of Prime rates. At low levels of Prime, the DPF coupon produces a yield advantage over a comparable maturity Prime FRN. However, this advantage rapidly vanishes for higher Prime rates.

EXHIBIT 5-5 Deleveraged Prime FRN

Note that the coupon index is now 50% of Prime rather than Prime. At the time of purchase, the DPF produced a high positive carry of 0.80% if the investor funds the purchase with overnight Fed funds. (In December 1993, Prime was 6%, and Fed funds was 3%.) However, that positive carry had all but vanished by August 1994 (Prime = 7.75%, Fed funds = 4.625%, resulting in a positive carry of only 0.05%). The other twist to this structure is the discrete once-a-quarter setting of the Prime rate, which is typically reset on a daily basis for most structured notes.

Issue Terms (Actual)

Issuer:	Federal Home Loan Bank
Principal amount:	US$25,000,000
Settlement date:	Dec. 17, 1993
Maturity date:	Dec. 17, 1996
Coupon paid in US$:	0.5 * Prime + 0.80%
Initial coupon:	3.80%
Day count basis:	Act/360 with no adjustment for period end dates.
Rate reset and payment dates:	Prime rate reset and paid quarterly. Payment dates are Mar. 17, June 17, Sept. 17, Dec. 17. First coupon paid on Mar. 17, 1994.
Prime rate determination:	Prime rate sets *discretely* two New York business days prior to reset dates. Source: Fed H.15(519).
Issue price:	100.00%

Performance

The performance of the DPF can be analyzed for a variety of final expectation Prime rates using LSE. The IRR results are shown in Exhibit 5-7. Similar to the coupon behavior, the IRR of the deleveraged Prime FRN outperforms a comparable maturity benchmark Prime FRN in low interest rate scenarios. This advantage is rapidly eroded as Prime rate begins to increase. The breakeven point between the two structures occurs at the Prime = 7 1/4% at maturity scenario. For higher interest rate scenarios, the Prime FRN begins to outperform the DPF significantly.

Risk

The DPF contains more interest rate risk than its unleveraged counterparty. Exhibit 5-7 shows that the DPF underperforms the Prime FRN in high interest rate scenarios. The risk of the note is thus to rising rates because it only

EXHIBIT 5-6   Deleveraged Prime FRN Coupon Versus Prime FRN Coupon

The deleveraged Prime FRN coupon is somewhat higher than a Prime FRN for low levels of Prime, but that advantage drops rapidly, reaching breakeven at a Prime rate of 6.7%.

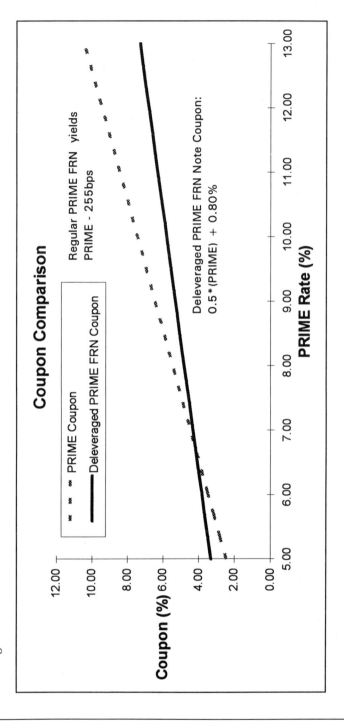

Coupon Comparison

Regular PRIME FRN yields
PRIME – 255bps

Deleveraged PRIME FRN Note Coupon:
0.5*(PRIME) + 0.80%

EXHIBIT 5-7 IRR of Deleveraged Prime FRN

Note that the DPF outperforms the Prime FRN in low interest rate scenarios. However, the note quickly underperforms the Prime FRN as interest rates begin to rise moderately. The breakeven between the two notes occurs at Prime = 7 1/4% at maturity scenario.

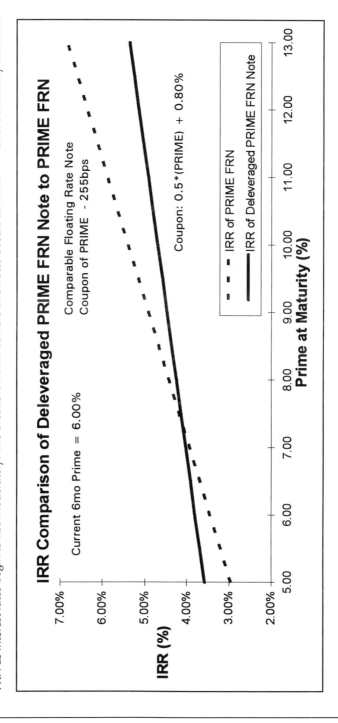

IRR Comparison of Deleveraged PRIME FRN Note to PRIME FRN

EXHIBIT 5-8 Duration of Deleveraged Prime FRN

The risk of the DPF is seen to be fairly constant across a wide range of final Prime rates with a duration of approximately 1.4. This shows that the note's interest rate risk is between that of a 3-year fixed coupon note and a 3-year Prime (or LIBOR) FRN.

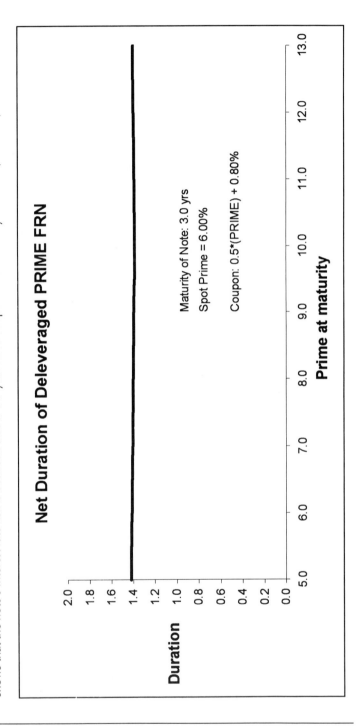

Net Duration of Deleveraged PRIME FRN

Maturity of Note: 3.0 yrs

Spot Prime = 6.00%

Coupon: 0.5*(PRIME) + 0.80%

provides 50% of the increase in Prime rate. Thus, one might expect the note to have a risk level that is between that of a fixed note and a Prime note. The actual risk of the note can be examined by interpreting the deterministic duration as shown in Exhibit 5-8. The duration is seen to vary little over a wide range of Prime scenarios. Exhibit 5-8 shows that the DPF has a duration that is not zero, but is approximately 1.4, which is half-way between that of a 3-year fixed note (2.8) and that of a Prime FRN (zero).

This result may be a surprise to investors who believe that a note that is reset off a floating rate index periodically should have the same durational risk as that of a LIBOR FRN, i.e., zero duration. As this chapter unfolds, the risk characteristics of other first generation structures will show that a non-zero duration is more often the rule rather than the exception.

STRUCTURE II. CAPPED AND FLOORED FLOATING RATE NOTE

The next level of structured note complexity introduces an optionality component, which can be either a cap or a floor on the coupon index. If the coupon is capped, the coupon index spread is increased to compensate the investor for giving up some potential upside. If the coupon is floored, the coupon index spread is likewise reduced to help pay for the protection of the coupon floor.

Capped Floating Rate Note (CapFRN)

Investor purpose: To obtain incremental higher yield for low risk.
Risk: In a fast rising rate environment, investor's coupon will be capped out.
Equivalent investor position: Long floating rate note, short cap option.

CapFRNs are FRNs that, like the regular floating rate note, reset off a floating rate index. The difference is that the CapFRN coupon no longer floats when the floating rate index rises above a certain level, but is fixed at the coupon cap level. By giving up the coupon upside above the coupon cap level, the investor receives, in return, an enhanced spread to the coupon index. A typical CapFRN has the following form:

Issuer: AA
Maturity: 3 years
Coupon: LIBOR + 0.50%, capped at 6%

The note described above would float at LIBOR + 0.50% until the coupon reaches 6.00%, i.e., LIBOR reaches 5.50%. If LIBOR rises above 5.50% on a coupon reset date, the investor's coupon would remain capped at 6.00%, hence the name CapFRN.

CapFRNs are popular among investors who believe that short-term rates will not rise as rapidly as predicted by the forward rates. These investors are willing to cap out their potential rate upside gains (sell off the cap option) in return for enhanced upfront yield. Because CapFRN investors have essentially sold an interest rate cap, the added implicit view of CapFRN investors is that current volatility is high.

History

CapFRNs became popular when the U.S. economy headed into and then stayed in a recession from 1990 through 1993. During that period, the U.S. yield curve was positive, implying that the forward predicted short-term rates would begin rising shortly.

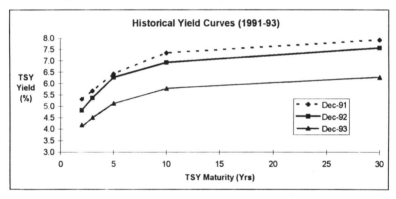

Since the U.S. economy at that time was mired in a recession, the expectation of a small segment of floating rate investors during that period was for the Federal Reserve to continue to lower short-term rates to stimulate the economy. These investors were willing to give up some potential yield upside by selling caps that have high value due to the upwardly sloping yield curve. In addition, because of the higher volatility associated with the Federal Reserve's easing actions during that period, the investor is also able to cash in on the high volatility at the same time by purchasing these CapFRNs.

It must be emphasized that only a small segment of all investors were of the opinion that interest rates would continue to drop. The CapFRNs were marketed to and sold to this select segment of the investor population. The view of the market in general was for short-term rates to rise, thus resulting in a positively sloped yield curve.

A significant fraction of investors who purchase regular FRNs refused to purchase the CapFRN even with the enhanced spread. In 1994, the market for CapFRNs was further dampened by both the interest rate hikes conducted by the Federal Reserve, and the SEC's letter in July 1994 to 2a-7 money market funds in which the SEC warned the funds that several structures (including the CapFRNs) cannot be reasonably assumed to be resettable back to par price at any time over its life.

Analysis

The sample terms of an actual CapFRN are given in Exhibit 5-9. The key features are summarized as follows:

1. The issuer is Sallie Mae, a U.S. Agency (with a AAA rating), and the maturity is five years. CapFRNs are typically issued by highly rated issuers whose new issue required funding spread to the floating rate index is usually quite low.
2. The floating rate index of the note is the 3-month Treasury bill rate, which resets weekly from levels set during the weekly Treasury auctions. Other popular CapFRNs use 3-month LIBOR as the floating rate index.
3. The coupon cap for the first year is 4.80% and rises 0.75% each year. CapFRN coupon cap levels can either be fixed or step up over time.
4. The notional amount of the deal was $500MM, which is a very large amount for a structured note.

The coupon behavior of the CapFRN in Exhibit 5-9 is calculated in Exhibit 5-10. The coupon rate rises with the Treasury bill rate until the coupon cap level is reached, after which the coupon remains fixed at the coupon cap level despite higher rates.

The characteristics of the CapFRN are analyzed using the simulation class of analysis. LSE is used to generate a set of intermediate rates from the initial rate and the final expectation rate. The performance of the note will be interpreted by examining the IRR for each base case scenario. Likewise, the interest rate risk of the note can be found by analyzing the duration characteristics for different expectation scenarios. Finally, the volatility risk of the note will be discussed via the volatility duration.

EXHIBIT 5-9 CapFRN

The investor receives an enhanced floating rate coupon in return for a coupon cap. The coupon cap is structured to step up each year, thus providing investors with added protection against rising rates.

Issue Terms (Actual)	
Issuer:	Student Loan Marketing Association (Sallie Mae)
Principal amount:	US$500,000,000
Settlement date:	July 16, 1992
Maturity date:	July 16, 1997
Coupon paid in US$:	3-month T-bill + 0.60% subject to coupon cap
Coupon cap:	4.80% for the first year, rising 0.75% each subsequent year
Day count basis:	Act/Act
Rate reset and payment dates:	3-month T-bill rate resets weekly, pays quarterly. Payment dates are Jan. 16, Apr. 16, July 16, Oct. 16. First coupon paid on Oct. 16, 1992.
T-bill determination:	3-month T-bill determination based on weekly T-bill auction rates. Source: Fed H.15(519).
Issue price:	100.00%

Performance

LSE is used to generate a series of final expectation rates and to calculate the intermediate rates and cash flows. The IRR of the CapFRN can then be calculated as a function of the final expectation rates and are plotted on Exhibit 5-11. As expected, the return of the CapFRN rises in a linear fashion up to a certain level and subsequently trails off after reaching a plateau. This is consistent with the scenarios in which the T-bill rate has risen and hit the cap level. When this occurs, the coupon is capped out and thus the IRR will no longer increase even for higher projected T-bill rate scenarios.

Risk

Interest Rate Risk. The interest rate risk of the note can be interpreted by examining the deterministic duration results plotted in Exhibit 5-12. For low interest rate scenarios, the coupon cap is not projected to be reached on any coupon reset date. Hence, for these scenarios the CapFRN would behave much like a regular T-bill FRN. The expectation is for the duration to be zero since the note would float off the weekly resetting T-bill rate.

EXHIBIT 5-10   CapFRN Coupon Versus LIBOR Coupon

The investor obtains a good spread to a regular LIBOR FRN when rates remain low. The investor receives a coupon enhancement of 0.45% and in return has a cap on the maximum coupon, which steps up each year by 0.75%.

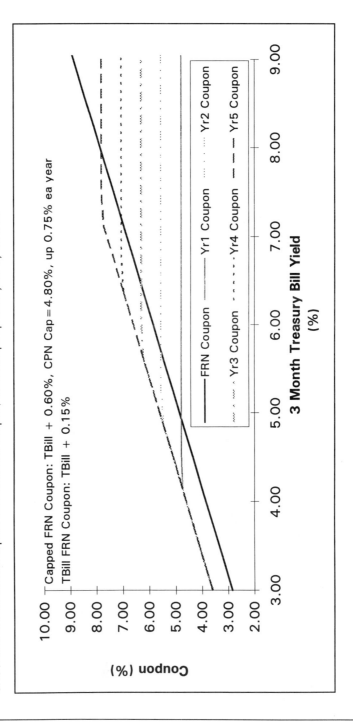

EXHIBIT 5-11   Capped T-bill FRN IRR

This 5-year SLMA step-up CapFRN outperforms a comparable maturity T-bill FRN when rates remain low or rise moderately. The step-up CapFRN levels provide an added measure of protection against the coupons being capped out.

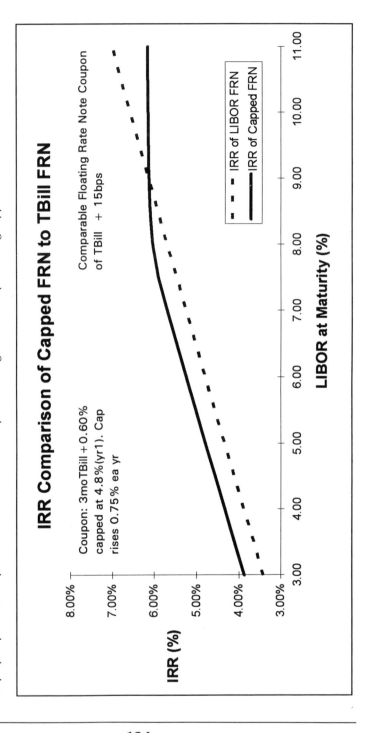

IRR Comparison of Capped FRN to TBill FRN

Coupon: 3moTBill +0.60% capped at 4.8%(yr1). Cap rises 0.75% ea yr

Comparable Floating Rate Note Coupon of TBill + 15bps

IRR (%)

- - - IRR of LIBOR FRN
—— IRR of Capped FRN

LIBOR at Maturity (%)

EXHIBIT 5-12 Capped T-Bill FRN Duration

Note that the duration does not start to pick up until the index first hits the coupon cap. As more coupons begin to be capped out, the note's duration will begin to approach that of a fixed note. The actual duration of the note as reflected by the simulation duration shows that the note begins to gain duration even prior to the level at which the first coupon is capped. 2000 simulations were conducted for each final expectation interest rate scenario.

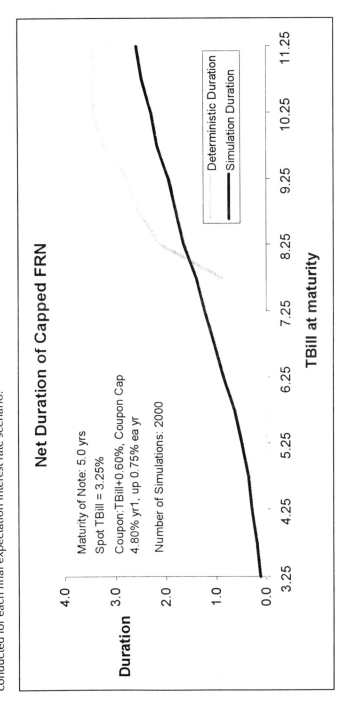

Net Duration of Capped FRN

Maturity of Note: 5.0 yrs
Spot TBill = 3.25%

Coupon: TBill+0.60%, Coupon Cap
4.80% yr1, up 0.75% ea yr

Number of Simulations: 2000

Duration

- - - - - Deterministic Duration
———— Simulation Duration

TBill at maturity

This is reflected in Exhibit 5-12, which shows that the deterministic duration is zero for low interest rate scenarios.

For very high interest rate scenarios in which all the coupon cash flows except the first coupon would be capped at the coupon cap level, the note will behave like a fixed note, with a duration close to that of a comparable maturity fixed note less the duration of the first coupon (which remains floating), or approximately 4.2. This is referred to as the asymptotic duration, or the duration in the limit of very high or very low rates. The deterministic duration results of Exhibit 5-12 are seen to rise up towards the asymptotic duration.

For intermediate interest rate scenarios, the duration of the note is expected to be between the zero duration of the floating rate note and the asymptotic duration of a fixed note minus the first coupon stub. This expectation is borne out by the deterministic duration.

The actual duration of the note as expressed by the simulation duration shows that the note begins to lose value and gain duration prior to any coupon having been capped. This is expected since the CapFRN's shorted cap option will start to lose value even prior to the coupon cap being reached. Thus, the CapFRN will gradually gain in duration for higher interest rate scenarios and not exhibit the rapid transition from zero to high duration as shown by the deterministic duration. However, the deterministic duration was useful in providing intuition into the behavior of the CapFRN. Like the deterministic duration, the simulation duration is also expected to rise towards the asymptotic duration for very high interest rate scenarios.

Volatility Risk.   Since the CapFRN includes the embedded optionality of shorted caps, changes in volatility will affect the value of the note. A 3000 simulation analysis using the same base case rate scenarios as the above interest rate duration analysis results in the volatility duration graph in Exhibit 5-13. The exhibit shows that volatility duration initially rises for higher interest rate scenarios. This behavior is due to the characteristics of the shorted cap. Recall from the discussion of option vega in Chapter 2 that the vega (change in value of an option with respect to changing volatility) increases as the rate approaches the strike and decreases as the rate moves farther away. This matches the volatility duration behavior of the note, which increases towards a maximum for higher interest rate scenarios and subsequently begins to drop. The volatility duration of the note represents the sum effect of all the individual cap vegas. The graph shows that the magnitude of

EXHIBIT 5-13 Volatility Duration of Capped FRN

The unit of volatility duration is defined as +1 when a 1% increase in volatility results in a 1 bp decrease in the price of a par bond. The positive and rising volatility duration signifies the shorted cap gaining in value as the T-bill index approaches the coupon cap strike level.

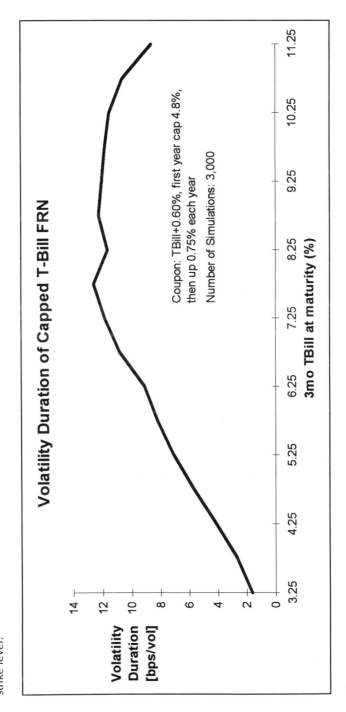

Volatility Duration of Capped T-Bill FRN

Coupon: TBill+0.60%, first year cap 4.8%, then up 0.75% each year

Number of Simulations: 3,000

3mo TBill at maturity (%)

Volatility Duration [bps/vol]

the volatility risk is not negligible: a 1% increase in volatility can, for the appropriate scenario, result in a decrease of as much as 13 bps of the note value.

Leveraged Capped FRN (LCFRN)

Investor purpose: Obtain yields higher than achievable with CapFRN over a fairly short risk period.

Risk: The investor has an equivalent short, leveraged position in cap options. In a rising rate environment, the note would lose yield extremely rapidly once the strike level has been exceeded.

Equivalent investor position: Long floating rate note, short $(m + 1)$ LIBOR cap options at initial strike, long (m) LIBOR cap options at higher strike (where m is the leverage factor).

Investors purchase LCFRNs for much the same reason as CapFRNs: yield enhancement. Short-term investors who wanted a higher return than is possible with the CapFRN were willing to take on more risk via the LCFRN to achieve that return.

LCFRNs have the following characteristic:

Coupon: LIBOR + A if LIBOR < STRIKE
          $B - 3 *$ LIBOR   if LIBOR > STRIKE

The note behaves like a floating rate note when LIBOR is below a preset STRIKE. However, once LIBOR exceeds the STRIKE rate, the note behaves like a leveraged inverse floating rate note. The leverage factor of 3 shown above can be tailored to reflect the investor's preferred risk level.

The enhanced leverage means that the coupon is extremely sensitive to rising interest rates. The coupon rapidly drops to zero once the strike level has been exceeded. The LCFRN is able to provide a better yield enhancement than the CapFRN, but at a considerably higher level of risk.

The investors who purchased LCFRNs were mainly money market 2a-7 investors. The SEC constraints on 2a-7 investors helped to define the terms of the typical LCFRN. These were:

1. **Short-term maturity.** Since a 2a-7 money market investor can purchase a corporate issued security for a maximum of only 397 days

from the trade date, that imposed a maximum maturity of less than 13 months for a corporate LCFRN.

2. **High credit issuers.** Money market investors have stringent credit requirements. Only U.S. Agencies and highly rated corporates (typically AA and better) were acceptable issuers.

3. **Frequent reset.** Typical reset frequency is 1 month as opposed to the 3-month resets of regular LIBOR FRNs. This requirement was originally envisioned as a mechanism that ensured a more rapid reset of assets back to par value. However, as employed in these LCFRNs, the frequent reset feature is actually disadvantageous to the investor, since any significant rate increase would be more rapidly reflected by a lower yield.

History

As interest rates dropped to all-time lows in 1993, short-term investors searching for ways of obtaining enhanced yields purchased many LCFRNs as a means of yield enhancement. Due to the short maturity of the notes that these investors are required to purchase, it was difficult to generate sufficient yield enhancement with a simple CapFRN, and hence the interest in the LCFRN. Three factors combine to make the LCFRN a popular instrument:

1. Historically low interest rate levels. The ever-lower short-term rates were a driving force behind many investors' search for higher yields.

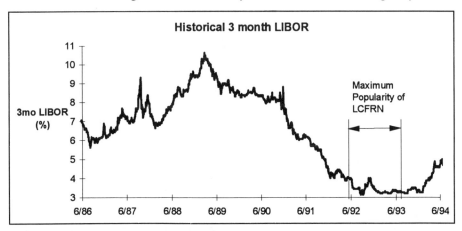

2. Historically steep yield curve. The yield curve was even steep in the short end of the curve (2-year Treasury to 3-month LIBOR). This provided even short-term investors with a means of extracting value from the curve via the LCFRN.

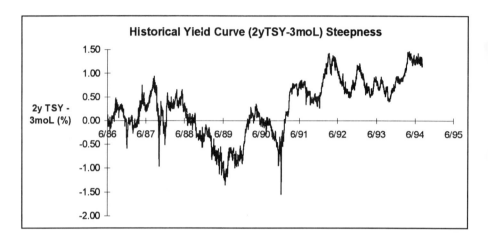

3. A large increase in short-term volatility. The Fed's sequence of interest rate cuts from 1991 through 1993 contributed to higher market volatility and resulted in higher levels of cap prices.

Analysis

The terms of a sample LCFRN in commercial paper (CP) form are described in Exhibit 5-14. The structure can be summarized as follows:

Issuer: Walt Disney Company Commercial Paper
Maturity: 6 months after settlement date
Coupon: Lower of 1-month LIBOR + 0.07%, or
                    18.82% – 4 * (1-month LIBOR)

The features of this structured commercial paper fit the criteria of the short-term money market investors perfectly. The note is issued by a well known and highly rated issuer. The maturity is relatively short at six months, and the structure provides a yield pickup based on a monthly resetting index.

The coupon behavior of this note is shown in Exhibit 5-15. The note behaves like a floating rate note prior to LIBOR exceeding the strike, but

EXHIBIT 5-14 Leveraged Capped Floating Rate Note

The investor receives an enhancement to LIBOR in return for diminished returns if LIBOR rises quickly. This LCFRN takes the form of commercial paper. The features required by money market funds are evident: an excellent issuer, short maturity, and a frequent (monthly) coupon reset.

Issue Terms (Actual)

Issuer:	The Walt Disney Company (A1/P1)
Form of note:	Commercial paper
Principal amount:	US$75,000,000
Settlement date:	Mar. 29, 1993
Maturity date:	Dec. 29, 1993
Coupon paid in US$:	Lower of: 1-month LIBOR + 0.07%, or 18.82% − 4 * (1-month LIBOR)
Day count basis:	Act/360 with no adjustment for period end dates.
Rate reset and payment dates:	1-month LIBOR resets monthly. Payment dates are monthly on the 29th. First coupon paid on Apr. 29, 1993.
LIBOR determination:	1-month LIBOR determination date is two New York and London business days prior to period end dates. Source: Telerate Page 3750.

becomes a leveraged inverse FRN once LIBOR has exceeded the strike. (Inverse FRNs will be discussed later in this chapter.)

Because the LCFRN's coupon decreases so rapidly beyond the strike, the presence of the zero coupon floor is an important factor in the risk and performance of the note. Since the LCFRN contains various option components, simulation and LSE are necessary to analyze the risk and performance of this note.

Performance

The performance of the note can be calculated for a variety of interest rate expectation scenarios. The result of the LSE analysis is shown on Exhibit 5-16. The IRR of the note is seen to rise with higher interest rates until the first coupon has exceeded the strike. Subsequent to that, the LCFRN's performance begins to deteriorate rapidly, with the breakeven point occurring for final expectation LIBOR of 4.05%. For higher interest rate scenarios, the LCFRN begins to underperform the benchmark LIBOR FRN by an increasingly larger margin due to the inverse leveraged coupon. The upside of this

EXHIBIT 5-15   LCFRN Coupon Versus LIBOR Coupon

The investor obtains a good spread to a regular LIBOR FRN when rates remain low. The LCFRN begins to lose yield very quickly when LIBOR exceeds the strike rate. As one can see, the investor is taking considerable interest rate risk for a relatively small yield advantage. This often was the only way that extra yield could be produced for short maturity notes.

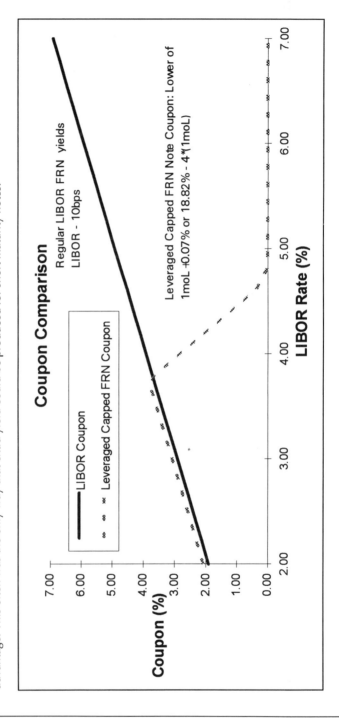

EXHIBIT 5-16 Performance of LCFRN Versus Comparable LIBOR FRN

The presence of the leveraged caps makes the LCFRN severely underperform the LIBOR FRN if rates should rise even moderately. The LCFRN thus contains large risk relative to its reward, which is a yield enhancement of approximately 17 bps over a comparable credit and maturity FRN.

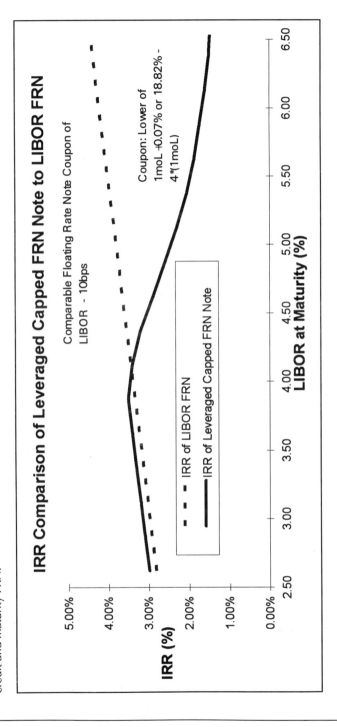

note is thus rather limited since the note ceases to behave as a floating rate note if rates rise above the strike.

Risk

Interest Rate Risk. The duration of the LCFRN for a variety of final LSE expectation scenarios is shown on Exhibit 5-17. The behavior of the note can be interpreted by examining the deterministic duration. For low interest rate scenarios, the note exhibits the behavior of a floating rate note, i.e., zero duration, when interest rates are low and the strike has not been exceeded. Once the strike is exceeded, however, the note's duration rises very rapidly, exhibiting a duration many times higher than that of a comparable maturity fixed note. This is due to the inverse and leveraged nature of the LCFRN. The note begins to drop in duration again for even higher interest rate scenarios, indicating that coupons are being reset to zero and that the note would, in a moderately high interest rate scenario, begin to behave like a zero coupon note of six months' maturity. Thus, the asymptotic duration for high interest rate scenarios is half, or the duration of a zero coupon half-year maturity note.

The actual duration of the note (as represented by the simulation duration) is qualitatively similar to the deterministic duration. Simulation duration shows that the LCFRN begins to gain duration prior to any index having exceeded the strike level of 3.75%. This is expected since the shorted cap options gain in value as the strikes are approached. The actual rise and subsequent drop in duration for higher interest rate scenarios is more gradual and not as pronounced as predicted by deterministic duration. The maximum duration of this LCFRN is approximately twice that of a 6-month fixed note. The reason that the maximum expected duration is less than the degree of leverage (four times) is due to the presence of the zero coupon floor option, which the investor is long. These zero coupon floor options gain in value even as the shorted cap options are losing value for the note, thus offsetting what would otherwise be an even higher duration.

Volatility Risk. The volatility risk of the note is reflected in the calculation of the volatility duration. The result of a 3000 simulation volatility analysis is shown in Exhibit 5-18. The behavior of the volatility duration is a result of the combination of options embedded in the note. Initially, the volatility duration is positive and increases for higher interest rate scenarios. This is due to the increasing vega of the leverage caps (which the note is short) as

EXHIBIT 5-17 Duration of LCFRN

The LCFRN is seen to behave like a LIBOR FRN when rates are low enough to allow all coupons to float. The behavior of the note can be seen by examining the deterministic duration. The note behaves as a regular FRN at low rates, hence zero duration. For higher interest rates, more components of the note become leveraged inverse coupons. These coupons have a duration five times that of a fixed coupon, adding significantly to the overall duration. Once interest rates have risen such that some coupons have been leveraged capped to zero, the duration of the note will begin to drop down. The asymptotic duration is 0.5, which is that of a zero coupon note.

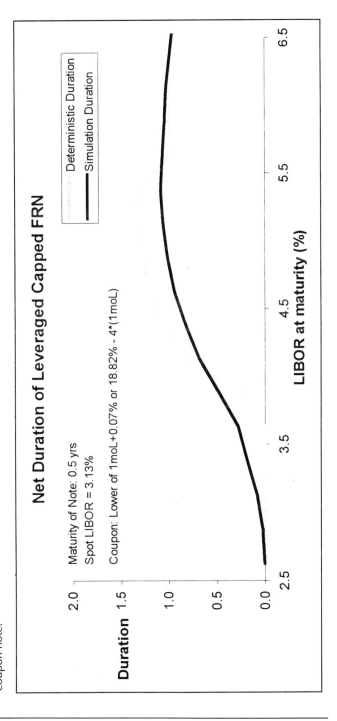

Net Duration of Leveraged Capped FRN

Maturity of Note: 0.5 yrs
Spot LIBOR = 3.13%

Coupon: Lower of 1moL+0.07% or 18.82% - 4*(1moL)

Legend:
---- Deterministic Duration
—— Simulation Duration

x-axis: LIBOR at maturity (%)
y-axis: Duration

EXHIBIT 5-18 Volatility Duration of LCFRN

The LCFRN shows positive volatility duration for low interest rate scenarios, signifying the loss in value due to the presence of the leverage caps. This positive duration begins to decrease and eventually becomes negative for higher interest rate scenarios. As rates move higher, the zero coupon floor becomes more in-the-money, and the increase in value of these zero coupon floor options will eventually overcome the shorted leveraged caps.

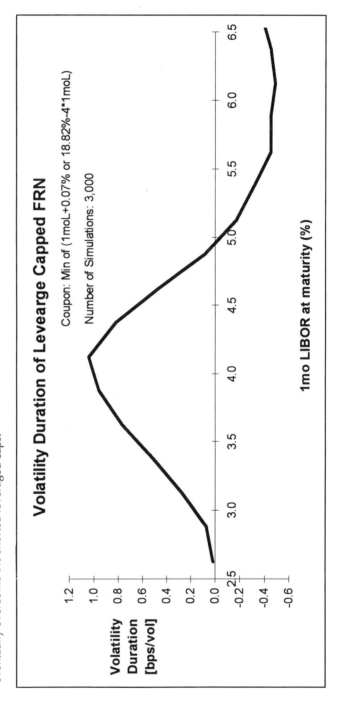

Volatility Duration of Levearge Capped FRN

Coupon: Min of (1moL+0.07% or 18.82%-4*1moL)

Number of Simulations: 3,000

1mo LIBOR at maturity (%)

Volatility Duration [bps/vol]

the index approaches the strike level of these leverage caps. The higher vega results in an increase in the value of the caps for an increase in volatility, and subsequently a decrease in the value of the note.

Volatility duration is seen to decrease beyond a maximum due to both the decreasing vega of the leverage cap beyond the strike as well as the increasing vega of the zero coupon floor. For higher interest rate scenarios, the vega of these zero coupon floor options (which the note is long) begin to increase for an increase in volatility, resulting in a gain in the value of the note and thus a negative volatility duration. The zero coupon floor option likewise attains a maximum vega close to the strike and subsequently decreases in amplitude for even higher interest rate scenarios.

Floored Floating Rate Note (FFRN)

Investor purpose: Obtain protection against lower short-term rates in the form of a high coupon floor.

Risk: In a rapidly rising rate environment, the floor will soon be out of the money.

Equivalent investor position: Long floating rate note, long floor options.

FFRNs are FRNs with an embedded coupon floor below which the coupon can never drop. Investors purchase FFRNs in order to obtain downside protection against lower interest rates. Many of these FFRNs have floors that provide higher-than-market yields, i.e., deep in-the-money floors. Because of the high cost of these deep in-the-money floor options, floored FRNs are generally issued by lower rated issuers whose large credit spreads can help pay for the floor. Issuers of FFRNs thus, in general, carry credit ratings that are substantially below that of U.S. Agencies. In return for a smaller floating rate spread, the investor obtains the protection of a coupon floor.

History

The popularity of FFRNs was confined to a few (albeit large) investors, typically pension funds that required protection against lowering yields. Because of the limited number of investors, the FFRN was never able to gain the prominence of the CapFRN. FFRNs are excellent performers in an upwardly sloping yield curve environment in which rates actually dropped (this occurred from 1991–93). The result of that environment was two-fold: first, the upwardly sloping yield curve means that floors are relatively cheap since future floors will contain less intrinsic value, resulting in a smaller yield decrement to the investor. Secondly, a falling rate environment results in the floor being further in-the-money, hence price appreciation.

The following graph illustrates the attractiveness of the FFRN in low interest rate environments. It shows the coupon performance of two hypothetical notes created in July 1993: a FFRN and a LIBOR FRN. The FFRN was able to provide an above-market coupon to the investor when rates were low and still retained some upside when interest rates turned around and began rising.

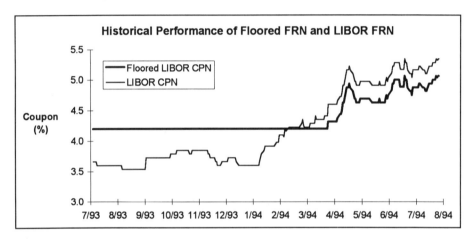

Analysis

An actual FFRN is described in Exhibit 5-19. The key features can be summarized as follows:

1. The issuer is Chemical Bank Corporation, which at the time of issuance was rated A3/A. This is in line with the expectation that FFRNs are typically issued by lower rated credits than those issuing CapFRNs.
2. The maturity of the FFRN is 10 years. A long maturity is typical of FFRNs so that the high cost of the floor can be amortized over a longer maturity.
3. The coupon floor is 4.20%, which is significantly above yields achievable through regular LIBOR FRNs at the time. This provides the investor with a higher coupon than typical FRNs in return for a smaller spread if the note does float. Most FFRNs are structured so

EXHIBIT 5-19 FFRN

The investor gives up part of the LIBOR spread in order to obtain downside protection and a high minimum coupon.

Issue Terms (Actual)

Issuer:	Chemical Banking Corp. (A3/A)
Principal amount:	US$150,000,000
Settlement date:	July 29, 1993
Maturity date:	July 29, 2003
Coupon paid in US$:	3-month LIBOR + 0.0625% subject to coupon floor
Coupon floor:	4.20%
Day count basis:	Act/360 with no adjustment for period end dates.
Rate reset and payment dates:	3-month LIBOR resets and pays quarterly. Payment dates are Jan. 29, Apr. 29, July 29, Oct. 29. First coupon paid on Oct. 29, 1993.
LIBOR determination:	3-month LIBOR determination date is two New York and London business days prior to period end dates. Source: Telerate Page 3750.
Issue price:	100.00%

that the floor is significantly higher than the coupon of a comparable maturity benchmark LIBOR FRN.

The coupon of the FFRN is plotted on Exhibit 5-20 for a range of LIBORs. The coupon is floored at 4.20% until LIBOR rises to such a point that the coupon exceeds the floor. After the coupon floor has been exceeded, the note behaves like a regular LIBOR FRN.

Performance

Since the FFRN contains optionality in the form of a coupon floor, the simulation class of analysis is appropriate. Employing LSE, a range of final LIBORs is selected and a set of base case scenarios is used for the simulation analysis.

The performance of the FFRN is calculated for a range of final expectation LIBORs and shown in Exhibit 5-21. The IRR of the FFRN is floored at 4.20% and slowly rises as more coupons begin to float off the floor. The note thus outperforms a comparable maturity LIBOR FRN for low interest rate scenarios. For higher interest rate scenarios, the FFRN will perform like a regular FRN, but its smaller floating rate spread contributes to its eventually underperforming the benchmark LIBOR FRN.

EXHIBIT 5-20   FFRN Coupon and LIBOR FRN Coupon

The FFRN outperforms the LIBOR FRN when rates remain low. FFRN investors give up some coupon spread in order to obtain the protection that a coupon floor offers.

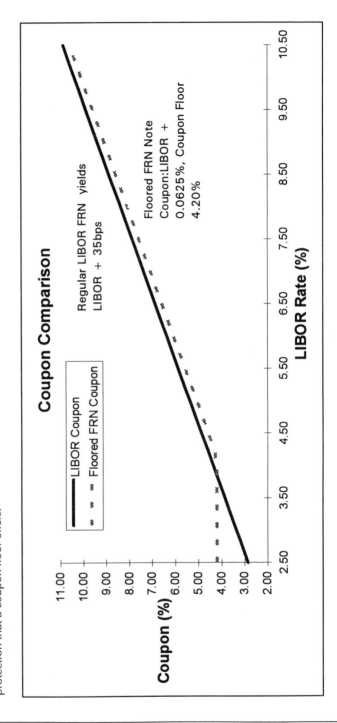

Coupon Comparison

LIBOR Coupon

Floored FRN Coupon

Regular LIBOR FRN yields
LIBOR + 35bps

Floored FRN Note
Coupon:LIBOR +
0.0625%, Coupon Floor
4.20%

Coupon (%)

LIBOR Rate (%)

EXHIBIT 5-21 FFRN IRR Versus a Comparable LIBOR FRN

The FFRN would outperform a comparable LIBOR FRN in low interest rate scenarios due to the presence of a coupon floor. However, that yield advantage rapidly vanishes for higher interest rate scenarios, resulting in the FFRN underperforming a LIBOR FRN.

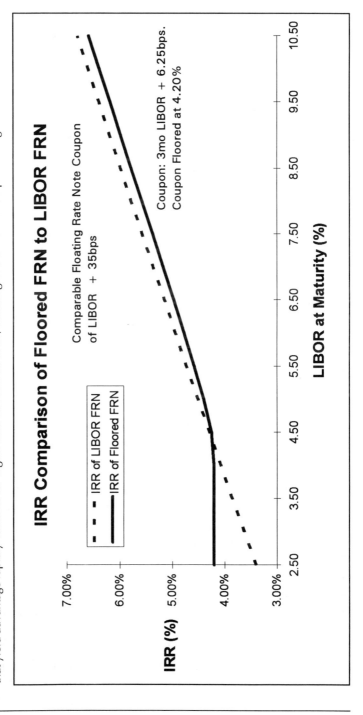

IRR Comparison of Floored FRN to LIBOR FRN

Comparable Floating Rate Note Coupon
of LIBOR + 35bps

Coupon: 3mo LIBOR + 6.25bps.
Coupon Floored at 4.20%

- - - IRR of LIBOR FRN
——— IRR of Floored FRN

LIBOR at Maturity (%)

IRR (%)

Risk

Interest Rate Risk. The interest rate risk of the FFRN can be found by interpreting the Deterministic durational characteristics of the note as shown in Exhibit 5-22. For low expectation scenarios, the future LIBORs will remain below the coupon floor, and thus the note will behave like a 10-year maturity fixed rate note. Deterministic duration reflects this expectation, exhibiting a duration approximately equal to that of a 10-year note for low interest rate scenarios.

For extremely high interest rate scenarios, the FFRN coupons will (with the exception of the first coupon) float off the coupon floor; hence the note would behave like a floating rate note with an asymptotic duration equal to the duration of a regular FRN (which is zero) plus the duration of the first fixed coupon, or 1/4. In between the two extremes, the duration is expected to decrease towards 1/4 for higher LIBOR scenarios. This expectation is again reflected in the deterministic duration.

The actual behavior of the FFRN as seen via the simulation duration is qualitatively similar to the deterministic duration results. The difference is that the note begins to decrease in duration prior to any coupons floating off the floor. This is due to the floor option (which the investor is long) losing value for higher rates. The rate of loss decreases for higher rates because the delta of each option decreases as the index moves away from the strike. The actual durational behavior thus shows a decrease that is slower and more gradual than depicted by the deterministic duration.

Volatility Risk. The volatility risk of the FFRN is the mirror image of the CapFRN. A 3000 run simulation analysis of the volatility duration is shown in Exhibit 5-23. Initially, the volatility duration of the FFRN is negative and decreases further for higher interest rate scenarios. This is due to the characteristics of the floor option embedded in the note. For all interest rate scenarios, the floor option (which the note is long) would gain value if volatility were to increase, thus the FFRN will always exhibit a negative volatility duration. From option theory, the vega of a floor option is at a maximum when the index is equal to the strike. Thus, the magnitude of the negative volatility duration would rise towards a "maximum" negative level and subsequently decrease.

The magnitude of the volatility duration of this note is quite large: a 1% change in volatility can correspond to as much as a 30 bp movement in the price of a par bond. The cause of this large volatility duration is the long maturity of the FFRN, which is 10 years. Option theory shows that longer

EXHIBIT 5-22 FFRN Duration

Note the difference between the deterministic duration and the simulation duration. When interest rates are low, deterministic duration indicates that the note would trade much as a fixed note. In reality, the note would have a smaller duration than a fixed note due to the delta of the floor option, which is less than one, i.e., the floored coupon would lose value slower than a fixed coupon, hence a lower duration. For high interest rate scenarios, both will converge towards an asymptotic duration of 0.25 (duration of a LIBOR FRN [zero] plus the first fixed period).

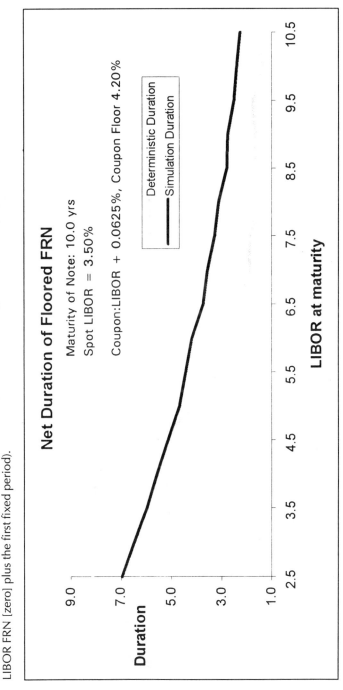

Net Duration of Floored FRN

Maturity of Note: 10.0 yrs
Spot LIBOR = 3.50%

Coupon:LIBOR + 0.0625%, Coupon Floor 4.20%

Deterministic Duration
Simulation Duration

Duration

LIBOR at maturity

EXHIBIT 5-23   Volatility Duration of FFRN

The volatility duration is negative, signifying that the floor option (which the investor is in effect long) gains value for higher volatility. The floor option reaches maximum vega when the index is closest to the strike for the majority of the quarterly floor options.

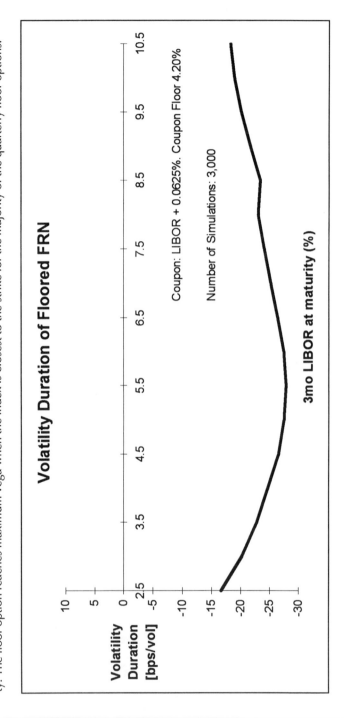

Volatility Duration of Floored FRN

Coupon: LIBOR + 0.0625%. Coupon Floor 4.20%

Number of Simulations: 3,000

3mo LIBOR at maturity (%)

Volatility
Duration
[bps/vol]

maturity options have larger vegas than their shorter maturity counterparts. This accounts for the larger volatility duration of the 10-year FFRN relative to the other structures examined thus far.

STRUCTURE III. COLLARED FLOATING RATE NOTE (CFRN)

Investor purpose: Pay for the protection of a high floating rate floor by giving up some floating rate upside via a coupon cap.

Risk: In a rising rate environment, the investor suffers doubly from both the decreasing value of the long floor and the increasing value of the shorted cap.

Equivalent investor position: Long floating rate note, short cap option, long floor option.

The hallmark of the collared floating rate note is the presence of a band or collar that restricts the movement of the underlying index for the life of the note. In order to provide a high minimum coupon floor to the investor without excessive penalty on the floating rate spread, the CFRN contains a coupon cap that helps to defray the cost of purchasing the coupon floor. The CFRN thus satisfied investors who demanded both a highly rated issuer and a high coupon floor, although a coupon cap had to be added to pay for the floor. Some CFRNs contain coupon caps and floors that step up over the life of the note.

History

From its humble beginnings as a poor cousin of the CapFRN, the CFRN has gained a stature unlike any other structured note. The first CFRN was issued in late 1992. By the end of 1993, the volume of CFRNs issued had ballooned to a notional amount of greater than $20 billion.[3] The great majority of CFRNs were purchased by investors in the Euromarket, while only a handful (less than $500 million) have been issued in the U.S. domestic market.

The issuer base of CFRN started out as stellar. Initially only AAAs and supranationals commanded the attention of the market. However, as interest rates dropped to levels that made coupon floors increasingly expensive, even single-A rated issuers were able to find good reception for their CFRNs.

---

3. See *Derivatives Week,* Nov. 15, 1993.

The success of the CFRN had an unexpected effect on the price of secondary market CFRNs. A larger supply of a particular type of structure enhances liquidity, but this abundant supply also created an impediment to price appreciation. When interest rates drop, the floor of a CFRN gains in value, while the cap becomes less likely to be hit. Thus, lower rates should result in the appreciation of the value of a CFRN. When U.S. rates dropped considerably in 1993, the expectation was that CFRNs would likewise appreciate significantly in price. However, due to the large supply, the price appreciation was less than the asset swap pricing (discussed in Chapter 9) would predict. This resulted in a supply of cheap secondary CFRNs, which provided good asset swap opportunities.

Analysis

The terms of an actual CFRN are described in Exhibit 5-24. The key features of the note are:

1. The issuer is the World Bank, arguably the most highly regarded issuer in the global capital markets. The World Bank reflects the quality of the initial issuers of CFRNs, which was uniformly sterling.
2. Long maturity. The typical maturity of CFRNs is 10 years, although some are as long as 12 years.
3. Coupon floor is significantly above spot LIBOR levels. This provides investors with the yield incentive and protection against lower rates.

The coupon of the CFRN of Exhibit 5-24 is calculated for a range of LIBORs and plotted on Exhibit 5-25.

CFRNs are higher in complexity than the CapFRNs and FFRNs discussed previously. Since the coupon can only move in a prescribed band, this produces a unique effect on the performance and risk of the note. Since the CFRN contains both floor and cap options, the simulation class of analysis is used in conjunction with LSE.

Performance

The performance of the CFRN is examined via an LSE analysis of the IRR. A series of final expectation rates are used to project intermediate rates and cash flows. The resulting IRR analysis is shown on Exhibit 5-26. The performance of the note is clearly superior to that of a comparable maturity bench-

EXHIBIT 5-24 CFRN

This was one of the very first CFRN deals issued in the Euro-markets to European investors. The issuer of this CFRN is one of the most highly regarded issuers in the global market, The World Bank.

Issue Terms (Actual)

Issuer:	International Bank for Reconstruction and Development ("The World Bank"; AAA/Aaa)
Form of note:	Euro medium-term note
Principal amount:	US$150,000,000
Settlement date:	Nov. 9, 1992
Maturity date:	Nov. 12, 2002
Coupon paid in US$:	6-month LIBOR – 0.25% subject to coupon cap and floor
Coupon cap:	8.25%
Coupon floor:	5.00%
Day count basis:	Act/360
Rate reset and payment dates:	Rate resets semiannually. Coupon payment dates May 9 and Nov. 9. First coupon paid on May 10, 1993.
LIBOR determination:	6-month LIBOR resets semiannually. Determination date is two London business days prior to reset date. Source: Telerate Page 3750.
Issue price:	100.00%

mark LIBOR FRN when rates are projected to remain low or rise moderately. However, for higher interest rate scenarios, the CFRN will underperform the benchmark LIBOR FRN due to the presence of the coupon cap. Exhibit 5-26 shows the breakeven expectation level of LIBOR (at maturity) as being 11%. This is the scenario for which the CFRN and benchmark LIBOR FRN would produce the same yield.

Risk

Interest Rate Risk.   The interest rate risk of the CFRN can be interpreted by examining the deterministic duration versus a range of LSE scenarios as plotted in Exhibit 5-27. Due to the presence of the collar, the interest rate risk of the CFRN bears careful interpretation. For low interest rate scenarios, the CFRN behaves like a fixed rate note since all future rates are below the coupon floor. Deterministic duration shows that for these low interest rate

EXHIBIT 5-25 CFRN Coupon Versus LIBOR FRN Coupon

The note outperforms a regular LIBOR FRN when short-term rates stay low. The CFRN will underperform a LIBOR FRN when the LIBOR has exceeded the coupon floor. The cap is used to provide additional proceeds to pay for the high cost of the in-the-money floor.

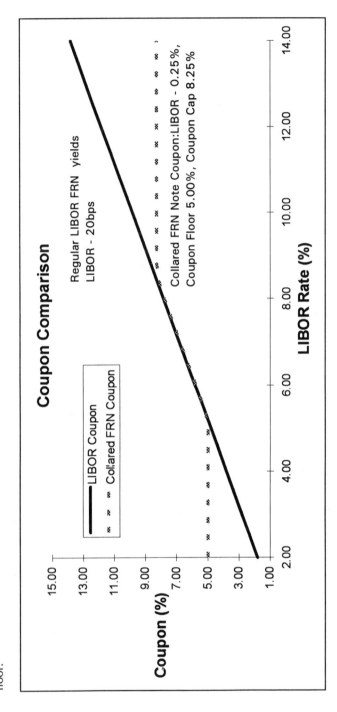

EXHIBIT 5-26 IRR Analysis of 10-Year World Bank CFRN

The CFRN outperforms a comparable LIBOR FRN when rates are low or rise moderately. The coupon floor provides a large yield cushion even when rates rise. When rates rise rapidly, the presence of the cap limits the performance of the CFRN, causing it to underperform the benchmark LIBOR FRN. The breakeven point at which the CFRN and LIBOR FRN performance are equal is the scenario of LIBOR (at maturity) = 11%.

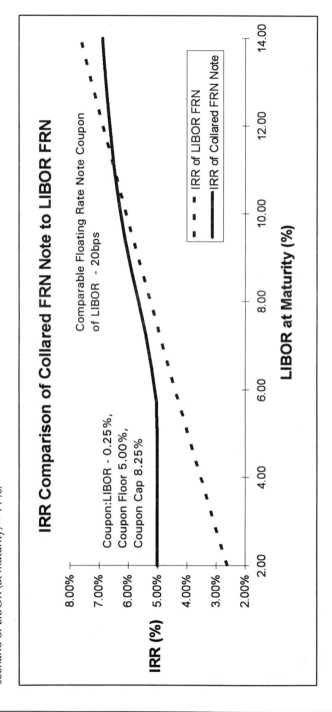

EXHIBIT 5-27 CFRN Duration

The CFRN has unique durational characteristics due to the presence of both a cap and a floor. When the rate scenario is low, the note behaves much as a fixed note, resulting in a high duration. Once rates rise enough for coupons to float, the note's duration decreases. Once the coupon cap is reached, the note's duration again increases. The actual duration of the note is seen to vary more smoothly, dropping moderately with rising rates from a high of eight to a minimum duration of approximately five. Due to the presence of the cap, the drop-off in duration for higher interest rate scenarios is modest compared to that of a FFRN (Exhibit 5-23).

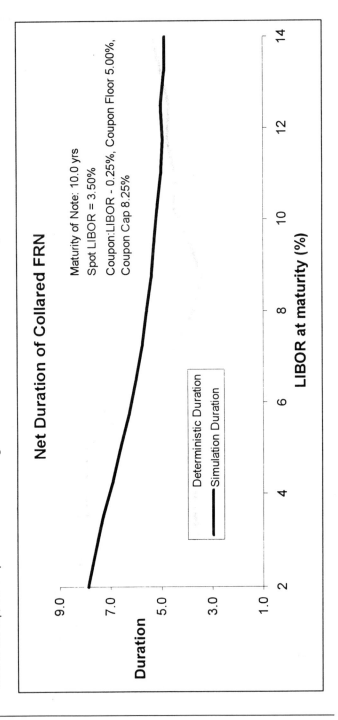

Net Duration of Collared FRN

Maturity of Note: 10.0 yrs
Spot LIBOR = 3.50%
Coupon:LIBOR - 0.25%, Coupon Floor 5.00%,
Coupon Cap 8.25%

Deterministic Duration
Simulation Duration

Duration

LIBOR at maturity (%)

scenarios, the CFRN will have a duration close to that of a fixed 10-year note, i.e., approximately eight.

For moderately rising interest rate scenarios, certain coupons will begin to rise above the coupon floor and float. This will cause the net duration of the CFRN to drop as more coupons begin to float off the floor.

Finally, for high interest rate scenarios, the coupon cap begins to be activated for certain coupons, and the result is that the CFRN will begin to gain duration again due to these coupons no longer floating. For extremely high interest rate scenarios, all the coupons will be fixed (the first coupon would be floored, the other coupons would be capped), and hence the asymptotic duration of the CFRN is also equal to that of a fixed 10-year note (minus the stub).

The actual duration of the note as reflected by the simulation duration is qualitatively similar, but contains some quantitative differences. For high interest rate scenarios, the duration does not drop off as dramatically. The presence of the cap affects the durational character of the note by limiting the minimum duration to approximately five. Compared to the 10-year FFRN of the previous section whose minimum duration dropped to below two, it is evident that the CFRN's durational variation is much less than its floored counterpart. Exhibit 5-27 shows that the CFRN's duration remains in a range of five to eight for a wide range of expectation LIBORs. Due to its consistently high duration, the CFRN contains a significantly higher level of interest rate risk than either a LIBOR FRN or a FFRN.

Some fixed income practitioners might be surprised by the consistently large duration exhibited by the CFRN. Upon further reflection, this high level of duration should not be unexpected. The CFRN contains a long floor option and a short cap option, both of which result in gains when rates drop and losses when rates rise. Thus, even for scenarios in which the base case LIBOR is projected to remain in the middle of the collared range for the entire maturity, the note should still exhibit considerable positive duration.

Volatility Risk. The volatility risk of the CFRN can be interpreted by examining the volatility duration. A 5000 run simulation analysis of the volatility duration is shown in Exhibit 5-28. For low interest rate scenarios, the volatility duration is negative, signifying that the floor option (which the note is long) gains greater value than the cap option (which the note is short) for an incremental increase in volatility. For low interest rate scenarios, the floating rate indices are closer to the strike of the floor than the cap, resulting in larger floor vega and thus a negative volatility duration.

EXHIBIT 5-28   Volatility Duration of CFRN

For low interest rate scenarios, the volatility duration is negative, signifying that the floor gains more value for incremental increases in volatility. For higher interest rate scenarios, the shorted cap option vega begins to increase as the index approaches the cap strike and moves away from the floor strike. The vega continues to increase, eventually becoming positive. At higher interest rate levels than shown, the vega will again decrease.

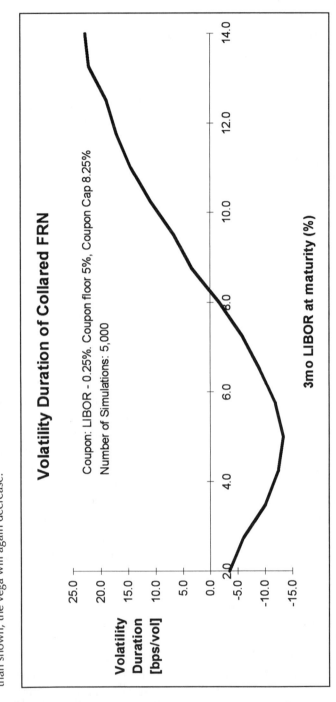

Volatility Duration of Collared FRN

Coupon: LIBOR - 0.25%. Coupon floor 5%, Coupon Cap 8.25%
Number of Simulations: 5,000

Volatility Duration [bps/vol]

3mo LIBOR at maturity (%)

For higher interest rate scenarios, the level of the future LIBOR indices begins to move further away from the floor strike and closer to the cap strike. The effect of this is that the vega of the floor option is expected to decrease and the vega of the cap would increase. The net volatility duration of the note thus increases and eventually becomes positive as the vega of the cap exceeds the floor vega.

For even higher interest rate scenarios, the vega of the cap is seen to completely dominate the behavior of the note, and the volatility duration likewise rises towards a maximum. For interest rate scenarios above the maximum scenario, the vega will once again decrease as the indices move further away from the strike, resulting in a decreasing vega.

Due to the two types of embedded options, the volatility risk of the CFRN is very much dependent upon market conditions. The analysis of this section illustrated that, depending upon the scenario, the CFRN can display volatility risk profiles that can be quite different from another scenario. The investor should thus continuously monitor market conditions as well as internal interest rate expectations to ensure that the volatility characteristics of the CFRN do not result in unanticipated changes in note value.

STRUCTURE IV. INVERSE FLOATING RATE NOTE (IFRN)

Investor purpose: Obtain high initial yield in an upwardly sloped yield curve environment.
Risk: In a rising rate environment, the note coupon quickly declines.
Equivalent investor position: Long fixed rate note, short floating rate note.

IFRNs are floating rate notes whose coupon resets based upon a floating index. Unlike an FRN, the IFRN's coupon increases when the floating index decreases, and vice versa. This property permits investors to benefit from a lowering rate environment. At the same time, this characteristic makes the IFRN markedly different from a regular FRN in that there is no longer any assurance that a coupon reset would bring the IFRN's value back towards par. As will be illustrated shortly, the interest rate risk inherent in IFRNs is not only higher than that of an FRN but is higher than even that of a fixed rate note.

Inverse floaters are popular in a positively sloped yield curve environment for those market participants who are expecting short-term rates to drop. It is a play against the occurrence of the forward rates, and expresses the belief that even though the yield curve implies higher forward rates in the future, the underlying economic picture implies the opposite.

History

The IFRN was the first relatively sophisticated structure to include more than simply one swap (the zero coupon floor guarantee involves an optionality). Inverse FRNs were popular in the bull markets of 1985–87 and 1990–93. As the accompanying graph clearly shows, investors who purchased IFRNs during the last bull market would have done exceedingly well against the performance of a LIBOR FRN.

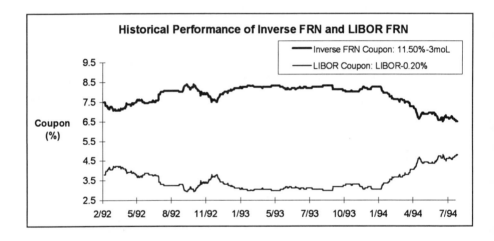

The issuance of an SEC letter in 1990 warning mutual, pension, and particularly money market funds against investing in IFRNs largely dampened investor enthusiasm for IFRNs. Although some speculative investors continued to purchase these notes, the acceptance of such instruments subsequently became more limited. The main concern of the SEC was that IFRNs are not floating rate notes in the sense that they would be reasonably expected to reset to par value at each coupon reset date. As will be seen shortly, this concern is justified.

In late 1993, investors began to purchase a variant of the IFRN. The note's coupon would first be fixed for a specified period. If the note is not called at the end of that period, the investor then receives an inverse-LIBOR based coupon. The motivation for investors is the above-market high upfront yield that the note initially pays. Many investors, unfortunately, have a short time horizon of two years or less and in purchasing this structure have sacrificed future performance for good current yield.

Analysis

The terms of an actual IFRN are described in Exhibit 5-29. The key features of the IFRN can be summarized as follows:

Issuer: U.S. Agency
Maturity: 3 1/2 years
Coupon: 10% – 6-month LIBOR (1st 6 months),
then 11, 12, 13% – 6-month LIBOR

The coupon behavior of the IFRN is calculated for a range of LIBORs in Exhibit 5-30. As expected, the IFRN coupon is higher for lower LIBORs and drops as LIBOR increases.

EXHIBIT 5-29 IFRN

This 3 1/2-year Agency note pays a coupon based on a constant minus 6-month LIBOR. The coupon constant rises by 1% each year after the first six months. The note also pays an unconventional coupon that accrues interest on a 30/360 basis, which is not the convention for LIBOR based coupons (Act/360).

Issue Terms (Actual)	
Issuer:	Federal National Mortgage Association (Fannie Mae)
Principal amount:	US$100,000,000
Settlement date:	Feb. 27, 1992
Maturity date:	Aug. 17, 1995. Non-call life.
Coupon paid in US$:	2/27/92–8/17/92: 10% – 6-month LIBOR
	8/17/92–8/17/93: 11% – 6-month LIBOR
	8/17/93–8/17/94: 12% – 6-month LIBOR
	8/17/94–8/17/95: 13% – 6-month LIBOR
Coupon floor:	0.00%
Day count basis:	30/360 (not conventional LIBOR)
Rate reset and payment dates:	Rate resets semiannually. Payment dates Feb. 17, Aug. 17. First coupon Aug. 17, 1992.
LIBOR determination:	6-month LIBOR resets semiannually. Determination date is two London business days prior to reset date. Source: Telerate Page 3750.
Issue price:	100.00%

EXHIBIT 5-30 Coupon Behavior of IFRN

The IFRN performs well in low interest rate environments. This particular FRN offers additional protection against rising rates in the form of a coupon whose spread steps up each year. However, the IFRN's coupon becomes lower for higher LIBOR. This behavior is quite different from a regular FRN.

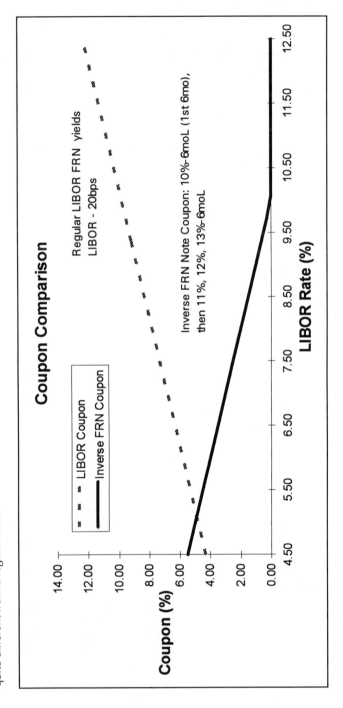

The IFRN contains optionality in the form of the zero coupon floor, thus requiring analysis via the simulation class of analysis.

Performance

Using LSE, a series of final expectation LIBORs is used to create a set of base case scenarios. Simulations about these base case scenarios are then performed.

The IRR performance of the IFRN is calculated for a range of base case scenarios and shown in Exhibit 5-31. As expected, the note outperforms the benchmark LIBOR FRN for low interest rate scenarios and underperforms in high interest rate scenarios. The breakeven final level of LIBOR is approximately 8%, beyond which the benchmark LIBOR FRN begins to gain significant yield advantage over the IFRN. The 8% breakeven point is quite high compared to the initial LIBOR of 4.375% and reflects the significant initial coupon advantage of the IFRN.

Risk

Interest Rate Risk. The risk of the note can be expressed by interpreting the results of the deterministic duration plotted in Exhibit 5-32. Recall that the net risk of the note is decomposed into two components: discounting and index.

The IR and DR are both equal to the to-maturity Treasury rate (3 1/2-year Treasury). The DRD is equal to that of a comparable maturity fixed rate note, which in this case is approximately 3.125. The IRD of the inverse LIBOR coupon carries the opposite sign of the IRD of a stream of regular LIBOR coupons, i.e., +3.125. Thus, the net duration of the note is expected to be approximately +6.25, which is twice that of a comparable maturity fixed rate note. This is summarized below.

Component	Key Rate	Duration of Component
Discounting	To-maturity Treasury rate	+3.125
Index	To-maturity Treasury rate	+3.125
	Net duration:	**+6.25**

The deterministic duration calculations shown in Exhibit 5-33 do indeed reflect the high duration. The one additional detail that deterministic duration shows is that the duration rises with higher rates. The cause of this effect is as follows: for a 1 bp rise in term rates, the absolute decrease in note value is the same regardless of the rate level. However, since the note loses value for higher rate scenarios, the decrease in value as a percentage of the

EXHIBIT 5-31 IRR of IFRN

The IRR rapidly drops off as expectation rates rise. The IFRN outperforms a comparable maturity LIBOR FRN when rates remain low or rise moderately, but underperforms the LIBOR FRN in high interest rate scenarios.

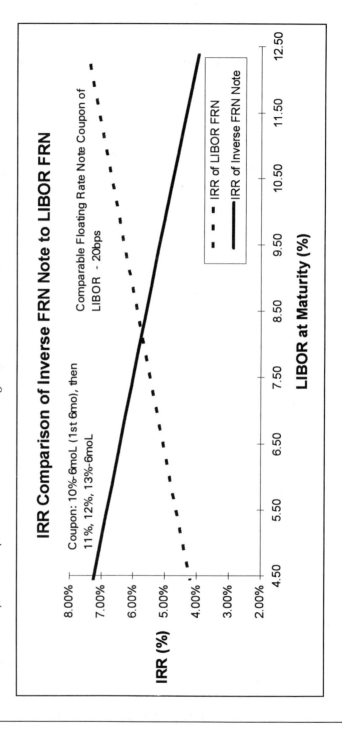

IRR Comparison of Inverse FRN Note to LIBOR FRN

Coupon: 10%-6moL (1st 6mo), then 11%, 12%, 13%-6moL

Comparable Floating Rate Note Coupon of LIBOR - 20bps

- - - IRR of LIBOR FRN
— IRR of Inverse FRN Note

IRR (%)

8.00%
7.00%
6.00%
5.00%
4.00%
3.00%
2.00%

4.50 5.50 6.50 7.50 8.50 9.50 10.50 11.50 12.50

LIBOR at Maturity (%)

EXHIBIT 5-32 Rate Duration of IFRN

The duration of the note is approximately six, which is twice as high as that of a comparable maturity fixed note. The duration increases for higher levels of expectation LIBOR since the absolute price change remains unchanged for a 1 bp increase in term LIBORs. The actual duration of the note as reflected by the simulation duration begins to drop lower after the 9% level. This precedes the first coupon being capped to zero. For extremely high rate scenarios (not shown), the note has an asymptotic duration of 3.5, equal to that of a zero coupon note.

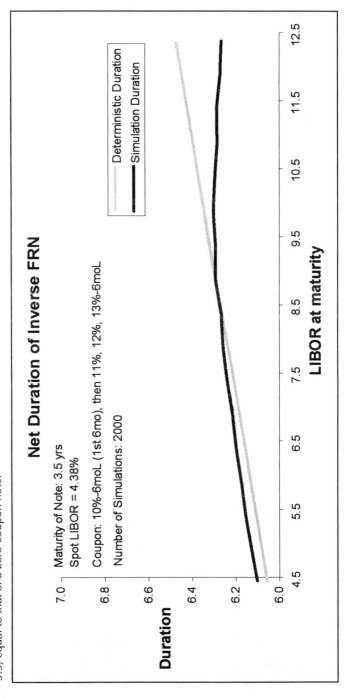

Net Duration of Inverse FRN

Maturity of Note: 3.5 yrs
Spot LIBOR = 4.38%

Coupon: 10%–6moL (1st 6mo), then 11%, 12%, 13%–6moL

Number of Simulations: 2000

Deterministic Duration
Simulation Duration

Duration

LIBOR at maturity

EXHIBIT 5-33   Volatility Duration of IFRN

The IFRN contains an embedded optionality in the form of the zero coupon floor. The negative volatility duration reflects the fact that this option gains in value when volatility rises for high interest rate scenarios. The peak in the amplitude of the volatility duration reflects the vega of the embedded cap.

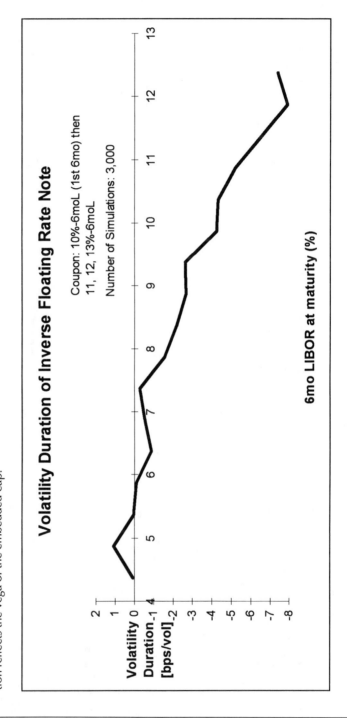

Volatility Duration of Inverse Floating Rate Note

Coupon: 10%-6moL (1st 6mo) then
11, 12, 13%-6moL

Number of Simulations: 3,000

Volatility Duration [bps/vol]

6mo LIBOR at maturity (%)

total value of the note becomes larger for higher interest rate scenarios. This is the cause of the small yet definitive increase in duration for higher rates.

The actual duration of the note as reflected by the simulation duration shows excellent agreement with the deterministic duration results for low interest rate scenarios. For higher interest rate scenarios, simulation shows that the duration of the note begins to decrease. This is due to the effect of the zero coupon option embedded in the note. This option (which the investor is long) gains in value as the index approaches the zero coupon level. Thus, the high duration of the note is lessened as a result of the gains to the investor from this option. The asymptotic duration for very high interest rate scenarios will be the duration of a zero coupon note, which in this case is 3.5.

Volatility Risk.   The IFRN contains volatility risk from the embedded zero coupon floor option. The volatility risk is calculated with a 3000 simulation analysis of the volatility duration and plotted on Exhibit 5-33. Since the only embedded optionality is a coupon floor, which the note is long, it is expected that the volatility duration of the IFRN should remain negative for all interest rate scenarios. The graph shows that the volatility duration for low interest rate scenarios is approximately zero, but begins to increase in magnitude (but is negative in sign) for higher interest rate scenarios. This is consistent with the expected vega behavior of the embedded zero coupon floor (which is actually a LIBOR cap option owned by the note). As the indices approach the strike, the vega of the embedded options increase, resulting in a note that gains value with increased volatility. For even higher interest rate scenarios than shown, the magnitude of the volatility duration will reach a maximum and subsequently decrease as the indices move further away from the strike.

The volatility risk of the IFRN is appropriate for a 3-year note, with the note gaining approximately 8 bps for every 1% increase in volatility for the LIBOR-at-maturity = 12% base case scenario. The investor should be aware that the volatility risk characteristic of the IFRN is not constant and changes significantly for different interest rate scenarios.

Comments.   The KTRD analysis performed in this section highlighted an interesting feature of the IFRN, namely, that its duration is actually *twice* that of a comparable maturity fixed rate note. KTRD was able to show that the source of this high duration can be linked, as expected, to the inverse nature of the coupon. This level of duration signifies that the IFRN does not behave in a similar manner to a regular FRN in that it cannot be reasonably assumed to reset back to a price of par on each coupon reset date.

STRUCTURE V. SUPERFLOATER

Investor purpose: Obtain high yield in a bearish environment in return for lower current yield.

Risk: If rates remain low, the investor will continue to receive a below-market coupon.

Equivalent investor position: Borrow cash at a fixed cost to purchase a leveraged amount of floating rate note.

The Superfloater is based upon a fairly simple concept: how one profits in a bearish environment when rates are rising higher. The original FRN was able to preserve value in a rising rate environment. The Superfloater takes the concept one step further and provides the investor with enhanced coupon and capital gains when rates rise. Because they are bear market structures, Superfloaters were not popular in the last bull market. They do enjoy moments of popularity when investors flock to Superfloaters in sporadic periods of panic over potentially rising inflation.

History

Superfloaters fell out of favor with investors in the bull market run of 1990–94. In rising rate environments, Superfloaters are often considered but not purchased because of the large yield sacrifice that has to be made by investors. This yield sacrifice is quite significant and is often more than most investors are willing to take in return for the promise of potential gains in the future. The graph below illustrates performance of a Superfloater if it had

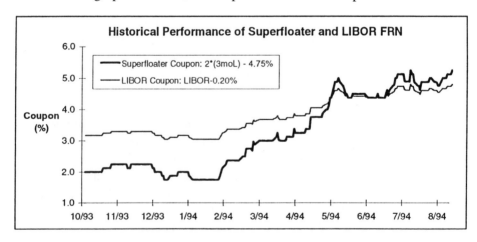

been purchased in October 1993. At the time of initial purchase, the Super-floater would have produced a significantly lower coupon than the regular LIBOR FRN. However, its enhanced performance subsequent to the initial Federal Reserve's interest rate hike in January 1994 shows that the Super-floater does indeed perform well in a bear market.

Analysis

The terms of an indicative Superfloater note are given in Exhibit 5-34. The note's coupon is two times LIBOR minus 7%, providing an initial coupon of 2.625%, which is 200 bps less yield than a comparable LIBOR FRN. The coupon behavior of the note is seen in Exhibit 5-35, which shows that for high interest rate scenarios, this Superfloater would eventually produce a higher coupon than the LIBOR FRN, the breakeven LIBOR being approximately 7%.

Since the Superfloater note involves optionality in the form of the zero coupon floor, the simulation class of analysis should be employed to examine the risks of the note. LSE will be employed to project the intermediate index levels of the base cases.

EXHIBIT 5-34 Indicative Terms of a LIBOR Superfloater
The coupon floats at twice LIBOR minus a fixed spread. The current coupon yield is considerably lower than that of a LIBOR FRN, which makes the purchasing decision a difficult one.

Issue Terms (Indicative)	
Issuer:	Single A
Principal amount:	US$100,000,000
Settlement date:	Aug. 15, 1994
Maturity date:	Aug. 15, 1996. Non-call life.
Coupon paid in US$:	2 * (3-month LIBOR) – 7.00%
First coupon:	2.625%
Coupon floor:	0.00%
Day count basis:	Act/360
Rate reset and payment dates:	Coupon resets and pays quarterly. Reset dates Feb. 15, May 15, Aug. 15, Nov. 15. First coupon Nov. 15, 1994.
LIBOR determination:	3-month LIBOR resets quarterly. Determination date is two London business days prior to reset date. Source: Telerate Page 3750.
Issue price:	100.00%

EXHIBIT 5-35 Superfloater Coupon versus Regular LIBOR FRN Coupon for U.S. Agency Note

The Superfloater outperforms the LIBOR FRN in high interest rate scenarios. However, investors have to sacrifice current yield in return for potential future gains.

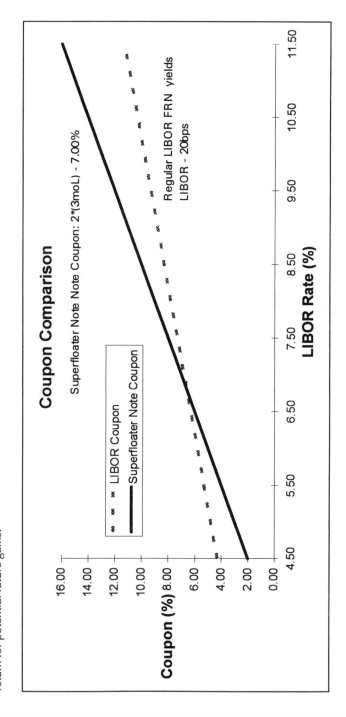

Performance

The performance of the Superfloater note can be calculated for a range of final expectation LIBORs and is shown in Exhibit 5-36. The IRR of the Superfloater remains significantly lower than that of a LIBOR FRN until LIBOR has risen significantly. The breakeven LIBOR-at-maturity scenario for which the Superfloater and LIBOR FRN returns are equal is approximately 9.5%. In other words, LIBOR would have to rise significantly higher than the current level of 4.8125% over its two years of life in order for the Superfloater to be a better purchase. This illustrates the reason that investors stay away from Superfloaters even in a rising rate environment: rates would have to significantly rise in order to make up the initial yield deficit.

Risk

Interest Rate Risk. The risk of the note can be interpreted by examining the deterministic duration results shown in Exhibit 5-37. In most interest rate scenarios, the note exhibits negative duration. This is expected since the IRD of the Superfloater should be twice that of a regular LIBOR FRN. This is shown in the following table.

Component	Key Rate	Duration of Component
Discounting	To-maturity Treasury rate	+1.9
Index	To-maturity Treasury rate	−3.8
	Net duration:	**−1.9**

The net duration of the Superfloater is thus expected to be the negative of a comparable maturity fixed rate note. This is indeed reflected by the deterministic duration results of Exhibit 5-37. This negative duration means that the Superfloater would gain value when rates rise because the multiplicative effect of the leverage will more than compensate for the lower value from the higher discounting rate.

How can a note exhibit negative duration? This result can be understood by considering the following example: if one were to combine a twice-leveraged Superfloater with a fixed rate note of the same notional amount and maturity, the resulting portfolio would be equivalent to a regular LIBOR FRN of twice the notional amount. Since LIBOR FRNs have been shown to have zero duration, the sum of the Superfloater's duration and the fixed note's duration must be zero. Thus, a twice-leveraged Superfloater should

EXHIBIT 5-36 IRR of Superfloater for a Range of Final Expectation Rates

As expected, the Superfloater underperforms a regular LIBOR FRN in low interest rate scenarios, but performs significantly better when rates rise higher.

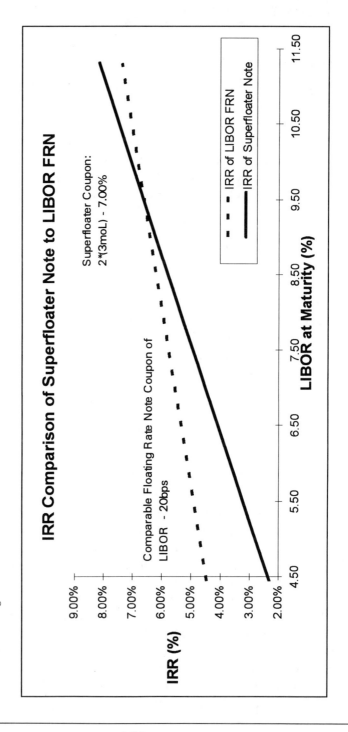

IRR Comparison of Superfloater Note to LIBOR FRN

Superfloater Coupon:
2*(3moL) - 7.00%

Comparable Floating Rate Note Coupon of
LIBOR - 20bps

IRR (%)

LIBOR at Maturity (%)

- - - IRR of LIBOR FRN
—— IRR of Superfloater Note

EXHIBIT 5-37 Deterministic and Simulation Duration for Superfloater

The note exhibits negative duration, i.e., it gains value when rates rise. This behavior is as expected since the coupon floats at twice LIBOR. Deterministic and simulation duration agree well with each other except for low interest rate scenarios. The difference is that the deterministic duration assumes that for LIBOR above 3.5%, all coupons will still be floating, and hence deterministic duration will remain high, whereas in reality the note would begin to lose value before any coupon has been floored, hence the lower simulation duration.

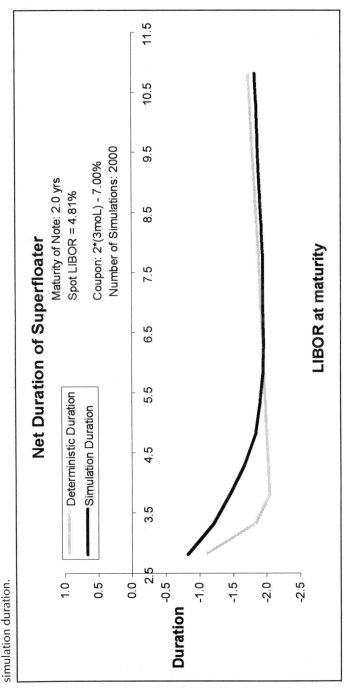

Net Duration of Superfloater

Maturity of Note: 2.0 yrs
Spot LIBOR = 4.81%

Coupon: 2*(3moL) - 7.00%
Number of Simulations: 2000

LIBOR at maturity

Duration

have a duration that is equal in magnitude but opposite in sign to a fixed note of comparable maturity. This negative duration is exactly what is observed in this chapter's analysis of the Superfloater.

The actual duration of the note as reflected by the simulation duration agrees quite well with deterministic duration except in low interest rate scenarios. The Superfloater in the example would yield zero coupon when LIBOR drops below 3.5%. Thus, for LIBORs above this level, deterministic duration should show a duration of –1.9. In reality, the note would begin to gain value as rates continue to drop even prior to the first coupon being floored at zero due to the presence of the zero coupon floor. This zero coupon floor is actually a floor option on LIBOR that is owned by the investor. As LIBOR drops lower, this floor gains value, and hence the note contains a contribution of positive duration from the embedded floor option. Thus, as rates drop, it is expected that the note's negative duration would begin to rise up. This is reflected in the simulation duration results. As LIBOR approaches zero, the duration of the note is expected to approach the duration of a zero coupon note of comparable maturity, which in this case is two.

Volatility Risk. The Superfloater contains volatility risk from the zero coupon floor option (which the note is long). The volatility risk of the Superfloater is calculated by performing a 3000 simulation analysis of the volatility duration. The result is plotted in Exhibit 5-38.

The volatility duration of the Superfloater is negative at low interest rate scenarios and rises towards zero for higher scenarios. This characteristic is due to zero coupon floor embedded in the note. For low interest rate scenarios, these coupon floors would gain value for incrementally higher volatility, resulting in higher value for the Superfloater and thus a negative volatility duration. The vega of these floor options decreases as rates rise away from the floor strike, resulting in a rising vega. The positive volatility at the high end of the interest rate spectrum is attributed to simulation noise.

CONCLUSION

This chapter described the first generation structures and outlined the risks and performance of these notes. Although the first generation structures are characterized by relatively simple and straightforward structures, the variety of first generation structures is quite abundant. These structures are capable of supporting a wide range of investor views and can be tailored for a variety of investor types from the very conservative to the high risk takers. This

EXHIBIT 5-38 Volatility Duration of Superfloater

The note exhibits a relatively large negative volatility duration for low interest rate scenarios. This is due to the large vega of the floor option when the indices are close to the floor strike. For higher interest rate scenarios, the indices move further away from the strike, resulting in a lower vega and thus a lower magnitude of volatility duration.

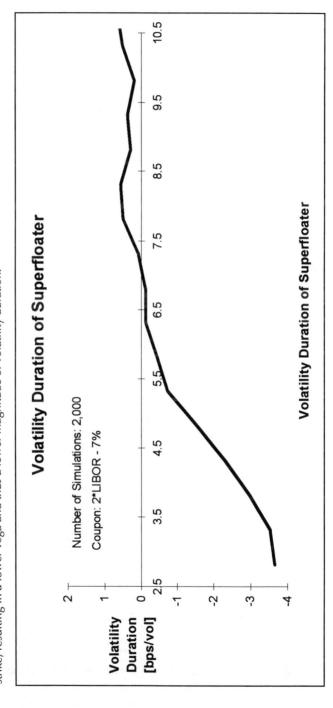

Volatility Duration of Superfloater

Number of Simulations: 2,000

Coupon: 2*LIBOR - 7%

EXHIBIT 5-39 Summary of First Generation Structures and Respective Interest Rate Durations

All interest rate durations are with respect to the IR/DR of the note, which is the to-maturity Treasury rate.

Structure	Sample Coupon	Minimum Duration*	Maximum Duration*
Floating Rate Note	Prime – 2.50%	0	0
Deleveraged FRN	0.5 * Prime + 0.80%	1/2	1/2
Floored FRN	LIBOR + 0.15%, Coupon floor = 4.25%	0 (if initial index > floor), else 0 + (duration of 1 cpn)	1
Capped FRN	LIBOR + 0.50%, Coupon cap = 8.00%	0	1
Leveraged Capped FRN	Min of (LIBOR + 0.25%, or $C - m$ * LIBOR)	0	$(m + 1)$**
Collared FRN	LIBOR + 0.10%, Coupon cap = 8%, Floor = 5%	~1/2	1
Inverse FRN	10% – LIBOR	2***	2
Superfloater	2 * LIBOR – 6.5%	–1	–1***

* Duration is expressed as a multiple of the duration of a comparable maturity fixed rate note.
** This maximum duration may not be attainable depending upon maturity, strike C, and interest rate scenario.
*** Except when all the coupons are zero and the note trades as a zero coupon note, in which case the note would have a duration equal to a zero coupon note of the same maturity.

chapter has also shown that the risk and performance characteristics of these structures are just as diverse and different as the underlying views.

Exhibit 5-39 summarizes the various first generation structures discussed in this chapter and their interest rate durational characteristics. The one conclusion that stands out is that these structures rarely have zero interest rate duration even though they can all be referred to as "Floating Rate Notes." This chapter has shown that most of these notes in fact do contain risks and these risks can change with different interest rate environments. A structured note should be analyzed via the methodologies described in Chapters 2, 3, and 4 to fully understand the risk and performance characteristics. Investors cannot assume that since the note's coupon resets quarterly, the note would have the same duration and risk as a LIBOR FRN.

6

Second Generation Structures

With the increased sophistication of issuers, investors, and structurers, second generation structured notes have gained in popularity because they provide a level of performance that cannot be attained via first generation structures. Due to the complexity of their design, second generation structures are typically more difficult to create and analyze than first generation notes. The key characteristics of second generation structures are as follows:

1. **Index maturity to reset frequency mismatch.** A common example of this structure is a constant maturity Treasury (CMT) FRN whose coupons float on the 10-year Treasury rate, but that are reset and paid on a quarterly basis.
2. **Multiple indices.** These are structures that pay an interest based on either the differential or sum of a combination of indices.
3. **Unconventional optionality payoff.** Some structures contain embedded options that do not fit traditional option payoff patterns. These exotic options include, but are not limited to, binary options, early prepayment options, and path-dependent options.
4. **The index is a non-native interest rate.** These are notes that provide investors with exposure to European or Japanese rates but that are denominated in U.S. dollars.
5. **Unusual leverage.** These include notes linked to an index raised to a power.

The bid-offer spread of second generation structured notes is typically larger than first generation notes because of the larger number of embedded derivatives. In addition, the risks of the second generation structures are often not easy to quantify. Nevertheless, despite these added complications, many investors gladly purchase these second generation structures because they provide payoff characteristics that cannot be obtained elsewhere.

The second generation structures discussed in this book are classified and listed in Exhibit 6-1. The list is by no means exhaustive. Because of the inventive nature of the structured note market, new structures are constantly being created to suit a client's needs or to take advantage of market movements. However, the structures discussed in this chapter do constitute a representative sample of some of the more popular second generation structures in recent times.

EXHIBIT 6-1 Second Generation Structured Note Classification

These structured notes are considerably more complicated to create, price, and analyze than first generation notes.

Category	Structure	Comments
Index maturity mismatch	CMT, CMS FRN, Deleveraged CMT	CMT/CMS notes are indexed to longer maturity indices to produce enhanced yield. Deleveraged CMT FRNs have high coupon floors to produce higher yields than LIBOR FRNs. CMS is used by European/Japanese investors as a proxy for the CMT index.
Multi-index (differential)	CMT-LIBOR, Prime-LIBOR	Mostly purchased in 1992–93 by investors seeking to obtain higher floating rate yields than either CMT or prime FRNs.
Exotic option	Accrual note	Permits investors with range views to obtain high yield. Accrual notes contain significantly higher risks than fixed rate notes.
	Index Amortizing Note, Ratchet Note	Purchased by bullish investors who believe rates will remain low. IANs purchased by mortgage buyers. These notes contain path-dependent options.
Quanto	Non-U.S. rates plays denominated in US$	Liked by sophisticated investors with views on non-domestic rates.
Unusual leverage	Inverse LIBOR squared, Inverse CMT/S squared	Very high risk, high return instrument purchased by investors who have a definitive view on the rate in question.

ANALYSIS OF SECOND GENERATION STRUCTURED NOTES

The analytics for the second generation structures are more complicated than required for first generation structures. First generation structures have identical IRs and DRs, resulting in risk exposure to only one key portion of the yield curve: the sector corresponding to the to-maturity Treasury rate. For the majority of second generation structures, this will usually not be true. For these notes, the methodology of key Treasury rate duration introduced in Chapter 2 will be required to fully analyze the yield curve risk.

The analysis of second generation notes will be performed in the same context as that of first generation. One of the three deterministic analyses—the forward analysis, the LSE analysis, or the historical analysis—and/or its simulation analysis counterpart will be selected to analyze structured note performance and risk.

The steps of KTRD analysis have been outlined in Chapter 2 and are briefly summarized here.

KTRD Analysis Methodology

1. Identify components of risk and the associated key indices.
2. Identify KTRs that correspond to each index.
3. Identify KTRD corresponding to each KTR.
4. Combine all components and generate a net KTRD spectrum of the structured note.
5. Update as required when rates and/or maturity change.

A special situation arises when the floating rate index and the currency in which the note is denominated are different. When the two are of the same currency, only one KTRD spectrum (that of the nation in which the currency is denominated) is required. Structures such as the Quanto note for which this is no longer true will require the introduction of a separate KTRD spectrum that corresponds to the non-domestic country of the coupon index. For example, the risk profile of a U.S. dollar denominated Quanto note whose coupon is based on the level of 3-month Peseta LIBOR will include both a key *U.S.* Treasury rate duration and a key *Spanish* Treasury rate duration (with the Spanish KTRD based on the CMS as the unit corresponding to the U.S. Treasury rate).

A. INDEX MATURITY TO RESET FREQUENCY MISMATCH

The first class of second generation structures includes structures whose index maturity does not match the reset frequency of the coupon. The complications that can arise from this situation were initially discussed in Chapter 2. This section completes the discussion of the risk and performance consequences of this mismatch by examining two structures that belong to this class of notes: the CMT/CMS note, and the deleveraged CMT (SURF) note.

STRUCTURE I. CONSTANT MATURITY TREASURY (CMT) AND CONSTANT MATURITY SWAP (CMS) FLOATING RATE NOTES

Investor purpose: Obtain higher floating rate yields than is possible with LIBOR FRNs while retaining full upside in a bear market.
Risk: The coupon is reset based upon the longer end of the yield curve. The note's yield advantage over a LIBOR FRN will quickly vanish if the yield curve should flatten significantly from initial levels.
Equivalent investor position: Buy short maturity fixed rate note, short longer maturity Treasury bonds.

CMT and CMS FRNs are floating rate notes that, like LIBOR FRNs, reset on a quarterly or semiannual basis. They are different from LIBOR FRNs in that their coupons are indexed off longer maturity indices such as the 10-year U.S. Treasury rate. A CMT or CMS FRN can, in a steep yield curve environment, produce a significantly higher yield relative to comparable maturity LIBOR FRNs.

History

As interest rates dropped to all-time lows in the bull market of 1990–94, investors sought to obtain higher floating rate yields by purchasing floating rate notes indexed to longer maturity indices. As shown in the graph on page 175, the historically low levels of LIBOR were accompanied by an unprecedented steepening of the yield curve. The net result was that investors who purchased the CMT FRNs were able to obtain a large yield advantage over LIBOR FRNs.

The shift in the Federal Reserve's policy to tighten monetary supply by hiking short-term rates resulted in a shift in investor preference from fixed rate notes to floating rate notes. Investors reasoned that in a rapidly rising

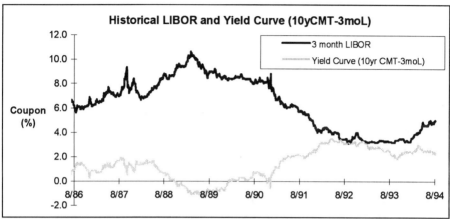

[Source: Sumitomo Bank Capital Markets]

environment, the durational risk of fixed rate notes would result in an equal-ly rapid drop in note value, and hence expressed a preference for floating rate notes. Since the yield curve remained relatively steep even after the Federal Reserve's interest rate hikes, investors who purchased CMT FRNs were still able to obtain a good yield advantage over LIBOR FRNs. This investor pref-erence for floating rate notes accounted for a surge in investor interest in CMT FRNs in the first quarter of 1994.

In Europe and Japan, the constant maturity swap (CMS) indices are often viewed as the counterpart to the CMT indices in the United States due to the lack of regularity with which many nations issue Government bonds. For the investors of these nations, the CMS index is the benchmark yield curve index.

Analysis

The terms of a sample CMT FRN are given in Exhibit 6-2. The key features of the note are summarized as follows:

1. Issuer is a U.S. Agency. The great majority of CMT FRNs are issued by U.S. Agencies.
2. Index is the 5-year CMT. The 5-year CMT is not the most popular index since most investors looking for higher floating rate yield gen-erally prefer the 10-year CMT.
3. Index resets and pays quarterly. CMT FRNs typically reset quarterly or semiannually on a 30/360 basis.

EXHIBIT 6-2 5-year Agency CMT FRN

The coupon is reset based upon the 5-year CMT rate and pays quarterly. This note produced an initial yield advantage of approximately 35 bps over a regular 3-month LIBOR FRN. (Rates on 8/12/92 were: 5-year CMT = 5.49%, 3-month LIBOR = 3.44%.)

Issue Terms (Actual)	
Issuer:	Federal Farm Credit Banks System
Principal amount:	US$25,000,000
Settlement date:	Aug. 14, 1992
Maturity date:	Aug. 14, 1997
Coupon paid in US$:	5-year CMT − 1.90%
Day count basis:	30/360
Rate reset and payment dates:	Rate resets quarterly. Payment dates Feb. 14, May 14, Aug. 14, Nov. 14. First coupon paid on Nov. 14, 1992.
5-year CMT determination:	The 5-year CMT rate shall be the 5-year constant maturity Treasury rate applicable on the determination day of the Fed H.15(519) publication. Determination date is two New York and London business days prior to reset dates. Source: Telerate Page 7059.
Issue price:	100.00%

Performance Analysis

The performance of a CMT FRN is analyzed with deterministic LSE analysis. A range of final expectation scenarios of CMT rates is used to create a set of intermediate CMT rates. The performance of the note as reflected by the IRR for each interest rate scenario can then be calculated and is plotted in Exhibit 6-3. As one might expect, the higher the final CMT rate is at maturity, the higher the IRR. This performance can be compared to that of a comparable maturity benchmark LIBOR FRN of the same issuer with a coupon of LIBOR − 0.20%. Exhibit 6-4 shows that, as expected, the CMT FRN outperforms the LIBOR FRN in high CMT, low LIBOR scenarios, and underperforms the LIBOR FRN in low CMT, high LIBOR scenarios. The performance graph shows that the CMT-at-maturity must be more than 2% larger than LIBOR-at-maturity in order for the CMT FRN to maintain a yield advantage over the LIBOR FRN.

Risk

Because the CMT FRN contains no embedded options, the note contains no volatility risk.

EXHIBIT 6-3 Performance of 5-Year Agency CMT FRN

As expected, the CMT FRN performs better for higher interest rate scenarios.

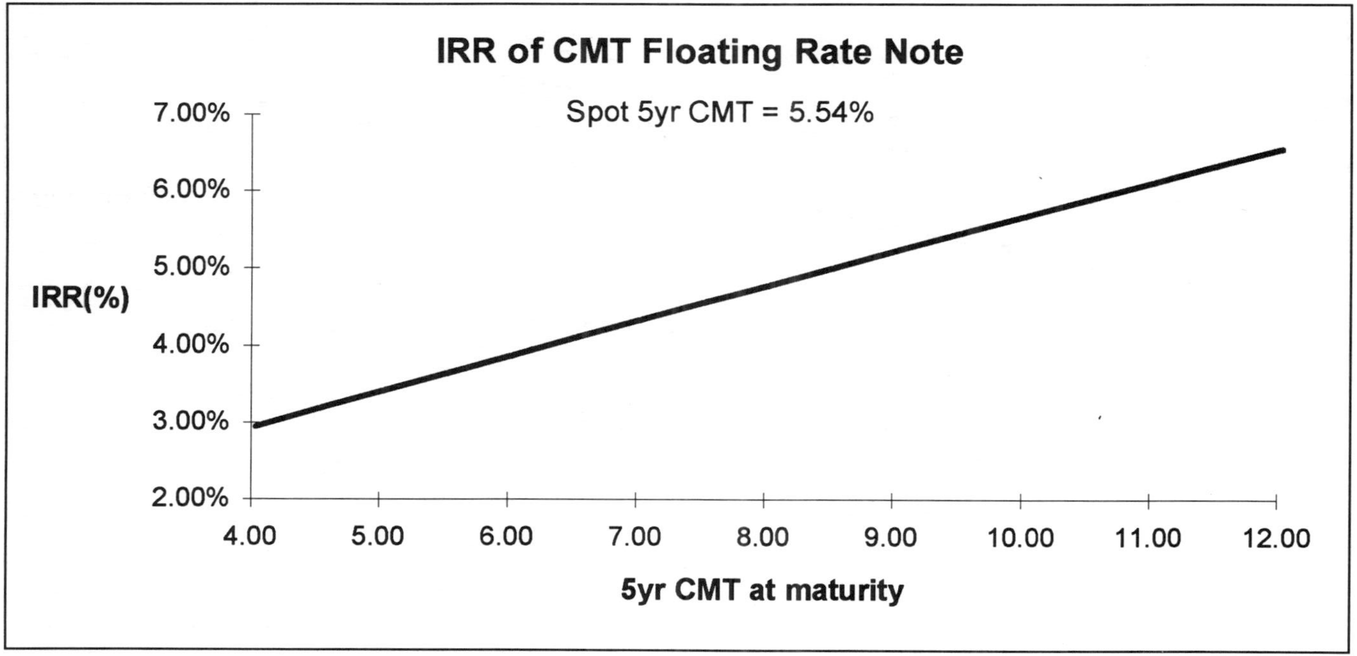

IRR of CMT Floating Rate Note
Spot 5yr CMT = 5.54%
IRR(%)
7.00%
6.00%
5.00%
4.00%
3.00%
2.00%
4.00
5.00
6.00
7.00
8.00
9.00
10.00
11.00
12.00
5yr CMT at maturity

EXHIBIT 6-4 Performance of CMT FRN Relative to Benchmark LIBOR FRN

For the linear scenarios chosen, the CMT FRN outperforms a comparable maturity LIBOR FRN (yielding LIBOR – 20 bps) if the spread between the CMT and LIBOR at maturity is greater than 2.00%. Thus, the yield curve would have to remain fairly steep in order for the CMT FRN to retain its yield advantage over the LIBOR FRN.

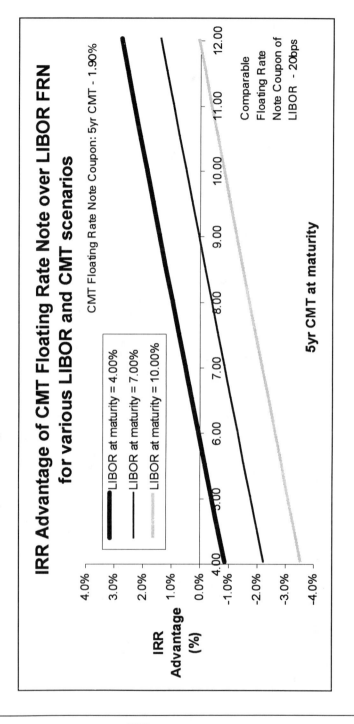

IRR Advantage of CMT Floating Rate Note over LIBOR FRN for various LIBOR and CMT scenarios

CMT Floating Rate Note Coupon: 5yr CMT - 1.90%

Interest Rate Risk.   As mentioned before, the use of KTRD is necessary to fully assess the risk of the CMT FRN. The use of KTRD is necessary because the mismatch between the index maturity and the reset frequency (i.e., a 5-year CMT rate is used as the index that resets and pays a quarterly coupon) results in yield curve risk.

The steps of the KTRD methodology are as follows:

Step 1.   Identify discounting and index components of risk:

Discounting component: The discounting rate is the to-maturity Treasury rate, or the 5-year maturity Treasury rate.

Index component: The floating rate index consists of five years of 5-year CMT coupon.

Steps 2 and 3.   Identify KTRs of each component and the corresponding KTRDs:

Discounting: The note's duration with respect to the discounting rate is equal to that of a comparable maturity fixed coupon note, i.e., a duration of 4.2 with respect to the 5-year maturity Treasury rate.

Index: The five years of 5-year CMT is composed of the spot 5-year CMT, the in-1-quarter-for-5-year rate, and the in-2-quarters-for-5-year rate, etc. The composite KTRD of these CMTs is shown in Exhibit 6-5.

The highlights of Exhibit 6-5 are that the negative duration contributions of the CMT index lie in the 5- to 10-year range, while the positive duration contributions are in the 0- to 5-year sector. This distribution is a result of the forward CMT index. Recall Equation (2-1), which was used to calculate the in-i-year-for-M-year forward Treasury rate $T_{M,i}$:

$$T_{M,i} = 2 * \{(1 + 1/2T_{M+i}) * [((1 + 1/2T_{M+i})/(1 + 1/2T_i))^{i/M}] - 1\}$$

The above equation shows that higher shorter maturity rates T_i will result in a lower forward rate $T_{M,i}$, while higher longer maturity rates T_{M+i} will result in a higher $T_{M,i}$.

Step 4.   Combine all components. The net composition of the KTRD spectrum of the CMT FRN is created by combining the discounting component with the index component. The composite KTRD spectrum of the CMT FRN is plotted in Exhibit 6-6 and summarized in the table on page 181.

EXHIBIT 6-5 KTRD of the 5-Year CMT Index for Five Years

Note that the durational contributions from the shorter maturity portion of the Treasury curve now cannot be ignored without losing valuable durational information.

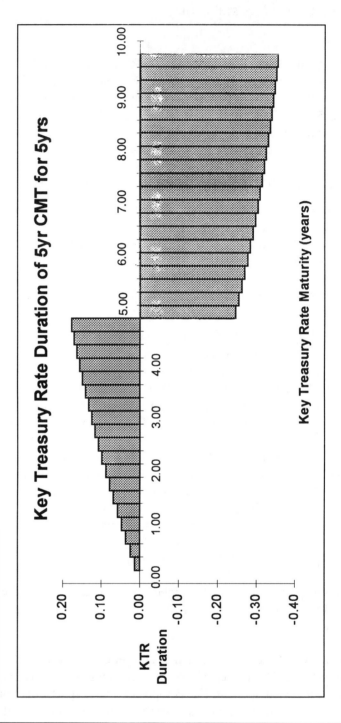

Key Treasury Rate Duration of 5yr CMT for 5yrs

Key Treasury Maturity Sector	Key Treasury Rate Duration of CMT Note with Respect to Treasury Sector
0.0 to 5.0 year	+6.1
5.25 to 10 year	–6.1

From the above table, it is evident that if the yield curve shifts in parallel, the note will behave like a LIBOR FRN with zero duration.[1] However, if the yield curve flattens, i.e., short-term rates rise more than long-term rates, the note will lose value. Specifically, if short-term rates (0- to 5-year maturity Treasury) rise by 1 bp over long-term rates (5.25- to 10-year maturity Treasury), a par valued CMT note would lose 6.1 bps of value.

Step 5. Update as rate and maturity change. The CMT note contains no embedded options and hence no associated volatility risk. The note's KTRD spectrum will, however, change as time goes by. As shown in Chapter 2, both the maturity of the KTRs and the corresponding KTRD will decrease as time increases.

The above KTRD risk analysis of the CMT FRN clearly illustrates that resetting coupons with an index whose maturity is different from the reset frequency results in yield curve risk. In the 5-year CMT FRN example, the interest rate risk can be summarized as follows: if the yield curve (0- to 5-year maturity Treasury sector versus the 5.25- to 10-year maturity Treasury sector) were to flatten by 1 bp, the note would lose 6.1 bps of value.

STRUCTURE II. DELEVERAGED CMT FRN, OR THE SURF NOTE

Investor purpose: Obtain higher floating rate yield than could be achieved with either CMT or LIBOR FRNs.

Risk: Any yield curve flattening will result in a lower yield advantage over LIBOR FRNs.

Equivalent investor position: Short Treasury bonds, long in-the-money Treasury bond call option.

---

1. Recall the definition in this book is for LIBOR FRNs to have zero duration since the analysis is assumed to be performed on new issue notes whose first coupon have not been set. If the first coupon were set, the LIBOR FRN would have a non-zero duration of 0.25, or that of the fixed stub.

EXHIBIT 6-6 The Net KTRD Spectrum of the 5-Year CMT FRN

Two features are worth noting: the large exposure of the investor to the 5-year maturity Treasury rate, and the relatively well spread-out distribution of the other KTRDs. The note has a net negative duration in the 5.25- to 10-year Treasury sector, and a net positive duration in the 0- to 5-year Treasury sector. This characteristic results in the note performing well in a yield curve steepening environment and losing value in a flattening one.

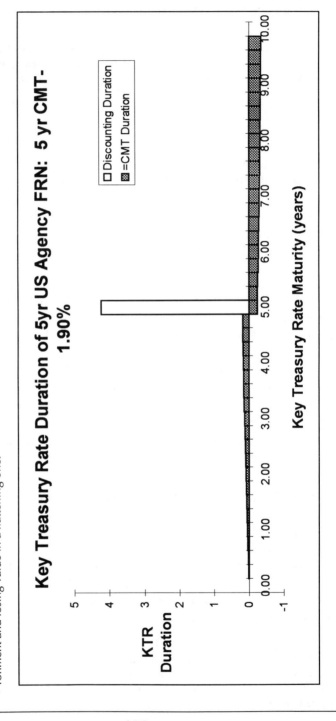

The deleveraged CMT FRN, popularly known as SURF, or step-up recovery floater,[2] combines two of the features desired by investors: a high coupon floor and a rise in the coupon rate if interest rates rise. A typical SURF note contains both an above market coupon floor as well as a fractional participation if rates should rise.

History

The SURF is a structure that first debuted in late 1992 and rapidly gained popularity among institutional as well as regional investors. The concept of the structure was simple: provide a high coupon floor and some participation if rates rise. When interest rates dropped to all-time lows in 1992–93, the SURFs were able to provide investors with an above-market coupon floor and promised a partial participation of interest rate upside if rates should rise again. The following graph of historical coupon performances illustrates the substantial yield pickup over both the CMT and the LIBOR FRN that the deleveraged CMT coupon was able to provide. The presence of the coupon floor also contributed to the SURF's enhanced performance.

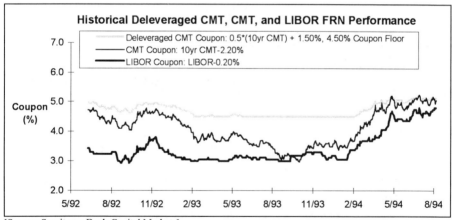

[Source: Sumitomo Bank Capital Markets]

Another reason for the structure's appeal was that since the coupon was reset each quarter based on the 10-year CMT rate, many investors were able

---

2. The term SURF was coined by Bob Lutey and Philippe Burke of Lehman Brothers on a particularly inventive afternoon in 1992. The term *Step-Up Recovery Floater* was selected because the initial variant of this structure had a coupon floor which stepped up over time.

to classify the structure internally as a floating rate instrument with three months of average life while earning a yield that was 100 basis points higher than a LIBOR FRN. Investors were thus able to boost the overall yield of their floating rate portfolio by adding SURFs. As will be shown shortly, classifying SURFs as a note with a duration of 0.25 is quite erroneous.

Analysis

The terms of an actual SURF note are described in Exhibit 6-7. The key features are summarized as follows:

Issuer:	U.S. Agency
Maturity:	5 years
Coupon:	0.5 * (10-year CMT) + 1.50%
Coupon floor:	4.50%

EXHIBIT 6-7   The Deleveraged CMT FRN

The investor obtains a very high coupon floor for a floating rate note and gives up part of any rate upswing. This is a fairly typical SURF note with a maturity of five years and a floating rate index of 0.5 times the 10-year CMT.

Issue Terms (Actual)	
Issuer:	Federal National Mortgage Association (Fannie Mae)
Principal amount:	US$100,000,000
Settlement date:	Feb. 25, 1993
Maturity date:	Feb. 25, 1998
Coupon paid in US$:	0.5 * (10-year CMT) + 1.50% subject to coupon floor
Coupon floor:	4.50%
Day count basis:	Act/Act
Rate reset and payment dates:	Rate resets quarterly. Payment dates Feb. 25, May 25, Aug. 25, Nov. 25. First coupon May 25, 1993.
10-year CMT determination:	The 10-year CMT rate shall be the daily 10-year constant maturity Treasury rate applicable on the determination day of the Fed H.15(519) publication. Determination date is two New York and London business days prior to reset dates. Source: Telerate Page 7059.
Issue price:	100.00%

This SURF structure illustrates two key SURF features: a coupon floor that is considerably higher than a benchmark LIBOR FRN, and some upside if 10-year CMT should rise.

Performance

The coupon behavior of the SURF note is plotted versus a range of CMTs in Exhibit 6-8. The minimum coupon is floored at 4.50%. For higher CMT rates, the coupon is able to float off the floor. Since the upside is based on only 50% of the CMT rate, the result is that the SURF note performs well in a stable and dropping rate environment but underperforms a benchmark CMT FRN in a rising rate environment.

The SURF note's IRR performance is shown in Exhibit 6-9. Reflecting the coupon behavior, the IRR of the SURF is able to outperform that of a benchmark CMT FRN for low interest rate scenarios. For high interest rate scenarios, the yield advantage of the SURF note will disappear, and the SURF note would underperform the benchmark CMT FRN, primarily due to its 50% deleverage factor, which reduces the investor's participation in a rate rise.

Risk

Interest Rate Risk.   Like the CMT FRN, the SURF contains yield curve risk due to the mismatch between the index maturity and its reset frequency. As will be shortly shown, this risk is quite complex. The net risk of the SURF note can be envisioned by examining the component risks separately.

1. **Risk components:** The risk components are the discounting risk and the index risk.
2. **Discounting component:** The DR is the 5-year Treasury rate, and the DRD is 4.2, or equal to that of a 5-year fixed rate note.
   Index component: The index risk is the 10-year CMT index subject to the coupon floor and leverage. The risk can be quantified in the following steps:
   a. The KTRD spectrum of five years of coupons based on the 10-year CMT is plotted at the top of page 188.

EXHIBIT 6-8 Deleveraged CMT Coupon Versus Regular Agency CMT Coupon

The coupon of a comparable maturity straight CMT FRN issued by a U.S. Agency would be 10-year CMT − 1.80%. SURF outperforms regular CMT floaters when rates remain low due to the protection of the coupon floor, but underperforms when rates rise.

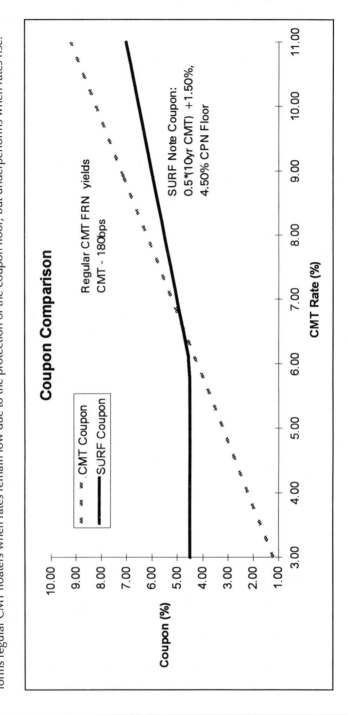

Coupon Comparison

Regular CMT FRN yields
CMT − 180bps

SURF Note Coupon:
0.5*(10yr CMT) +1.50%,
4.50% CPN Floor

CMT Coupon
SURF Coupon

Coupon (%)

CMT Rate (%)

EXHIBIT 6-9 IRR Performance of a CMT SURF Note

The IRR of a SURF note is computed for a range of final expectation CMT rates. It is seen that the IRR is floored at 4.5% since the coupon is floored at that level. For higher interest rate scenarios, the SURF note is seen to underperform the CMT FRN due to its only 50% upside participation. The breakeven final expectation CMT level, which would result in equal returns by the SURF and the CMT FRN, is the CMT-at-maturity = 7% scenario.

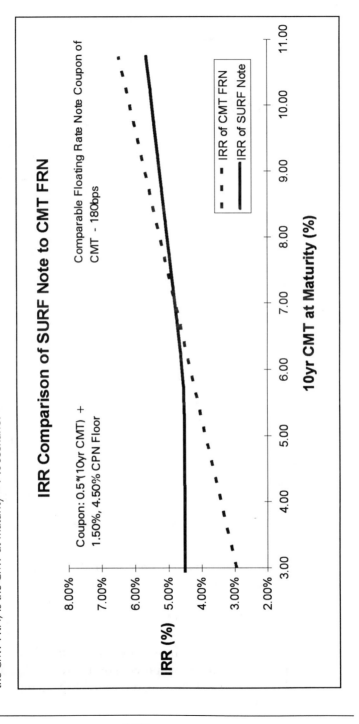

IRR Comparison of SURF Note to CMT FRN

Coupon: 0.5*10yr CMT) +
1.50%, 4.50% CPN Floor

Comparable Floating Rate Note Coupon of
CMT - 180bps

- - - IRR of CMT FRN
—— IRR of SURF Note

IRR (%)

10yr CMT at Maturity (%)

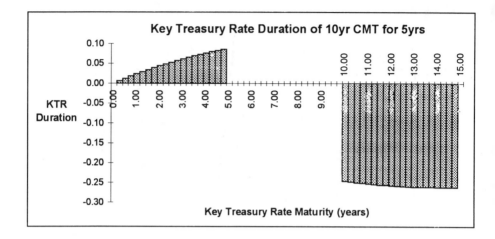

b. The KTRD spectrum of the 10-year CMT index leveraged by 0.5
times has half of the above amplitudes:

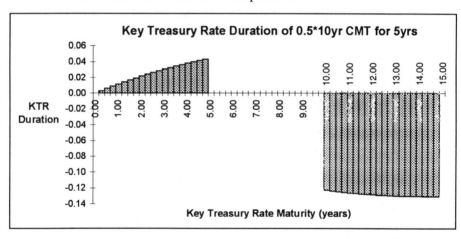

c. Assuming the *natural coupon* of the SURF, i.e., the leveraged
index plus the coupon spread, is always below the coupon floor,
the note will never float, and thus the index's KTRD spectrum
shown above would all have zero amplitudes. If the natural
coupon exceeds the coupon floor for all coupon resets, the KTRD
of the index would be exactly equal to the above spectrum. Thus,
for a note whose natural coupon is projected to float above the
floor at some future time, the KTRD of the index would be
between the above two extremes.

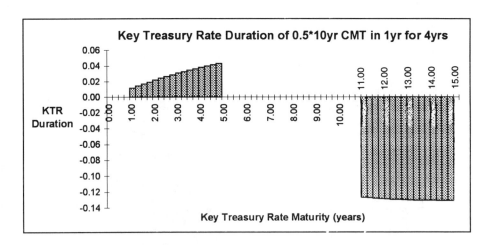

In the above KTRD spectrum, the natural coupon of the note is portrayed as rising above the coupon floor after one year. Thus, the CMT index component contains risk exposure with respect to the in-1-year-10-year CMT, the in-1.25-year-10-year CMT, etc. For different interest rate scenarios, the starting point of the interest rate exposure of the index will vary as well.

The composite behavior of this note is shown in Exhibit 6-10. The behavior of the note for low and high interest rate scenarios is clearly seen. Higher interest rate scenarios will result in the natural coupon floating off the coupon floor earlier in the life of the note. The effect of this is a larger negative duration in the 10- through 15-year maturity sector of the Treasury curve. Lower interest rates will result in a later floating of the natural coupons, and hence less negative duration contribution. In the limit of very low interest rates, all the natural coupons would be below the coupon floor. In this situation, the KTRD of the index will be zero, and the note would behave like a fixed rate note of comparable maturity.

One item to note is that regardless of the interest rate scenarios, the SURF's DRD of 4.2 with respect to the 5-year Treasury rate remains unchanged.

The aggregate durational behavior of the note for parallel yield curve shift is shown in Exhibit 6-11 versus different interest rate scenarios. Deterministic duration shows that the note will have a duration that is approximately that of a fixed rate note for low interest rate scenarios. The aggregate duration of the note will fall with higher rates as more coupons float off the floor. The asymptotic duration of the SURF will be reached when all coupons float

EXHIBIT 6-10 KTRD of 5-Year SURF Note

For high interest rate scenarios, most of the SURF coupons are floating off the floor at 0.5 * CMT. Thus there is negative duration contribution from the 10- through 15-year maturity Treasury sector. For lower interest rate scenarios, the coupons will float off the coupon floor at a later time, resulting in negative duration at longer maturity Treasury sectors. For interest rate scenarios where all the coupons are expected to be floored, the note will exhibit no negative duration in the longer maturity sector and will have the duration of a 5-year fixed rate note, or 4.2. The KTRD at the 5-year maturity Treasury sector has an amplitude of 4.2.

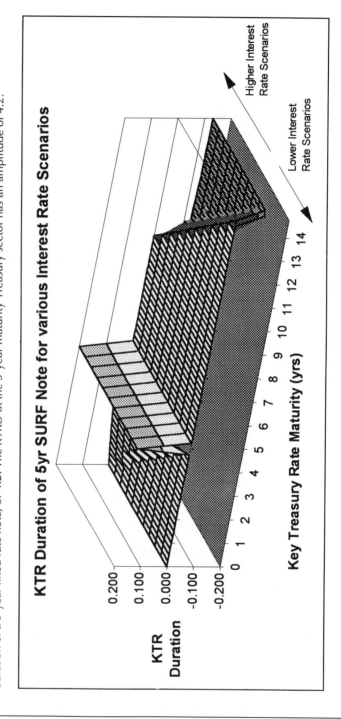

KTR Duration of 5yr SURF Note for various Interest Rate Scenarios

EXHIBIT 6-11   Deterministic and Simulation Duration of a CMT SURF (for Parallel YC Shift)

The duration of a SURF note is computed for a range of final expectation CMT rates. The deterministic duration of the SURF is seen to vary between 4.2 when rates are low and the coupons are essentially floored, to a minimum of 2.1 when all coupons are floating at 50% of the CMT rate. The actual duration of the note as reflected by the simulation duration is similar in nature to the deterministic duration, except with a lower initial duration and a more gradual decrease in duration for higher rates.

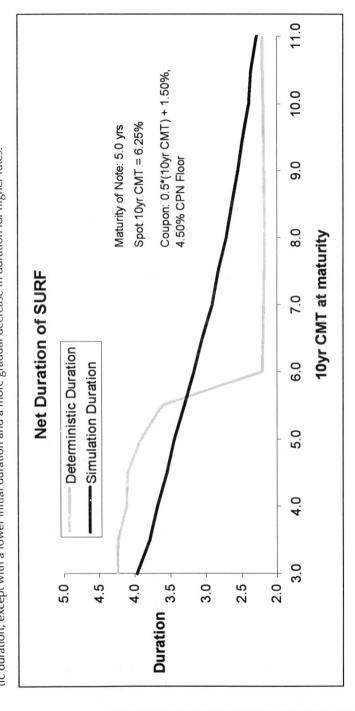

off the floor. In this example, the asymptotic duration of the note would be half of that of a fixed rate note, or 2.1. The actual duration is reflected by the simulation duration, which agrees qualitatively with the deterministic duration, except that the transition from fixed to floating is much more gradual.

Volatility Risk.   The volatility risk of the SURF note is calculated by performing a 3000 run simulation analysis with the same base case scenarios as the above durational analysis. The results are graphed on Exhibit 6-12. The results can be understood by examining the behavior of the vega of the embedded coupon floor (which the note is long). The vega increases as the index approaches the strike, resulting in an increase in the value of the floor for higher volatility and thus a higher negative volatility duration. For higher interest rate scenarios, the vega becomes lower as the index moves away from the strike. This results in a lower magnitude of the negative volatility.

The volatility risk of the SURF note is smaller than might be expected for a comparable maturity CapFRN or FFRN. This is due to the amount of floor option embedded in the note. As will be demonstrated in Chapter 8, only half the notional amount of the CMT floor option is required. This reduces the volatility risk of the SURF note.

B. MULTI-INDEX NOTES

The second class of the second generation structures is the multi-index notes. These notes reset based on the sum or difference between multiple indices. The two most popular and representative notes of this class are the CMT-LIBOR differential note and the Prime-LIBOR differential note.

STRUCTURE III. CMT-LIBOR DIFFERENTIAL NOTES

Investor purpose: Obtain higher spot floating rate yields than is possible with either the CMT FRN or the LIBOR FRN.
Risk: Yield curve flattening will rapidly erode this note's yield advantage over CMT or LIBOR FRNs.
Equivalent investor position: Long CMT FRN, long Eurodollar futures.

The CMT-LIBOR differential note pays the investor the difference between a CMT rate (typically the 10-year CMT) and a short-term LIBOR (typically 3-month LIBOR). Its popularity springs from its high floating rate

EXHIBIT 6-12   Volatility Duration of SURF

The SURF note contains a high coupon floor. Higher volatility would thus result in a gain in the value of the coupon floor, and subsequently a gain in the value of the note.

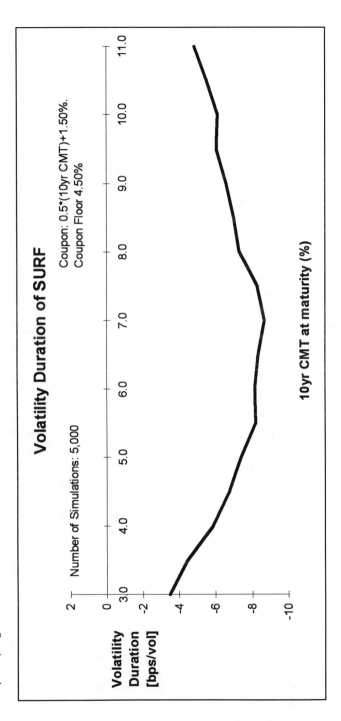

yield. The price of this higher yield is that, unlike a regular FRN, the CMT-LIBOR FRN contains yield curve risk. The sample terms of a CMT-LIBOR note are as follows:

Issuer: U.S. Agency
Maturity: 3 years
Coupon: 10-year CMT – 3-month LIBOR + 1.95%, reset quarterly

The maturity of the CMT-LIBOR differential notes was often short relative to other FRNs, with three years being a typical maturity.

History

CMT-LIBOR differential notes gained considerable popularity among floating rate investors in 1993. The chief reason behind the purchase of such notes was a search for higher yield. As both short- and long-term rates dropped close to all-time lows, floating rate investors searching for higher yield flocked to CMT-LIBOR FRNs for the high upfront coupon.

The historical graph below compares the historical coupon performance of a CMT-LIBOR differential note to a CMT FRN and a LIBOR FRN, all of which are assumed to have been structured in July 1992. The graph provides ample motivation for investor preference of CMT-LIBOR differential notes: the CMT-LIBOR note was able to produce yields that could not be obtained via either the CMT or the LIBOR FRN. This yield advantage of the hypothetical July 1992 vintage CMT-LIBOR differential note was sustained until the end of the first quarter of 1994.

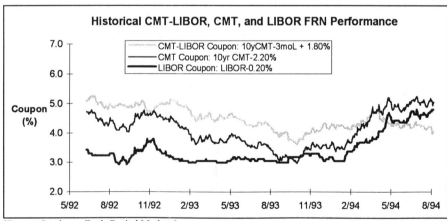

[Source: Sumitomo Bank Capital Markets]

EXHIBIT 6-13 CMT-LIBOR Differential Note

This note is different from typical CMT-LIBOR notes in that it provided a "teaser" above-market coupon of 5% for the first year before switching to a CMT-LIBOR differential coupon for the last two years.

Issue Terms (Actual)

Issuer:	Federal Home Loan Bank System
Principal amount:	US$100,000,000
Settlement date:	July 1, 1993
Maturity date:	July 1, 1996
Coupon paid in US$:	Year 1: 5.00% Years 2–3: 10-year CMT – 3-month LIBOR + 1.60%
Day count basis:	30/360
Rate reset and payment dates:	Rate resets quarterly. Payment dates Jan. 1, Apr. 1, July 1, Oct. 1. First coupon paid on Oct. 1, 1993.
10-year CMT determination:	The 10-year CMT rate shall be the daily 10-year constant maturity Treasury rate applicable on the determination day of the Fed H.15(519) publication. Determination date is two New York and London business days prior to reset dates. Source: Telerate Page 7059.
LIBOR determination:	3-month LIBOR resets quarterly. Determination date is two New York and London business days prior to period end dates. Source: Telerate Page 3750.
Issue price:	100.00%

Since the CMT-LIBOR differential note contains yield curve risk due to the mismatch of its IR and DR, KTRD analysis will be required to fully assess the risks inherent in this structure.

Analysis

The terms of an actual CMT-LIBOR note are described in Exhibit 6-13. This note is an interesting variant on the CMT-LIBOR theme in that the CMT-LIBOR differential component of the coupon only applies in the last two years. The first year of the note is an above-market fixed rate coupon. This complication will be useful in illustrating the effect of such complications on the KTRD spectrum of a note.

The note pays an above-market "teaser" coupon of 5% for the first year, followed by last two years of CMT-LIBOR + 1.60%. A similar CMT-LIBOR differential note was analyzed in Chapter 2. As mentioned before, the added complications for this note are:

1. Coupon resets quarterly (as opposed to yearly in the example of Chapter 2). The resolution of the Treasury maturity spectrum will be adjusted finer to accommodate this quarterly reset.
2. Floating component does not start until one year from settlement. This will introduce additional considerations into the index risk calculations.

Performance

The performance of the note can be examined using LSE to generate a series of base case scenarios for the CMT-LIBOR differential. The IRR for each of these base case scenarios is plotted on Exhibit 6-14. As expected, the note performs well when the CMT-LIBOR spread at maturity remains relatively large and poorly when the spread contracts significantly from initial levels.

Risk

Interest Rate Risk

Step 1: Components

a. **Discounting component:** The maturity of the note is three years; hence the DR is the 3-year Treasury rate.
b. **Index component:** The coupon is composed of two components: 10-year CMT and LIBOR. The IR is the aggregate of the in-1-year-for-2-year stream of quarterly cash flows of 10-year CMT as well as the stream of quarterly LIBORs.

Steps 2 and 3: Components and the Corresponding KTRs and KTRDs.
The components of this CMT-LIBOR differential note are:

a. **Discounting rate.** As mentioned above, the DR is the 3-year Treasury rate. The DRD is the duration of a comparable maturity fixed coupon note, or approximately 2.7.
b. **Index 1: 10-year CMT.** The 10-year CMT component consists of the component of the coupons that depend upon the 10-year CMT rate. These are the 10-year CMT rate starting in 1 year, 1.25 years, and so forth until the last coupon set based on the 10-year CMT rate in 2.75 years. The KTRD of the CMT component is seen in Exhibit 6-15.
c. **Index 2: LIBOR.** The floating portion of the cash flow does not start until the end of the first year. Hence the LIBOR component of

EXHIBIT 6-14 IRR Performance of CMT-LIBOR FRN

The performance of the CMT-LIBOR note improves for steeper final CMT-LIBOR spreads.

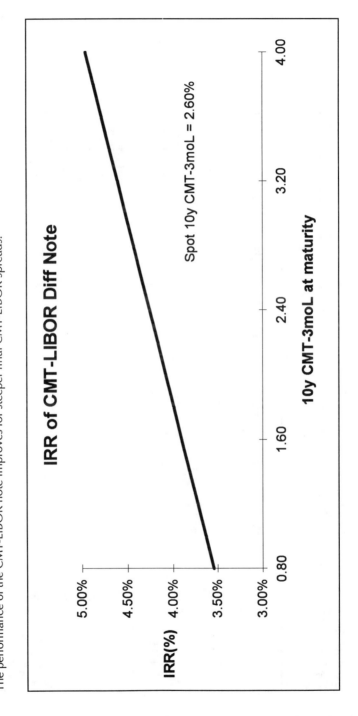

EXHIBIT 6-15   KTRD of CMT Component of Coupon
The CMT component shows a positive duration with respect to short-term rates and negative duration with respect to long-term rates.

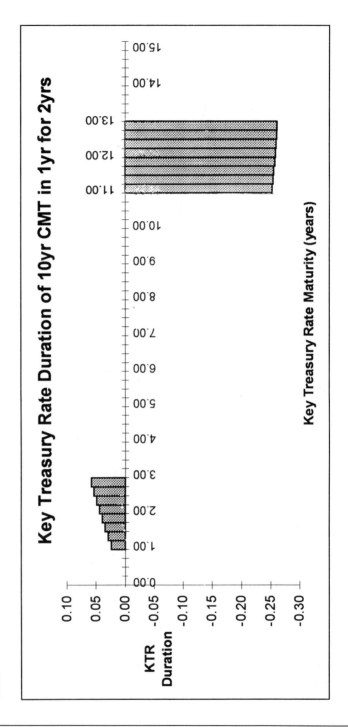

Key Treasury Rate Duration of 10yr CMT in 1yr for 2yrs

the coupon is no longer the 3-year swap rate, but rather the in-1-year-for-2-year swap rate. This is calculated as:

$$(1 + T_{2,1}/2)^4 * (1 + T_1/2)^2 = (1 + T_3/2)^6$$

This is again the bootstrap relationship linking the in-1-year-for-2-year forward swap rate $T_{2,1}$ to the spot 1- and 3-year swap rates T_1 and T_3. Solving for the forward rate:

$$T_{2,1} = 2 * \{[(1 + T_3/2)^6/(1 + T_1/2)^2]^{1/4} - 1\}$$
$$= 2 * \{(1 + T_3/2) * [(1 + T_3/2)/(1 + T_1/2)]^{1/2} - 1\}$$

Since no distinction is made between the swap rate and the Treasury rate, the LIBOR component of this note has KTRD with respect to the 1-year and 3-year sector of the Treasury yield curve.

Estimates of the variability of the $T_{2,1}$ rate with T_3 and T_1 can be made based on the above formula. Two good estimates are:

$$T_{2,1} \approx 1.5 \ T_3, \quad \text{and}$$
$$T_{2,1} \approx -0.5 \ T_1$$

The LIBOR component's IRD with respect to each of these KTRs could then be calculated by multiplying the above variability of the forward rate $T_{2,1}$ by the duration of the in-1-year-for-2-year stream of cash flows, or approximately 1.7 years. In other words, the LIBOR component of the note has a KTRD of positive 2.5 (1.5 * 1.7 duration) with respect to the 3-year Treasury rate, and a KTRD of *negative* 0.7 (–0.5 * 1.7 duration) with respect to the 1-year Treasury rate.

Steps 4 and 5.   The net aggregate of the KTRD spectrum of the note is calculated and plotted in Exhibit 6-16. The KTRD spectrum of the note can be summarized as follows:

Key Treasury Maturity Sector	Duration of CMT-LIBOR Note with Respect to Treasury Sector
0.0 to 1.0 year	–0.7
1.25 to 3 year	+5.5
10 to 15 year	–2.1
For parallel YC shifts:	Net duration: +2.7

EXHIBIT 6-16   Net KTR Durational Spectrum of CMT-LIBOR Spread Note

Note that the contribution of the CMT component to the KTRD spectrum in the shorter maturity sector is negligible in the overall risk profile. The fixed-for-1-year characteristic of this note adds a negative duration contribution from the LIBOR component in 1-year maturity Treasury sector.

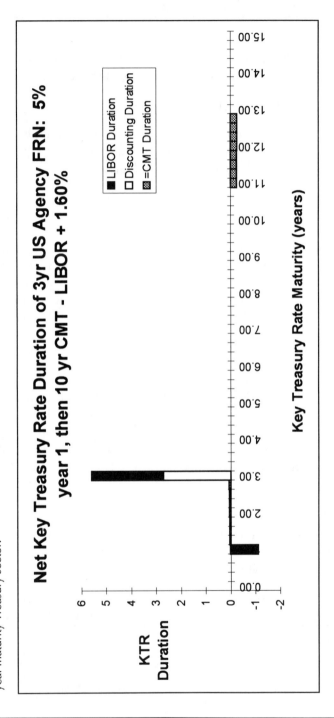

From the above table and Exhibit 6-16, it is evident that the CMT-LIBOR differential note in question increases in value only when the longer maturity Treasury rates (10+ years) rise and the shorter maturity Treasury rates (under three years) drop, i.e., if the yield curve steepens. Another important feature is that the note behaves like a 3-year fixed rate note with a duration of 2.7 when the yield curve shifts in parallel. This is an expected result since the CMT-LIBOR spread would remain constant for a parallel yield curve shift, resulting in the note being exposed to only changes in the DR of the 3-year Treasury rate.

Volatility Risk. The volatility risk of the CMT-LIBOR differential note will be examined via a 5000 run simulation analysis of the volatility duration. Recall from Chapter 4 that any simulation involving two indices must account for a correlation factor between the two indices. Thus, in addition to the usual volatility duration, the note will also exhibit characteristic changes for different correlations.

Exhibit 6-17 displays the result of the 5000 run volatility analysis for two assumed correlation levels. The first characteristic that emerges is that the note exhibits negative volatility duration throughout the assumed interest rate scenarios. Since the note is long the zero coupon option, which is a spread option between the two indices, any incremental rise in volatility will result in this option gaining in value, and hence a negative volatility duration.

The CMT-LIBOR differential note exhibits the largest volatility duration for scenarios in which the CMT-LIBOR differential-at-maturity are negative. Since lower differential scenarios result in the CMT-LIBOR differential approaching the zero coupon floor strike, this results in a larger vega and thus a larger magnitude of volatility duration. For higher differential index scenarios, the differentials are further away from the floor strike; hence the magnitude of the volatility duration decreases towards zero.

The interesting characteristic of this note that is not observable for other single-index notes is the effect of correlation on the note characteristics. Exhibit 6-17 also shows that higher correlation results in a lower volatility duration. Since a higher correlation effectively ties the movement of the two indices closer together, the likelihood of the two indices diverging is not as great as for a low correlation case. Thus, for a given differential scenario and a high correlation, the probability of the differential moving away from the base case scenario and closer to the floor strike would be lower; thus, a higher correlation results in lower volatility risk.

EXHIBIT 6-17   Volatility Duration of CMT-LIBOR Differential Note

Due to the embedded zero coupon floor option, the note exhibits negative volatility duration. The volatility duration of the note is also different if the correlation between the two indices change. The 5000 run simulation analysis shows that a higher correlation will result in a lower magnitude of volatility duration.

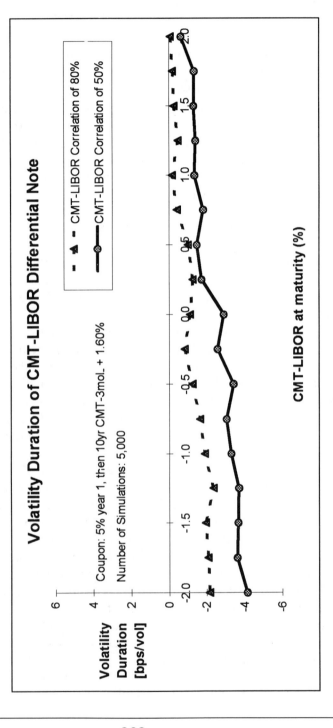

Volatility Duration of CMT-LIBOR Differential Note

Coupon: 5% year 1, then 10yr CMT-3moL. + 1.60%

Number of Simulations: 5,000

- ▲ - CMT-LIBOR Correlation of 80%
—⊗— CMT-LIBOR Correlation of 50%

Volatility Duration [bps/vol]

CMT-LIBOR at maturity (%)

The volatility risk of this note is comparatively low versus other structures. Part of this low volatility risk is due to the forward starting indices. Since the note is fixed for the first year and only floats off the differential for the last two years, the effective maturity of the floating rate period is only two years. This forward start results in a note with lower volatility and durational risk than a CMT-LIBOR note that floats off the differential for the full three years.

STRUCTURE IV. PRIME-LIBOR DIFFERENTIAL NOTES

Investor purpose: Obtain higher floating rate yield than is possible with either the Prime or the LIBOR FRN.
Risk: Prime-LIBOR spread contains interest rate and yield curve risks that are not intuitively obvious.
Equivalent investor positions: Long Prime FRN, long Eurodollar futures.

Prime-LIBOR differential notes pay a floating rate coupon based upon the spread between the Prime rate and 3-month LIBOR. In 1992–93, the spread between the two indices was high by historical standards, resulting in Prime-LIBOR differential notes whose yields were considerably higher than obtainable by either LIBOR or Prime FRNs.

Despite the presence of two indices that are familiar to most investors, the note contains risks that are not immediately obvious. This section will demonstrate that the Prime-LIBOR note, unlike the CMT-LIBOR note, contains risks that are difficult to assess.

History

During the bull market of 1990–94, many investors were increasingly disappointed by the low (and ever-dropping) yields generated by traditional floating rate notes. Even CMT and Prime FRNs did not provide much yield enhancement over the low (and fast dropping) short-term rates such as LIBOR. Investors seeking out higher yielding floating rate securities thus purchased Prime-LIBOR differential notes for the same reason as the CMT-LIBOR differential notes: the high floating rate yield. Prime-LIBOR notes were popular among regional investors who are familiar with the Prime rate from their association with bank loans denominated in Prime (either as a lender or a borrower).

The historical graph clearly shows that investors purchased Prime-LIBOR FRNs in 1993 because they provided a very high yield pickup relative to either the Prime or the LIBOR FRN. This yield advantage proved fairly constant until the Federal Reserve's tightening action in 1994 drove up short-term rates and closed the yield gap.

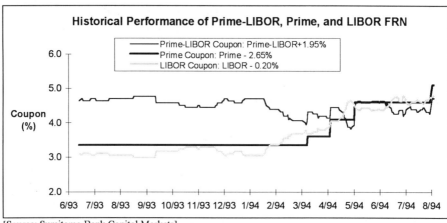

[Source: Sumitomo Bank Capital Markets]

Analysis

This section will illustrate the earlier assertion that the purchase of a Prime-LIBOR differential note should be carefully considered because the inherent risk is not obvious to the investor. At first glance, there appears to be no obvious mechanism that drives the behavior of the spread between Prime and LIBOR. This results in many investors having difficulty in adequately assessing the risk associated with the structure.

The appropriate methodology for the analysis of Prime-LIBOR differential notes is the historical analysis. By examining how this differential changes in historical context, one can gain insight into the behavior of the differential and find some hidden mechanism that could drive this differential.

The terms of a Prime-LIBOR spread note are described in Exhibit 6-18 and can be summarized as follows:

Issuer: U.S. Agency
Maturity: 3 years
Coupon: Prime – 3-month LIBOR + 1.95%, reset quarterly

The terms of this note are quite representative of most Prime-LIBOR differential notes. The majority of these notes were issued by U.S. Agencies.

EXHIBIT 6-18 Prime-LIBOR Differential Note

This note produced an initial coupon of 4.64%, which is 1.53% higher than the initial coupon of a comparable maturity benchmark LIBOR FRN.

Issue Terms (Actual)	
Issuer:	Federal Farm Credit Bank System
Principal amount:	US$150,000,000
Settlement date:	July 29, 1993
Maturity date:	July 29, 1996
Coupon paid in US$:	Prime – 3-month LIBOR + 1.95%
Day count basis:	Act/360
Rate reset and payment dates:	Rates reset and pay quarterly. Payment dates Jan. 29, Apr. 29, July 29, Oct. 29. First coupon paid on Oct. 29, 1993.
Prime determination:	The Prime rate shall be the Prime rate as published in the Fed H.15(519) publication. Determination date is two New York and London business days prior to reset dates. Source: Telerate Page 7059.
LIBOR determination:	3-month LIBOR resets quarterly two New York and London business days prior to reset date. Source: Telerate Page 3750.
Issue price:	100.00%

The average maturity of these structures tended to be short since investors were uncomfortable with taking spread risk for long maturities. Finally, the coupon of the note is reset quarterly based on rates at the beginning of the period. This type of coupon rate setting is the same as for LIBOR FRNs but differs from the daily rate setting of Prime FRNs.

Recall that the historical analysis described in Chapter 3 was able to establish a historical relationship between a relevant index (chosen to be the spread between the 10-year CMT and 3-month LIBOR) and the Prime-LIBOR spread via linear regression. This linear regression relationship between the two spreads was found to be:

$$(\text{Prime-LIBOR}) = 0.32 * (\text{CMT-LIBOR}) + 1.46\%$$

The linear regression relationship indicate that, if past history is a guide, the Prime-LIBOR differential note's risks are similar to, but less leveraged (due to the 0.32 regression factor) than, that of a CMT-LIBOR note.

One possible explanation for this relationship is as follows: as the yield curve flattens, longer-term loan demand begins to pick up, while shorter-term loan demand begins to go down. This increase in longer-term loan demand is due to the fact that borrowers can now obtain long-term fixed loans at the same level as the floating rate of short-term loans, resulting in many borrowers locking in more attractive long-term fixed rate loans. Since Prime is an indication of shorter-term floating rate bank loan demand, the Prime rate is usually lowered to attract more short-term borrowing. The lowering of the Prime rate thus results in the narrowing of the Prime-LIBOR spread.[3]

Performance

The performance of the Prime-LIBOR differential note can be examined by employing LSE to project a series of final expectation levels of the relevant index (10-year CMT–3-month LIBOR). For each final scenario of the relevant index, a final level of the Prime-LIBOR spread can be calculated via the regression relationship. The intermediate spreads and coupons can then be calculated. The IRR of the note is plotted in Exhibit 6-19 versus final CMT-LIBOR expectation scenarios. As expected, the Prime-LIBOR spread note performs well in yield curve steepening scenarios but badly in flattening scenarios. Because of the deleveraged relationship between the Prime-LIBOR and the CMT-LIBOR, this drop-off in performance is not as dramatic as exhibited by the CMT-LIBOR differential note.

Risk

Interest Rate Risk.   With the establishment of the relationship between the Prime-LIBOR spread and the relevant index of CMT-LIBOR, KTRD methodology can be employed to fully assess the risks of this note. Exhibit 6-20 shows the KTRD spectrum of the Prime-LIBOR spread note. The risks of the note are summarized as follows:

Key Treasury Maturity Sector	Duration of CMT-LIBOR Note with Respect to Treasury Sector
0.0 to 3.0 year	+3.7
10 to 12.75 year	−1.0
For parallel YC shifts:	Net duration: +2.7

---

3. This explanation was espoused by Rick Ziwot of Lehman Brothers.

EXHIBIT 6-19 **IRR Performance of Prime-LIBOR Differential Note**

The analysis of the note is calculated for a variety of final expectation levels of (10-year CMT-3-month LIBOR) spreads using the regression relationship of (Prime-LIBOR) = 0.32 * (CMT-LIBOR) + 1.46%. The note is seen to perform well in yield curve steepening environments but suffers in yield curve flattening scenarios.

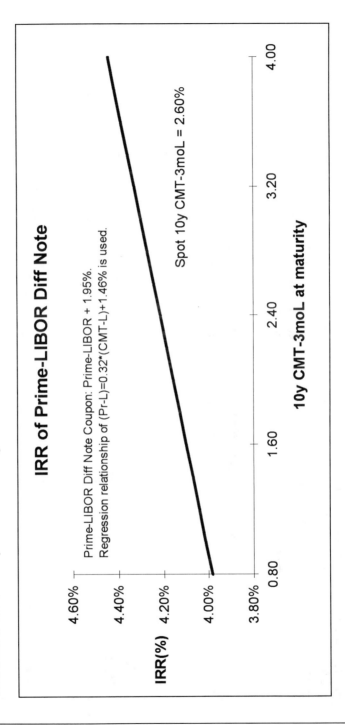

IRR of Prime-LIBOR Diff Note

Prime-LIBOR Diff Note Coupon: Prime-LIBOR + 1.95%.
Regression relationship of (Pr-L)=0.32*(CMT-L)+1.46% is used.

Spot 10y CMT-3moL = 2.60%

10y CMT-3moL at maturity

IRR(%)

4.60%
4.40%
4.20%
4.00%
3.80%

0.80   1.60   2.40   3.20   4.00

EXHIBIT 6-20   KTRD of 3-Year Agency Prime-LIBOR Differential Note

The linear regression relationship of (Prime-LIBOR) = 0.32 * (10-year CMT–3-month LIBOR) + 1.46% is used to create the following spectrum. The Prime-LIBOR spread note thus has a positive duration with respect to the 0- to 3-year maturity Treasury sector, and a smaller positive duration of –1 with respect to the 10- through 12.75-year maturity sector. The net aggregate duration for parallel yield curve shift is 2.7, which is equal to the duration of a 3-year fixed rate note.

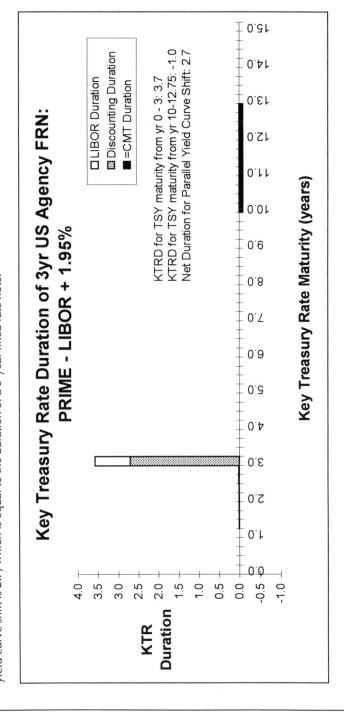

Key Treasury Rate Duration of 3yr US Agency FRN:
PRIME - LIBOR + 1.95%

KTRD for TSY maturity from yr 0 - 3: 3.7
KTRD for TSY maturity from yr 10-12.75: -1.0
Net Duration for Parallel Yield Curve Shift: 2.7

□ LIBOR Duration
▨ Discounting Duration
■ =CMT Duration

Key Treasury Rate Maturity (years)

KTR Duration

The risks of the note are observed to lie predominantly in the zero to 3-year Treasury maturity sector. Each basis point of rising long-term rates (10- to 12.75-year maturity Treasury) will result in only a 1 bp gain in value of the par note, while each basis point of rising short-term rates (0- to 3-year maturity Treasury) will result in 3.7 bps loss in the value of a par note.

One important fact to remember is that the risks described for the Prime-LIBOR note are *contingent upon the applicability of the relevant index*. In this case, the relevant index (10-year CMT–3-month LIBOR) is a relevant index because there is both historical and anecdotal evidence to support the linkage. When analyzing structures such as the Prime-LIBOR note, it is the responsibility of the analyzer to select a relevant index that not only has good historical correlation with the index in question, but that also has good reason for this correlation.

Volatility Risk. The volatility risk of the Prime-LIBOR differential note in question is quite negligible. The volatility risk of the note is minimal due to the high strike of the coupon floor. Examine the coupon formula:

CPN = Prime-LIBOR + 1.95%

Employing the linear regression relationship linking the relevant index of CMT-LIBOR to Prime-LIBOR:

CPN = 0.32 * (10-year CMT – 3-month LIBOR) + 1.46% + 1.95%

In order for the note coupon to be at zero, 3-month LIBOR would have to exceed 10-year CMT by 10.65%! This is an extremely low probability event and most reasonable interest rate scenarios would not be close enough to this strike to result in the zero coupon floor option gaining vega of any significant magnitude.

In addition, the 0.32 deleveraging coefficient multiplying the relevant index (10-year CMT–3-month LIBOR) further reduces the effect of volatility on the note. Thus, the combination of a very high strike and a deleveraging factor result in a negligible volatility risk of the Prime-LIBOR differential note.

C. EXOTIC OPTIONS

The exotic option class of structured notes is the most diverse of all the second generation structures. The large and ever-increasing number of exotic options have increased both the performance capabilities and the level of confusion of investors. Some representative structures involving exotic options that are analyzed in this section are the accrual note, the one-way collared (OWC) note, and the index amortizing note.

STRUCTURE V. ACCRUAL NOTES
(ALSO KNOWN AS RANGE NOTES)

Investor purpose: Obtain enhanced yield if short-term rates remains within the prescribed range.

Risk: Dramatically lower (even zero) yield if rates move outside range.

Equivalent investor positions: Long fixed note or FRN, short binary cap and/or floor options.

Accrual notes were created to meet the requests of short-term investors who do not wish to invest in inverse floating rate notes but nevertheless wanted a bullish rate play. The coupon of the accrual note can either be fixed rate or floating rate.

Accrual notes have the following coupon structure:

Coupon: $X\%$ when *Index* is within RANGE
             $Y\%$ when *Index* is outside RANGE

The *Index* is the accrual index and is generally a short-term index such as LIBOR, although CMT rates have also been used. The maximum coupon $X\%$ can either be fixed or floating, while the minimum coupon $Y\%$ is typically zero or a small fixed floor.

If the accrual index remains within the prescribed range for the life of the note, the investor would obtain a much larger yield than is possible with typical fixed or floating rate notes. The downside is that the yield becomes dramatically lower (even zero) when the accrual index moves outside the prescribed range.

The three main variants of the accrual note are the LIBOR enhancement Accrual Note (LEAN), fixed accrual note, and the yield curve accrual note. The most popular variant is the LEAN, and hence it will be the subject of analysis in this section.

LIBOR Enhancement Accrual Note (LEAN)

The version of the accrual note that has received the most investor interest and attention is the LEAN. The coupons of the LEAN have a much higher spread to LIBOR (or some other index) than comparable FRNs, but do not accrue interest when the accrual index is outside an accrual range.

A typical LEAN is as follows:

Issuer: AAA
Maturity: 3 years
Coupon: LIBOR + x% each day LIBOR is within a preset range
            0.00% each day LIBOR is outside preset range

where x is the coupon spread. This spread x is usually significantly higher than comparable maturity FRNs of the same issuer. One key distinction that is made is that the accrual index LIBOR used to determine the accrual condition is set each day, whereas the coupon index LIBOR for the coupon accrual is set at the start of the period.

History

The story of the LEAN is one of explosive growth followed by dramatic decline. The note rapidly caught the attention and interest of investors when it was first unveiled in January of 1994. Within a short span of two weeks, over US$1 billion in new issue had been created and purchased by investors globally. What drove investors to purchase these notes was the then-prevailing low volatility of LIBOR and the belief that there would not be any rate hikes since signs of inflation were still not apparent. As the graph below illustrates, LIBOR had been trading in a tight range for the previous two years, which contributed to investor optimism.

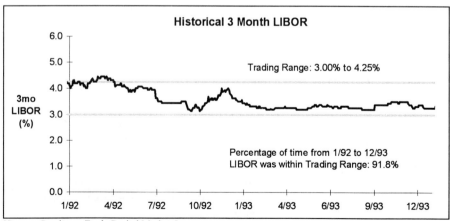

[Source: Sumitomo Bank Capital Markets]

Unfortunately, the Federal Reserve did not view inflationary fears as optimistically as these investors. The subsequent interest rate hikes in the first quarter of 1994 took many investors by surprise and has resulted in a considerable amount of outstanding LEANs with accrual indices that are out of the accrual range.

Analysis

The terms of an actual LEAN are provided in Exhibit 6-21. This particular note has an accrual range that widens periodically, providing investors some protection in a rising rate environment. The coupon structure of this LEAN is plotted versus LIBOR on Exhibit 6-22. As expected, the LEAN produces a

EXHIBIT 6-21 LEAN

This is a typical accrual note with two key features: a highly rated issuer, and a short maturity. This note provides investors with a coupon of LIBOR + 0.80% (considerably higher than a comparable benchmark Agency FRN) when the accrual condition is met.

Issue Terms (Actual)	
Issuer:	Federal Home Loan Bank System
Principal amount:	US$25,000,000
Settlement date:	Apr. 11, 1994
Maturity date:	Apr. 11, 1995
Coupon paid in US$:	LIBOR + 0.80% each day ACCLIBOR is within RANGE 0.00% otherwise
RANGE:	4/11/94 to 7/10/94: 3.50% to 4.875% 7/11/94 to 10/10/94: 3.50% to 5.125% 10/11/94 to 1/10/95: 3.50% to 5.375% 1/11/95 to 4/10/95: 3.50% to 5.625%
Day count basis:	Act/360
Rate reset and payment dates:	Coupon rates reset and pay quarterly. Payment dates Jan. 11, Apr. 11, July 11, Oct. 11. First coupon paid on July 11, 1994.
ACCLIBOR:	ACCLIBOR, the 3-month LIBOR for coupon accrual determination, resets daily as of 11 A.M. London time. Source: Telerate 3747.
LIBOR for coupon determination:	3-month LIBOR for coupon rate determination resets quarterly two New York and London business days prior to reset date. Source: Telerate Page 3747.
Issue price:	100.00%

EXHIBIT 6-22 LIBOR Enhanced Accrual Note (LEAN)

Although the coupon yields a very high spread to LIBOR (100 bps higher than where comparable Agency LIBOR FRN would theoretically trade), the yield drops to zero once LIBOR is outside the prescribed range. This note thus has a range in which it would outperform a comparable LIBOR FRN, but would underperform when LIBOR moves outside the range.

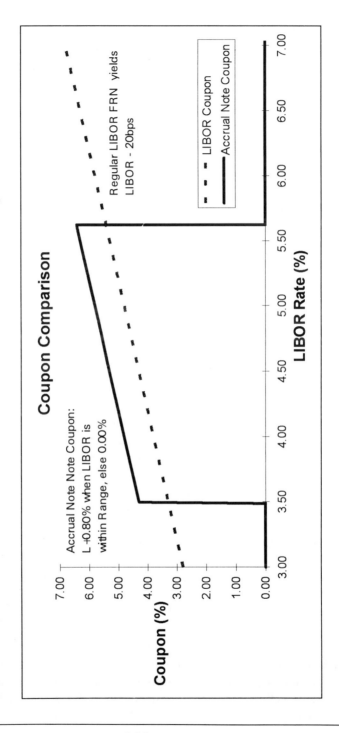

Coupon Comparison

Accrual Note Note Coupon:
L +0.80% when LIBOR is
within Range, else 0.00%

Regular LIBOR FRN yields
LIBOR - 20bps

- - - LIBOR Coupon
—— Accrual Note Coupon

LIBOR Rate (%)

Coupon (%)

large spread to LIBOR FRN coupons within the accrual range, but falls to zero outside. Because the LEAN includes binary options, the simulation class of analysis is appropriate for examining the risk of the note.

Performance

Employing LSE analysis, a range of final LIBORs at maturity is selected and the associated IRR of each scenario calculated and shown in Exhibit 6-23. The note provides enhanced yields over the benchmark LIBOR FRN as long as LIBOR remains within the prescribed range. However, as soon as the LIBORs drop outside the range, the note begins to lose an increasingly larger portion of the coupon, hence the lower yield for higher or lower scenarios of the accrual index.

Risk

Interest Rate Risk.   Investors who purchased LEANs in January 1994 saw firsthand the large drop in the bid price of the notes when the Federal Reserve sent both short- and long-term rates soaring in February with its tightening policy. The risk of the note can be interpreted by examining the deterministic duration behavior in Exhibit 6-24. The KTR of both the index and discounting components of risk is the 1-year Treasury rate.

The presence of negative duration when LIBOR is below the low end of the accrual range illustrates an interesting risk point. The accrual note loses part of the coupon when the accrual index falls outside the accrual range. The negative duration thus means that for low interest rate scenarios in which a significant portion of the accrual index is projected to be below the lower limit of the accrual range, any rise in rates will cause the value of the note to increase.

When LIBOR is within the preset range, the note behaves just like a regular FRN. However, once the accrual rate exceeds the preset range, the coupon behavior changes radically and the note begins to lose value very quickly. The deterministic duration is seen to rise very rapidly to a very high level before a gradual decline. This large duration is a result of the rapid drop in value when LIBOR rises out of the accrual range. For very high interest rate scenarios, the deterministic duration approaches the asymptotic duration, which is equal to the duration of a 1-year maturity zero coupon note, or 1.

The risk of the note as reflected by the simulation duration is qualitatively the same as that of the deterministic duration. The actual durational changes are not as drastic as might be expected from deterministic calculations. The

EXHIBIT 6-23 IRR of LIBOR Accrual Note

The maximum IRR is achieved if LIBOR remains within the accrual range. Once LIBOR drops outside the accrual range, the performance drops off dramatically.

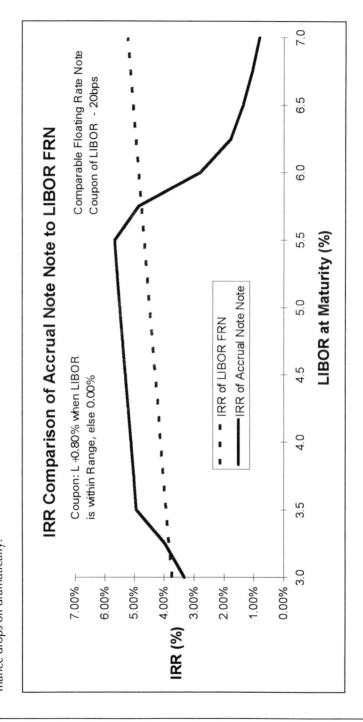

215

EXHIBIT 6-24 Duration of LIBOR Accrual Note

The deterministic duration of the note is zero when LIBOR is within the accrual range for the life of the note. The note's duration changes dramatically as soon as rates move out of the accrual range, reflecting the loss of value due to the non-accruing coupon. For interest rate scenarios below the accrual range, this note exhibits negative duration. The actual duration of the note as reflected by the simulation duration is similar to, but does not change as dramatically as, the deterministic duration, rising to a maximum duration of approximately 4.

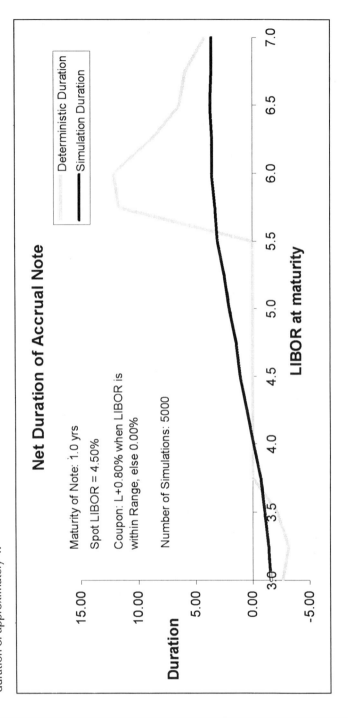

Net Duration of Accrual Note

Maturity of Note: 1.0 yrs

Spot LIBOR = 4.50%

Coupon: L+0.80% when LIBOR is within Range, else 0.00%

Number of Simulations: 5000

Duration

15.00

10.00

5.00

0.00

-5.00

3.0 3.5 4.0 4.5 5.0 5.5 6.0 6.5 7.0

LIBOR at maturity

Deterministic Duration

Simulation Duration

note begins to lose value even prior to any forward LIBOR crossing the upper limit of the accrual range. This is due to the binary option (which the investor is short) having a non-zero delta, which causes it to increase in value as the rate approaches the strike. The actual maximum duration level is lower than that predicted by the deterministic duration, reaching a maximum level of approximately four upon crossing the upper limit of the accrual range. This *duration* of four, however, is still *quadruple* that of a comparable maturity 1-year fixed rate note. This unexpectedly large duration is the cause of investors' sticker shock from trying to sell the note after the Federal Reserve's initial interest rate tightening moves in 1994.

For final expectation LIBORs above the upper limit of the accrual range, Exhibit 6-24 shows that the note exhibits positive duration. Likewise, for final expectation LIBORs below the lower limit of the accrual range, the note exhibits negative duration. The note thus contains an implicit view that interest rates will remain stable, since interest rate movement in either direction will result in the note losing significant value.

Volatility Risk.   The volatility risk of the LEAN is calculated using a 5000 run simulation analysis of the volatility duration for the same base rate scenarios as the above durational calculations and is graphed in Exhibit 6-25. The volatility risk profile is quite interesting and requires some thought to understand the embedded risk.

For very low interest rate scenarios, the note exhibits negative volatility duration. The reason for this is as follows: these low rate scenarios would result in most of the coupons not accruing interest. A higher volatility would enhance the likelihood that some of these coupons would be back in the accrual range and thus result in a higher expected value. This higher expected value is thus reflected in the negative volatility duration.

For very high interest rate scenarios, the same logic applies. Most of the coupons in the base rate scenario would fall outside the accrual range and accrue no interest. A higher volatility would thus enhance the probability that these coupons can begin accruing interest again. Thus an increase in volatility for these scenarios would result in a higher expected value of the note and thus negative volatility duration.

For intermediate interest rate scenarios, the reverse of the above is true. The intermediate base rate scenario would dictate that most of the coupons be within the accrual range. An increase in volatility would thus result in a higher probability that the note accrue less coupon. Hence, for the intermediate interest rate scenarios, an increase in volatility results in a drop in the

EXHIBIT 6-25   Volatility Duration of LIBOR Enhancement Accrual Note

The note exhibits negative volatility duration for low interest rate scenarios. Since low interest rate scenarios have less coupon accrual, an increase in volatility would tend to result in a gain in the value of the note by bringing more rates into the accrual range. The volatility duration is also negative for higher interest rate scenarios due to the same reason. For the medium range of interest rate scenarios, an increase in volatility would introduce higher probability of the note attaining higher or lower rates, thus bringing the coupons outside the accrual range.

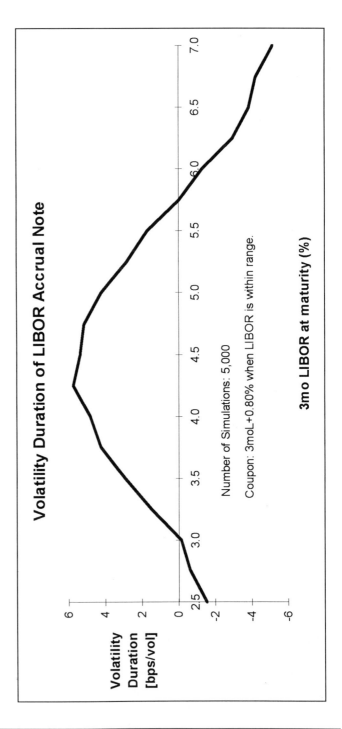

Volatility Duration of LIBOR Accrual Note

Number of Simulations: 5,000

Coupon: 3moL+0.80% when LIBOR is within range.

3mo LIBOR at maturity (%)

Volatility Duration [bps/vol]

expected value of the note, resulting in positive volatility duration. The maximum positive duration should occur when the majority of the interest rates reset in the middle of the accrual range. This is when the investor has the most to lose from higher volatility.

The magnitude of the volatility risk of the LEAN is large compared to comparable structures of similar maturity. This is due to the nature of the embedded optionality within the LEAN. The binary options have larger vegas than regular cap or floor options, and thus the note exhibits higher volatility risk.

Other Accrual Structures

Binary Accrual Note

The binary accrual note differs from the LEAN described earlier in that its coupons are fixed. The accrual condition will determine that fixed range at which the note accrues interest. A typical binary accrual note has the following structure:

Maturity: 3 years
Coupon: 5.50% each day 3-month LIBOR is within accrual range
                2.00% each day 3-month LIBOR is outside accrual range
Range: 3.00% to 5.50%

The binary accrual note produces a large fixed rate coupon if the accrual index remains within the accrual range.

Yield Curve Accrual Note (YCAN)

The yield curve accrual note (YCAN) concept arose from the accrual note described in the previous structure. Both evolved from an investor demand for higher yield. The YCAN is a combination of the CMT-LIBOR differential note and the binary note. A sample YCAN has the following structure:

Maturity: 3 years
Coupon: Year 1:   4.75%
                  Years 2–3:   7.125% if the yield curve is between 1.25% and
                               2.25%
Yield curve: 10-year CMT – 6-month LIBOR

This structure produces a higher yield when the yield curve (defined here as the spread between the 10-year CMT and 6-month LIBOR) is within the accrual range. The advantage of using the spread between two indices as the accrual condition is that the spread has a much lower absolute volatility than either index by itself.

STRUCTURE VI. ONE-WAY COLLARED (OWC) NOTE (ALSO KNOWN AS RATCHET, OR STICKY FLOATER)

Investor purpose: Obtain a FRN with downside protection in return for giving up rate rises beyond 25 basis points each reset period.

Risk: If rates rise quickly, the coupon cap will be reached each reset period, producing a yield that is low relative to a LIBOR FRN. The note has limited upside and downside potential. Due to the presence of the embedded path-dependent options, the interest rate and volatility risk of the note may not be obvious to the investor.

Equivalent investor position: Long FRN, short path-dependent LIBOR cap option, long path-dependent LIBOR floor option.

The OWC note was created to provide intermediate maturity investors with a high coupon floor as protection against coupon erosion when rates dropped. These coupon floors, however, are quite expensive in a short maturity (<10 years) setting and would result in a FFRN with a large negative spread to LIBOR. Even the imposition of a coupon cap could not offset this negative spread for a short maturity note. The OWC note provided a solution by subjecting the note to a path-dependent cap. The typical OWC has the following structure:

Issuer: U.S. Agency
Maturity: 5 years
Coupon: LIBOR + 0.25% subject to Condition.
Condition: Coupon cannot rise by more than 25 basis points from previous coupon nor fall below previous coupon.

The above Condition distinguishes the OWC from the collared FRN discussed in the previous chapter. The distinguishing feature of the OWC is that the coupon can never reset to a level that is lower than the previous coupon, nor can it reset to a level higher than a fixed spread over the previous coupon. This path dependency of the option constitutes the exotic option component of the OWC.

History

The OWC was popular during the bull market of 1990–94. Investors looking for protection against further drops in interest rates flocked to the OWC because it was perceived as a cheap and shorter maturity alternative to a FFRN or CFRN. Because rates continued to drop over most of that period, investors were more worried about obtaining protection against lowering rates than about giving up potential interest rate upside if rates rose. The historical graph of 3-month LIBOR below clearly illustrates the plight of investors who had ample reason to be worried about lower floating rate yields.

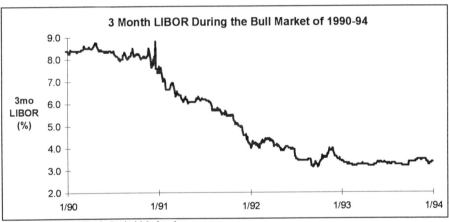

[Source: Sumitomo Bank Capital Markets]

OWCs attained a high level of popularity among investors who want downside protection for a floating rate security and are willing to put up with periodic caps to pay for this downside protection. The upside of the OWC is extremely limited since the note's maximum IRR is typically only a few basis points higher than the issuer's fixed rate note even if the coupons were set at the maximum cap levels each period. The OWC thus provided investors with protection against interest rate declines at the expense of a severely limited upside.

Analysis

The coupon behavior of the OWC note for a scenario of LIBORs is shown on page 222. The OWC coupon will never fall below the previous period coupon nor rise by more than a fixed spread over the previous coupon.

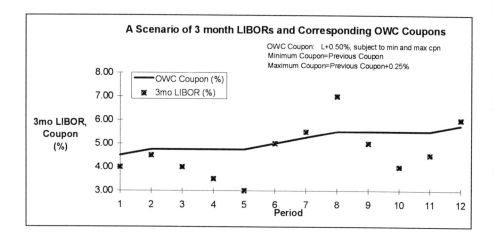

The terms of an actual OWC note are described in Exhibit 6-26. The relevant features are summarized as follows:

Issuer:	U.S. Agency
Maturity:	3 years
Coupon:	LIBOR + 0.655% subject to coupon cap and floor
Coupon cap:	Previous coupon + 0.25%
Coupon floor:	Previous coupon; first coupon at 4.655%

The majority of OWCs were issued by U.S. Agencies, although a select number of highly rated and well-known corporates were also able to find buyers for their OWCs.

Since the OWC contains embedded path-dependent options, the appropriate analysis is the simulation class of analysis.

Performance

The performance of the OWC note is calculated using LSE for a series of final expectation LIBORs and is plotted on Exhibit 6-27. The performance of the OWC is characterized by the presence of a collar on IRR. Because the note's coupon cannot drop below the previous period's coupon, the note has a minimum IRR of 4.655%, or equal to the initial coupon. Also, since the coupons cannot rise more than 25 bps per quarterly period, the maximum IRR is also constrained. In this case, the maximum IRR that can be attained is approximately 6%.

EXHIBIT 6-26 3-Year FHLB OWC Note

The coupon of LIBOR + 0.655% is significantly higher than a benchmark Agency FRN. The OWC shown in this example is quite typical of other OWC structures: the coupon can never drop below the previous coupon, and can never exceed the previous coupon plus 0.25%.

Issue Terms (Actual)	
Issuer:	Federal Home Loan Bank System
Principal amount:	US$50,000,000
Settlement date:	Apr. 21, 1994
Maturity date:	Apr. 21, 1997
Coupon paid in US$:	LIBOR + 0.655% subject to coupon cap and floor
Coupon cap:	Previous coupon + 0.25%
Coupon floor:	Previous coupon
First coupon:	4.655%
Day count basis:	Act/360
Rate reset and payment dates:	Coupon rates reset and pay quarterly. Payment dates Jan. 21, Apr. 21, July 21, Oct. 21. First coupon paid on July 21, 1994.
LIBOR determination:	3-month LIBOR for coupon rate determination resets quarterly two New York and London business days prior to reset date. Source: Telerate Page 3747.
Issue price:	100.00%

Risk

Interest Rate Risk. The deterministic and simulation duration of the note is calculated for a variety of LSE scenarios and plotted on Exhibit 6-28. The risk of the OWC can be examined by interpreting the deterministic duration. For low interest rate scenarios, the base case scenarios will result in all of the natural coupons being lower than the coupon floor, and hence the note would behave as a 3-year maturity fixed rate note with a duration of 2.7. For very high interest rate scenarios, all the future LIBORs will result in natural coupons above the coupon cap; hence, the note would again behave as a 3-year fixed rate note with a duration of 2.7. For intermediate interest rate scenarios, some of the coupons of the note can float off the coupon floor yet not exceed the coupon cap, and the duration of the note is expected to be in between that of a fixed and floating rate note. This is indeed the observed deterministic duration result.

The actual duration of the note as represented by the simulation duration is qualitatively similar to the deterministic duration with some quantitative differences. For most scenarios, the actual duration of the OWC note is relatively stable and remains within a duration range of 1 to 2. The actual duration does drop

EXHIBIT 6-27 IRR of OWC Note

The performance of the OWC is similar to the CFRN due to the presence of the coupon floor and cap. The two features of the OWC note are the coupon floor, which is initially the first coupon, and the coupon cap, which is limited by the 25 bps per quarter rise.

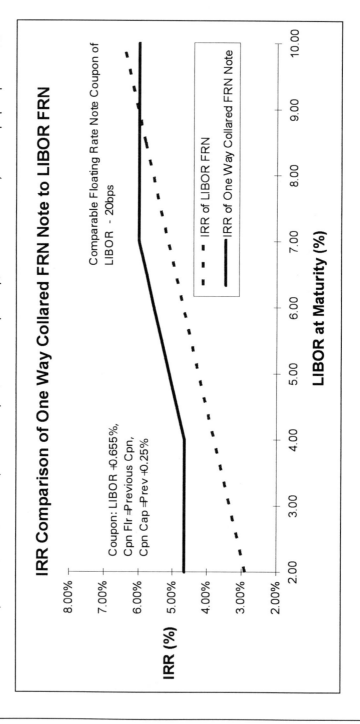

IRR Comparison of One Way Collared FRN Note to LIBOR FRN

Comparable Floating Rate Note Coupon of LIBOR - 20bps

Coupon: LIBOR +0.655%,
Cpn Flr =Previous Cpn,
Cpn Cap =Prev +0.25%

- - - IRR of LIBOR FRN
—— IRR of One Way Collared FRN Note

IRR (%)

LIBOR at Maturity (%)

EXHIBIT 6-28   Duration of OWC Note

The deterministic duration of the note shows a fixed duration of 2.7 for high and low interest rate scenarios. This reflects the fully-capped or -floored nature of the coupons for these scenarios, resulting in the note's behaving like a fixed rate note. For intermediate interest rate scenarios, the duration drops to reflect the floating of the coupons. Simulation duration results are similar to deterministic duration, but vary more smoothly and remain within a stable duration range for the interest rate scenarios selected.

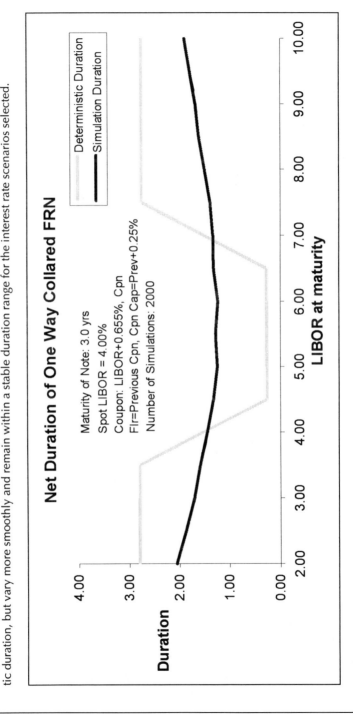

Net Duration of One Way Collared FRN

Maturity of Note: 3.0 yrs
Spot LIBOR = 4.00%
Coupon: LIBOR+0.655%, Cpn
Flr=Previous Cpn, Cpn Cap=Prev+0.25%
Number of Simulations: 2000

Legend:
- Deterministic Duration
- Simulation Duration

Y-axis: Duration (0.00, 1.00, 2.00, 3.00, 4.00)
X-axis: LIBOR at maturity (2.00, 3.00, 4.00, 5.00, 6.00, 7.00, 8.00, 9.00, 10.00)

to a minimum for intermediate scenarios in which all the base case coupons are expected to float, but that minimum duration of one is still considerably larger than the zero duration of a LIBOR FRN.

The OWC note attests to the power of the simulation analysis. By conducting simulation analysis, the investor is able to capture the risk of the note without having to understand the full details of the structure of the embedded option, which in the case of the OWC note is a path-dependent option. This capability makes the simulation analysis a very powerful tool for understanding risk.

Volatility Risk.   The volatility risk of the OWC is calculated by performing a 3000 run simulation analysis of the volatility duration with the same base case scenarios as the durational calculations above. The result of the volatility risk is plotted in Exhibit 6-29. The volatility risk of the OWC is quite straightforward to comprehend.

For low interest rate scenarios, the OWC exhibits high negative volatility duration. This is due to the high vega of the coupon floors (which the note is long). When rates are low, the index is close to the option strike, resulting in high option vega and a comparatively large gain in note value for an incremental increase in volatility.

For higher interest rate scenarios, the vega of the floor options decreases as the indices move further away from the strike. At the same time, the coupon cap option (which the note is short) vega begins to increase as the index approaches the cap strike (of 25 bps increase each period). The result is that for higher interest rate scenarios, the note will lose value for an incremental increase volatility due to the increasing vega of the cap, and thus the volatility duration of the note becomes positive. Note that for very high interest rate scenarios (not shown), the volatility duration of the note would again decrease as the index moves away from the strike.

The magnitude of the volatility risk of the OWC is comparable to the risk of CapFRNs or FFRNs of comparable maturity.

STRUCTURE VII. INDEX AMORTIZING NOTES

Investor purpose: Obtain high upfront yield in the expectation that rates will remain low enough for the note to be called after the expiration of the lockout period.

Risk: In a rising rate environment, the note maturity will extend, leaving the investor with a note whose coupon is considerably lower than a comparable full-term fixed note. The investor thus loses value due to both the durational losses as well as to the higher duration due to the maturity extension.

EXHIBIT 6-29 Volatility Duration of OWC Note

The negative volatility duration for low interest rate scenarios represents the gain in value of the coupon floor for higher volatility. For higher interest rate scenarios, the positive volatility duration represents the gain in value of the shorted coupon cap for higher volatility, resulting in the OWC note losing value.

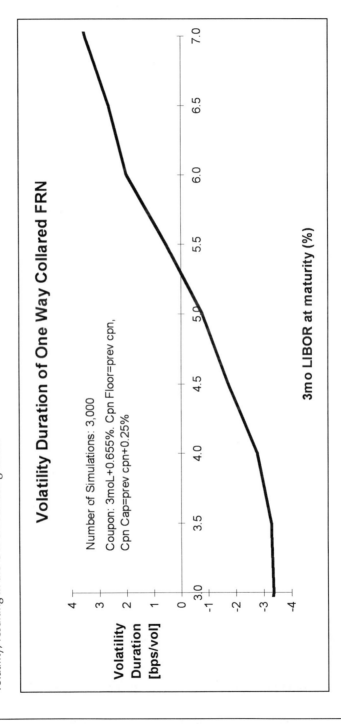

Volatility Duration of One Way Collared FRN

Number of Simulations: 3,000

Coupon: 3moL+0.655%. Cpn Floor=prev cpn, Cpn Cap=prev cpn+0.25%

Volatility Duration [bps/vol]

3mo LIBOR at maturity (%)

Equivalent investor position: Long fixed or floating rate note, short pre-payment option.

Although this book does not include discussions of mortgage derivative products such as interest-only (IO) and principal-only (PO) strips (which are not structured notes), the index amortizing notes (IANs) are included because unlike IOs and POs, IANs are created via the swaps market and qualify as structured notes. The IANs are different from typical mortgage products in two ways: the amortization rate for various interest rate scenarios is fully specified on an amortization table, and they are not backed by any mortgages or underlying assets. Because they are not backed by prepayable assets, IANs do not contain the prepayment uncertainty that is embedded in standard mortgage products. If the amortization index reaches a certain level on a specified date, the amount of amortization is defined on a lookup table and cannot be changed. IANs thus remove prepayment uncertainty for investors who like the yield of mortgage products but wish to quantify the prepayment risk. Unlike mortgage products, IANs are not backed by any underlying assets and are of the same form as other structured notes, i.e., backed by the faith and credit of the issuer. For this reason, most investors purchase IANs issued by the U.S. Agencies for their high credit rating.

A sample IAN has the following form:

Issuer:	U.S. Agency
Maturity:	5 years maximum life, 1 year minimum lockout. Maturity subject to call condition.
Coupon:	Fixed at 4.25% (1-year T-bill rate + 100 bps)
Call condition:	The note is called in its entirety if 3-month LIBOR does not rise by more than 100 bps from the current level at the end of one year. Otherwise, the note remains outstanding for the full five years.

The above note illustrates the basic characteristics of an IAN. The issuer is typically a U.S. Agency, since most purchasers of IANs are mortgage buyers who prefer the AAA credit of U.S. Agencies. The maturity of the note is contingent upon a certain call condition, in this case the level of 3-month LIBOR one year from the issue date.

History

IANs grew in popularity in the bull market of 1990–94. They were originally created to simulate the performance of mortgages. As more investors became acquainted with mortgage products, there arose a demand for synthetic mortgage products such as IANs. Like the mortgage products that they simulate, IANs perform extremely well for the investor in a low and stable rate environment where forward rates predict sharply higher rates but where investor expectation is for rates to remain low. The IAN coupon is typically fixed and are large relative to the notes maturing on the first call date, but can be significantly lower relative to notes maturing on the stated maximum maturity date. The major risk of IANs to investors is the extension risk. In high interest rate environments, IANs typically will extend to full maturity. Thus, in addition to durational losses associated with higher rates, the investor also owns a longer maturity note, which has higher duration.

In the aftermath of the Federal Reserve's interest rate hikes of the first quarter of 1994, demand for IANs and other synthetic mortgage products dropped precipitously. Part of this is due to the linkage of IANs to the mortgage market, which was decimated by market illiquidity and mortgage prepayment extensions that rendered previous prepayment assumptions obsolete. As of the middle of 1994, the IAN market has yet to mount a sustained recovery from this lull.

Analysis

The terms of an actual IAN are provided in Exhibit 6-30. As mentioned, the terms of this IAN differ from most IANs because of the one-time all-or-nothing call feature. Most IANs have a graduated amortization schedule, which stipulates the amount of principal that is amortized at each quarterly reset. The note in the exhibit was selected for clarity to illustrate the concept of analyzing the performance and risk.

Performance

The performance of an IAN can be calculated for a range of LIBORs at the end of 3/4 years. This result is seen in the deterministic IRR in Exhibit 6-31. The deterministic IRR shows that the IAN would perform well until LIBOR at the end of 3/4 years exceeds the LIBOR call threshold of 5.00%. Since the note extends at 1% for the last 2 1/4 years, the IRR is seen to drop sharply to approximately 2% once LIBOR-in-3/4-years crosses the call threshold.

The actual expected performance of the note can be observed via the simulation IRR. Qualitatively, the simulation IRR is in agreement with the deterministic IRR, with some key differences. The actual expected performance of the note will deviate from the deterministic IRR because the expected performance includes results of deviations from the base case scenario. Therefore, the expected performance is reflected by the simulation

EXHIBIT 6-30 3 Non-Call 3/4-year Agency IAN

This note is somewhat different from the typical IAN because its amortization is a one time all-or-nothing event.

Issue Terms (Actual)	
Issuer:	Federal Home Loan Bank
Principal amount:	US$35,000,000
Settlement date:	Mar. 7, 1994
Maturity date:	Mar. 7, 1997. Callable one time on Dec. 7, 1994 based on CALL CONDITION.
Coupon paid in US$:	3/7/94–12/6/94: LIBOR + 1.40%
	12/7/94–3/7/97: 1.00% if not called
CALL CONDITION:	On Dec. 7, 1994, the note will be called in its entirety if 3-month LIBOR as of 11 A.M. London time 10 New York and London business days prior to Dec. 7, 1994, is AT or BELOW 5.00%.
Day count basis:	3/7/94–12/6/94: Act/360
	12/7/94–3/7/97: 30/360 (if not called)
Rate reset and payment dates:	Coupon rates reset and pay quarterly. Payment dates Mar. 7, June 7, Sept. 7, Dec. 7. First coupon paid on June 7, 1994.
3-month LIBOR determination:	3-month LIBOR for coupon rate determination resets quarterly two New York and London business days prior to reset date. Source: Telerate Page 3750.
Issue price:	100.00%

IRR, which begins to decrease prior to the base case scenario exceeding the call threshold. The expected performance of the note changes smoothly and less dramatically than predicted by the deterministic IRR. In the limit of high interest rates, the asymptotic IRR would be approximately 2%.

Risk

Interest Rate Risk.   The risk of the IAN is not entirely obvious to most investors. At first glance, the investor's risk is mainly to the 3-month LIBOR in 3/4 years. In reality, the note has exposure to a variety of different rates.

To fully understand the risk, the IAN will be examined via KTRD. The risk of the note can be clarified by the following two scenarios:

Scenario 1. LIBOR ≤ 5% in 3/4 years, and the note is called.   For this scenario, the risk of the note is clear since the note becomes a 3/4-year maturity FRN. The DR is thus the 3/4-year Treasury, while the coupon's LIBOR

EXHIBIT 6-31   Deterministic and Simulation IRR of the IAN

The performance of the note as portrayed by the deterministic IRR shows that the note would perform well for rising LIBOR until the threshold of extension at LIBOR = 5%. Beyond 5%, the investor's IRR is expected to drop sharply to approximately 2%. In reality, the note would perform somewhat differently, with the expected return showing a smooth drop-off prior to the note actually being extended.

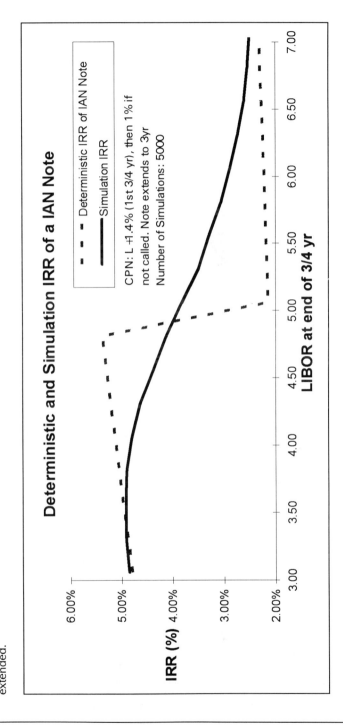

Deterministic and Simulation IRR of a IAN Note

- - - Deterministic IRR of IAN Note
——— Simulation IRR

CPN: L +1.4% (1st 3/4 yr), then 1% if
not called. Note extends to 3yr
Number of Simulations: 5000

LIBOR at end of 3/4 yr

IRR (%)

based cash flows have an IR that is also equal to the 3/4-year Treasury rate. The net KTRD spectrum is then as follows:

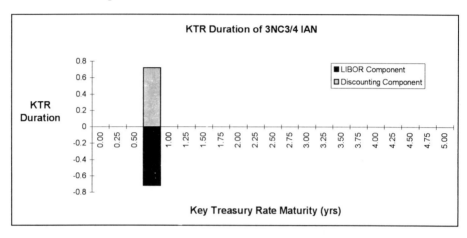

The above chart shows the risk for a 3/4-year LIBOR FRN. For this scenario, the IAN has zero yield curve risk and zero duration since the LIBOR contribution to the durational spectrum cancels out the discounting term contribution, resulting in a net duration neutral note.

Scenario 2. LIBOR > 5% in 3/4 years, and the note extends. For this scenario, the note would be certain to extend in maturity, resulting in the following KTR durational profile:

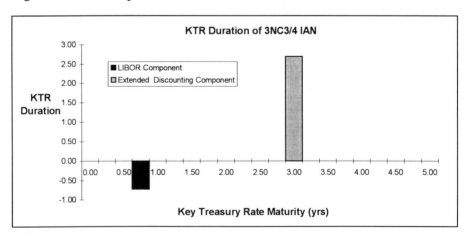

The above chart shows the durational profile of the three-NC3/4 note, which is fully extended out to three years of maturity. The note now has yield curve risk due to the mismatch between the 3-year final maturity discounting rate and the 3/4-year LIBOR floating coupon.

In reality, the note has call uncertainty and would exhibit a behavior that is a combination of the above two scenarios. This is shown in the graph below:

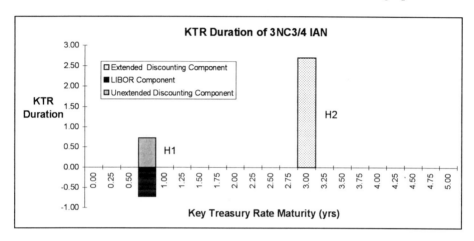

H1 and H2 represent the height of the discounting components of the note. H1 represents the probability that the note will be fully called in 3/4 years, while H2 represents the probability of extension to three years. Both H1 and H2 are normalized to their respective maturity durations.

Employing simulation, one can find the behavior of H1 and H2 as a function of the call condition, i.e., LIBOR in 3/4 years. The result of 2000 simulation runs are shown below.

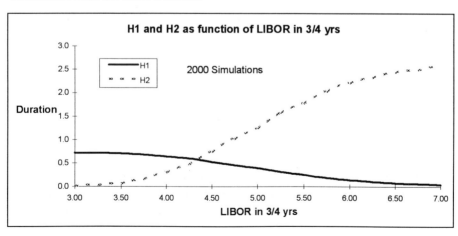

This graph shows that in addition to the KTRD profile, the height of H1 and H2 are also dependent upon 3-month LIBOR at the end of 3/4 years.

The combined KTRD of the note is plotted in Exhibit 6-32. For low interest rate scenarios, the entire KTRD spectrum of the note tends to zero amplitude because the note is more likely to be below the call threshold and thus be called. If the IAN were called, it would have behaved like a LIBOR FRN that has a zero net duration. For high interest rate scenarios, the note would more likely exceed the call threshold and not be called. The KTRD spectrum would thus tend towards the spectrum shown in Scenario 2 above.

The IAN contains an additional complication that will significantly affect the risk characteristics discussed above. If the scenario is such that LIBOR is exactly 5% in 3/4 years, the note will be called. For a 1 bp movement in LIBOR, i.e., if LIBOR were 5.01%, the note would undergo a severe change in character by extending out to three years. In addition to the usual durational extension, the note has extended at a sub-market coupon rate of 1% for the last 2 1/4 years. Thus, the note loses considerably more in value than a simple maturity extension would imply. In fact, the note would lose approximately 10% of value due to this 1 bp increase. Thus, there would be a sharp durational spike of a height of 1000 in the durational spectrum of H1 for LIBOR = 5% in 3/4 years.

The sharp spike in deterministic duration around the call threshold manifests itself in the simulation duration as shown in Exhibit 6-33. Simulation duration is seen to rise prior to the call threshold being reached, eventually reaching an expected duration of approximately five before decreasing towards the asymptotic level of two. This behavior is due to the effect of this rapidly changing characteristic around the call threshold. The note's maximum duration of five is twice as high as one might expect by simply examining the deterministic duration.

Volatility Risk. The volatility risk of the IAN is calculated by performing a 5000 run simulation analysis of the volatility duration. The result is plotted on Exhibit 6-34. Like the accrual note, the volatility risk of the IAN is not intuitively obvious and must be carefully interpreted.

For low interest rate scenarios, the note exhibits positive volatility duration. Since these base case scenarios predict the note would be called at the end of 3/4 years (LIBOR < 5%), a higher volatility would generate a higher probability of LIBOR exceeding 5%, resulting in the extension of the note. It has been demonstrated that an extension of this particular note would

EXHIBIT 6-32 KTRD Spectrum of 3NC3/4 IAN for Various LIBOR-at-End-of-3/4-Year Scenarios

The higher the LIBOR-at-end-of-3/4-year scenario, the more likely the IAN is to extend. The asymptotic duration for high interest rate scenarios is a KTRD of +2.7 with respect to the 3-year maturity Treasury, and −0.7 with respect to the 3/4-year maturity Treasury. For low interest rate scenarios, the note will be more likely to be called; thus, the note's behavior tends towards that of a LIBOR FRN, i.e., zero net duration.

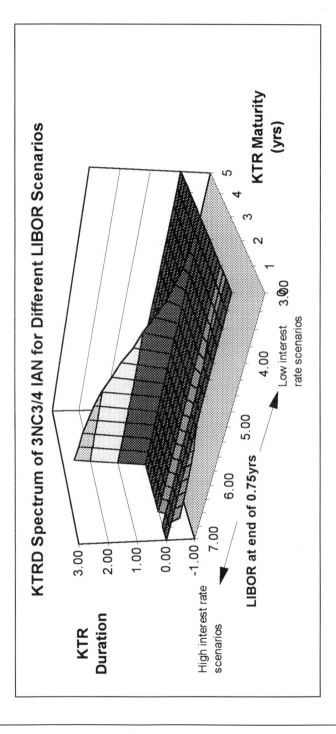

KTRD Spectrum of 3NC3/4 IAN for Different LIBOR Scenarios

EXHIBIT 6-33   Deterministic and Simulation Duration of the IAN

Deterministic duration shows that the note would behave like a floating rate note with zero duration until the extension threshold of LIBOR > 5% has been breached. Beyond that, it is expected that the note would behave as a fixed note of a duration of approximately two. In reality, the note begins to gain duration even at low rates and the duration climbs to a maximum of five before dropping lower. As discussed, this is due to the large spike in duration around the LIBOR = 5% call threshold.

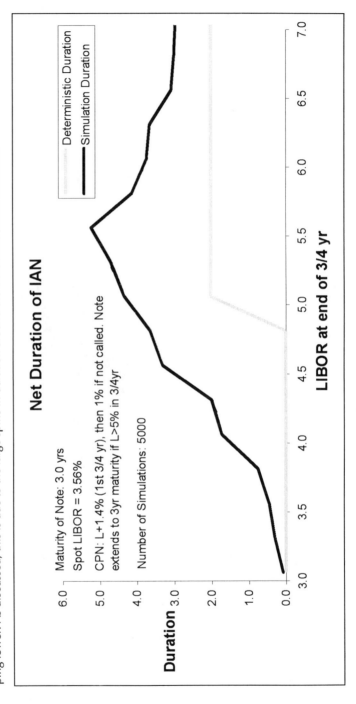

Net Duration of IAN

Maturity of Note: 3.0 yrs

Spot LIBOR = 3.56%

CPN: L+1.4% (1st 3/4 yr), then 1% if not called. Note extends to 3yr maturity if L>5% in 3/4yr

Number of Simulations: 5000

Deterministic Duration

Simulation Duration

Duration

LIBOR at end of 3/4 yr

EXHIBIT 6-34 Volatility Duration of IAN

The volatility duration of the IAN is positive for low interest rate scenarios, signifying that a higher volatility would bring LIBOR at the end of 3/4 years closer to the 5% call threshold. As the base case scenario exceeds the call threshold, the note is more likely to be extended. Thus, for high interest rate scenarios, an increase in volatility would more likely bring LIBOR at the end of 3/4 years back to below the call threshold, resulting in a gain. The volatility duration for high interest rate scenarios is thus negative, representing a gain in note value if volatility increases.

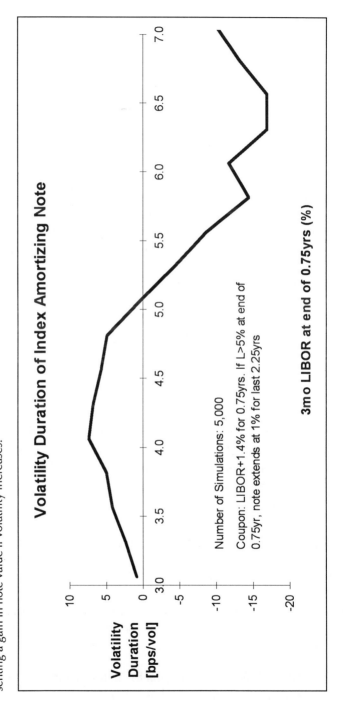

Volatility Duration of Index Amortizing Note

Number of Simulations: 5,000

Coupon: LIBOR+1.4% for 0.75yrs. If L>5% at end of 0.75yr, note extends at 1% for last 2.25yrs

3mo LIBOR at end of 0.75yrs (%)

result in a significant decrease in expected value. Thus, an increase in volatility for these low interest rate scenarios would result in a lower expected value of the note, and thus a positive duration.

For high interest rate scenarios, the reverse of the above is true. Since these base case scenarios would predict an extension of the note, a higher volatility would generate a higher probability that LIBOR would be lower than 5%, resulting in a call. Thus, an increase in volatility for these high interest rate scenarios would result in a higher expected value of the note, and thus a negative duration. For very high interest rate scenarios, the volatility duration of the note would decrease but still remain negative since any increase in volatility can only result in a higher probability of call.

The volatility risk of the IAN with a maximum magnitude of approximately 20 is quite high for a 3-year maturity note. This high risk is due to the rapid change in the characteristics of the note close to the LIBOR-at-end-of-3/4-year = 5% scenario.

The results of this section showed that the IAN contains both yield curve risk as well as major complications due to the rapid change in note characteristics between extension and call. These complications result in a larger-than-expected interest rate and volatility risk.

D. QUANTO NOTES

This class of second generation structures provides investors with a cross-country play on rates. Investors interested in either hedging or speculating in the interest rate of another country but who wish to be paid in the native currency purchase Quanto notes.

STRUCTURE VIII. LIBOR DIFFERENTIAL (QUANTO) NOTES

Investor purpose: Obtain rate play of one currency, but paid in another currency.
Risk: Rates of other nations move according to dynamics that may not be obvious to a typical domestic buyer. Interest rate risk is now in two markets.

LIBOR differential, or Quanto, notes arose from investor desire to obtain either a hedge or a rate play in a non-domestic interest rate. The typical investor requires that the payoff from this rate play be made in the native currency. Thus was born the Quanto note.

The basic form of a Quanto note is as follows:

Issuer:	AA Bank
Maturity:	2 years
Coupon:	9.11% minus 6-month Sterling LIBOR
	paid in US$
6-month Sterling LIBOR:	5.375%
Indicative first coupon:	3.735%

The Quanto note described above is tailored for an investor with a bullish view on Sterling rates. This particular structure provides a coupon that is enhanced if Sterling LIBOR should drop further than its spot rate of 5.375%. All the cash flows of this note are in US$. Only the index itself is based on a non-domestic currency. This example illustrates the simplest variant of the Quanto note.

History

The bullish LIBOR Quanto note was popular from 1992 to 1994 when European rates were perceived as being extremely high and susceptible to large downward rate cuts. Most European rates were supported at extremely high levels despite the overall European recession due to the ERM system of lock-step monetary policy. Since the yield curves of these European nations were essentially flat to slightly inverted in 1992, an inverse bullish play indexed to short-term rates was possible and yielded large upfront coupons. The collapse of the ERM in the crisis of 1992 created opportunities whereby many European nations (led by Great Britain) felt free to cut rates to relieve high unemployment rates and economic recessions. As seen in the graph on page 240, the effect of the ERM crisis on European yield curves such as the Gilt curve was quite dramatic.

The upheaval in European yield curves in the aftermath of the ERM crisis had two immediate implications for the structured note arena: First, investors who purchased bullish non-German Quanto notes prior to the ERM were able to obtain significant capital gains due to the lower rates, and secondly, the yield curve of most European nations subsequently became positive with an inversion between short-term LIBOR rates and two- to three-year rates. The result of this inversion is that an inverse bullish note based on

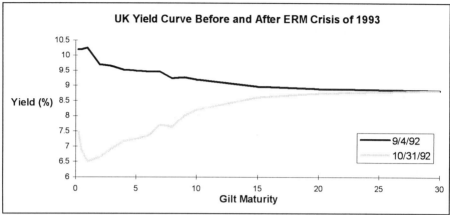

[Source: Sumitomo Bank Capital Markets]

short-term rates would produce a small initial coupon. Quanto bullish plays, which reset based on longer-term rates such as the CMS (constant maturity swap) rates, were subsequently introduced to provide both a bullish play as well as a good upfront coupon.

The three basic variants of the Quanto note are:

1. The non-domestic index is a short maturity rate such as LIBOR.
2. The non-domestic index is a longer maturity rate such as the CMS rate.
3. The coupon is linked to the sum of or differential between two non-domestic indices, e.g., $LIBOR_{UK} - LIBOR_{DM}$.

Analysis

The Quanto note contains coupons that reset based upon a non-domestic interest rate. The IR and DR would thus be based on the yield curve of different countries. In addition, if the coupon index is not a short-term rate but a longer-term rate such as the CMS, there will also be yield curve risk and the KT (or swap) RD analysis would be required to analyze the risk.

The terms of an actual Quanto note are described in Exhibit 6-35 and is summarized as follows:

Issuer: U.S. Agency
Maturity: 3 years
Coupon: 8.25% + (6-month DM LIBOR – 6-month US$ LIBOR
                                          – 3.5625%)   (in US$)

EXHIBIT 6-35 3-Year SLMA DM Quanto Note

The coupon pays the differential between 6-month DM and 6-month US$ LIBOR. All cash flows are denominated in U.S. dollars.

Issue Terms (Actual)	
Issuer:	Student Loan Marketing Association
Principal amount:	US$110,000,000
Settlement date:	Aug. 26, 1991
Maturity date:	Aug. 26, 1994
Coupon paid in US$:	4.6875% + (6-month DM LIBOR – 6-month US$ LIBOR)
Minimum coupon:	0.00%
Day count basis:	Act/360
Rate reset and payment dates:	Coupon rates reset and pay semiannually. Payment Feb. 26, Aug. 26. First coupon paid on Feb. 26, 1992.
6-month US$ LIBOR determination:	6-month US$ LIBOR for coupon rate determination resets semiannually two New York and London business days prior to reset date. Source: Telerate Page 3750.
6-month DM LIBOR determination:	6-month DM LIBOR for coupon rate determination resets semiannually two New York and Frankfurt business days prior to reset date. Source: Telerate Page 3750.
Issue price:	100.00%

The above note illustrates the concept of the Quanto note quite well. The typical issuer of the Quanto note can be a U.S. Agency or a large highly rated corporate. The coupons are reset based on the differential between the 6-month DM LIBOR and US$ LIBOR, with all cash flows denominated in U.S. dollars.

Performance

The performance of the Quanto note can be examined via the LSE analysis for different final expectation levels of 6-month DM and US$ LIBORs. The IRR of the note under different scenarios is shown in Exhibit 6-36. As expected, the note performs well in high DM and low U.S. interest rate scenarios.

EXHIBIT 6-36 IRR Performance of DM-US$ Quanto Note

The note performs well for lower US$ rate scenarios and higher DM rate scenarios.

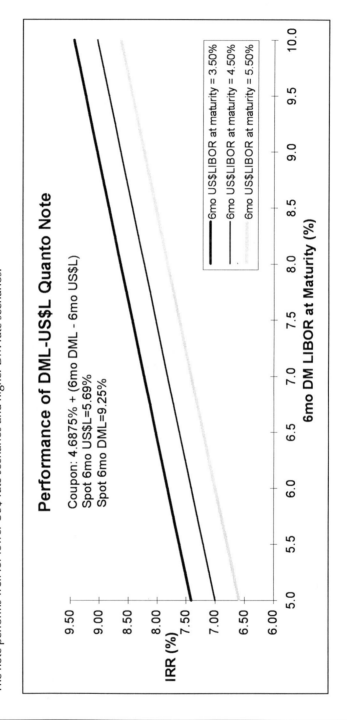

Performance of DML-US$L Quanto Note

Coupon: 4.6875% + (6mo DML - 6mo US$L)
Spot 6mo US$L=5.69%
Spot 6mo DML=9.25%

6mo US$LIBOR at maturity = 3.50%
6mo US$LIBOR at maturity = 4.50%
6mo US$LIBOR at maturity = 5.50%

6mo DM LIBOR at Maturity (%)

IRR (%)

Risk

Interest Rate Risk. The interest rate risk of the Quanto note can be found by performing KTRD analysis.

Step 1. Identify component risks. The three risk components of this note are:

a. Discounting
b. DM LIBOR
c. US$ LIBOR

Steps 2 and 3. Identify KTR and KTRD of components:

a. Discounting: The DR of the 3-year Quanto note is the 3-year Treasury rate. The KTRD with respect to the 3-year Treasury rate is that of a 3-year fixed rate note, or 2.7.
b. DM LIBOR. The IR representing the aggregate of three years of DM LIBOR coupon flows is the 3-year DM swap rate. The KTRD with respect to the 3-year DM swap rate is –2.7. The sign is negative since increases in DM rates will result in higher coupons and thus higher PV.
c. US$ LIBOR. Likewise, the IR representing the aggregate of three years of US$ LIBOR coupons is the 3-year swap rate, which corresponds to a KTR of the 3-year maturity Treasury rate. The KTRD with respect to the 3-year Treasury rate is +2.7. The sign is positive to reflect the inverse US$ LIBOR component of the coupon.

Step 4. Combine all components. The KTRD spectra of the note are plotted in Exhibits 6-37(a) and (b). As noted before, *two* KTRD spectra are needed: a U.S. KTRD, and a German KTRD. The note contains interest rate risk in the form of KTRD with respect to both the 3-year U.S. rate as well as the 3-year German rate. The interest risk of the Quanto note can be summarized in the following table:

Key Treasury (Swap) Rate	Key Treasury (Swap) Rate Duration
3-year US$ Treasury rate	+5.4
3-year DM CMS rate	–2.7

The large KTRD with respect to the U.S. rate is due to the combination of the inverse US$ LIBOR coupon and the DRD. Thus, this note will perform well in a bullish U.S. market even if German rates remain unchanged. Since German rates actually rose significantly during the life of this note while U.S. rates dropped, this note was able to perform quite well for its investors.

EXHIBIT 6-37(a)   U.S. Component of DM-US$ LIBOR Differential Quanto Note

The overall duration is large due to the superposition of the discounting duration and the LIBOR duration.

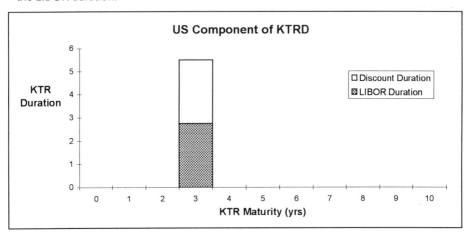

EXHIBIT 6-37(b)   German KSRD Component of DM-US$ LIBOR Differential Quanto Note

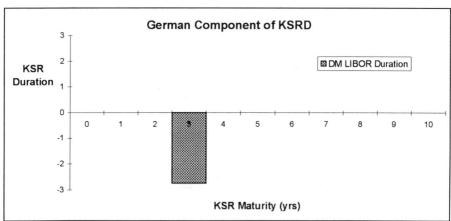

Step 5. Monitor changes in KTRD. The KTRD of this note will be altered as the note approaches maturity. The KTRs will shift down the maturity spectrum and the associated KTRDs will decrease in height, reflecting both the shorter maturity discounting index and the lower durational effects of a shorter maturity.

The overall risk of Quanto notes must be carefully monitored by investors since they contain risk exposure to multiple KTRD spectra: a KTRD spectrum for the domestic interest rate market, and one (or more) for the non-domestic floating rate index (indices).

Volatility Risk. The volatility risk of the Quanto note will be interpreted by examining the result of a 10,000 run simulation analysis of the volatility duration. For high final differential scenarios, the resulting volatility duration is close to zero. Since the strike of the zero coupon floor option (which the note is long) is at DM LIBOR − US$ LIBOR = −4.6875%, these scenarios result in differentials that are still far from the strike level, and thus the vega of the option is quite low. This low vega translates into low volatility risk for these high final differential scenarios.

For lower and negative final differential scenarios, the differential begins to approach the zero coupon floor option strike. As this occurs, the vega of the floor option will increase, resulting in a rising magnitude of volatility duration. Since the note is long the option, the result is a larger magnitude of negative volatility duration.

As with the CMT-LIBOR differential note, a high degree of correlation between DM LIBOR and US$ LIBOR effectively ties the movement of the two indices closer together and reduces the likelihood of the divergence of the two indices beyond the base case scenario. Thus, a high correlation will reduce the probability of the differential moving away from the base case scenario and closer to the floor strike, resulting in lower volatility risk. This is reflected by the results shown on Exhibit 6-38.

E. UNUSUAL LEVERAGE

This class of second generation structures include structures that pay off based on unusual leverage. Although all the structures discussed thus far can be created in leveraged form, the term *unusual leverage* is used in this book to refer to leveraged payoffs that differ from linear leverage. A representative structure of this class is the power note.

EXHIBIT 6-38   Volatility Risk of DM-US$ LIBOR Quanto Differential Note

The graph shows the result of a 10,000 run simulation analysis. The volatility duration is negative for all scenarios since the zero coupon floor option (which the note is long) gains in value for incremental increases in volatility. For low interest rate differential scenarios, the magnitude of the volatility duration of the note is seen to increase. Higher final differential scenarios will result in the indices moving further away from the floor, hence lower vega and lower volatility duration. Higher correlation produces lower volatility duration.

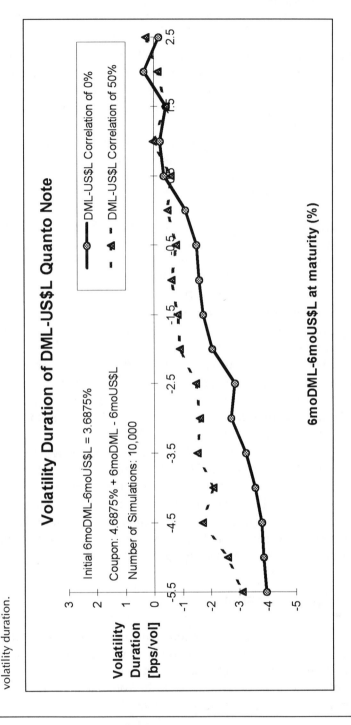

Volatility Duration of DML-US$L Quanto Note

Initial 6moDML-6moUS$L = 3.6875%
Coupon: 4.6875% + 6moDML - 6moUS$L
Number of Simulations: 10,000

DML-US$L Correlation of 0%
DML-US$L Correlation of 50%

Volatility Duration [bps/vol]

6moDML-6moUS$L at maturity (%)

246

STRUCTURE IX. POWER NOTES

Investor purpose: Obtain extremely high return over short period of time.

Risk: Power notes have extremely large duration and negative convexity. The highly leveraged nature of power notes introduces very high risk.

Equivalent investor position: Long fixed rate note, short highly leveraged (and changing) amount of FRN, long highly leveraged (and changing) amount of out-of-the-money interest rate cap options.

Power notes are structured notes that pay a coupon that is linked to a power of the underlying index. A typical power note has the following structure:

Issuer: AA
Maturity: 2 years
Coupon: $C -$ (3-month LIBOR squared)
Minimum coupon: 0.00%

The above structure illustrates the features of power notes. The coupon constant C is large enough such that the initial coupon is extremely large. The downside risk of this note is that, if rates do rise, the inverse squared formula causes the coupon to decrease rapidly towards zero. The investor must thus be willing to face extremely high durational risk when considering power notes.

History

The power note is a relatively rare structure that was purchased on a custom-tailored basis by investors. Because the power note was able to provide a high coupon at a high risk, the typical power note investor is highly sophisticated and driven by the need to generate high returns.

Analysis

Exhibit 6-39 describes the indicative terms of the power note outlined above in greater detail. The salient features are:

1. Issuer is a AA bank. Highly leveraged structures such as this are typically issued by highly rated issuers because the typical investor does not wish to simultaneously manage a credit risk and a large rate risk.

EXHIBIT 6-39   Indicative Terms of a Power Note

Issue Terms (Indicative)

Issuer:	AA Bank
Principal amount:	US$25,000,000
Settlement date:	Mar. 1, 1994
Maturity date:	Mar. 1, 1996
Coupon paid in US$:	25.00% – (3-month LIBOR)^2
Day count basis:	Act/360
Current 3-month LIBOR:	3.75%
Indicative first coupon:	10.94%
Minimum coupon:	0.00%
Rate reset and payment dates:	Rate resets quarterly. Coupon payment Mar. 1, June 1, Sept. 1, Dec. 1. First coupon paid on June 1, 1994.
3-month US$ LIBOR determination:	The 3-month US$ LIBOR shall be the 3-month LIBOR on determination date. Determination date is two London business days prior to quarterly period end dates. Source: Telerate Page 3750.
Issue price:	100.00%

   2. Maturity is two years. The typical maturity of a power note is quite short.
   3. The investor receives a large initial coupon of 10.94%. This is also typical of power notes, which initially produce extremely high coupons in return for the high risks.

Due to the power note's highly leveraged nature, a small change in LIBOR would result in a large change in the coupon. The presence of the zero coupon floor option is thus an integral component of the risk analysis. The simulation class of analysis is thus required to fully analyze the risk of the note.

Performance

The coupon behavior of the power note is calculated in Exhibit 6-40 and illustrates the interest rate risk described above. The investor receives a very high coupon if rates remain low, but the coupon advantage over a benchmark LIBOR FRN shrinks rapidly as rates increase. For the note in question, the investor would receive zero coupon if LIBOR exceeds 5%. Exhibit 6-40 also illustrates the convex nature of the coupon behavior in the shape of the coupon curve.

EXHIBIT 6-40   Coupon of Power Note

Although the coupon can never drop to below 0.00%, the principal can be at risk due to the negative accruals that are tabulated and netted against the next coupon or principal (if any negative accruals remain at maturity). Zero coupon occurs when LIBOR exceeds 5%.

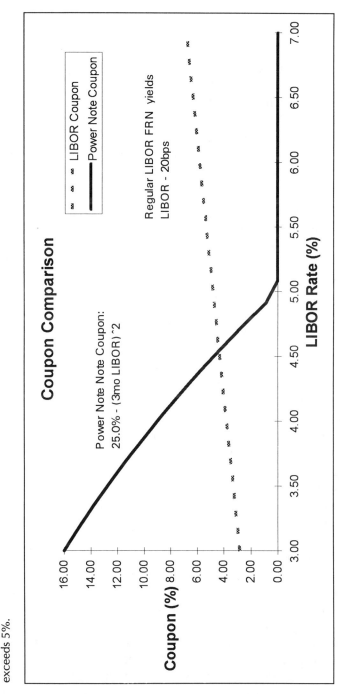

Coupon Comparison

Power Note Note Coupon:
25.0% - (3mo LIBOR)^2

Regular LIBOR FRN yields
LIBOR - 20bps

· · · LIBOR Coupon
—— Power Note Coupon

The IRR of the power note is shown on Exhibit 6-41 using LSE to project a set of final expectation 3-month LIBORs. For low interest rate scenarios, the note produces a high level of IRR. The yield advantage of the power note over a benchmark LIBOR FRN rapidly declines as interest rates rise. The breakeven LIBOR-at-maturity scenario at which the performance of the power note and a LIBOR FRN are equal is 5.5%. For higher interest rate scenarios, the return of the power note will further lag that of a LIBOR FRN.

Risk

Interest Rate Risk. Since LIBOR squared increases at a higher rate for higher levels of LIBOR, it is expected that the note would exhibit higher levels of interest rate duration for higher interest rate scenarios. This is reflected by the deterministic duration calculations in Exhibit 6-42. The duration increases until the final LIBOR reaches 5%. For final LIBOR scenarios greater than 5%, more coupons reach the zero coupon floor, resulting in a decline in the deterministic duration. For high interest rate scenarios, the duration will approach the asymptotic duration, which is that of a 2-year zero coupon note, or a duration of two.

The real duration as reflected by simulation duration shows a much more gradual increase in duration than predicted by the deterministic duration. The decrease in duration as more LIBORs are floored at zero is also reflected by the simulation duration, although not in as dramatic a fashion as the deterministic duration. For very high interest rate scenarios, the actual duration will likewise approach the asymptotic duration of two.

The 2-year power note exhibits a maximum expected duration of approximately 14, which is higher than the duration of even a 30-year Treasury bond. This illustrates the key feature of the power note: high risk and high return.

Volatility Risk. The volatility risk of the power note is calculated by a 5000 run simulation analysis of the volatility duration and is graphed on Exhibit 6-43. The volatility risk of the note stems from the embedded zero coupon floor option (which the note is long).

For higher interest rate scenarios, the LIBOR indices begin to approach the zero coupon strike. Since the option vega increases as the index approaches the strike, the embedded zero coupon options would gain in value for higher volatility, resulting in negative volatility duration. The magnitude of the volatility duration would increase towards a maximum, eventually reversing

EXHIBIT 6-41   IRR of Power Note

The return of the power note, as expected, drops as 3-month US$ LIBOR rises. The breakeven point occurs when rates have have risen to approximately 5.75% at maturity, which exceeds the level at which the power note coupons become zero. This is due to the fact that the investor has a high upfront coupon of 10.94%, which acts as a cushion against the rapid drop in coupon. The note thus greatly outperforms a comparable FRN in low interest rate scenarios, but rapidly loses yield as rates rise.

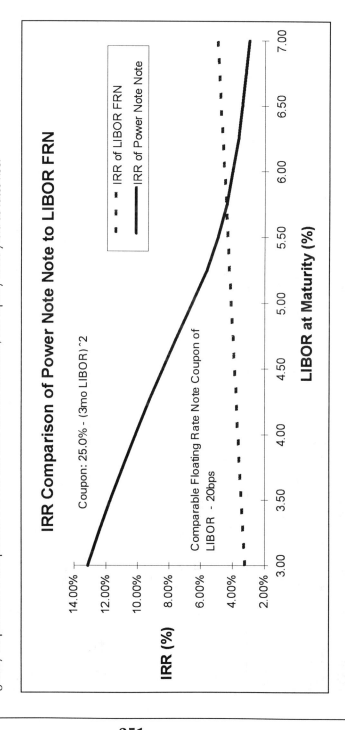

IRR Comparison of Power Note Note to LIBOR FRN

Coupon: 25.0% - (3mo LIBOR)^2

Comparable Floating Rate Note Coupon of
LIBOR - 20bps

- - - IRR of LIBOR FRN
— IRR of Power Note Note

IRR (%)

14.00%
12.00%
10.00%
8.00%
6.00%
4.00%
2.00%

3.00   3.50   4.00   4.50   5.00   5.50   6.00   6.50   7.00

LIBOR at Maturity (%)

EXHIBIT 6-42   Simulation and Deterministic Duration of Power Note

The duration of the power note is very high, reflecting the leveraged risks inherent in power notes. The duration increases with higher rates until some coupons hit the zero coupon floor. The duration will continue to decrease for higher rates until all coupons are set to zero, at which time the note behaves as a 2-year zero coupon bond with a duration of two. Simulation duration is shown with the deterministic duration due to the presence of the zero coupon floor, which can contribute significantly to the behavior of the note.

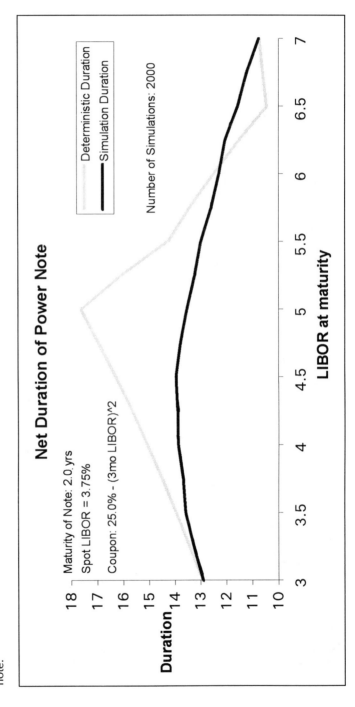

Net Duration of Power Note

Maturity of Note: 2.0 yrs
Spot LIBOR = 3.75%
Coupon: 25.0% - (3mo LIBOR)^2

Number of Simulations: 2000

Deterministic Duration
Simulation Duration

LIBOR at maturity

Duration

EXHIBIT 6-43   Volatility Duration of Power Note

The large negative duration represents the value of the zero coupon floor. Because the LIBOR-squared index is so highly convex, the zero coupon option exhibits a large value of volatility duration.

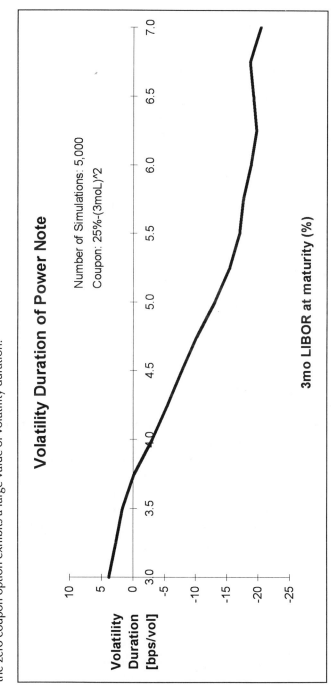

Volatility Duration of Power Note

Number of Simulations: 5,000
Coupon: 25%-(3moL)^2

Volatility
Duration
[bps/vol]

3mo LIBOR at maturity (%)

direction as the vega drops off when the index is further away from the strike. For lower interest rate scenarios, the index would also be further away from the strike, resulting in a lower magnitude of the negative volatility duration.

The unusual leverage class of structures defines both unusual performance and risk. This high risk and high performance characteristic was well illustrated by the power note. The 2-year power note provided a high potential return (10% initial coupon) if rates remained low. However, the inherent risk of the note is correspondingly high as reflected by the large interest rate duration, which reaches a maximum of 14. Likewise, the volatility risk of the note is high: a 1% decrease in volatility would result in a maximum decrease of 20–25 bps of price.

CONCLUSION

This chapter introduced the readers to the second generation structures. These structures usually contain more interest rate risk and/or volatility risk than first generation structures. Second generation structures are more varied and can thus provide performances and express views that would be impossible to accomplish with first generation structures.

The characteristics of the second generation structures are demonstrated from the performance and risk analyses. The performance of many second generation structures can be considerably higher than that of first generation structures. However, this superior performance is accompanied by higher (or different) risks. In order to fully benefit from the enhanced performance provided by second generation structures, investors must push the analysis envelope out further to fully comprehend the associated risks and pitfalls of these notes. Investors who do not perform an adequate amount of risk assessment will pay the price of being unpleasantly surprised by the changes in the performance and value of these structures once interest rate or volatility conditions change.

Cross-Category Notes

7

The explosive growth in the number of investment alternatives in the 1990s has fueled investor demand for structured notes that provide returns based on indices not typically found in the domestic fixed income market. To meet this demand, cross-category structures were created to provide returns based on the performance of other fixed income or non-fixed income markets.

Due to their cross-category nature, all the structures discussed in this chapter require extensive reviews of the regulatory, legal, tax, and accounting issues by both the issuer and the investor. As will be mentioned later in this chapter, regulators and rating agencies do not look kindly upon certain structures that can be viewed as being used to skirt the regulatory restrictions that protect investors.

MOTIVATION FOR PURCHASING CROSS-CATEGORY NOTES

Investors purchase cross-category structured notes for one of three main reasons: risk capital arbitrage, hedging requirements, and asset allocation.

Risk Capital Arbitrage

A major driving force behind the growth of the cross-category notes is risk capital utilization. In order to control the risk of the overall portfolio, investment companies require portfolio managers to allocate a portion of their overall risk capital when purchasing assets. Readers interested in further details concerning risk capital are directed to the article by Raghavan, Miller, and Askin,[1] which is briefly summarized here.

Bank risk capital requirements are based on the guidelines approved by supervisory authorities of 12 major nations (known as the Basle committee) and the Federal Reserve Bank in 1989. The guidelines assigned various risk weighting to different classes of assets. Exhibit 7-1 outlines the risk weightings of various asset classes.

The concept of risk capital arbitrage is illustrated by examining the following exhibit. Exhibit 7-1 shows that the risk capital weighting for corporate bond investments is 100%. By contrast, the risk capital requirements for OECD Bank certificates of deposit are much lower, requiring only 20% risk weighting. Investors wishing to obtain a play in corporate bonds could thus purchase a bank-issued structured CD, which provides a return tied to a basket of the desired corporate bonds and obtains the 20% risk weighting of bank CDs. This "risk capital arbitrage" is one of the main reasons why certain investors who could transact in the underlying markets prefer to purchase cross-category structured notes instead. It permits investors to leverage their limited risk capital and obtain the same play with greater efficiency.

Although these risk capital weighting guidelines were designed for banks, other investment companies use similar guidelines as a method of controlling and allocating risks among different portfolios. Thus, the use of structured notes as a means of risk capital arbitrage is by no means limited only to the banking sector.

Hedging Requirements

Many investors have found that they are restricted from participating in certain market segments. Unfortunately, these investors may own assets that require access to these markets in order to hedge and limit their risks. For example, a fund that invests in European bonds may be limited by its prospectus against investing in futures, options, or swaps. However, in order to hedge some of the foreign exchange risks on its holdings, an investor has to purchase some cross-currency swaps. If the investor is not permitted to engage in swap transactions, one alternative would be to purchase currency indexed structured notes with the embedded requisite hedge.

---

1. Raghavan, Vijay, Llewellyn Miller, and David Askin. "The New Bank Capital Guidelines and Their Implications, " pp. 329–365 in Frank J. Fabozzi and Atsuo Konishi (eds.), *Asset/Liability Management.* Chicago, IL: Probus, 1991.

EXHIBIT 7-1   Risk Capital Weighting for Various Asset Classes

Risk Weighting	Asset Type
0%	U.S. Treasury and obligations of central governments of OECD countries* Cash held Gold bullions held
20%	Cash in process of collection Claims on U.S. depository institutions and OECD banks U.S. Agency securities Agency CMO Investment in funds whose portfolio contains securities that qualify for either 0% or 20% risk weighting Municipal general obligation bonds
50%	Municipal revenue bonds
100%	Corporate bonds Equity LDC debt Claims on non-OECD banks exceeding 1 year Claims guaranteed by non-OECD central governments that do not qualify for 0% or 20% categories Plant and equipment Real estate Claims on commercial firms owned by a government Mortgage strips and residuals

Source: Fabozzi and Konishi. *Asset/Liability Management*. Probus Publishing, 1991.

* The Organization for Economic Co-operation and Development. The 25 member countries are: Australia, Austria, Belgium, Canada, Denmark, Finland, France, Germany, Greece, Iceland, Ireland, Italy, Japan, Luxembourg, Netherlands, New Zealand, Norway, Portugal, Saudi Arabia, Spain, Sweden, Switzerland, Turkey, U.K., and U.S.A.

Asset Allocation

The globalization of international capital markets in the 1990s resulted in an explosive growth in the variety of investment opportunities and possibilities. In order to take advantage of these investment opportunities, a portfolio manager must strategically allocate the limited amount of risk capital. Structured notes offer an alternative to actually investing in each of the underlying markets. Instead of investing considerable capital to start up operations in each of the targeted countries and markets, an investor can obtain the same play by purchasing cross-category structured notes with the added benefit of removing the foreign exchange risks that accompany non-domestic investments.

CROSS-CATEGORY STRUCTURE CLASSIFICATION

The four classes of cross-category notes are:

1. **Currency indexed notes (CINs).** These permit an investor to participate in the foreign exchange market via structured notes.
2. **Commodity linked notes (CLNs).** Commodity linked notes are relatively rare and are often linked to either gold and/or crude oil as good inflation hedge plays.
3. **Equity linked notes (ELNs).** These are popular among investors who are limited by risk capital weighting requirements and can better leverage their risk capital via ELNs.
4. **Bond index notes.** Investors can easily track the return of an index by purchasing a bond index note, which provides such a total return. Its use has extended (with controversy) to investors who use bond index notes to make plays in certain credit classes that are not permitted to the investor.

Risk Analysis

The risk analysis of cross-category notes is based upon expectation analysis (and its simulation counterpart). The structure's performance is calculated for a range of final expectation interest rate and currency/commodity scenarios. This chapter will perform risk and performance analysis on only the cross-currency and commodity linked notes.

The risk and performance of total return index notes such as the bond and equity index notes will not be analyzed in this book since investors who purchase these structures typically measure themselves against the total return of these indices. The performance of these total return index notes is thus measured as a spread to the desired index. Likewise, the investor's risk in purchasing an index note is limited to the credit risk of the issuer since the index risk is considered a benchmark.

STRUCTURE I. CURRENCY INDEXED NOTE (CIN)

Investor purpose: Obtain gains when FX rates move in an anticipated direction.
Risk: Investor is exposed to both FX and interest rate risk.
Equivalent investor position: Long fixed or FRN, long or short forward FX contracts and FX options.

The currency indexed note (CIN) found ready acceptance among investors because it was one of the first fixed income instruments that permitted investors to profit from their views in another market sector. The two main variants of the CIN are the coupon currency indexed note (CCIN), or the principal currency indexed note (popularly known as PERLs, or principal exchange rate linked notes[2]). The basic structure of a CIN is as follows:

Notional: $10MM
Maturity: 1 year
Coupon: 10% in US$
Principal: $100\% * [1 + 2 * (FX^{\S} - 1.50)/1.50]$
Minimum principal: 90%
Maximum principal: 120%
§FX: US$/GBP FX rate at maturity

The above terms illustrate the key features of a CIN: a small notional amount due to its highly customized nature, a short maturity of one year, and the linkage of the principal at redemption to a then-spot FX rate. Most CINs will also provide a minimum principal to limit the investor's exposure. A maximum principal return that caps the investor's maximum return may also be present.

History

Many investors purchased CINs from 1991 to 1992 to obtain gains from their views concerning FX rates. In particular, many investors focused on the predicted forward FX rates between European countries. Because the cross FX between European countries were limited to a narrow trading band by the Exchange Rate Mechanism (ERM) of the European Monetary System (EMS), investors sold options on either side of the trading band in the belief that the ERM will remain intact for a long period of time.

The onset of the ERM crisis of 1992, which eventually culminated in the effective dissolution of the ERM also resulted in many investors suffering large losses from CINs. The historical Lira/DM FX rate below illustrates the state of the ERM prior to and after the crisis of September 1992. Prior to September 1992, most European-to-DM FXs traded within a specified band. The ERM crisis resulted in the effective dissolution of the trading band.

---

2. The term *PERL* was coined by Morgan Stanley, which originated the CIN.

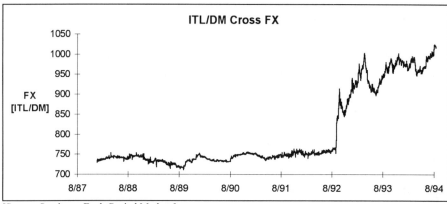

[Source: Sumitomo Bank Capital Markets]

Demand for FX linked structured notes in the post-ERM era fell dramatically. Less than 10% of all new issue structured notes by notional amount are FX linked, and a reversal of this downward trend does not appear likely. The other factor contributing to the demise of the FX linked structured note is the growing sophistication of investors. Most fixed income investors can now replicate such plays directly in the forward FX and swap market without having to resort to structured notes.

Analysis

The terms of an actual CIN are described in Exhibit 7-2. Although the analysis of FX linked notes can be performed with either expectation or forward analysis, most CIN investors have views that run contrary to forward predictions. Thus, the most appropriate analysis for FX linked notes is usually the expectation analysis. Because CINs contain embedded options, the simulation class of analysis is required to examine the risks.

As mentioned earlier, the risk of a CIN straddles multiple markets. In addition to the spot FX risk, the CIN also contains interest rate risk. Recall the famous interest rate parity relationship linking the spot FX rate to future FX rates:

Future FX rate [in units of x/y] = Spot FX rate [x/y] $* (f_y/f_x)$

where f_x and f_y are the relevant period discounting factors for currency x and y respectively. The discounting factor can be calculated (assuming money market yield basis) as:

$$f_x = \frac{1}{1 + R_x * (\text{Days in period}/360)}$$

where R_x is the money market discounting rate in currency x for the relevant period from note settlement date to maturity date.

From the above discussion, it is evident that CINs that have cash flows linked to FX rates on future dates will expose investors to three distinct risks: movement in the *spot* FX rate, movement in the interest rate of currency x, and movement in the interest rate of currency y.

The principal behavior of this CIN with respect to the DM/US$ FX rate at maturity is plotted on Exhibit 7-3. The complication that is not shown on the graph is that this particular CIN will lock in a principal return of 108% if the FX rate exceeds 1.9233 on any day during the life of the note.

EXHIBIT 7-2 Currency Indexed Note

This note provides no coupon, but the principal is linked to the DM/US$ FX rate at maturity. The additional complication is that if the DM/US$ FX rate exceeds 1.9233 on *any day* during the life of the note, the principal is automatically locked in at 108%. If DM/US$ FX does not exceed 1.9233 on any day during the year, the investor would receive a principal based on a leveraged formula specified below, subject to a minimum of 90%, and a maximum of approximately 117.99%.

Issue Terms (Actual)

Issuer:	Federal Home Loan Bank Systemwide Note
Principal amount:	US$25,000,000
Settlement date:	Mar. 28, 1994
Maturity date:	Mar. 28, 1995
Coupon paid in US$:	0.00%
Principal:	
If FX > 1.9233 during year:	108%
Otherwise:	100% * [1 + 1.5 * (FXmat − 1.6925)/FXmat]
FX definition:	Daily DM/US$ mid-market FX rate as of 10 A.M. New York time. Source: Reuters Page 1FED.
FXmat definition:	DM/US$ mid-market FX rate as of 10 A.M. New York time on the day that is 10 New York banking days prior to the maturity date.
Minimum redemption:	90.00%
Maximum redemption:	117.9934484%
Issue price:	100.00%

EXHIBIT 7-3 Principal Behavior of the DM/US$ Currency Indexed Note

The principal returned increases with increasing FX rate at maturity until the level of 1.9233 is reached. Once the FX rate exceeds 1.9233, the principal of 108% is locked in. This note also locks in the principal of 108% if the FX rate exceeds 1.9233 on *any day* of the period.

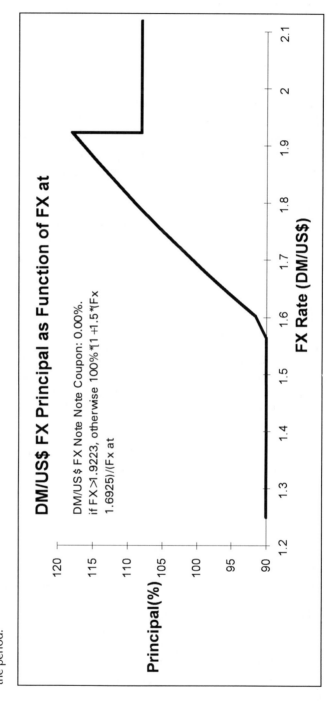

DM/US$ FX Principal as Function of FX at

DM/US$ FX Note Note Coupon: 0.00%.
if FX >1.9223, otherwise 100%*[1 +1.5*(Fx
1.6925)/(Fx at

FX Rate (DM/US$)

Principal(%)

The examination of the risks of this note will require three separate analyses. First, the note's risk with respect to the spot DM/US$ FX rate will be examined, followed by the analysis of the note's risk with respect to both US$ and DM interest rates. For all three analyses, the simulation class of analysis will be used with the expectation analysis to generate a set of base case scenarios.

Conditions on the trade date (3/14/94) were:

DM/US$ FX: 1.6925
12-month DM LIBOR: 5.50%
12-month US$ LIBOR: 4.50%

Simulation 1. FX Rate Variation

Interest rate parity imposes the following relationship between spot and forward FX rates:

$$\text{FX maturity} = \text{Spot FX} * (f_{\text{US\$}}/f_{\text{DM}})$$
$$= \text{Spot FX} * (1 + 5.5\% * 365/360)/(1 + 4.5\% * 365/360)$$
$$\text{FX maturity} = \text{Spot FX} * 1.0097 \tag{7-1}$$

When analyzing the risk and performance with respect to the spot FX rate, it will be assumed that the two discounting factors $f_{\text{US\$}}$ and f_{DM} do not change. A range of base case spot FX rate scenarios can then be selected, each with a corresponding final FX rates at maturity calculated from Equation (7-1). For each of these scenarios, simulation and LSE analysis will be performed.

Performance

The IRR performance of the CIN for a range of initial FX rates is plotted in Exhibit 7-4. The behavior of the note can be interpreted by examining the deterministic IRR. For low spot FX scenarios, the note produces low yields. The breakeven (IRR of 0%) FX-at-maturity occurs at 1.6925 DM/US$, which, according to Equation (7-1), corresponds to a spot FX of 1.6762 DM/US$. For spot FX lower than 1.6762, the performance of the CIN would continue to degrade until the principal floor is reached, at which time the IRR is floored at approximately −10%. The investor's return rises with higher rates, rising to a maximum of approximately 20% for the FX rate at maturity to be 1.9232 DM/US$.

EXHIBIT 7-4 IRR of the DM/US$ Currency Indexed Note

Due to the extremely skewed nature of the payoff, simulation analysis is required to fully determine the performance of the note. The note performs well when the DM/US$ FX rate rises. Note that the deterministic IRR shows the return if the interest rate path follows the LSE projection exactly, while the simulation IRR projects the expected IRR over 3500 simulations using the LSE projection as the base case.

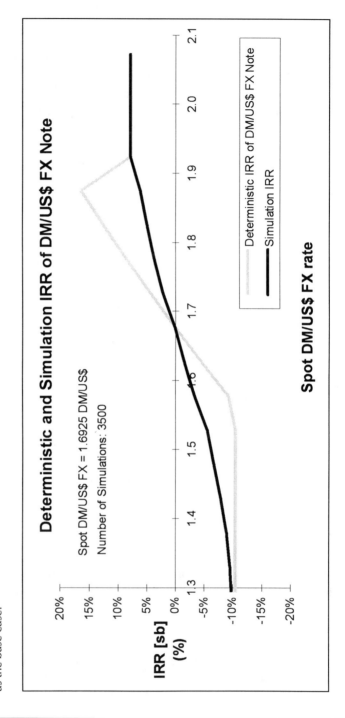

Deterministic and Simulation IRR of DM/US$ FX Note

Spot DM/US$ FX = 1.6925 DM/US$
Number of Simulations: 3500

IRR [sb]
(%)

Spot DM/US$ FX rate

Deterministic IRR of DM/US$ FX Note
Simulation IRR

That maximum return as calculated via deterministic IRR, however, is not realistic because it is highly probable that the FX rate at maturity will reach 1.9233 if it reaches 1.9232, at which time the principal return is locked in at 108%. The simulation IRR reflects the expected return given 2000 simulations about the spot FX base case scenarios. The simulation IRR deviations from the deterministic IRR for base case FX scenarios close to the lock-in level of 1.9232. This reflects the higher probability that the principal will be locked in at 108% for higher FX base case scenarios. Although there is a finite probability that the investor would be able to obtain a return of 20% without locking in the principal at 108%, simulation results show that this is not likely, and that the investor should not expect to receive a principal higher than 108%. For spot FX base case scenarios beyond 1.9233, both the simulation and deterministic IRR are locked in at 7.862% (semiannual BEY) due to the principal being locked in at 108%.

Risk

Spot FX Risk. The FX risk of the CIN as reflected by the FX duration is shown on Exhibit 7-5. In keeping with the conventions of duration, the FX duration is defined as follows: an FX duration of +1.00 is defined as representing the note *losing* 1% of its current value for a 0.01 *increase* in DM/US\$ FX rate. Exhibit 7-5 shows that the deterministic FX duration of the CIN is negative for all scenarios, signifying that the note would *increase* in value for *increasing* levels of DM/US\$ FX rate. For low interest rate scenarios, the negative duration implies that the note would lose value for an incremental decrease in FX rates until the principal reaches the floor of 90%. For spot FX scenarios below this principal floor level, the value of the note would no longer change for incremental increases in FX, resulting in a zero FX duration. For high FX scenarios, the negative duration implies that the note would gain value for an incremental increase in the spot FX until the FX reaches the principal lock-in level of 1.9233 DM/US\$, beyond which the principal is locked in at 108%, resulting in the FX duration again returning to zero.

The actual duration of the note as reflected by the simulation duration is qualitatively similar. Simulation results show that the note begins to gain value for incremental increases in FX levels even for base case scenarios in which the FX would result in the principal being floored at 90%, resulting in a small but increasingly larger negative FX duration at low FX rates. The simulation duration does not attain as high a level as the deterministic duration, attaining a maximum durational magnitude of –0.4. Above spot

EXHIBIT 7-5 Duration of FX Accrual Note with Respect to Spot Movement in DM/US$ FX Rate

The duration of the note is taken with respect to the change in the FX rate. A duration of 1 is defined here as 1% change in note price for 1 Pfennig change in DM/US$ FX rate. The note exhibits negative duration, meaning that higher FX rates will cause the note to gain value. The FX volatility used in the analysis is 12%.

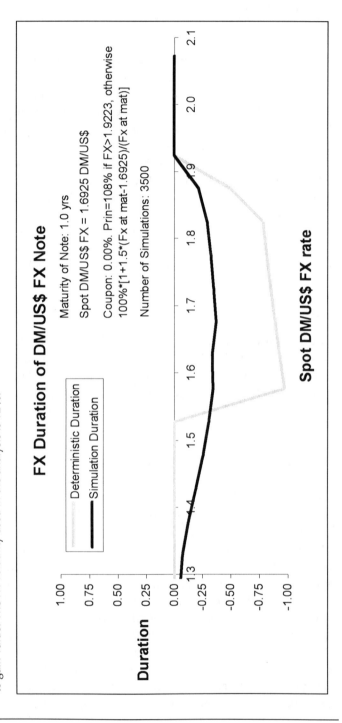

FX Duration of DM/US$ FX Note

Maturity of Note: 1.0 yrs

Spot DM/US$ FX = 1.6925 DM/US$

Coupon: 0.00%. Prin=108% if FX>1.9223, otherwise
100%*[1+1.5*(Fx at mat-1.6925)/(Fx at mat)]

Number of Simulations: 3500

Deterministic Duration
Simulation Duration

Duration

Spot DM/US$ FX rate

FX base case scenarios of 1.9233 DM/US$, the principal is likewise locked in at 108% and the note exhibits no further durational risk beyond this level.

Volatility Risk. The volatility risk of the note is reflected in the 3500 run simulation analysis of the volatility duration. Exhibit 7-6 shows that for low spot FX base case scenarios, the note exhibits negative volatility duration. Since the note is long a floor option in the form of a minimum principal limit, incremental increases in volatility for low spot FX scenarios will result in higher floor vega and thus negative volatility duration. For higher spot FX scenarios, the index moves further away from the floor option towards the maximum principal cap (which is a cap option that note is short). For these scenarios, the floor vega decrease combined with the cap vega increase will result in a gradual increase in volatility duration. The note attains a maximum positive volatility duration of approximately 25 at a spot FX level of 1.85. For higher spot FX scenarios, the volatility duration drops off rapidly until the lock-in level of 1.9233, beyond which the note's principal is locked in at 108% and thus will exhibit no volatility risk.

As expected, this note exhibits a large level of volatility risk for its 1-year maturity. This is a result of the high leverage embedded in the redemption formula. Investors should also be aware of the note's rapidly shifting volatility risk profile, which can shift very rapidly from +25 to –35 over a small range of spot FX scenarios.

Simulation 2. Duration with Respect to U.S. Interest Rate

As noted earlier, this note contains U.S. interest rate risks even though the note is indexed to an FX rate. In addition to the dependence of the FX rate at maturity on U.S. interest rates (from interest rate parity considerations), the note also contains duration with respect to the to-maturity rate, which in this case is the 12-month LIBOR (which is equivalent to a KTR of 1-year maturity Treasury).

Performance

The performance of the FX note for a range of 12-month US$ LIBOR scenarios in Exhibit 7-7 illustrates the effect that changing U.S. interest rates has on the note. From interest rate parity, higher U.S. rates will result in lower future DM/US$ FX rates, consequently the note should perform worse for

EXHIBIT 7-6 Volatility Risk of DM/US$ FX Note

Due to the presence of the maximum and minimum principal restrictions, the note contains optionality. For spot FX scenarios in which forward FX is close to the minimum principal level, the note exhibits maximum negative volatility duration, while for spot FX scenarios that result in forward FX being close to maximum principal level, the note exhibits maximum positive duration. For spot FX levels past the lock-in FX level of 1.9233 DM/US$, the note exhibits no duration since the principal would be locked in at 108%.

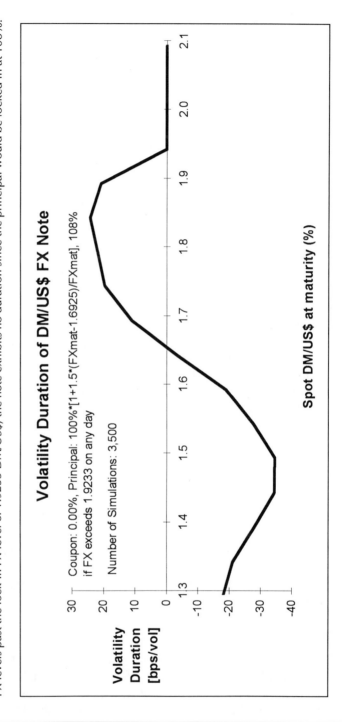

Volatility Duration of DM/US$ FX Note

Coupon: 0.00%, Principal: 100%*[1+1.5*(FXmat-1.6925)/FXmat], 108% if FX exceeds 1.9233 on any day

Number of Simulations: 3,500

Volatility Duration [bps/vol]

Spot DM/US$ at maturity (%)

EXHIBIT 7-7 Deterministic and Simulation IRR of DM/US$ FX Note for Range of Final US$ LIBORs

Note that both agree well with each other. This signifies that the effects of the embedded options are minimal at the current level of the FX rate, which is assumed to be constant at 1.6925 DM/US$. Both the spot FX rate and the DM LIBOR are assumed to be constant in this calculation.

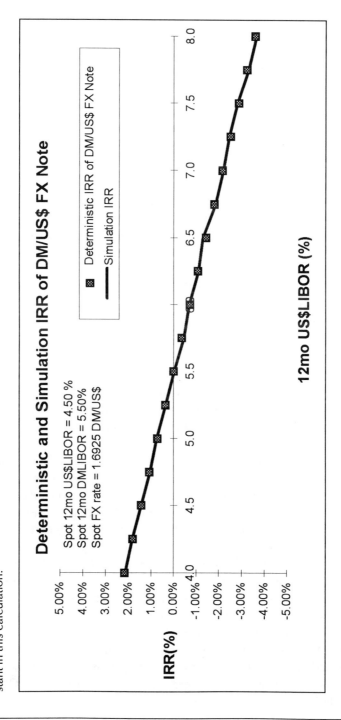

Deterministic and Simulation IRR of DM/US$ FX Note

Spot 12mo US$LIBOR = 4.50 %
Spot 12mo DMLIBOR = 5.50%
Spot FX rate = 1.6925 DM/US$

Deterministic IRR of DM/US$ FX Note
Simulation IRR

12mo US$LIBOR (%)

IRR(%)

higher U.S. interest rate scenarios. This is exactly the scenario depicted by both the deterministic and simulation IRR in Exhibit 7-7. The performance of the CIN is seen to deteriorate for higher U.S. interest rate scenarios. The breakeven 12-month US$ LIBOR at which the CIN yield is zero is 5 1/2%, which is 100 bps higher than the initial 12-month US$ LIBOR.

Risk

Interest Rate Risk. The risk of the note with respect to the U.S. interest rate can be clarified by examining the two components of risk: the discounting component and the index component.

The discounting rate of the CIN is equal to the to-maturity 1-year U.S. Treasury rate. The CIN has a discounting rate duration equal to the duration of a 1-year fixed rate note, or approximately 0.95.

The CIN's index rate (IR) is equal to the 12-month LIBOR (which equates to a KTR of the 1-year U.S. Treasury rate). The index rate duration (IRD) with respect to the 1-year Treasury rate is based on the leverage-principal formula. In the sample note, the leverage factor of 1.5 and spot FX of 1.6925 DM/US$ produce an IRD of approximately 1.4. The note's net KTRD with respect to the 1-year Treasury rate is then the sum of the two components, or approximately equal to 2.35. Exhibit 7-8 plots the actual calculated KTRD of the note with respect to the 1-year Treasury rate. The note shows a relatively constant duration level of 2.35 over a wide range of interest rates.

The actual duration of the CIN as reflected by the simulation duration shows little deviation from the deterministic results described above. The reason for this is that the interest rate would have to change quite dramatically before resulting in the FX-at-maturity approaching either the minimum principal floor or the lock-in-principal cap. The 12-month US$ LIBOR must exceed 12.44% in order for the FX-at-maturity to be low enough that the principal is floored at 90%. The level of 12.44% is almost 800 bps higher than current levels and is outside most reasonable interest rate scenarios. The highest FX-at-maturity that could be produced as a result of different U.S. rates would be 1.7869 DM/US$ due to a 12-month US$ LIBOR of 0%. Thus, even at a practically impossibly low interest rate level, the resulting FX-at-maturity is still quite far from the lock-in level of 1.9233. For the range of selected interest rate scenarios, the note exhibits very little non-deterministic effects and hence the U.S. interest rate volatility risk of the CIN is negligible for these interest rate scenarios.

EXHIBIT 7-8 Deterministic and Simulation Duration of DM/US$ FX Note with Respect to 12-Month US$ LIBOR

For the spot FX rate of 1.6925 DM/US$, the note has a fairly constant duration of approximately 2.4. Again, both the spot FX rate and the DM LIBOR are assumed to be constant during the calculation. 2000 simulations are run for each scenario.

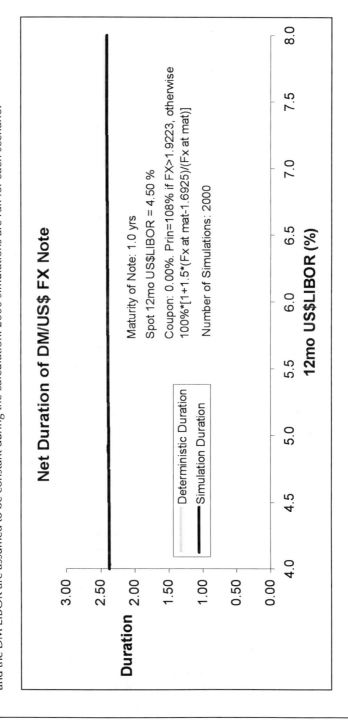

Net Duration of DM/US$ FX Note

Maturity of Note: 1.0 yrs

Spot 12mo US$LIBOR = 4.50 %

Coupon: 0.00%. Prin=108% if FX>1.9223, otherwise 100%*[1+1.5*(Fx at mat-1.6925)/(Fx at mat)]

Number of Simulations: 2000

Legend:
Deterministic Duration
Simulation Duration

X-axis: 12mo US$LIBOR (%) — 4.0, 4.5, 5.0, 5.5, 6.0, 6.5, 7.0, 7.5, 8.0

Y-axis: Duration — 0.00, 0.50, 1.00, 1.50, 2.00, 2.50, 3.00

Simulation 3. Duration with Respect to DM Interest Rate

Interest rate parity shows that the FX-at-maturity depends upon both the term U.S. rates and term DM rates. Thus the risk of the CIN with respect to DM interest rates has to be assessed as part of the overall risk picture.

Performance

The IRR of the CIN for a range of 12-month DM LIBORs illustrates the effect of different DM interest rates on the performance of the CIN. From interest rate parity, higher DM rates will result in higher future DM/US$ FX rates, consequently the note should perform better for higher DM interest rate scenarios. Exhibit 7-9 shows that the performance of the CIN does indeed improve for higher DM interest rate scenarios.

Risk

Interest Rate Risk.   The risk of the note with respect to the DM rates is seen by examining the DM index component. Since this CIN is denominated in U.S. dollars, the note contains no discounting component of risk with respect to the DM rates.

The CIN contains only an index component of risk with respect to DM interest rates. The IR is the 12-month DM LIBOR, and hence the corresponding key swap rate is the 1-year DM swap rate. The IRD of the CIN with respect to the 1-year DM swap rate is the result of the 1.5 times leverage and the spot DM/US$ FX rate, and is approximately -1.4. The duration is negative because higher DM rates result in higher FX-at-maturity and thus a higher principal return. The deterministic duration in Exhibit 7-10 fully reflects this expectation.

The simulation duration is almost exactly equal to the deterministic duration over the range of selected DM interest rate scenarios. This is due to the same effect as observed for U.S. interest rates: DM interest rates would have to move by a very large amount before the resulting FX-at-maturity would even approach either end of the principal corridor. The 12-month DM rate would have to rise to 18.56% in order for the FX-at-maturity to be at 1.9232 DM/US$. The level of 18.56% is 13.06% greater than the initial 12-month DM LIBOR, and is outside a reasonable range of interest rate scenarios. Likewise, the lowest FX-at-maturity of 1.6186 DM/US$ would result from a 12-month DM LIBOR of 0%. This level is still significantly far away from the FX level required to produce a minimum 90% principal return.

EXHIBIT 7-9 Deterministic and Simulation IRR of DM/US$ FX Note for Range of Final DM LIBORs

Again, both IRRs are in agreement with each other, signifying little skewness at the current level of the FX rate, which is assumed to be constant at 1.6925 DM/US$. Both the spot FX rate and the US$ LIBOR are assumed to be constant in this calculation. A volatility of 20% is assumed for the DM LIBOR volatility.

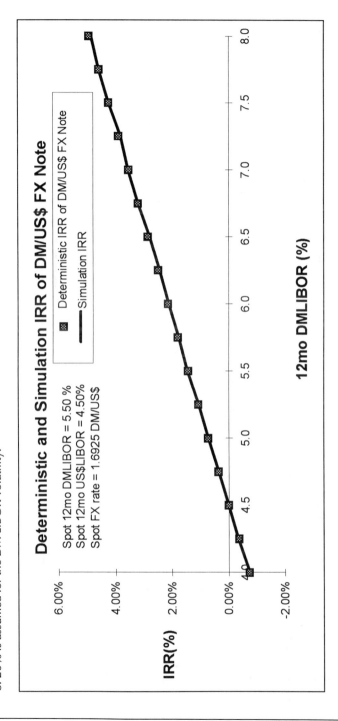

EXHIBIT 7-10 Deterministic and Simulation Duration of DM/US$ FX Note with Respect to 12-Month DM LIBOR

Note that compared to the durational results with respect to US$ LIBOR, this duration is negative. The note thus increases in value with larger DM rates. The other feature is that the magnitude of the note's DM duration is about one smaller than its US$ duration, which is accounted for by the contribution from the discounting component of duration.

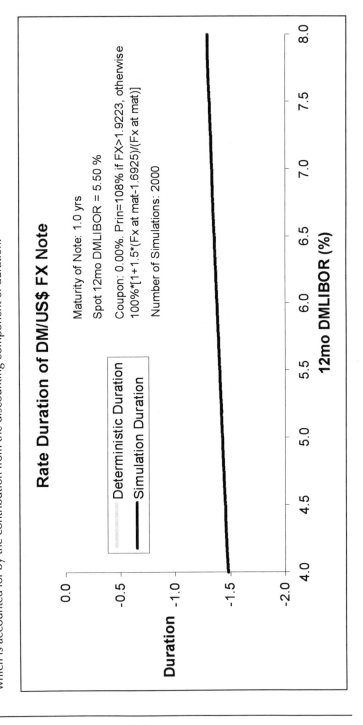

Rate Duration of DM/US$ FX Note

Maturity of Note: 1.0 yrs

Spot 12mo DMLIBOR = 5.50 %

Coupon: 0.00%. Prin=108% if FX>1.9223, otherwise
100%*[1+1.5*(Fx at mat-1.6925)/(Fx at mat)]

Number of Simulations: 2000

Deterministic Duration

Simulation Duration

Thus, over a reasonably wide interest rate range, the CIN's actual duration contains little deviation from deterministic duration; hence, the DM interest rate volatility risk of the note is quite negligible over this range of scenarios.

Composite Risk. The overall risk of the note can then be summarized in the following table:

Market	Index Rate	Duration with Respect to Index Rate
Currency (FX)	Spot FX [DM/US$]	0 to −0.40*
US$ interest rate	1-year U.S. Treasury rate	~ +2.40**
DM interest rate	1-year DM swap rate	~ −1.40**

* FX duration: +1.00 when note loses 1% of current value for 0.01 increase in spot FX.
** Interest rate duration: +1.00 when note loses 1 bp of current value for 1 bp increase in interest rate.

This note also contains considerable volatility risk with respect to the spot FX rate.

Market	Volatility Duration
Spot FX	−35 to +20*

*FX volatility duration: +1.00 when note loses 1 bp of current value for 1% increase in volatility of spot FX.

The assertion made at the beginning of this section stating that the note contains exposure to three different market sectors has now been duly verified. The value of the CIN will change with respect to the spot DM/US$ FX rate, the 1-year U.S. Treasury rate, and the 1-year DM swap rate. Given the multiple market exposures, the purchaser(s) of this note must monitor the three market sectors, as well as their associated volatilities, in order to track the changes in the value, performance, and risk profile of the CIN.

STRUCTURE II. COMMODITY LINKED NOTE (CLN)

Investor purpose: Obtain exposure or hedge to either commodities or a commodity index of a basket of commodities.

Risk: Investor is exposed to both commodity risk as well as interest rate risk.

Equivalent investor position: Long fixed/floating rate note, long/short underlying either commodity contracts and options, or long/short commodity index options.

Commodities have been a favorite refuge of investors in times of inflationary worries. In times of high inflation, commodities such as gold are regarded as good hedges that retain value well. Investors can purchase a CLN linked to either the underlying commodity or a composite index of a basket of commodities.

As with the CINs, CLNs are often purchased for the purpose of either risk capital arbitrage or hedging exposure.

History

Fixed income investors flock to CLNs in times of inflationary concerns. The latest rally of investor interest in CLNs occurred in 1994 in the midst of the series of Fed tightening action. Investors worried about renewed heightening of inflation sought out commodity linked notes to provide a pseudo-hedge.

In notional amount terms, CLNs continue to account for less than 5% of the overall structured note market. That does not discount the importance of this class of investments to investors since they are typically smaller-sized, custom-tailored products designed for only one investor. As such, CLNs fulfill a function that is unique to structured notes: they are structured to meet specific individual investor requirements.

Commodity Index

Investors can purchase CLNs indexed to changes in either the price movement of an underlying commodity, or the appreciation in the value of a commodity index. The advantage of a CLN linked to a commodity index is the diversification of risk away from one particular commodity into a basket of commodities. However, a composite index may introduce risks from other less desirable commodity components of the index.

Exhibit 7-11 lists some of the exchange-traded commodities that are of interest to CLN investors. The two basic commodities that have garnered the lion's share CLN investor interest are gold and crude oil. Gold is the benchmark precious metal that is regarded as a stable asset in inflationary times. Crude oil, on the other hand, is often seen as a major component of inflation, since it affects not only the underlying energy prices, but also production costs of foods and goods.

EXHIBIT 7-11 List of Some Exchange-Traded Commodities (by No Means Exhaustive) and Their Relevance to Commodity Linked Notes

The commodities that have generated the greatest amount of interest from investors have been gold and crude oil, although other raw and processed materials are also available to the interested investor.

Commodity	Comments
Gold (100 troy oz.)	Commodity of the highest interest among structured note purchasers. Often sought out in inflationary times as the best inflation hedge.
Crude oil (WTI), heating oil (no. 2), unleaded gasoline	Crude oil is considered a good proxy for inflation because energy cost is a major component of the CPI. Heating oil and unleaded gasoline as refined products have not garnered much demand from investors.
Silver, platinum	Some interest in these precious metals as a distant cousin to gold. However, the high supply of silver and the abandonment of platinum as a key element in automobile catalytic converters have depressed investor interest in these metals.
Aluminum, copper, etc.	Industrial metals typically exhibit low volatility and stability for long periods of time with intermittent periods of high volatility. Can be popular with more speculative investors who wish to take advantage of momentary market trends.
Orange juice, pork bellies, corn, soybeans, wheat, etc.	Food-based commodities typically do not generate much interest among structured note investors.

Exhibit 7-12 lists some of the composite commodity indices that are often desired by investors. The main index that has attracted investor interest is the KR-CRB index, which is the geometric average of 21 commodity prices (each price is the mathematical average of futures prices up to nine months from spot). Investors often regard the CRB index as a useful precursor to inflation.

Analysis

The indicative terms of a "gold bull note" indexed to the price of gold at maturity are described in Exhibit 7-13. Because of the presence of minimum and maximum redemption limits, the note contains embedded optionality and thus must be analyzed with simulation analysis.

**EXHIBIT 7-12 Commodity Composite Indices of Interest to Structured
Note Investors**

These are the most publicized commodity basket indices. The three newest commodity
indices introduced in 1994 were an attempt to provide a more tradable and hedgeable
commodity index.

Commodity Index	Comments
KR-CRB	The Knight-Ridder Commodity Research Bureau Index of 21 traded commodities. The CRB index is often regarded by fixed income investors as a good precursor to inflation, although its recent track record as a predictor of inflation has actually been quite poor. The CRB index is the geometric average of 21 commodity prices (each individual price being the mathematical average of all contracts for the following nine-month period). This makes the CRB index tremendously difficult for structurers to replicate. The CRB index futures are traded out to a maturity of one year, but even these contracts are exceedingly illiquid.
Goldman Sachs Commodity Index (GSCI)	One of the longest-running commodities indices other than the CRB. Composed of a basket of 20 commodities composed of the following sectors: energy, livestock, agricultural, and metals. GSCI was launched in 1991, followed by GSCI futures contracts trading in 1992. GSCI thus far has a good trading track record, which the other three newer indices (ENMET, JPMCI, and BTCI, below) do not yet have.
Merrill Lynch Energy and Metals Index (ENMET)	Launched in July 1994. Composed of 55% energy, 45% metals. Geometric average.
Bankers Trust Commodity Index (BTCI)	Launched in July 1994. Composed of 54% metals, 46% energy. Arithmetic average.
JP Morgan Commodity Index (JPMCI)	Launched in October 1994. Arithmetic average of 11 industrial commodity futures based on energy and base and precious metals. Excludes "soft" commodities.

Sources: KR-CRB, Goldman Sachs, Merrill Lynch, Bankers Trust, JP Morgan.

The relationship linking forward commodity price to the spot price is as
follows:[3]

$$\text{Forward price} = (\text{Spot price} + \text{STOR}) * f_{\text{disc}} * f_{\text{conv}}$$

3. Readers are directed to an excellent discussion of forward and future commodity prices in
Hull, John, *Introduction to Futures and Options Markets.* Englewood Cliffs, NJ: Prentice
Hall, 1991.

EXHIBIT 7-13 A Commodity Linked Note

This particular note is linked to the price of gold at maturity.

Issue Terms (Indicative)	
Issuer:	AA Bank
Principal amount:	US$10,000,000
Settlement date:	Oct. 1, 1994
Maturity date:	Oct. 1, 1995
Coupon paid in US$:	0.00%
Redemption:	100.00% + 10% * (GOLDPX – $350)/$10
Current price of gold:	$350/troy oz.
Minimum principal:	60%
Maximum principal:	140%
GOLDPX determination:	GOLDPX, the price of gold, is determined as the spot price ($/troy oz.) for 100 troy oz. of gold at 5 P.M. New York time on determination date. Determination date is two New York business days prior to maturity date. Source: COMEX.
Minimum redemption:	80.00%
Issue price:	100.00%

where STOR is the cost of storage of the commodity, f_{disc} is the period discounting factor, and f_{conv} is the *convenience yield factor*. The forward price of a commodity thus is a function of three factors: interest rate, storage cost, and convenience yield. The period discounting factor f_{disc} is

$$f_{disc} = \frac{1}{1 + r_{disc} * (\text{No. of days in period}/360)} \qquad (7\text{-}2)$$

where r_{disc} is the to-maturity discounting rate expressed as a money market yield. The convenience yield factor likewise can be related to a convenience yield, which is usually expressed as a continuously compounded rate, i.e.

$$f_{conv} = \exp(-yt)$$

where y is the convenience yield. The implications of the convenience yield factor will be addressed in detail later in this chapter.

The convenience yield, while not always quantifiable, is an important factor in the determination of the forward price of certain commodities. In the analysis performed in this chapter, it will be assumed that this convenience yield factor does not change over the life of the CLN.

Because of the embedded option providing the investor with a minimum and maximum principal return, the note will be analyzed with the simulation class of analysis.

The examination of the risks of this note will require two separate analyses. The note's risk with respect to changes in the spot gold price will be examined, followed by the analysis of the note's risk with respect to U.S. interest rates. LSE will be employed to generate a set of base case FX and interest rate scenarios.

The following conditions on the trade date of the note are *assumed*. These values are not the actual levels such as those employed in the analyses performed in the previous chapters, but are selected to illustrate the concepts of storage and convenience yield factors:

Spot gold price (as of 9/29/94):	$350/troy oz.
Forward gold price on 9/29/95:	$340/troy oz. (as of 9/29/94)
12-month US$ LIBOR:	5.00%
Storage cost of gold:	$1/oz., payment made at start of storage period.

Since gold is not a commodity that could be used, it usually does not exhibit the effect of the convenience yield factor. However, for the sake of illustration, the forward price is set to be lower than the spot price to demonstrate the effect of including the convenience yield factor.

Simulation 1. Performance and Risk with Respect to Spot Gold Prices

Performance

LSE is used to generate a series of spot gold price scenarios. The performance of the note can subsequently be determined by calculating the corresponding gold-price-at-maturity, which could then be used to calculate the principal return.

Equation (7-2) is first employed to resolve the implied convenience yield factor:

$$\text{Forward price} = (\text{Spot price} + \text{STOR}) * f_{\text{disc}} * f_{\text{conv}}$$
$$340 = (350 + 1) * (1 + 5\% * 365/360) * f_{\text{conv}}$$
$$340 = (368.79) * f_{\text{conv}}$$
$$f_{\text{conv}} = 0.922$$

In the risk analysis, this convenience yield factor will be assumed to be constant. Given that, the forward price for a given spot price is calculated as

Forward price = (Spot price + STOR) $* f_{disc} * f_{conv}$
             = (Spot + 1) * 1.0507 * 0.922

Forward price = 0.9687 * (Spot + 1)   (7-3)

Equation (7-3) will be used to calculate the corresponding forward gold prices for a given range of spot gold prices.

For a range of spot gold price scenarios, the performance of the note is calculated and plotted on Exhibit 7-14. As expected, higher spot gold price scenarios result in correspondingly higher gold-prices-at-maturity, hence a higher principal return and a higher yield.

Risk

Commodity Risk.   The risk analysis of CLNs is similar to the analysis of the CINs discussed previously. CLNs are usually indexed to commodity prices on some future dates, and hence the note not only contains risk exposure with respect to the spot price levels of the underlying commodity, but also contains risk exposure with respect to interest rates. Equation (7-2) shows that higher spot gold prices result in higher levels of forward price of gold. Thus, the note is expected to perform better for higher spot gold price.

The duration of the CLN with respect to the spot gold price is calculated for a range of spot prices and shown in Exhibit 7-15. The duration with respect to spot gold price is defined as one when a $1/oz. rise in gold price results in a 1% decline in PV. The deterministic duration of Exhibit 7-15 shows that for spot gold prices that result in forward gold prices being outside the minimum or maximum principal band, the note is not expected to change in value for incremental changes in the spot gold price. When spot gold price results in forward prices that are within the band, the note exhibits negative deterministic duration, i.e., the CLN gains in value for higher spot gold prices.

The actual risk of the note as reflected in the simulation duration is qualitatively similar to the deterministic duration with some quantitative difference. Simulation duration shows that for spot gold price scenarios with corresponding gold-price-at-maturity levels that would result in the principal being outside the minimum principal restriction, the note would still gain in

EXHIBIT 7-14 Performance of Gold Bull Note for a Range of Spot Gold Prices

The breakeven point is at a spot price of $360. This is due to the assumed convenience yield factor, which depresses the forward price relative to the spot price.

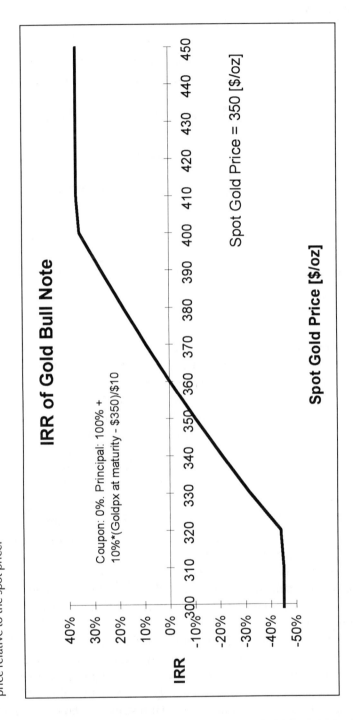

IRR of Gold Bull Note

Coupon: 0%. Principal: 100% + 10%*(Goldpx at maturity - $350)/$10

Spot Gold Price = 350 [$/oz]

Spot Gold Price [$/oz]

EXHIBIT 7-15 Risk of Gold Bull Note for a Range of Spot Gold Prices

Deterministic duration (defined as +1 when $1 increase in gold price results in 1% decrease in PV) shows that the note gains in value for higher levels of gold prices within the minimum and maximum principal range. Simulation results are similar, but show that the note will always increase in value when gold prices rise, even for base case scenarios outside the minimum and maximum principal range.

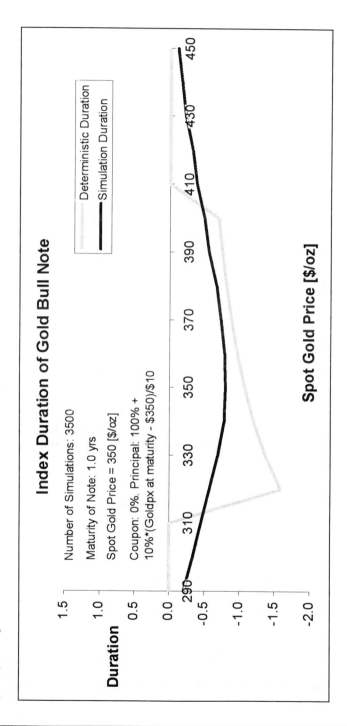

Index Duration of Gold Bull Note

Number of Simulations: 3500

Maturity of Note: 1.0 yrs

Spot Gold Price = 350 [$/oz]

Coupon: 0%. Principal: 100% + 10%*(Goldpx at maturity - $350)/$10

Spot Gold Price [$/oz]

Duration

Deterministic Duration
Simulation Duration

value for incrementally higher spot gold prices. This is expected since an increase in the spot gold prices would result in a higher probability that gold-price-at-maturity would result in a principal above the minimum principal restriction.

Volatility Risk.   The volatility risk of the gold linked note is reflected in the 3500 run simulation analysis of the volatility duration. Exhibit 7-16 shows that the volatility risk of the gold linked note is quite similar in shape to that of the FX linked note of the previous section. For low spot gold scenarios, the resulting base case principal is close to the minimum principal floor (which is an option that the note is long). For incrementally higher volatility, the rise in floor vega is considerably higher than the rise in the cap vega of the maximum principal cap (which the note is short), resulting in a net negative volatility duration.

For higher spot gold price scenarios, the index moves away from the floor strike and closer to the strike of the maximum principal cap. The result is that the volatility duration begins to increase towards a maximum of +150 at approximately the base case spot gold price scenario of $400/oz. (Recall the unit of volatility duration is +1 when a 1% increase in spot gold price volatility results in a 1 bp decrease in the percentage of price.) Thus, at maximum volatility duration, a 1% increase in volatility will result in a 1.5% decrease in note value. This is an extremely large volatility duration and points out the importance of taking into consideration the volatility component of risk.

Simulation 2. Performance and Risk with Respect to U.S. Interest Rate

Performance

LSE is again used to generate a range of base case U.S. interest rate scenarios. From Equation (7-2), the forward gold price can be expressed as a function of the appropriate maturity discounting rate r_{disc}.

$$\text{Forward price} = (\text{Spot price} + \text{STOR}) * f_{disc} * f_{conv}$$
$$= (350 + 1) * (1 + r_{disc} * 365/360) * 0.922$$
$$\text{Forward price} = 323.622 + 3.28117 * r_{disc} \qquad (7\text{-}4)$$

where r_{disc} is the 12-month US$ LIBOR expressed in percent terms.

EXHIBIT 7-16 Volatility Risk of Gold Linked Note

The note exhibits negative duration for low spot gold price scenarios and positive duration for higher spot gold price scenarios. Note that the unit of volatility duration is +1.00 when a 1% increase in volatility results in 1 bp fractional decrease in the value of the note.

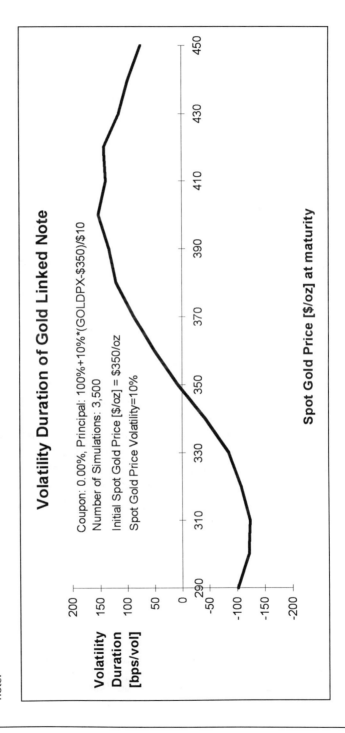

Volatility Duration of Gold Linked Note

Coupon: 0.00%, Principal: 100%+10%*(GOLDPX-$350)/$10
Number of Simulations: 3,500
Initial Spot Gold Price [$/oz] = $350/oz
Spot Gold Price Volatility=10%

Volatility Duration [bps/vol]

Spot Gold Price [$/oz] at maturity

The above relationship will be used in calculating the forward price of gold corresponding to different term discounting rate.

The performance of the gold bull note for a variety of interest rate scenarios is shown in Exhibit 7-17. The note performs better for higher interest rates since the forward price of gold is proportional to the term discounting rate. Thus, a higher interest rate would result in a larger forward gold price, a higher principal return, and thus better performance.

Risk

Interest Rate Risk.   The risk analysis of the CLN with respect to U.S. interest rates is similar to the interest rate risk analysis of the CIN. For this CLN, the DR and the IR are both equal to the 1-year maturity Treasury rate.

The DRD of the CLN is approximately equal to the duration of a 1-year fixed rate note, or 0.95. The IRD is the result of the combination of the leveraged redemption formula and Equation (7-4). For a par bond, the IRD is approximately –3.2. The net aggregate duration of the two durations is thus approximately –2.2.

The deterministic duration of the note is calculated for a variety of to-maturity LIBORs and plotted on Exhibit 7-18. As expected, the deterministic duration is negative for the range of interest rate scenarios. As in the case of the CIN, even a wide range of interest rate scenarios would not result in the principal approaching the maximum or minimum constraints. The simulation and deterministic durations reflect this effect by showing very good agreement with each other. Since these scenarios would result in gold-price-at-maturity levels that are far from the strike of the embedded options of the CLN, the U.S. interest rate volatility risk of this CLN is negligible for this range of interest rate scenarios.

Composite Risk.   The composite of the risk components of the gold linked note are summarized as follows:

Market	Index Rate	Duration with Respect to Index Rate
Commodity	Spot gold price ($/oz.)	0 to –0.7*
US$ interest rate	1-year U.S. Treasury rate	~ –3**

* Commodity duration: +1.00 when note loses 1% of current value for $1 increase in spot gold price ($/oz.).
** Interest rate duration: +1.00 when note loses 1 bp of current value for 1 bp increase in interest rate.

EXHIBIT 7-17 Performance of Gold Bull Note for a Range of To-Maturity Rates

Based on current interest rate and spot gold price, the to-maturity rate would have to rise from 5% to 11% before the note would achieve a breakeven yield of 0%. This illustrates the fact that the spot gold price is a much larger driving force in determining the behavior of the note.

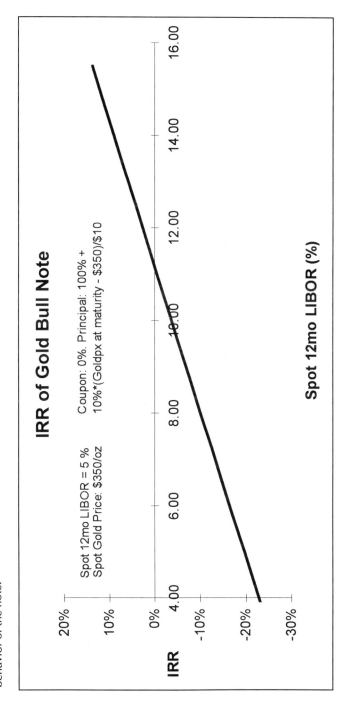

IRR of Gold Bull Note

Spot 12mo LIBOR = 5 %
Spot Gold Price: $350/oz

Coupon: 0%. Principal: 100% +
10%*(Goldpx at maturity - $350)/$10

EXHIBIT 7-18 Risk of Gold Bull Note for a Range of Term Discounting Rates

Deterministic duration shows that the note gains in value for higher levels of U.S. interest rates. This result reflects the gain in value of the note from higher expected forward gold prices when interest rates rise. Because the value of the note is still far from either the minimum principal floor and maximum principal cap, the deterministic and simulation durations are practically identical.

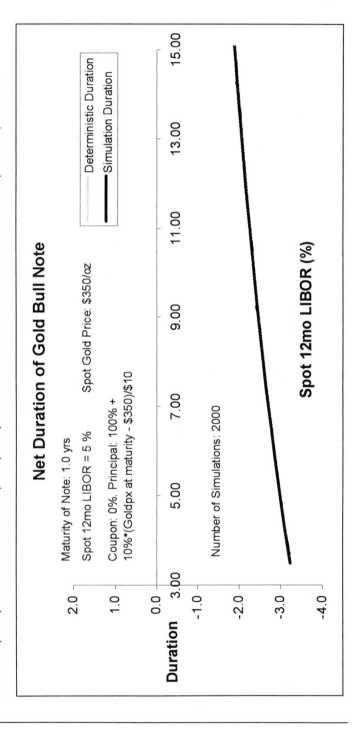

Net Duration of Gold Bull Note

Deterministic Duration
Simulation Duration

Maturity of Note: 1.0 yrs

Spot 12mo LIBOR = 5 %   Spot Gold Price: $350/oz

Coupon: 0%. Principal: 100% +
10%*(Goldpx at maturity - $350)/$10

Number of Simulations: 2000

Duration

Spot 12mo LIBOR (%)

In addition to the index risk, the note also exhibits a large volatility risk with respect to the spot price of gold.

Market	Volatility Duration
Commodity	−125 to +150*

* Commodity volatility duration: +1.00 when note loses 1 bp of current value for 1% increase in spot gold volatility.

The risk of the gold bull note has been demonstrated to straddle two markets: the spot gold commodity market, as well as the U.S. interest rate market.

Comments on Convenience Yield and Forward Commodity Prices

What factors drive the convenience yield, and why is it different across differing commodities? The paragraphs below summarize Hull's reasoning.[4]

Commodities such as gold and silver often do not exhibit any signs of convenience yield, i.e., their forward prices are almost always higher than spot prices. Investors typically purchase these commodities for investment purposes and thus can conduct arbitrage trades if the forward-to-spot prices deviate too much from the relationship:

$$\text{Forward price} = (\text{Spot price} + \text{STOR}) * f_{\text{disc}} \qquad (7\text{-}5)$$

This is simply Equation (7-2) without the convenience yield factor.

Commodities that can be purchased for reasons other than investment exhibit forward price behaviors that are consistent with the presence of a convenience yield factor since owning the underlying commodity carries with it the benefit of instant utilization. For example, an investor who purchases crude oil on the spot market has the right to use that crude oil, whereas an investor purchasing the crude for forward delivery does not possess that right. For these commodities, the right of instant utilization is the driving force behind the convenience yield factor.

---

4. Hull, John. *Introduction to Futures and Options Markets*. Englewood Cliffs, NJ: Prentice Hall, 1991, pp. 70–71.

STRUCTURE III. EQUITY LINKED NOTE (ELN)

Investor purpose: Obtain equity linked returns with fixed income instruments. Obtain benefits of lower risk capital weighting.

Risk: Regulatory, legal, tax, and accounting issues have to be thoroughly investigated. The credit risk of the issuer is the major risk.

Equivalent investor position: Long fixed/floating rate note, long or short equity index forwards and options.

Typical ELNs are linked to a broad basket equity index such as the S&P 500 Index. The typical structure will provide the investor with the upside movement of the equity index and in return the investor will give up part or all of the coupon interest that such a note would usually pay. In other words, ELNs permit investors to reallocate the typical interest rate return from fixed income instruments into a return based on the equity class of assets.

The regulatory and legal covenants that govern most fixed income investors typically prohibit direct participation in the equity market. The ELN was created to provide a measure of equity participation to the investor without violating such regulatory and legal covenants.

Many purchasers of ELNs are investors who are constrained by risk capital limits. The typical risk capital weighting for equity is 100%, while structured ELNs typically require much lower risk weighting. This is a powerful inducement for investors to look to ELNs instead of trading in the underlying equities because ELNs permit a more efficient utilization of their limit risk capital.

History

Equity linked structured notes were first created in the late 1980s. They provided investors with the aforementioned capital arbitrage ability as well as provided good asset allocation capabilities. Recent interest from investors has centered around the small capitalized company indices and the non-U.S. equity indices.

Indices

Readers interested in a discussion of the evolution of stock index options and futures are directed to the works of Luskin[5] and Berlin.[6] The indices of inter-

---

5. Luskin, Donald L. *Index Options and Futures: The Complete Guide.* New York, NY: John Wiley & Sons, 1987.

6. Berlin, Howard M. *The Handbook of Financial Market Indexes, Averages, and Indicators.* Homewood, IL: Dow Jones-Irwin, 1984.

est to ELN investors are summarized in Exhibits 7-19 and 7-20. These two exhibits illustrate the wide selection of U.S. and global equity indices that can be available to the ELN investor. Some of these composite equity indices cannot be used in structured notes or even traded on exchanges because the creator of the index has not granted permission for such use.

The above ELN structure provides the investor with an enhanced fraction of the ABC Index appreciation over three years. The investor receives no coupon interest, but does receive a return based on the appreciation of the ABC index over the maturity of the note. This structure is typical of ELNs, which expose the investor to none of the downside of typical equity index futures contracts, and whose return is similar in form to equity index options.

EXHIBIT 7-19 U.S. Stock Indices

The following lists some of the major U.S. equity indices.

Index	Comments
Dow Jones Industrial Average	Best-known index of leading industrial companies. Was the first stock index whose future was traded on the Philadelphia Exchange. Dow Jones subsequently litigated and the index was removed from trading. Dow Jones has refused to grant permission for use of this index in either exchange or OTC products.
S&P 500	Based on the 500 companies from NYSE, AMEX, and NASDAQ. Consists of four subgroups: industrial, financial, utilities, and transportation. Accounts for approximately 80% of the total value of all stocks on the NYSE. Base level of 100 from 1941 to 1943 base period.
NASDAQ Composite	Indicator of 4300 OTC traded stocks, mainly high-tech companies. 35% of NASDAQ composite have capitalization under $10MM.
Russell 1000, 2000, 3000	Russell 1000 is the index of the highest capitalized companies in the U.S. market, all with market capitalization of $300MM. Russell 2000 is the index of the 2000 next highest (after the Russell 1000) capitalized companies in the U.S., with market capitalization between $20MM to $300MM. Russell 3000 is the list of the 3000 largest capitalized companies (combines Russell 1000 and Russell 2000).
Wilshire 5000	Index of over 6000 issues composed as follows: NYSE (86%), AMEX (3%), and OTC (11%). Base level 1404.596 set on 12/31/80.

EXHIBIT 7-20   European and Asian Stock Indices

The largest European and Asian stock markets and the relevant indices of these markets. Some indices such as the Nikkei are tightly controlled and unauthorized uses of such indices are prohibited.

Country	Index	Comments
U.K.	FT-SE 100	Index of the 100 largest companies on the London Stock Exchange as tabulated by the *Financial Times*. Represents about 72% of total capitalization of U.K. stocks.
Japan	Nikkei 225	Price-weighted index of 225 blue chip stocks listed in the First Section of the Tokyo Stock Exchange.
	Nikkei 300	Reconstituted Nikkei Index with 300 companies.
Germany	DAX	Index based on 30 top-rated German stocks traded on the Frankfurt Stock Exchange. Replaced the Borsen Zeitung Index in 1987 with a base level of 1000.
France	CAC	Narrow-based capitalization-weighted index of 40 stocks listed on Paris Bourse. Base of 1000 in 1987.
Hong Kong	Hang Seng	Index of 33 companies traded on the Hong Kong Stock Exchange, representing 70% of the capitalization of the stock exchange. Base of 100 in 1964.

EXHIBIT 7-21   Equity Linked Note

The following indicative ELN returns 120% of the S&P upside over the next three years.

Issue Terms (Indicative)	
Issuer:	AA Bank
Principal amount:	US$25,000,000
Settlement date:	Jan. 27, 1994
Maturity date:	July 27, 1997
Coupon paid in US$:	0.00%
Redemption:	100.00% + 1.20 * (S&P Upside)
S&P Upside definition:	[S&P index on maturity – Spot S&P]/[Spot S&P index]
S&P Index determination:	The S&P index is the S&P 500 average at 5 P.M. New York time on determination date. Determination date is two New York business days prior to maturity date.
Minimum redemption:	80.00%
Issue price:	100.00%

STRUCTURE IV. TOTAL RETURN INDEX NOTES (TRIN)

Investor purpose: Match return of note with the client's targeted return index, diversification of credit risk.

Risk: Complicated regulatory and legal implications. TRINs that provide cross-ratings plays will not automatically earn the default rating of the issuer.

Equivalent investor position: Long fixed/floating rate note. Long basket of bonds that constitute the index.

Many fixed income investors have target indices against which their performance are measured. These targets or investment objectives have to be met or exceeded over certain periods. For example, an investment grade bond investor may have a target rate of return goal that has been set to the Merrill Lynch Corporate Bond Index (MLCBI) plus 0.25%. This return target has to be met or exceeded each quarter. For this investor, TRINs are a relatively straightforward way of achieving this goal. For example, if the above investor were able to purchase a note issued by a single-A issuer that provides a return of the MLCBI plus 0.25%, his or her task of achieving the target of MLCBI + 0.25% becomes much simpler. Instead of having to replicate the bond index to the best of his or her ability and having to worry about the mix of credit risk, the investor now only has to be comfortable with the credit risk of the single-A issuer that issued the note and be safe in the knowledge that if no default occurs, his or her return will perfectly track the MLCBI.

From the above discussion, one of the obvious advantages of purchasing a TRIN is the elimination of *tracking error.* Investors who have to track the returns of an index resort to a variety of asset allocations to minimize the tracking error. This error, however, can never be completely eliminated unless the investor exactly duplicates the weighting of all the bonds within the index. Since each broad index class typically consists of hundreds and sometimes thousands of bonds, zero tracking error can be an almost impossible goal. By purchasing TRINs, the investor is able to eliminate the tracking error and pass the tracking error risk onto the structurer creating the TRIN.

The purchaser of a TRIN essentially owns the basket of notes that form the underlying index. The typical structure of a TRIN pays the total return over a specific period out in coupon form. Because the investor cannot receive less than zero coupon, any negative return is pushed off to maturity, at which time it is taken out of the principal. Thus, although the investor's coupons have a floor of zero, the principal returned is typically not guaranteed at 100, but would reflect any gain or losses on the underlying index.

Cross-Credit Structures

The original intent of these TRINs was to provide the investor with a note that eliminated their target return tracking error. TRINs rapidly evolved from this original use to providing cross-credit plays. Variations of the basic TRIN were created in 1993 to permit an investment grade investor to purchase TRINs issued by single-A issuers, which provide returns linked to high yield indices. Both the SEC and the rating agencies have and continue to scrutinize the investors who purchase such cross-credit notes. In several instances, the underwriters of such notes were unable to obtain a rating from the rating agencies reflecting the credit rating of the issuer.

Effects of Issuer Upgrade and Downgrade

Bond indices and TRINs carry a credit movement effect that should be considered by the client prior to purchase. A simple example will illustrate this effect. An investor purchased a BBB TRIN whose index consists of the bonds of five BBB rated issuers. One of these issuers, XYZ Corp, is upgraded by both Moody's and S&P to single-A minus (or A3). Because the bonds of XYZ Corp are now in the single-A category, they are no longer part of the BBB bond index calculation. The investor thus loses out on some of the capital gain he or she would have received had he or she actually purchased the notes. By the same token, if XYZ's bonds were to be downgraded to junk bond status, they would disappear from the BBB index as well, thus saving the client from capital loss. The exception to this effect are the high yield indices. Since the high yield indices encompass notes that are rated below investment grade, notes cannot be downgraded out of the index, but can be upgraded out of the index.

This credit movement effect is not as dramatic in practice as the above paragraph may suggest, since upgrades and downgrades are usually not instantaneous, i.e., notes are usually first placed on positive watch, and the actual upgrade may come after several months have passed. However, dramatic downgrades and upgrades sometimes do occur without prior notice, and this credit movement effect needs to be understood by the investor before investing in the bond index of interest.

Sample Bond Index Note

The terms of a sample bond index note are described in Exhibit 7-22. The terms are somewhat more complicated than the typical structured note due to the provisions for the rolling over of any negative returns to the next period. An investor who purchases this note could replicate the return of ABC's bond index with the exception that any negative return would be netted on a future coupon date against future positive returns. Note that the entire negative return is netted against the principal at maturity, resulting in both potential principal risk.

EXHIBIT 7-22 A Sample Bond Index Note

The note returns the total return of the ABC bond index minus 0.25% over three years. Negative returns are carried forward to be netted against any positive future returns and the principal. The note thus contains principal risk.

Issue Terms (Indicative)	
Issuer:	AA
Principal amount:	US$25,000,000
Settlement date:	Aug. 1, 1994
Maturity date:	Aug. 1, 1997
Coupon paid in US$:	TOTRET – 0.25% – NEGCPN
Minimum coupon:	0.00%
TOTRET:	Total return of the ABC Bond Index (ABCBI). Calculated as follows:
	TOTRET = (ABCBI at end of period – ABCBI at start of period)/(ABCBI at start of period)
NEGCPN:	If the coupon calculated above is negative for any period, the coupon is set to zero, but the absolute value of the negative accrual is added as a positive amount to the NEGCPN. At the end of each period, the NEGCPN is compounded as follows:
	NEGCPN = (NEGCPN at start of period) * COMPF
COMPF:	Compounding factor is calculated as:
	COMPF = [1 + 6-month LIBOR * (No. of days in period/360)]
Redemption:	100.00% – NEGCPN
ABCBI:	ABC's bond index applicable on determination date. Determination date is two New York business days prior to either period start or end date.

CONCLUSION

This chapter discussed a sector of structured notes that can be the most custom-tailored and arcane of all structures. These cross-category notes provide investors with the ability to allocate and reallocate assets to the desired asset class without many of the complications associated with performing the transactions directly in the underlying markets. Because of their nature, cross-category notes should be carefully examined for their regulatory, legal, tax, and accounting characteristics prior to any purchase decision.

These cross-category notes, by their very nature, expose investors to a multitude of market risks. This chapter demonstrated that, in addition to risks in the desired market, investors still retain exposure to the interest rate market of the underlying note. The investor must carefully monitor these markets to ensure no performance surprises.

In conclusion, the cross-category notes provide investors with an entry into alternative investment sectors, but in return these structures must be analyzed carefully prior to purchase (for their regulatory and accounting characteristics) as well as during the life of the note due to their multiple market risks.

8

Creation and Customization
of Structured Notes

The ability of structured notes to be customized to produce a desired risk/ reward profile makes them unique among fixed income instruments. An investor is no longer obligated to select from a fixed menu of existing instruments to find the components with which to build a portfolio that suits his or her views. Instead, the investor can purchase a single custom-tailored security that encompasses the desired view.

Recent news of investors taking losses from derivative instruments and the current environment of impending regulatory and legislative actions makes it even more imperative for the investor to comprehend the risks and rewards of structured notes. The previous chapters addressed the topic of structured note risk and performance under various market scenarios. This chapter will complete the risk picture by describing the process of structured note creation. By understanding the process by which a structured note is created, investors can gain further insight into the risk and performance of these notes.

Structured note creation can be decomposed into three main steps: the conceptual stage, the identification process, and the structuring or construction stage.

1. **Conceptual stage.** An investor can have one or more of the following requirements, which can be met by purchasing a structured note.
   a. View
   b. Risk management
   c. Cash flow

        d. Arbitrage/timing
        e. Diversification
        f. Asset allocation

2. **Identification process.** Once the idea has been conceptualized, the equivalent views that are necessary to the construction of a structured note can be distilled from these concepts. The general type of the structure can then be selected based on these views, and the components required for the assembly of the structure are identified.

3. **Structuring or construction stage.** The final step of the creation process involves obtaining the correct market price of each underlying component, and the assembly of these components into the final product.

This chapter is organized as follows. First, the three stages of the structured note creation process are described in greater detail. Following the description of the stages of creation, several different structured notes are created based upon typical market information that would be supplied to structurers.

I. CONCEPTUAL

The first step in the creation of a structured note is the conceptual phase. An investor can have one or more of the following requirements, which need to be fulfilled:

1. **View.** The investor may have certain economic, interest rate, currency, commodity, or other views and wish to profit if these views come to pass.

2. **Risk management.** Investors may have risks to be hedged, but are prohibited from executing the required type of hedge transaction.

3. **Asset-liability management.** Investors may have either fixed or contingent liability cash flows on specific dates and need a security that can meet the liability requirements.

4. **Arbitrage/timing.** Market conditions may be such that a specific sector of a particular market is at a level that is rarely reached on a historical basis. An investor may wish to arbitrage that specific component. Another investor may believe that within a short time, market conditions will exist that would result in a dramatic shift of certain indices from currently predicted forward levels. Structured notes can provide such a timing play on different indices.

5. **Diversification and asset allocation.** With the globalization of markets, many investors need to diversify and allocate assets among different classes of investments. As mentioned in Chapter 7, these alternative asset classes include the domestic and non-domestic fixed income market, as well as the equity, currency, and commodity markets. Structured notes can be an efficient vehicle to achieving that goal without the expense of setting up a global trading operation.

II. IDENTIFICATION

This stage of the structured note creation process requires the identification of the underlying components that are combined in the final stage to create a structured note. The identification of the components of a structured note is based on the requirements of the investor as identified in the conceptual stage. This requirement is divided into answers to the five customization factors to be shortly discussed. Once the five factors have been sufficiently defined, the framework of the structure can be fully constructed.

Five Customization Factors

1. Nationality

The first factor to be gleaned from the requirements expressed in the conceptual stage is the nationality factor. This factor defines the country upon which the investor has a conceptual requirement. The answer to the nationality factor reduces the scope of potential products by limiting the indices or payoffs to a small number of countries and indices. The structurer should remember that the great majority of investors have views or requirements based only upon their respective domestic rates. Thus, for the majority of cases, the answer to the nationality factor is often the native country itself.

Investors may also have views or requirements based on the divergence or convergence of a combination of the rates of two or more nations. This requirement can be accommodated within the structured note framework.

2. Rate Profile

The identification of the investor's interest rate profile is a major component of the structuring process. The rate factor is critical in the determination of the directional play (bearish or bullish) that is contained within the structure.

EXHIBIT 8-1 Rate View Matrix and the Structured Notes That Fit Those Views

The investor's rate view can be distilled into one of the four quadrants and a potential structure can be selected from the list of appropriate structures within that quadrant.

Short-Term Rates		Yield Curve	
		Flatten	**Steepen**
	Economic View →	Low inflation expectation Slow economic growth	Some inflation Slow economic growth
Remain Low	Suitable structured notes	SURF Floored FRN LEAN Index amortizing notes Yield curve accrual note Inverse FRN Prime FRN	CMT-LIBOR differential note Prime-LIBOR differential note CMT, CMS floating rate note Capped/leveraged capped FRN
	Economic View →	Low to fair inflation expectation Strong economic growth	Fair to high inflation Strong economic growth
Rise High	Suitable structured notes	LIBOR, Prime FRN LIBOR minus CMS/CMT Superfloater (based on LIBOR) Accrual note (based on CMT)	CMT-LIBOR differential note Leveraged CMT-LIBOR differential note CMT, CMS FRN Superfloater (based on CMT or CMS)

The various interest rate view possibilities are provided in Exhibit 8-1 along with the currently available structures that can express such a view. Once the investor's views have been translated, the appropriate rate view quadrant can be found in Exhibit 8-1 and a structure that provides the desired rate profile can either be selected from the list in that quadrant or custom-tailored for the investor.

3. Risk/Return

The investor's risk and return profile is crucial in determining the amount of risk embedded in the note. The following table illustrates the combination of risk/return profiles that can be achieved by adjusting the location of the play (either coupon or principal), the minimum coupon, and principal risk.

Risk/Return	Coupon Structure	Principal Structure
Low	Minimum coupon > 0, Incremental yield pickup	No principal risk
Medium	Minimum coupon = 0, Medium yield increment	No principal risk
High	Minimum coupon = 0, Low to very high yield increment	Principal risk

The above table shows that a single rate view can generate a myriad of structures for investors ranging from extremely low-risk pension funds to high-risk, high-return hedge funds.

Strategic Views and the Impact on Structure. Embedded within the risk/return profile is the investor's strategic view. The two basic strategies are the buy-and-hold, and trading. The table below briefly summarizes the two types of investor strategy and the structural implications associated with each.

Strategy	Structure	Time Horizon
Buy-and-hold	Low leverage Enhanced coupon at low risk Typically no principal risk	Maturity
Trading	Higher leverage High risk/High return May have principal risk Some protection on minimum return of principal	Intermediate date

Buy and Hold Strategy. Many investors purchase structured notes with the intention of holding the note until maturity. The essential risk elements of the buy-and-hold strategy are:

1. **Low leverage.** These investors often wish to obtain a steady level of return over the life of the note and thus prefer to avoid high leverage.
2. **Enhanced cash flow.** A buy-and-hold investor is willing to take a relatively low measure of risk in order to achieve incremental yield enhancement. Depending upon the structure and maturity, yield enhancement can range from 5 to 200 basis points of yield.
3. **Minimum coupon protection.** Typical buy-and-hold investors prefer a non-zero minimum coupon to minimize risk if interest rates move in an adverse direction.

4. **No redemption rate risk.** Not having any redemption risk allows the buy-and-hold investor to be able to recover par at redemption. Thus, even if rates moved against the investor, the investor can be assured (within the limits of the issuer's credit) that regardless of the coupon performance, the note would be able to return par at maturity.

Typical buy-and-hold investors include pension funds, banks, and small regionally based investors.

Trading. A smaller class of investors engages in a trading strategy when considering the purchase of structured notes. These investors require a structure that can gain value very quickly if rates move in a certain direction. This rapid gain in value enables the investor to sell out at a profit within a relatively short period of time. Since a trading time horizon is typically one year or less, the trading investor usually has little intention of holding the structured note for an extended period of time. However, the maturity of the note can be longer than one year in order to provide the investor with higher duration and the associated higher implied leverage.

Structured note features that appeal to a trading investor are:

1. **High risk.** The trading structure has a higher level of leverage than buy-and-hold structures. This leverage results in high durational risk.
2. **High return.** The trading structure must provide capital appreciation very rapidly if rates move in the right direction. By the same token, the note would depreciate in value just as rapidly if rates move in the opposite direction.
3. **Redemption linked structures.** A trading structure usually contains some measure of redemption risk in order to produce the desired leveraged gains. However, some investors will require a minimum redemption level (typically around 60–70% of par) to ensure some downside protection.

Typical trading investors include mutual funds, total return funds, and certain hedge funds.

4 and 5. Maturity and Credit

The last two customization factors provide the finishing touch to the basic framework of a prospective structure. The investor's maturity profile has implications on both the form of the note as well as the issuer ratings. The table below summarizes the maturity profile and the associated note form and issuer type.

Maturity	Typical Form of Security	Typical Issuer
Under 1 year	CP	A1/P1
1 to 3 years	CD, Bank notes, MTN	Banks, corporations
Greater than 3 years	Corporate bond, MTN	U.S. Agencies

Typical short-term investors are willing to purchase corporate commercial paper (CP) because shorter term instruments usually have lower duration (with some notable exceptions addressed in Chapters 5 and 6). CP is a good vehicle for short-term money market purchasers due to its short maximum maturity of 270 days or less. Since 2a-7 money market funds are restricted from purchasing notes whose maturities are longer than 397 days (unless the note contains periodic investor puts), the CP is the perfect structured investment vehicle for these investors.

For investors with longer maturity profiles, the credit rating of the issuer becomes increasingly important. Structured notes of three years and longer are mostly issued by U.S. Agencies since investors who have views longer than three years often do not want to take credit risk in conjunction with rate risk.

The great majority of new issue structured notes have relatively short tenures. As the following graph shows, almost 80% of these newly issued structured notes have maturities shorter than three years.

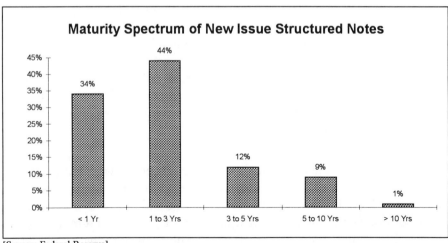

[Source: Federal Reserve]

The following example illustrates the combination of the conceptual and identification stages of the structured note creation process by creating the basic framework of a structured note from an investor's requirements.

Example 8-1

An investor believes that the U.S. economy will continue to recover for the next three years. The investor has some concerns about inflation but does not believe that the Fed will move in the foreseeable future to again tighten money supply. The investor can tolerate some risk but cannot take either credit or redemption rate risk. What structured note would be appealing under these circumstances?

Solution

The above statement summarizes the conceptual stage and represents the investor's views and requirements. These views can be summarized via the identification stage into the following five customization factors.

Nation view:	U.S.
Rate view:	Inflation worry: Rising long-term rates.
	Fed not tightening money policy: Short-term rates remain stable.
	Net rate view is that short-term rates will remain relatively low, and the yield curve will steepen.
Risk/return:	No redemption risk, all coupon linked.
Maturity:	3 years
Credit:	Not being able to take any credit risk, the highest rated note that the investor can purchase is one that is issued by a U.S. Agency, which carries the implied guarantee of the U.S. Government.

Once the five customization factors have been answered, a potential structure that fits the client's view can be selected from the appropriate view quadrant in Exhibit 8-1. The low short-term rate and yield curve steepening view corresponds to the upper right quadrant of the table. From the list of potential structures in that quadrant, one possible structure that can be proposed to the investor is the CMT-LIBOR differential note:

Issuer:	U.S. Agency
Maturity:	3 years
Coupon:	(10-year CMT – LIBOR) + x
Redemption:	100%

Creating an actual structured note would require the calculation of the spread x. The third and final step of the structured note creation process will describe the structuring or construction stage.

III. STRUCTURING OR CONSTRUCTION

In order to fully define a structure, relevant market and issuer information have to be obtained. Some of the required information is described below:

Issuer funding target: The issuer's cost of funding is an integral part of the structuring process. If the funding target is not met, the issuer has little incentive to issue a structured note.

Desired coupon/principal structure: The process of determining the appropriate structure for the investor is described in the previous two steps.

Extraneous hedging cost: This can be an important but overlooked factor because even the offered-side of the market may be insufficient to cover the continuously incurred hedging costs incurred by the structuring swap counterparty.

Underwriting fees: The underwriting fees and profits have to be figured into the overall structure of the note.

Bid/offered side of the underlying components: The appropriate bid and offered prices must be used.

Other pertinent correction factors: Certain rates require additional information such as correlation and convexity. These can greatly affect the underlying swap and option pricing.

Creation of First Generation Structures

The first note to be customized will be the FRN. An FRN is considered structured when the issuer is swapped out of the coupon that it pays on the note into another funding index of choice.

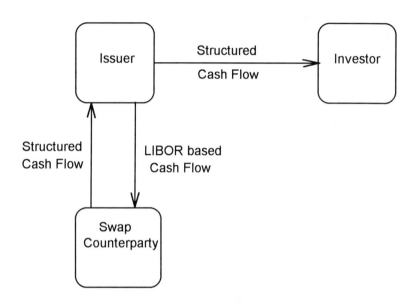

The above diagram illustrates the swap transaction underlying a structured note. The issuer pays a structured coupon to the investor who purchased the structured note. A swap counterparty would pay the same structured coupon to the issuer, and receive a LIBOR based cash flow from the issuer. In this manner, the issuer is *swapped out* of any interest rate risk and is able to obtain funding at a LIBOR based funding level. An issuer is capable of issuing essentially any index as long as it is comfortable with both the structured index and the credit-worthiness of the swap counterparty.

The following example will illustrate the structuring of a first generation structure, the FRN.

Example 8-2

An investor who believes that rates will remain low nevertheless wishes to purchase a floating rate note. The issuer preference is XYZ Corp. (rated Aa2/AA). The investor does not like the low yields currently generated by LIBOR FRNs and would prefer a note based on another floating rate index. The investor is comfortable only with U.S. domestic rates.

Market Specifications

3-month LIBOR:	3.25%
Prime:	6.00%
3-year Prime-LIBOR swap:	Prime – 2.55% versus LIBOR

Issuer Specifications

Issuer:	XYZ Corp. (Aa2/AA)
Maturity:	3 years
Issuer funding target:	LIBOR – 0.15%

The underwriter/structurer would like to make 20 bps of upfront profit on this transaction.

Solution

Based on the investor's views, the following answers to the five customization factors can be generated:

Nation view:	U.S.
Rate profile:	Believes short-term rates will remain low.
Risk/return:	No redemption risk, all coupon linked.
	Only want floating rate note—no leverage
Maturity:	3 years
Credit:	XYZ Corp. (Aa2/AA)

The investor's bullish rate views place the rate profile in the two left quadrants of Exhibit 8-1. Out of the potential structures in the two quadrants, a Prime-based FRN can be recommended. The diagram on the next page shows the details of the structuring transaction. The issuer pays a structured note coupon of Prime – x to the investor. In order to obtain funding on a LIBOR basis, the issuer would simultaneously enter into a swap with a swap counterparty. This swap agreement stipulates that the swap counterparty would pay the issuer the Prime index (minus a swap spread, shown as 2.55%) and receive from the issuer the LIBOR index.

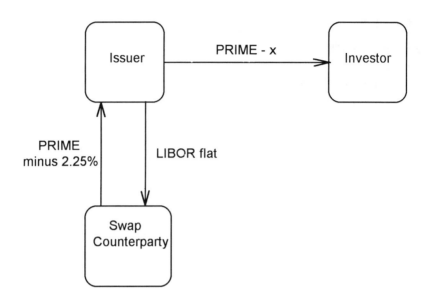

The above diagram shows that the swap counterparty is willing to pay Prime – 2.25% and receive LIBOR flat on a quarterly basis for three years.

The value of x, the note's negative spread to Prime, must now be calculated. The calculation is performed in two steps.

1. **Net cash flow paid by issuer.** The net cash flow paid out by the issuer is calculated by netting all the cash flows in the diagram, with positive being outflows, and negative being inflows.

   Net CF out = Prime – x – (Prime – 2.25%) + LIBOR

             = 2.25 + LIBOR – x

2. **Equating net cash flow to issuer funding cost.** The above calculation describes the issuer's net interest cost after issuing the note and performing the swap transaction. This net outflow should equate to the issuer's funding cost. If the net outflow were any higher, the issuer would refuse to issue since the funding cost for issuing this structured note would exceed the desired funding target.

   Equating the issuer funding target to the net outflow calculated in Step 1,

   $$\text{LIBOR} - 0.15\% = 2.25 + \text{LIBOR} - x \qquad (8\text{-}1)$$

The Prime negative spread x is found to be:

$x = 2.40\%$

The above calculation did not include the necessary underwriting fees of the note. Including the cost of the underwriting fees results in a modification of Equation (8-1):

LIBOR $- 0.15\% -$ Fees $= 2.25 +$ LIBOR $- x$

resulting in the following Prime negative spread x:

$x = 2.40\% +$ Fees

Note that the upfront underwriting fee of 20 bps must be expressed in terms of yield in order to calculate the negative coupon spread x.

Fees = yield equivalent of 0.20%, discounted by 3-year swap rate
   = 7 bps of yield over 3 years

The 3-year swap rate is used as the discounting rate to calculate a yield equivalent of the 20 bps fees, resulting in a yield equivalent of 7 bps.
   The value of the negative Prime spread after adjusting for fees is

$x = 2.47\%$

Care must be taken to ensure that, while summing up the cash flows, all the spreads are converted to the same yield basis. Since Prime is an index that pays quarterly on an Actual/360 basis, and 3-month LIBOR is an index that also pays quarterly on an Actual/360 basis, there is no problem in simply adding the spreads together. However, if the two indices use different day counting and payment basis, conversion of one index's spread into another must be carefully performed to ensure that all the spreads are on the same basis.

Once the spread x has been determined, the entire structure of the note has been defined. However, the work of a structurer does not stop there. The investor and issuer must now be sent the necessary *termsheets* describing the proposed transaction. The first termsheet is the "issue termsheet" specifying the terms of the proposed structured note and is sent to both the issuer and the prospective investor. The second termsheet is the "swap termsheet," which specifies the terms of the swap that the swap counterparty performs with the issuer and is sent only to the issuer since the swap agreement between the issuer and the swap counterparty is transparent to the investor.

Exhibit 8-2 is the issue termsheet of the note, which was structured in the above example. Note the multitude of necessary details such as the definition of the Prime rate, the day count convention used, and the reset conventions. This is a preliminary description of the terms of the note. In the event of a trade, the investor would be sent both a trade confirmation from the underwriter as well as the "prospectus," sometimes referred to as the "pricing supplement" from the issuer specifying in full detail the terms of the structured note.

Exhibit 8-3 is the swap termsheet which is sent to only the issuer. Like the issue termsheet, it is only a preliminary summary of the proposed swap terms. In the event of a trade, the actual documents to be signed by the issuer and the swap counterparty would usually be the full ISDA (International Swaps and Derivatives Association) swap agreement, which is signed shortly after the trade occurs.

EXHIBIT 8-2 Issue Termsheet of CapFRN of Example 8-2

The issue termsheet is sent to both the investor and the issuer. Since no underwriting fees are specified, the note would be purchased (by the underwriter) from the issuer at 100% and sold to the investor at 100%. Since the underwriting fees were originally included in the quoted spread of Prime − 2.47%, LMN's underwriting fees would be paid by the structuring swap counterparty.

Issue Terms	
Issuer:	XYZ Corp. (Aa2/AA)
Principal amount:	US$25,000,000
Settlement date:	Nov. 4, 1993
Maturity date:	Nov. 4, 1996
Coupon paid in US$:	Prime − 2.47%
Day count basis:	Act/360 with no adjustment for period end dates.
Rate reset and payment dates:	Prime rate resets daily, paid quarterly. Payment dates are Feb. 4, May 4, Aug. 4, Nov. 4. First coupon paid on Feb. 4, 1994. Source: H.15(519). Standard two London and New York business days cutoff prior to period end dates.
Issue price:	100.00%
Underwriter:	LMN Underwriter, Inc.

EXHIBIT 8-3 Swap Termsheet for Example 8-2

A summary of the swap agreement between the issuer and the swap counterparty. Note that the arranger of the swap (LMN) is the underwriter of the structured note and can be a completely different entity from the swap counterparty. The swap counterparty must, however, pay the underwriter from the structuring proceeds.

Swap Terms

Notional amount:	$25,000,000
Swap counterparty:	ABC Swaphouse, Inc.
Trade date:	Oct. 13, 1993
Settlement date:	Nov. 4, 1993
Maturity date:	Nov. 4, 1996. Non call life.
Issuer receives:	Amount equal to bond coupon payments on coupon payment dates.
Issuer pays:	3-month LIBOR – 0.15%
Reset and payment dates:	Feb. 4, May 4, Aug. 4, Nov. 4. First coupon payment date Feb. 4, 1994.
LIBOR determination:	3-month LIBOR resets quarterly. Determination day is two London business days prior to reset date. Source: Telerate Page 3750.
Day count basis:	Act/360 with adjustment for period end dates.
All-in financing cost:	3-month LIBOR – 0.10%
Swap arranger:	LMN Underwriter, Inc.

The next example will illustrate the embedding of optionality into structured note, thereby creating a more complex first generation structured note.

Example 8-3

An investor informs you, a structurer for ABC Structurehouse, that her view is for the U.S. economy to remain in a slow growth mode for the next three years, that inflation will continue to remain low, and that there will be no further move by the Fed to tighten the money supply given the slow growth. The investor would like to obtain some good spread to LIBOR but cannot take a large amount risk. In addition, the investor would like to maintain a portfolio of only AA or better issuers. What structure might you propose to this investor?

Solution

The investor's views can be distilled into the following five customization factors:

Nation view: U.S.
Rate profile: No inflationary worries: Low long-term rates.
                          Fed not tightening money policy: Low short-term rates.
                          Net view is that short-term rates will stay low, and long-term
                          rates will remain low or drop even further.
Risk/return: No redemption risk, all coupon linked.
Maturity: 3 years
Credit: Investor can buy a AA issued note.

Given the above rate views, Exhibit 8-1 can be used to provide a list of potential structures that appeal to the rate view. From the rate view quadrant of the investor (upper left), a specific structure is selected: the CapFRN.

The answers to the customization factors form the basic framework of a structure:

Issuer: AA Bank (Issuer funding target: LIBOR-0.15%)
Maturity: 3 years
Structure: Capped LIBOR FRN
Coupon in US$: US$ LIBOR + 0.15% (15 bps higher than a comparable
                            maturity AA floating rate note, which currently trades at
                            LIBOR flat)

Since the issuer funding index and the coupon index are both LIBOR, the only component the structurer needs to provide is the cap.

A CapFRN is essentially the selling of a cap by the investor to the issuer since the investor is selling off the gain in the coupon beyond a certain level of LIBOR. The cap is paid for in the form of enhanced yield to the investor. The unknown pieces of the structure are the LIBOR cap strike X, and the corresponding bid price of the cap. The diagram on the next page illustrates the swap process required to create this note.

The coupon cap is $X + 0.15\%$, which is the actual LIBOR cap strike X plus the coupon spread.

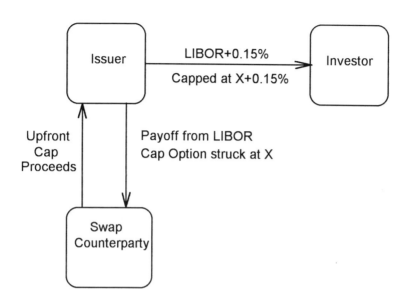

1. The starting level for the coupon is the issuer's funding target:

$$CPN = LIBOR - 0.15\%$$

If the desired coupon level after selling a cap is LIBOR + 0.15%, a difference of 30 basis points of yield must be generated from the proceeds of selling a cap. The present value of 30 bps of yield over three years (present valuing at the current 3-year swap rate of 4.75%) is 83 bps upfront. The structurer must thus find the strike of a 3-year LIBOR cap whose bid price is approximately 83 bps to create the structure (with no fees).

2. The required cap proceeds would have to include the necessary underwriting fees. In this case, the underwriter would like to make as close to 20 bps upfront as possible, bringing the net cost to 103 bps upfront (83 + 20).

3. Next, the correct strike level of the cap has to be found to provide a bid of 103 bps upfront. A 3-year maturity LIBOR cap option at a strike of 5.50% is currently being bid in the broker market at 100 bps upfront.

4. Once the appropriate LIBOR cap strike is found, the structure has been fully determined. Since only 83 bps is required to bring the issuer funding level of LIBOR − 0.15% to the desired coupon of LIBOR + 0.15%, the remaining 17 bps constitutes the underwriting fees.

5. Summarizing the above, the terms of the structure are:

Issuer:	AA Bank
Maturity:	3 years
Coupon:	LIBOR + 0.15% subject to coupon cap
Coupon cap:	5.65% (5.50% LIBOR strike plus the 0.15% coupon spread)
Underwriter fees:	17 bps of price upfront

6. An investor who purchases this note thus has the equivalent net positions of:

Long 3-year maturity LIBOR FRN
Short 3-year maturity cap on LIBOR struck at 5.50%

The issue termsheet is shown in Exhibit 8-4. The swap termsheet is not given, but it would be similar in form to Exhibit 8-3.

Creation of Second Generation Structures

As noted in Chapter 6, second generation structures are typically more difficult to both create and analyze. Some second generation structures will be constructed in the following examples.

EXHIBIT 8-4 Issue Termsheet of the CapFRN of Example 8-3

As with the previous structure, the underwriter fee is being paid out of the structuring proceeds.

Issue Terms	
Issuer and form of note:	AA Bank Certificate of Deposit
Principal amount:	US$25,000,000
Settlement date:	Nov. 15, 1993
Maturity date:	Nov. 15, 1996
Coupon paid in US$:	3-month LIBOR + 0.15% subject to coupon cap
Coupon cap:	5.65%
Rate reset and payment dates:	Rate resets and pays on Feb. 15, May 15, Aug. 15, Nov. 15. First coupon payment date Feb. 15, 1994.
Day count:	Act/360 with no adjustment for period end dates.
LIBOR determination:	3-month LIBOR resets quarterly. Determination day is two New York and London business days prior to period end dates. Source: Telerate Page 3750.
Issue price:	100.00%

Example 8-4

An investor believes that the high inflationary scenarios of the late 1970s and early 1980s will not be repeated again and that inflation will continue to remain low for the foreseeable future. The investor believes that rates will remain stable but does not like the low yield that LIBOR based coupons currently provide. The investor also requires significant downside coupon protection, and is comfortable with AA issuers for as long as 10 years. What structured note would appeal to this investor?

Solution

From the above conceptual requirements, the investor's views can be distilled into the following five customization factors:

Nation view: U.S.
Rate view: No inflationary worries: Low long-term rates.
                  Rates remain stable: Yield curve will not change much.
Risk/return: Low risk tolerance: only coupon linked structures. Wants high coupon floor protection, but wants some upside participation if rates do rise.
Maturity: 10 years
Credit: AA

As in the previous example, the appropriate rate view quadrant of Exhibit 8-1 is selected and a suitable product can be chosen from the list in the quadrant. Given the required high coupon floor protection, a potential structure is the SURF (deleveraged CMT FRN) note.

From the five customization factors, the framework of the proposed structure is:

Issuer: AA Bank (Issuer funding target: LIBOR – 0.125%)
Maturity: 10 years
Structure: Deleveraged CMT FRN with a 5.25% coupon floor and a coupon spread of X

The construction stage is now implemented to solve for the coupon spread X.

Step 1: Swap the issuer out of CMT into LIBOR by performing a CMT/LIBOR basis swap on half the notional amount. This balances the 1/2CMT of the coupon index.

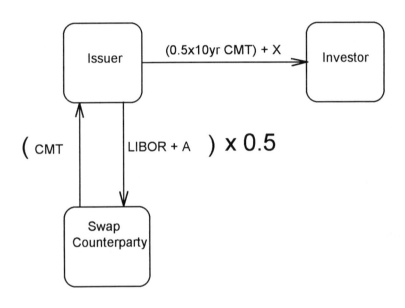

The net cash flow paid by the issuer after performing this swap is:

$$\text{CF paid by issuer} = 1/2 * \text{10-year CMT} + X - 1/2 * \text{10-year CMT} + 1/2 * (L + A)$$

$$= 1/2L + 1/2A + X$$

The result of this swap is to replace the issuer's 1/2 * CMT coupon payments by 1/2 * LIBOR cash flows. Since the issuer's funding is LIBOR based, another swap transaction is necessary to transform the 1/2 * LIBOR into LIBOR.

Step 2: Swap the issuer out of fractional LIBOR into LIBOR. The second swap is a fixed-floating rate swap on half the notional amount.

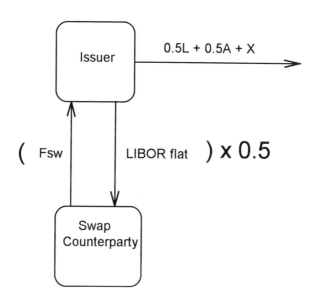

where F_{sw} is the fixed 10-year swap rate versus LIBOR flat. The net cash flow paid by the issuer is then:

$$\text{CF paid by issuer} = 1/2L + 1/2A + X + 1/2L - 1/2F_{sw}$$
$$= L + 1/2(A - F_{sw}) + X$$

This cash outflow must equal the issuer's funding level, making allowances for underwriter fees and the coupon floor.

$$L + 1/2(A - F_{sw}) + X = L - 0.125\%$$

Step 3: Solve for the coupon spread X. Current market levels are as follows:

10-year swap rate F_{sw} = 6.00%,
10-year CMT-LIBOR swap: CMT flat versus LIBOR + 0.95%.

The basis of these spreads must be made consistent. Since the CMT index of the SURF note are paid on a quarterly 30/360 basis, while LIBOR is paid on a quarterly Act/360 basis, the two LIBOR spreads must be converted to quarterly 30/360 basis:

$$X = 1/2[F_{sw} - 0.95 * (365/360)] - 0.125\% * (365/360)$$
$$= 1/2F_{sw} - 0.6083\%$$

where the (365/360) is the factor to convert Act/360 basis to 30/360 basis.

Likewise, the swap rate F_{sw} must also be converted to a quarterly 30/360 basis. Since the fixed leg of a swap is quoted on a semiannual 30/360 basis, decompounding is required:

$$F_{sw,qtrly} = 4 * [((1 + 1/2F_{sw})^2)^{1/4} - 1]$$
$$= 4 * (1.4889\%)$$
$$= 5.9557\% \text{ quarterly } 30/360$$

The spread X can then be calculated:

$$X = 1/2(5.9557) - 0.6083\%$$
$$= 2.3696\% \text{ quarterly } 30/360$$

This value of X does not include structurer profit, upfront bond underwriting fees, or the proceeds to pay for the coupon floor. The next step will incorporate the effect of the coupon floor.

The calculation of the coupon floor and cost is an iterative process. An anticipated floor cost amount F_{fl} is first set aside to pay for the floor option. This amount is subtracted from the above coupon spread X, and the strike of the CMT floor option can be calculated from the preset coupon floor of 5.25%. The cost of the floor at this strike is computed and compared to the original set-aside amount. If the two are different, the set aside amount F_{fl} is changed and the process repeated until the two costs converge.

Step 4: Floor strike calculation. Setting aside an anticipated floor cost of $F_{fl} = 0.3696\%$ yield leaves

$$X_{actual} = X - F_{fl} = 2.00\%$$

Using the preset coupon floor level of 5.25%, the CMT floor strike is calculated to be:

$$\text{Coupon floor} = 1/2\text{CMT} + X = 5.25\%$$
$$1/2\text{CMT} + 2\% = 5.25\%$$
$$\textbf{CMT floor strike} = \textbf{6.50\%}$$

This is the strike of the CMT floor option that is provided to the investor.

Step 5: Floor cost calculation. The cost of a 10-year floor option on the 10-year CMT rate struck at 6.50% is calculated to be 450 bps upfront. However, only half the notional amount of the floor is required due to the deleveraged coupon. To illustrate why only half a floor is required, examine the effect on the coupon when CMT drops 100 basis points from 6.50% to 5.50%. The natural coupon without the floor would be

$$\text{Natural CPN} = 1/2\text{CMT} + 2.00\% = 1/2(5.5\%) + 2\%$$
$$= 4.75\%$$

Since the coupon floor is struck at 5.25%, the floor we structured has to pay (5.25% − 4.75%), or 50 bps. Thus for a 100 bp drop in rates, the floor would only pay 50 bps; hence, only half a floor is required. The cost of this half floor is then:

$$\text{Floor cost} = 1/2 * (450 \text{ bps upfront})$$
$$= 225 \text{ bps}$$

Expressing this upfront amount in terms of yield on the 10-year note:

$$\text{Floor cost (yield)} = 30 \text{ bps of yield}$$

This is less than the 36.96 bps originally set aside for the floor purchase. The structurer can then change the amount set aside F_{fl}, iterating through steps 4 and 5 until that amount agrees with the actual cost of the floor.

Step 6: Fees. Some underwriting fees have to be considered as part of the structuring process. Since the floor cost is 30 bps, and 36.96 bps had been set aside (F_{fl}) originally, the 6.96 bps that is left over can be used for fees, which include both the structurer fees and the bond underwriting fees.

Combining the above steps, the specifications of the proposed structure are:

Issuer:	AA Bank
Maturity:	10 years
Coupon:	1/2CMT + 2.00% subject to coupon floor
Coupon floor:	5.25%
Fees:	6.96 bps of yield, or 52.2 bps upfront

An investor purchasing this note has the following equivalent positions:

Long the notional amount of a 1/2CMT FRN
Long half the notional amount of a CMT floor struck at 6.50%

In summary, the market pricing data required to price this structure are:

1. **Issuer funding level:** This is the final funding level to which the issuer must be hedged.
2. **CMT-to-LIBOR basis swap spread.** This transaction has the role of swapping the issuer out of the deleveraged CMT coupon into deleveraged LIBOR.
3. **Fixed-to-floating swap rate.** This swap transforms the issuer's cash flow payments from deleveraged LIBOR into an unleveraged LIBOR based funding cost.
4. **CMT floor cost.** This component ensures that the coupon spread of the note is consistent with the coupon floor.
5. **Underwriter/structurer fees.** This last piece completes the equation required to solve for the spread to the deleveraged CMT coupon.

Once the above market data are known, the exact structure of the SURF is easily found.

The above example illustrates how even a fairly complicated structure such as the SURF can be created without much difficulty when the structuring process is performed in a stepwise manner. The key point of the construction stage is that the structurer's train of thought should be directed towards swapping the issuer's net payment into LIBOR based funding.

The next structured note to be created is the Quanto note. The issue of how structurers hedge the underlying Quanto swap is not addressed in this book, but interested readers are directed to Das's succinct discussion of the Quanto swap and the associated hedges.[1]

Example 8-5

An investor believes that the European economies will be in a full growth mode for the next few years and would like to participate in the anticipated interest rate rise that usually accompanies such recoveries. The investor can take limited coupon risk but no principal risk.

---

1. See article by Das, Satyajit, "Differential Swaps," in Ravi E. Dattatreya and Kensuke Hotta (eds.), *Advanced Interest Rate and Currency Swaps.* Chicago, IL: Probus, 1994, pp. 25–52.

Solution

From the above conceptual requirements, the investor's views can be distilled into the following customization factors:

Nation view: Europe. Spain is a good candidate for the recovery view because smaller economies usually lead in a recovery due to their low turnaround momentum. Larger economies require longer time to turn around.

Rate view: Believes that Peseta rates will rise quickly.

Risk/return: No redemption risk, all coupon linked. Wants some minimum coupon protection

Maturity: 3 years

Credit : AA

A structure that might be suitable for this investor is a note indexed to Peseta LIBOR but paid in U.S. dollars.

Using the above five customization factors, the framework of the proposed structured note is:

Issuer: AA Bank (Issuer funding target: LIBOR – 0.125%)
Maturity: 3 years
Coupon: 3-month Peseta LIBOR – Y paid in U.S. dollars.

This is actually a relatively simple structure to create. The only swap that is required is shown in the diagram below.

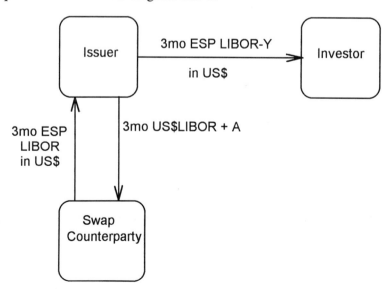

The swap that is required to hedge the issuer back to a LIBOR based funding target is a Quanto swap. The diagram above shows the form of this swap, which requires that a swap counterparty pay the issuer a quarterly coupon based on 3-month Peseta LIBOR but paid in U.S. dollars. In return, the issuer pays the swap counterparty a quarterly coupon based on 3-month US$ LIBOR plus a swap spread A. The net cash flow paid by the issuer is then:

$$\text{Net CF paid by issuer} = \text{3-month ESPL} - Y - (\text{3-month ESPL})$$
$$+ \text{3-month US\$ LIBOR} + A$$
$$= \text{3-month US\$ LIBOR} - Y + A$$

This net cash flow paid by the issuer is equal to the funding target, i.e.,

$$\text{3-month US\$ LIBOR} - 0.125\% = \text{3-month US\$ LIBOR} - Y + A$$

Solving for the negative coupon spread Y yields:

$$Y = A + 0.125\%$$

The only piece of market information required to solve for the coupon spread is the swap spread of the Quanto swap.

Assume a friendly swaps trader ("Trader B") has informed you that he could perform the following swap:

Trader B pays you 3-month ESP LIBOR and receives 3-month US$ LIBOR + 3.00%, 3 year maturity, all cash flows in U.S. dollars.

The resulting coupon spread Y is then

$$Y = 3.00\% + 0.125\%$$
$$= 3.125\%$$

The full structural details of the proposed note are as follows:

Issuer: AA
Maturity: 3 years
Coupon: 3-month Peseta LIBOR − 3.125% paid quarterly in US$.

Since the spread of 3.125% is not zero, a zero coupon floor is also required. However, a quick check of Peseta Quanto option prices shows that the cost of this floor is quite negligible. Nevertheless, the structurer should not forget that this note includes a zero coupon floor, which must be provided.

The above example showed that even though the Quanto note is a relatively exotic structure, the structuring process itself is relatively straightforward. The complicated aspect of creating a Quanto note is the hedge of the underlying Quanto swap. Das showed that this swap is neither simple nor a perfect hedge and must be dynamically managed by the swap counterparty.

The final example will involve the creation of a cross-category structured note for asset allocation purposes.

Example 8-6

An investor who currently holds $100MM of 10-year Treasury notes wants to reallocate the coupon return from $50MM of the 10-year notes into a return on the Hang Seng Index for one year. The investor is willing to take any and all risks associated with a return linked to the Hang Seng. The investor does not want to sell out his holdings, and would like to regain the return from all $100MM of the Treasury notes after one year. The investor can only purchase AAA rated notes. What structure might be appropriate for this investor?

Solution

This asset allocation problem is relatively straightforward to structure. Based on the above conceptual requirements, the five customization factors are as follows:

Nation view: Hong Kong
Rate view: Bullish on Hang Seng
Risk/return: All associated risk of the HS Index: Can take redemption risk if negative returns are carried to maturity.
Maturity: 1 year
Credit: AAA Bank

In addition, the proposed structure must also accomplish the following:

1. Remove the coupon return from the $50MM 10-year Treasury notes.
2. Provide exposure to the Hang Seng Index for a notional amount of $50MM.

Given the above requirements, the framework of a proposed structure would be as follows:

Issuer: AAA Bank (Issuer funding target: LIBOR – 0.25%)
Notional: US$ 50MM
Maturity: 1 year
Coupon: 0.00%
Redemption: 100% + (Total return of Hang Seng Index
                            – Coupon return of 10-year Treasury note) + X
Total return: (Index at maturity – Index at start)/(Index at start)
Current 10-year
TSY CPN: 5.00%

Current market levels are:

10-year Treasury coupon CPN = 5.00% semiannual 30/360
Total return swap spread S = 1.50% quarterly Act/360
Issuer credit spread I = 0.25% quarterly Act/360

The construction stage of the creation process will provide the solution of the negative coupon spread X.

Step 1. The first swap involves swapping the issuer out of the Hang Seng Index exposure into a LIBOR based exposure. A swap quote is obtained whereby the swap counterparty pays the issuer the total return on the Hang Seng Index over one year (paid in US$) and receives in return 3-month LIBOR plus a spread. (See the illustration on page 325.)

The net cash flow paid out by the issuer after the swap is:

$$\text{Issuer cost} = (\text{Total return of HS} - \text{Coupon return of } 10y + X)$$
$$+ (\text{LIBOR} + S) - (\text{Total return of HS})$$
$$= (\text{LIBOR} + S + X - \text{Coupon return of } 10y)$$

Step 2. Equating this swapped cost to the issuer's required funding target produces the equation required to solve for the negative spread X.

$$\text{LIBOR} + S + X - \text{CPN} = \text{Issuer funding cost}$$
$$= \text{LIBOR} - 0.25\%$$
$$X = \text{CPN} - S + 0.25\%$$

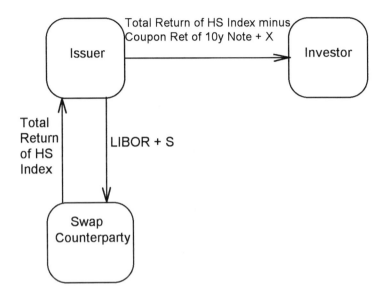

The market swap levels must now be converted into the same basis as the proposed coupon structure. Since the Hang Seng Index return is only paid at the end of the first year, the two spreads must be converted into an annual 30/360 basis. Without going through the particulars, these are:

$$CPN = 5.0625\% \text{ annual } 30/360$$
$$S = 1.5295\% \text{ annual } 30/360$$
$$I = 0.2537\% \text{ annual } 30/360$$

The coupon spread X is calculated to be

$$X = 5.0625\% - 1.5295\% + 0.2537\%$$
$$X = 3.7867\%$$

assuming 0.2867% of fees results in a spread X of 3.50%. This means that the spread is actually positive. Summing the positive spread X with the negative coupon return of −5.0625% annual 30/360 (5.00% semiannual 30/360) produces the net coupon spread to the Hang Seng Index of −1.5625%.

Issuer:	AAA Bank
Notional:	US$ 50MM
Maturity:	1 year
Coupon:	0.00%
Redemption:	100% + (Total return of Hang Seng Index) – 1.5625%
Total return:	(Index at maturity – Index at start)/(Index at start)

This note will permit the investor to pay away the coupon return on $50MM 10-year Treasury note and in return receive the total return of the Hang Seng Index minus 2.50% over one year. At the end of the one year, the note matures, and the investor recovers the coupon return on the entire $100MM of the 10-year Treasury note.

CONCLUSION

This chapter describes the methodology of the structured note creation process. The creation process consists of three stages: conceptual, identification, and construction. The conceptual stage is the fact-finding stage. The structurer must understand the needs, requirements, and limitations of the investor in order to create a customized structure. Identification breaks down the investor requirements into five customization factors. Construction combines the basic framework provided by the identification phase with market information of the underlying components and produces the actual final structure.

In many instances, the structurer works closely with the end investor to custom tailor an end product specifically for the investor. This stepwise process of understanding an investor's needs and using those requirements to create a structure that fits the investor's needs is what sets structured notes apart from other fixed income instruments.

Understanding the structured note creation process is vital for investors to gain further insight into the behavior of these notes. This chapter provided readers with a view of the structured note creation process from the structurer's perspective. By combining knowledge of the structured note creation process with knowledge of the risk and performance characteristics from the previous chapters of this book, an investor can synthesize a clear view of all the potential pitfalls and benefits of a structured note.

9

Structured Notes
and Portfolio Management

The topic of portfolio and asset/liability management is one which has been frequently and ably addressed.[1,2] This chapter will summarize some of the basic portfolio management goals and demonstrate how these concepts apply to investments involving structured notes.

This chapter will be organized as follows: first, a brief overview of portfolio management concepts will be provided. Following the overview, the use of structured notes within the context of the two portfolio management philosophies will be introduced. Finally, the role of structured notes in simplifying and expanding the role of the portfolio management process will be examined via the examples provided.

PORTFOLIO MANAGEMENT: AN OVERVIEW

A portfolio manager has two overriding priorities. The first is to protect the portfolio against adverse market conditions, and the second is to enhance the return of the portfolio. Within that general context, most portfolio managers adhere to one of two distinctly different lines of philosophy: passive portfo-

---

1. Dattatreya, Ravi E., and Frank J. Fabozzi. *Active Total Return Management of Fixed Income Portfolios.* Chicago, IL: Probus, 1989.
2. See Dattatreya, Ravi E. "A Practical Approach to Asset/Liability Management," pp. 37–59 in Frank J. Fabozzi and Atsuo Konishi (eds.), *Asset/Liability Management.* Chicago, IL: Probus, 1991.

lio management, and active portfolio management.[3] Structured notes can be an important component of either methodology. Prior to examining the role of structured notes within either portfolio management context, a brief overview of both methodologies will be first presented.

Passive Portfolio Management

The role of the passive portfolio manager is to manage a portfolio to produce a return which matches that of a target index. The goal of the passive manager is therefore to replicate an index return with minimal risk. The passive investor's risk profile is as follows:

Nationality: Domestic.
Rate view: None. Obtain a return which closely matches the total return of an index.
Risk/return: Minimal risk to achieve target index return.

The term "passive portfolio management" brings to mind a portfolio manager with feet up on a desk reading a magazine. Nothing could be further from the truth. Since passive portfolio management requires that a manager produce a portfolio return as close to an index return as possible, constant monitoring and vigilance is required to accomplish this task.

Passive investors represent a relatively small fraction of all investors and include index funds and pension funds.

Passive Management Methodology

The two steps taken by a passive portfolio manager in creating and maintaining an index portfolio are:

1. **Index portfolio selection.** Select assets whose yield, duration, and convexity closely match that of the index. Because the passive manager's role subsequent to the initial purchase is to maintain adherence to the index, the initial selection process is extremely important.

---

3. See articles by Fong, Gifford, "Bond Management: Past, Current, and Future," pp. 875–881, and Dialynas, Chris, "The Active Decisions in the Selection of Passive Management and Performance Bogeys," pp. 882–887 in Frank J. Fabozzi (ed.), *The Handbook of Fixed Income Securities.* Homewood, IL: Business One Irwin, 1991.

2. **Index portfolio maintenance.** Continuously rebalance the investments within the portfolio to ensure the above characteristics continue to match the index.

The selection of assets will first be discussed. Portfolio adjustment, rebalancing, and rehedging will be addressed shortly in the asset/liability management section of this chapter.

Index Portfolio Selection

The selection of the original portfolio is an important component of the passive manager's role. Readers interested in the issue of index portfolio selection are directed to the work of Mossavar-Rahmani,[4] which is briefly summarized here.

There are three basic approaches to creating an indexed portfolio: stratified sampling, linear optimization, and quadratic optimization.

Stratified Sampling Methodology, or the Cellular Approach. The simplest approach to assembling an index portfolio is via stratified sampling. The investor attempts to replicate an index by separating the index into several classes or sectors. Sectors can be based on coupon, maturity, duration, issuer rating, and issuer type. Within each of these sectors, an investor can then select representative investments. The initial portfolio selection is complete when all the sectors have been filled. The following table illustrates the stratified sampling methodology replicating a bond index with two sectors: industry and maturity.

	Industry	
Maturity	*Agency*	*Corporate*
0 to 3 years	Bond 1a	Bond 2a
3 to 5 years	Bond 1b	Bond 2b
5 to 10 years	Bond 1c	Bond 2c

The above table shows that in order to replicate a bond index by stratification into two sectors, the investor would select an appropriate investment for each cell of the table. Once all the cells have been filled, the passive manager's initial task is complete.

4. See article by Mossavar-Rahmani, Sharmin, "Indexing Fixed Income Assets," pp. 898–911 in Frank J. Fabozzi (ed.), *The Handbook of Fixed Income Securities*. Homewood, IL: Business One Irwin, 1991.

Stratified sampling offers a simple, straightforward, and flexible approach to achieving index replication. Its weaknesses are that the subsequent rebalancing and rehedging require considerable effort, and that the portfolio which is so created is not optimized (optimization being defined as a portfolio with maximum yield and convexity).

Linear Optimization.   The next level of sophistication in index portfolio selection methodology is the linear optimization. It introduces the concept of maximizing the conformity to the index within certain constraints. It is a more structured and systematic approach to the construction of an index portfolio. Linear optimization seeks to maximize the adherence to an index within the constraints of the cellular structure of stratified sampling and a given universe of investment possibilities.

Quadratic Optimization, or Variance Minimization.   Variance minimization is the most complex of the three portfolio selection methodologies. It requires the maximization of a utility function, which expresses the difference between the expected return and the risk. The investor thus identifies investments which, when combined into a portfolio, will maximize this utility. At the same time the portfolio manager must act to minimize the variance, or deviation from the expected return of the index. The risk of potential investments is calculated from historical data.

Advantages of Indexing and Passive Management

The advantages of a passive portfolio management philosophy are as follows:[5]

1. Indexing permits the ultimate investor some means of control over independent portfolio managers.
2. Indexed fund managers typically charge lower management fees than active investment managers.
3. Indexed portfolios typically exhibit lower turnover than actively managed portfolios and hence the embedded transaction costs are likewise lower.
4. Indexed portfolios permit easy evaluation of investment advisors. The advisors can be easily judged by how well they have met or exceeded the index target.
5. Investors can limit the maximum deviation from the index return to further limit risk.

---

5. Ibid.

Active Portfolio Management

Active portfolio managers have no fixed target index to follow. Their mandates are less clear: obtain the maximum yield for the risk taken. In other words, active managers take risks and expect to be rewarded for these risks. Active investors constitute the majority of fixed income investors and include asset/liability managers, mutual funds, total return funds, cash managers, and hedge funds.

The management of an active portfolio consists of the following tasks:

1. **Asset selection.** This includes the decision of the relevant asset class and the initial selection of the risks which would be taken.
2. **Risk monitoring.** The portfolio manager must continuously monitor and adjust the risks of the portfolio and its components.

The issue of asset selection will first be addressed. Risk management is a process which is common to both the active and passive managers and will be discussed shortly.

Asset Selection

The asset selection process is further divided into two considerations: the asset allocation decision and risk selection (see Exhibit 9-1).

Asset Allocation.   Given the limited amount of risk capital that is available, how does the active manager select from the multitude of investment possibilities? The following is a brief summary of the selection process.

1. **Country selection.** Investors have the choice of investing in multiple countries, each with its own associated risks and returns. If investing in a non-domestic country, country risks such as political volatility must be taken into consideration.
2. **Analysis and selection of asset class.** Within each country, the investor can select different asset classes for investment. The ramifications of investing in these markets must be carefully examined. The market sectors available (in most developed countries) to investors are:
   a. Fixed income (taxable and tax exempt)
   b. Equity
   c. Currency

EXHIBIT 9-1   Asset Selection Considerations
The two main components of the asset selection process are asset allocation and risk
selection.

Asset Selection	Considerations
Asset allocation	Country determination
	Asset class determination
	Fixed income
	Equity
	Currency
	Commodity
	Other indices
	Asset class switching
Risk selection	Interest rate risk
	Maturity risk
	Credit risk
	Index risk
	Currency risk
	Volatility risk
	Correlation risk

      d. Commodity
      e. Real estate
   3. **The switching decision.** The markets have to be monitored and
reevaluated periodically. Decisions to switch into or out of asset
classes should be made as part of an overall strategic plan.

Risk Selection.   After making a decision to allocate risk capital to a particular class of assets, the active portfolio manager must next select the desired
risks to be taken in order to achieve the maximization of return within this
asset class. Some of the risks which can be selected by the active manager are:

   1. **Interest rate.** This is the most common of risks taken by fixed
income portfolio managers.
   2. **Maturity.** Certain investments carry maturity uncertainty. The
investor can obtain enhanced yield in return for selecting maturity risk.
   3. **Credit.** This is a risk which is quite familiar to most fixed income
investors. By descending the ratings ladder, an investor can obtain a
higher level of yield for a lower rated issuer with a higher risk of
default.

4. **Index.** This is the risk associated with the asset class selected. Some indices which can be selected are bond indices, equity indices, and commodity indices.
5. **Currency.** If an investor decides to invest in non-domestic markets, any profit or loss would be in the non-domestic currency. This currency risk can be further tailored to obtain additional gains. For example, an investor who believes that the British pound will increase in value against the U.S. dollar can purchase high-yielding British Gilts and receive a high coupon return complemented by additional FX gains when the coupon interest is FX'd from pounds into U.S. dollars (assuming that the pound does indeed increase in value versus U.S. dollars; otherwise the investor would suffer a corresponding FX loss).
6. **Volatility.** Some investors may wish to capitalize on a level of volatility which is high or low by historical standards. These investors can sell or purchase options on either interest rate or any of the above risks, thereby taking on volatility risk in addition to the risk of the underlying index.
7. **Correlation.** Certain indices may show historical correlation to other indices. Investors can take advantage of such correlation risks by purchasing assets which provide payoffs linked to either higher or lower future correlation.

A very important complication which arises from purchasing securities to take a particular risk is that the security can often contain other risks. This is true whether the investment is a simple callable bond or a cross-category structured note. The goal of an active manager should thus be to select the desired risks and at the same time eliminate or manage the undesired residual risks. The issue of risk assessment and management will be discussed in the next section.

PORTFOLIO RISK AND ASSET/LIABILITY MANAGEMENT (ALM)

Once an active or passive portfolio manager has selected a particular avenue towards achieving a return goal, the risks of such a portfolio must be analyzed, deemed acceptable, and managed.

Risk Measurement

Prior to purchasing any investment instrument, the risks of the proposed investment must be understood and deemed acceptable and appropriate for the level of enhanced return. The risks to be initially quantified are the measurable risks and the scenario risks.

Measurable Risk

These are risks which can directly result in gains or losses in the value of the investment.

1. **Interest rate risk.** Interest rate risk should be analyzed in the context of the risk analysis methodologies addressed in Chapters 2–4. The main considerations should be the yield curve risk of each note which can be calculated via KTRD.
2. **Index (currency, commodity, equity) risk.** These risks are only present in structured notes which are tied to these markets.
3. **Maturity risk.** Certain notes can have embedded maturity risks which must be quantified.
4. **Volatility risk.** Notes with embedded optionality can change in value for incremental changes in volatility.
5. **Credit Risk.** What is the effect on the value of an investment when the issuer is downgraded? Interested readers are directed to a discussion of analyzing credit risk in a portfolio context by Frye.[6]

Scenario Risks

These are the "what-if" risks which an investor must initially quantify. Knowing the scenario risks allows the investor to prepare for what can occur if rates deviate from expectations.

1. **Hedge risk.** If the note is designed as a hedge, the note should be analyzed over a range of scenarios and shown to be adequate to the hedging task.
2. **Cash flow mismatch risk.** If the note is designed to produce an anticipated stream of cash flows to meet liability, the analysis should

---

6. See article by Frye, Jon, "Portfolio Approach to Credit Risk Evaluation," pp. 3–23 in Ravi Dattatreya and Kensuke Hotta (eds.), *Advanced Interest Rate and Currency Swaps.* Chicago, IL: Probus, 1994.

ensure that the cash flow is anticipated and the liability is met over a range of scenarios.
3. **Worst-case scenario.** Can the portfolio survive a worst-case performance by the structured note? What is the maximum loss associated with such a scenario?
4. **Index mismatch risk.** This is a concern of passive managers who have to constantly ensure that the portfolio is as close in characteristics to the index as possible.

Suitability

Once the risks have been quantified, the first question that should be posed by the portfolio manager is whether the investment with its associated risk and performance profiles is an appropriate investment instrument for this portfolio. Are the embedded views of the structured note compatible and consistent with the other securities in the portfolio? Is the risk appropriate to the reward? In light of the recent publicity surrounding losses by 2a-7 money market funds investing in derivative products, the suitability question is an important issue which should be addressed in the context of portfolio strategy and investment philosophy.

Risk Monitoring

The risks of the investments should be continuously monitored to ensure that the initially assessed risk characteristics do not rapidly change. Not monitoring these risks can result in a portfolio whose risk and performance profiles are quite different from initial assessments.

A risk monitoring system[7] is essential in enabling the portfolio manager to continuously monitor the performance and risks of the note. A risk monitoring system must contain the following components.

Performance Monitoring System

This system monitors the past and present performance of both the overall portfolio and any particular security in question. The following characteristics should be monitored:

---

7. See Dattatreya, Ravi E., "A Practical Approach to Asset/Liability Management," pp. 37–59 in Frank J. Fabozzi and Atsuo Konishi (eds.), *Asset/Liability Management.* Chicago, IL: Probus, 1991.

1. **Cash flow.** The actual cash flow performance should be monitored and weighted against any liability requirements. A consistent mismatch between cash flow and liability or anticipated income is a good indication that the investment is not performing as planned.
2. **Market value.** The market value of the portfolio and individual securities should be continuously monitored. The investor would be well served to obtain frequent mark-to-market supplied by external sources as well as perform internal calculations in order to properly and consistently monitor the market values of the securities. Investors should never rely solely on either an external valuation or an internal calculation.

Risk Analyzer

The risk of the investments within the portfolio have to be constantly monitored.

1. **Interest rate and index risk.** The risk characteristics of structured and non-structured investments can change with different market conditions. These risks must be constantly monitored.

EXHIBIT 9-2 Risk and Liability Management Considerations of a Portfolio Manager in the Context of Structured Notes

A full consideration of all the inherent risks must be made.

Risk and Liability Management	Considerations
Risk measurement	Measurable risk: Interest rate, duration, volatility, credit, index.
	Scenario risk: Hedge, index mismatch, cash flow, worst case.
Suitability	Decide appropriateness of SN investment:
	Are the risk and return profiles consistent with overall portfolio strategy?
	Is the structure compatible with existing portfolio?
	Are the risks manageable?
Risk monitoring	Continuous monitoring of risk via a risk monitoring system.
Adjustments	If the risk of the note exceeds initial expectations, adjustments must be made to compensate.

2. **Maturity risk.** As mentioned in Chapter 2, the durational characteristics of structured notes can change not only with market movements, but also with time. As notes mature and new investments are made, the risk profiles of the portfolio will change.
3. **Volatility risk.** Many structures do contain a significant level of volatility risk which can change significantly with different interest rate conditions. Volatility risk should be monitored in conjunction with measuring the underlying volatility so that the investor is not caught off-guard by rapid shifts in volatility.
4. **Credit risk.** The credit rating of the issuer should be continuously monitored for signs which could point to a ratings downgrade or upgrade.

Scenario Analyzer

The risk management system must have the capacity for performing scenario analysis and observing the resulting effect on all of the above monitored items. In particular, the investor should examine worst-case scenarios to ensure that if such an event does occur, the damage to the portfolio is still manageable. Worst-case scenarios are events in which conditions deviate by three standard deviations (in the direction to cause the most harm) from an expected level.

Adjustments

In the event that the risk of the note is greater than expected, adjustments must be made in order to reduce the risk to a manageable level.

Advantages of Active Portfolio Management

Active portfolio managers offer certain advantages over passive index portfolio managers.

1. **Risk selection.** Index portfolio management philosophy does not allow portfolio managers their own selection of risks. Many investors may wish to take on specific risks. Active portfolio managers are permitted such leeway.
2. **More flexibility.** Active portfolio managers set their own investment goals and targets. This permits greater flexibility and allows a rapid transition into areas of new investment opportunity.

3. **Investors may not wish to track an index in certain market conditions.** When market conditions change from a bull market into a bear market, the relevant fixed income and equity indices will produce low or negative total returns. In this situation, investors may not wish to track these indices.

4. **Liquidity.** Passive index portfolio managers are almost always invested fully in the markets, while active managers usually keep a core of cash or liquid securities as a reserve against adverse conditions. This liquidity core can act to soften the impact of a bear market.

ROLE OF STRUCTURED NOTES IN PORTFOLIO MANAGEMENT

What is the role of structured notes in the scheme of portfolio management in the 1990s? What benefits do structured notes provide that cannot be obtained from other investments? Structured notes offer some tangible benefits to both the passive and active portfolio manager. These include:

1. **Risk management.** Structured notes can greatly simplify the task of passive portfolio managers who must produce results as close to a target index as possible. Structured notes can also contain the necessary ingredients to help limit the risks of active portfolio managers.

2. **Enhanced views.** Structured notes can enhance the role of the active portfolio manager by offering the investor a variety of types, combinations, and degrees of risk. Many of these risks are not available to fixed income investors.

3. **Customization.** A portfolio manager is no longer constrained to purchase whatever is currently available on the market to create a portfolio. Structured notes offer investors the benefit of customized solutions.

4. **Diversification.** Structured notes can provide investors with a diversification of risks. Rather than purchase a variety of different securities in different markets, an investor can purchase a single customized structured note based on a basket of such indices.

This section will outline the role of structured notes within the context of the two portfolio management philosophies. Examples will serve to illustrate some of the benefits described above.

Structured Notes for Passive Portfolio Managers

Structured notes are perfectly suited for portfolio managers who track the returns of certain indices. As mentioned in Chapter 7, cross-category notes can provide the desired exposure to various markets and indices. The following classes of indices can be embedded in cross-category notes:

Bond index: An investor who tracks the total return of a particular bond index can purchase a total return indexed note which provides such returns.

Equity index: Likewise, an investor who tracks a return based on an equity index can purchase an equity linked note to provide the same exposure.

Commodity index: Although few fixed income investors measure themselves against a commodity index, the ability to track such an index can be provided by structured notes via a commodity linked note.

The advantage of purchasing a cross-category structured note to accomplish the task of index replication is that, unlike the traditional index portfolio methodologies of stratified sampling, linear optimization, and quadratic optimization, the tracking error can be totally eliminated. The index portfolio manager could purchase such an index linked note and be worried only about the credit of the issuer since payment of the total return of the index is, in effect, guaranteed by the good faith and credit of the issuer.

The following short example will illustrate this capability.

Example 9-1

A passive portfolio manager tracks the total return of the ABC Government Bond Index. She would like to create a new portfolio which closely replicates this index. Although the duration of the index is nine years, she would like to purchase notes of maturities shorter than five years. She can purchase finance company notes with ratings as low as BBB, but is willing to sacrifice as much as 20 bps of yield to purchase single-A rated notes. What structured note would assist this manager in her task?

Current market swaps. Swaphouse A pays ABC Government Bond Index – 0.35% and receives LIBOR flat.

Current issuer levels. Following is a list of finance companies and their funding targets for five years:

Issuer	Funding Target
XYZ Finance Corp. (A1/A+)	LIBOR flat
NOP Inc. (Baa1/A–)	LIBOR + 0.25%
UVW Broker Dealer Inc. (A3/A–)	LIBOR + 0.40%
Abc Banking Corp. (Baa3/BBB)	LIBOR + 0.50%

Solution

The investor's customization factors are as follows:

Country: U.S.
Rate view: No explicit view
Risk/return: Wants return based on the ABC Government Bond Index
Maturity: 5 years
Credit: BBB (but single-A if possible) finance company

Combining the issuer funding targets with the swap spread and assuming 5 bps (yield) in underwriting fees, the following structures can be created for each of the issuers:

Issuer	Coupon: Total Return of ABC Government Bond Index +
XYZ Finance Corp. (A1/A+)	–0.40%
NOP Inc. (Baa1/A–)	–0.15%
UVW Broker Dealer Inc. (A3/A–)	+0.00%
Abc Banking Corp. (Baa3/BBB)	+0.10%

The investor has shown a definite preference for single-A issuers. From the list of prospective issuers, UVW Broker Dealer Inc. is a single-A entity that can provide a yield that is only 10 bps lower than another BBB issuer (Abc Banking Corp.). Based on the investor's issuer preference, the following structured note can be proposed to the investor:

Issuer: UVW Broker Dealer Inc.
Maturity: 5 years
Coupon: Total return of ABC Government Bond Index + 0.00%
Redemption: 100% – Accrued negative returns (if any)

This note provides the portfolio manager with the entire exposure of the ABC Government Bond Index over five years. By purchasing the above note, the passive portfolio manager has, in effect, shifted the risk of replicating the index return to the structurer. In return, the investor gains the credit risk of the issuer, UVW. The role of the portfolio manager is now dramatically simpler: the portfolio manager must periodically track the credit rating of the issuer to ensure that the investor can be reasonably expected to continue paying the total return of the index.

Structured Notes for Active Portfolio Managers

As mentioned earlier, structured notes offer active portfolio managers the ability to profit from their views. Since the goal of active portfolio managers is to maximize the return for a degree of selected risk, structured notes can constitute a useful component of the investment strategy of such investors. Structured notes are often able to provide exposure to various types and degrees of risks which are not available to fixed rate note investors. Depending on the investor's views or requirements, a structure usually can be tailored to meet those specific needs.

Although structured notes can be easily customized to meet the active portfolio manager's selected risk, the customization process can introduce additional risks which may not be transparent. This underscores the importance of the initial risk analysis.

The following example will illustrate how structured notes can fit the active portfolio manager's selected risks profile and how the initial risk analysis can shed light on all the embedded risks of a structured note.

Example 9-2a

A portfolio manager wishes to maximize his floating rate yield and believes that rates will remain stable for the next two years. He is willing to take high interest rate risk but prefers AAA rated issuer. What investment might meet the portfolio manager's risk profile, and what are the risks associated with this investment?

Solution

The investor's requirements are summarized in the following customization factors:

Nationality: U.S.
Interest rate view: Rates will remain stable: Range view
Risk tolerance: High
Maturity: 2 years
Issuer: AAA

Given the above customization factors, a possible investment instrument is the LIBOR enhanced accrual note (LEAN). The details of a potential structure are:

Issuer:	AAA
Maturity:	2 years
Coupon:	3-month LIBOR + 1.00% when LIBOR is in range;
	0.00% when LIBOR is outside range
Range:	3.50% to 6.00%
Current LIBOR:	4.75%

As with any structure, the above note introduces risks in addition to the investor's selected rate view risk. These additional risks must be analyzed and deemed acceptable by the investor. The following asset/liability management risk measurement analyses should be performed by the portfolio manager prior to the purchase:

I. Performance analysis
II. Risk analysis: Measurable risk
   1. Durational analysis
   2. Volatility analysis
   3. Credit analysis
III. Risk analysis: Scenario risk
   4. Cash flow analysis
   5. Worst-case analysis

Performance Analysis

The characteristics of the LEAN have been described in detail in Chapter 6. In the present example, the performance of the LEAN for a range of final expectation LIBORs is shown at the top of page 343. The LEAN provides a good yield advantage over comparable issuer and maturity floating rate note provided LIBOR remains within the 3 1/2% to 6% accrual range.

Risk Analysis: Measurable Risk

1. Durational Analysis. The durational behavior of the LEAN is illustrated in Chapter 6. The KTR for this LEAN is the 2-year maturity Treasury rate. As observed earlier in Chapter 6, the accrual note can attain rather high duration. This is reflected by the durational calculations from the 5000 run simulation analysis. The maximum duration of the LEAN can be as high as 4 1/2,

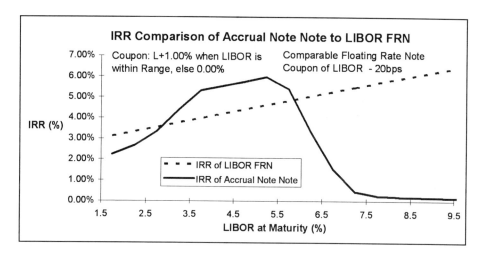

IRR Comparison of Accrual Note Note to LIBOR FRN

which is more than twice the duration of a comparable maturity fixed rate note. The portfolio manager must thus be prepared to manage this high level of interest rate risk.

For low interest rate scenarios, the note exhibits negative duration. This phenomenon was likewise discussed in Chapter 6 and represents an increase in note value for an incremental rise in interest rates.

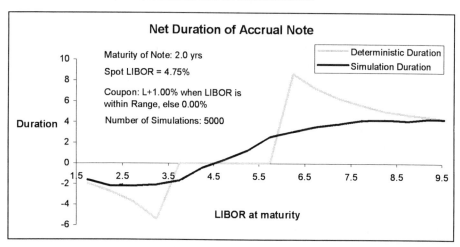

Net Duration of Accrual Note

2. Volatility Analysis.   The mechanics of the LEAN's volatility risk have been discussed in detail in Chapter 6. From the graph below, the key risk features of the LEAN are that the maximum and minimum volatility duration are approximately +15 and –10 respectively. This is a very high volatility duration for a 2-year maturity note and reflects the high volatility risk of the LEAN.

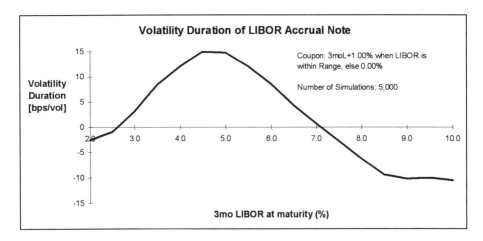

The large positive volatility duration for medium interest rate scenarios points out that the note is particularly vulnerable to *increases* in volatility for these scenarios. Likewise, the large negative volatility duration for higher interest rate scenarios point out the note's vulnerability to *decreases* in volatility. In summary, the LEAN exhibits volatility duration profile which is large in magnitude and which can, depending upon the interest rate scenario, reverse directions. In order to avoid surprises, the investor must be vigilant against the rapidly changing characteristic of the LEAN's volatility risk profile.

3. Credit Analysis. For the purposes of the credit risk discussions in this book, it will be sufficient to simply consider the results of a downgrade. The credit analysis of structured notes is no different from the credit analysis of a fixed rate note.[8]

The following is a range of credit spreads for a 2-year maturity note. The associated change in the value of the note due to the downgrade action is calculated by multiplying the spread widening by the duration of the note with respect to credit spread widening. This credit spread widening duration is equal to that of a regular 2-year fixed note, or 1.9.

---

8. A downgrade of a structured note issuer can result in some additional side effects on the price of the note. This effect will be discussed in Chapter 11.

Ratings	Credit Spread to TSY	Change in Value of 2-yr. Note Due to Downgrade from AAA
AAA	+10 bps	0.000%
AA	+25 bps	−0.285%
A	+50 bps	−0.950%
BBB	+85 bps	−1.610%

Based on the above table, the price implications of a single issuer ratings downgrade is approximately a 28.5 bps drop in price.

Risk Analysis: Scenario Risk

4. Cash Flow. The cash flow of the accrual note is shown below for a range of final LIBOR scenarios. It is seen that for LSE based scenarios, it is most likely that the accrual index will move out of the accrual range towards the latter part of the note's life.

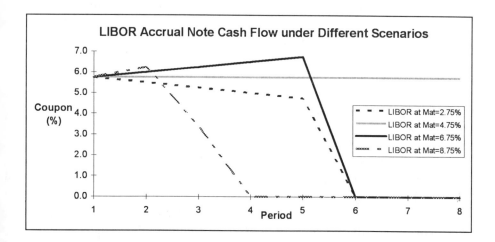

In either a rising or dropping rate environment, the coupon cash flows of the accrual note would most likely be weighted towards the front periods. Due to the contingent nature of the note's cash flow and the minimum coupon of 0%, it should not be used as a hedge for fixed liability cash flows.

5. Worst-Case Analysis. The note performs badly if the accrual rate (LIBOR) moves outside the accrual range very rapidly. The worst-case sce-

nario is that if LIBOR should move out of the accrual range in the first period and remain outside for the tenure of the note.

LIBOR at End of First Period	Fraction of First Period Which Accrued at L + 1.00%	IRR of Note
1.50%	38.4%	0.28%
2.50%	55.5%	0.40%
3.50%	100%	0.72%
6.00%	100%	0.72%
7.00%	55.5%	0.40%
8.00%	38.5%	0.28%
9.00%	28.4%	0.21%

* Spot LIBOR = 4.75%

Based on the above projections, it is seen that in cases where LIBOR
exits the accrual range during the first period, the note can produce yields
which are close to zero. The absolute worst case occurs if the accrual LIBOR
moves out of the accrual range the day after the note is purchased and
remains outside the range for the remainder of the note's life. The portfolio
manager should thus be prepared for this worst-case scenario in which the
LEAN is effectively a zero coupon note, producing little or no coupon cash
flows during its life. This conditional and volatile nature of the cash flow of
this note makes the LEAN an unsuitable candidate for offsetting a stream of
fixed liability.

To recap, the stable rate view risk originally selected by the investor led
to a proposed structure, the LEAN. The risk measurement conducted by the
investor illustrates the performance and risk characteristics of the note under
various scenarios. After performing the above risk measurements, the portfolio manager must make a suitability decision regarding the acceptability of
these risks and the appropriateness of these risks to the overall portfolio and
investment philosophy.

Based on the above analyses, the portfolio manager now has a good
understanding of the potential risks and benefits of the note. If the LIBOR
accrual note should be deemed a suitable investment for the portfolio and
purchased, the portfolio manager must continue to periodically monitor the
risk and performance of the note to ensure that these characteristics do not
rapidly change.

Example 9-2b

The portfolio manager decided that the risks are acceptable and purchased the above LEAN. Soon thereafter, a situation arose whereby the portfolio manager must set aside 2% of the note's interest to offset an unforeseeable liability. What can be done?

This situation illustrates the flexibility of structured notes. As mentioned, many issuers are willing and able to effect either a buyback of the original structured note or to restructure the note in another form. It will be assumed in this example that the issuer can and will restructure the note. The investor's additional requirement is thus:

Minimum coupon: 2.00%

The new proposed LEAN would be similar in structure to the original note. However, to generate the higher minimum coupon floor, the accrual range and coupon spread must be reduced. The following structure can be produced:

Issuer:	AAA
Maturity:	2 years
Coupon:	3-month LIBOR + 0.75% when LIBOR is in range;
	2.00% when LIBOR is outside range
Range:	4.00% to 5.50%
Current LIBOR:	4.75%

Of course, this new structure requires that the portfolio manager undertake a full reassessment of risk and performance characteristics. These analyses are shown below.

Performance

The performance of the new structure is similar to that of the previous structure. The key difference is that the breakeven range between which the LEAN's performance is superior to that of a LIBOR FRN is noticeably narrower. This is a reflection of the narrower accrual range and the lower coupon spread. The drop-off in performance for very high interest rate scenarios is significantly less as well, dropping to an asymptotic return of 2.00% (coupon floor) rather than the 0% of the previous structure.

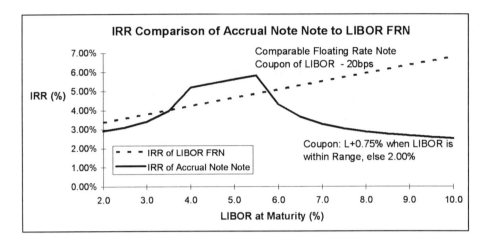

Risk Analysis: Measurable Risk

1. Interest Rate Risk.   From the result of the simulation analysis below, the maximum duration of the new structure is now approximately 3 1/4. This is considerably lower than the 4 1/2 duration of the previous structure. The higher minimum coupon accounts for this change in behavior. Since the loss in value between being inside the accrual range and outside the accrual range is lessened, an incremental increase in interest rates would likewise result in a lower magnitude of loss or gain.

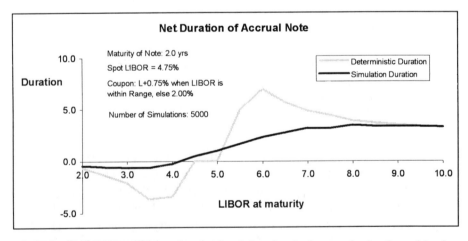

2. Volatility Risk.   From the result of the simulation analysis plotted in the next graph, the maximum and minimum volatility duration of this note are approximately +7 and −7 respectively. This is significantly lower than the

+15 and –10 of the previous structure. The higher coupon floor is again the cause of this behavioral change. The loss in value between being inside the accrual range and outside the accrual range is now considerably less, resulting in a lower change in note value for an incremental change in volatility and hence a lower volatility risk.

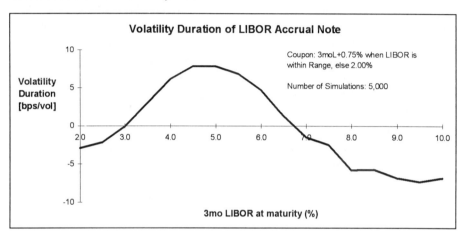

3. Credit Risk. Since the issuer is not changed, the credit component of the note's risk remains the same.

Risk Analysis: Scenario Risk

4. Cash Flow. The cash flow generated by the new LEAN structure for a variety of scenarios is shown in the graph below. As expected, the coupon

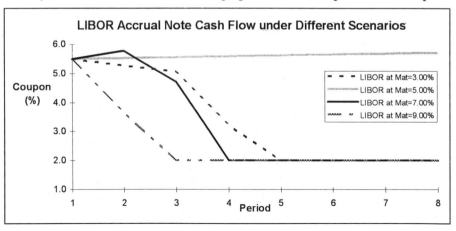

cash flow characteristics are quite different from the previous note. The key
difference is that, as expected, the minimum coupon cash flow is now
floored at 2%. This new structure is quite able to meet the annual liability
cash flow requirement of 2%.

5. Worst-Case Scenario. The worst-case scenario remains the same: the
accrual index would exit the accrual range the day after settlement and
remain outside the accrual range for the life of the note. However, the performance of the note under this worst-case scenario is now quite different
due to the presence of the 2% minimum accrual coupon floor. The worst-
case scenario is thus for the note to be a fixed rate note yielding 2% for its 2-
year life.

This example illustrated the ability of structured notes to be customized
to an investor's views as well as the task of risk determination which all portfolio managers must undertake. This particular structure introduced significant levels of risk in addition to the desired risk of the investor. The example
illustrated the importance of the process of initial risk determination which
was able to quantify the various embedded risks and permit the investor to
make an informed investment decision.

This example also illustrated the flexibility of structured notes as an
investment whose characteristics can be fine-tuned and reshaped to an
investor's changing needs. This is one of the many benefits which structured
notes provide. This flexibility cannot be matched by fixed rate notes.

Final Consideration: Liquidity

A risk that is not obvious and does not fall under the above risk analysis categories but that needs to be considered by investors is *liquidity*. As evi-
denced by the well-publicized collapse of a large mortgage fund, the market
for any product, be it government bonds, mortgages, or structured notes, has
the potential of turning illiquid in times of crisis. The astute portfolio manager should first determine the liquidity condition of the secondary market for
the structured notes within the portfolio. Once the secondary market liquidity is known, a reserve of highly liquid cash instruments in combination with
other less liquid securities would be maintained in order to avoid a liquidity
crisis. By maintaining this liquidity core, the investor can avoid having to
sell a security into an illiquid market to generate cash and suffering the large
bid-offer spreads demanded by dealers or other investors.

CONCLUSION

Portfolio managers generally adhere to one of two investment philosophies: active and passive. This chapter briefly illustrated the role of these portfolio managers and how structured notes can both simplify and amplify the portfolio manager's role. Investors should bear in mind that although structured notes can greatly simplify the investment process, they can also introduce unforeseen risks. For this reason, a thorough initial analysis of the embedded risks of structured notes is extremely important to identify and control these undesired risks.

Structured Notes versus
Cash and Futures

INTRODUCTION

The ability of structured notes to provide investors with active investment strategies often leads to comparisons with alternatives in the cash and futures markets. At first glance, the exchange-traded cash and futures instruments might seem to be cost-effective alternatives to implementing such a strategy. This chapter will illustrate the comparative advantages and disadvantages of structured notes versus such exchange-traded instruments. By the end of this chapter, it will be clear that while exchange-traded products do, in certain situations, offer definitive advantages over structured notes, it is often difficult and sometimes impossible to re-create all the investment possibilities provided by structured notes in the cash, bond, futures, and options markets.

It is worth repeating the statement that investors seeking to engage in any new product or market should ascertain fully the tax, accounting, regulatory, and legal consequences of such action. In the discussion of the pros and cons of structured notes versus cash and futures, these non-economic issues constitute a significant component of the investment decision process.

OVERVIEW OF THE FUTURES AND OPTIONS MARKET

A brief review of the futures and options market is in order, with the main emphasis being on the interest rate index exchange-traded products. Readers interested in a full discussion of the futures and options markets are directed to Burghardt.[1]

Futures

In the interest rate arena, 3-month LIBOR is currently the most popular short-term floating rate index. It has supplanted the 3-month Treasury bill as the benchmark short-term U.S. interest rate. The relevant futures contract for LIBOR is the Eurodollar time deposit futures ("Eurodollar futures," or "ED"). The first traded financial futures contract was the 3-month Treasury bill futures, which were first traded on the IMM (International Monetary Market, a division of the Chicago Mercantile Exchange) in 1976, while Eurodollar futures contracts were first permitted to trade in 1982. The number of Eurodollar futures contracts currently stands at 40, extending in maturity to 10 years. Eurodollar futures contracts are actively traded on the IMM, the SIMEX (Singapore International Monetary Exchange), and the LIFFE (London International Financial Futures Exchange).

Although it was the first financial futures index contract to be traded, the popularity of the 3-month T-bill futures has faded since the introduction of the Eurodollar futures contracts. Three-month Treasury bill futures are still being traded, but the longest maturity is only one year, and market liquidity is far less than that of Eurodollar futures contracts.

Options

Options on Eurodollar futures have been traded on the IOM (Index and Options Market division of the Chicago Mercantile Exchange) since 1985. The unit of trading in Eurodollar options is half that of the Eurodollar futures, namely in increments of 1/2 basis points. Each basis point change in price reflects $12.50 in profit or loss to the investor. The expiration of the Eurodollar options is, like the Eurodollar futures contract, on the second London business day prior to the third Wednesday of the contract month.

Eurodollar options are American-style options, i.e., they can be exercised at any time during the period. They differ from interest rate caps in that on option expiration date, the payoff is made on the expiration date based on

1. Burghardt, Galen, Terry Belton, Merton Lane, Geoffrey Luce and Richard McVey. *Eurodollar Futures and Options.* Chicago, IL: Probus, 1991.

the then-current setting of LIBOR, whereas interest rate caps pay three months *after* the final determination of the LIBOR.

The size of the exchange-traded Eurodollar options market is tremendous. As far back as 1989, over 6 million Eurodollar options contracts were traded[2] during the year. With each contract controlling $1 million, that equates to over $6 trillion in notional amount terms traded in one year. This tremendous liquidity and volume is one of the key advantages of exchange-traded products.

Growth of OTC and Exchange-Traded Products

The growth of both the over-the-counter (OTC) derivatives market and the exchange-traded market from 1990 to 1994 has been explosive. However, as shown in Exhibits 10-1 and 10-2, the OTC market has far outstripped the exchanges in its growth. This is due in part to the flexible nature of the OTC market, which has great capacity for generating new products, compared to the exchanges, which by their nature have difficulty creating customized structures.

The exchanges continue to make attempts to compensate for the inflexible nature of exchange-traded products and to compete with the OTC market, the latest attempt being the introduction by the Chicago Board Options Exchange (CBOE) of *Flex options* in 1993.[3] The Chicago Board of Trade (CBOT) has likewise introduced "Flex-like" options on Treasury bonds and notes. The Flex system permits investors to specify the following contract characteristics:

1. **Underlying index.** Investors can select from a fixed menu of traded indices such as the S&P 100.
2. **Option type.** Investors can select a call or a put, but nothing more exotic.
3. **Expiration date.** Investors can, with some exception, select a maturity date up to five years from trade date.
4. **Strike price.** Investors have considerable flexibility in selecting the strike level.
5. **Exercise style.** The exercise can be American, European, or capped.

---

2. Ibid.
3. See *Euromoney,* June 1994.

EXHIBIT 10-1 The Over-the-Counter Derivatives Market

The growth in the notional amount of OTC-traded products from 1989 to 1992 has been nothing less than phenomenal.

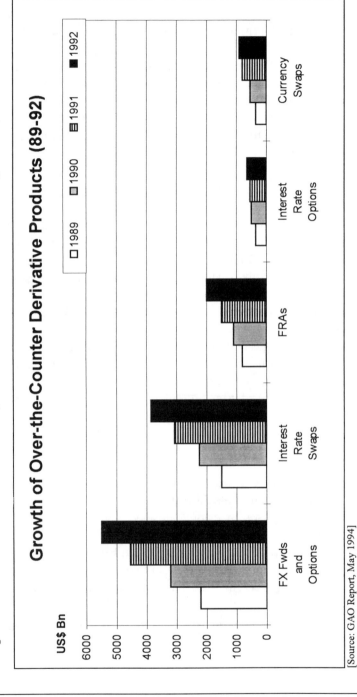

Growth of Over-the-Counter Derivative Products (89-92)

☐ 1989 ☐ 1990 ☰ 1991 ■ 1992

US$ Bn

6000
5000
4000
3000
2000
1000
0

FX Fwds and Options | Interest Rate Swaps | FRAs | Interest Rate Options | Currency Swaps

[Source: GAO Report, May 1994]

EXHIBIT 10-2 The Exchange-Traded Products

Exchange-traded derivative products have, compared to the OTC derivatives market, seen comparatively lower growth both in absolute and notional amounts. The amounts in the graph represent the amount of outstanding open interest of the listed products.

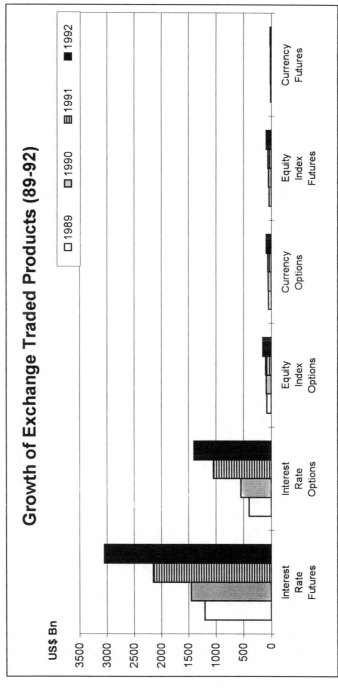

Growth of Exchange Traded Products (89-92)

US$ Bn

Legend: □ 1989 □ 1990 ⊞ 1991 ■ 1992

Categories: Interest Rate Futures, Interest Rate Options, Equity Index Options, Currency Options, Equity Index Futures, Currency Futures

[Source: GAO Report, May 1994]

For CBOE-traded Flex contracts, the minimum contract size required to initiate a new Flex series is US$10 million, with subsequent trades limited to notional amounts of US$1 million or larger.

The above customizations are an improvement from the standard exchange-traded options and futures contracts. However, the flexibility of these Flex options is limited at best, in that investors are still constrained to the traditional options and futures payoffs and cannot obtain nontraditional exotic-type payoffs such as those found in the second generation and cross-category structured notes.

Although the Flex options are traded on the floor of the exchanges in the open-outcry style, the Flex market makers are by nature smaller in number than those participating in standard Exchange-traded contracts. The introduction of flexibility thus sacrifices the advantages provided by standard exchange-traded products, namely liquidity, small contract size requirements, and ease of execution. Hence, the introduction of the Flex option has, if anything, made the exchanges more like another OTC dealer.

INVESTOR CRITERIA FOR EXCHANGE-TRADED PRODUCTS

Not all investors can transact in the exchange-traded products directly. Investors wishing to transact in the future and options exchanges must possess the following characteristics.

1. **Sophistication.** The investor must be sophisticated enough to understand and accept the risks associated with transacting in exchange-traded products. For example, municipal retirement funds may not want to transact directly in crude oil futures because of the high volatility and risk of the product. By the same token, a cautious investor may not wish to transact in a non-domestic market, such as the Gilt futures, of which he or she has little or no knowledge.
2. **Ability to transact in cash and futures market.** The investor must be equipped to transact in the exchanges. This typically means that an investor must be able to transact through an intermediary (broker) on the exchange floor who can execute transactions discreetly on behalf of the investor. The term "ability" also implies that the investor must have the proper record-keeping, cash management, trade analysis, and any other systems set up to support these futures and options transactions.

3. **Capital and liquidity.** Investors must have sufficient reserve capital to post margins against exchange-traded positions. Depending upon market conditions, the investor may have to post additional margins to offset a loss in the underlying positions. Investors who do not possess a sufficient amount of liquid reserves should be extremely careful about monitoring their outstanding positions.
4. **Legal and regulatory permission.** The investor must be legally permitted to transact in the market in question. Certain investors may be prohibited from taking non-hedging positions directly in the future and options exchanges. This requirement must be thoroughly researched by the investor prior to proceeding.

EXCHANGE-TRADED PRODUCTS VERSUS STRUCTURED NOTES

Advantages of Exchange-Traded Products Over Structured Notes

A good discussion of some of the strengths of exchange-traded products over OTC products such as structured notes is presented by Konishi and Dattatreya[4] and is summarized here.

1. **Standardization.** The contracts traded on the exchanges are created along standard expiration dates, strikes, and sizes. This standardization eliminates confusion about the terms of a traded contract.
2. **Cost.** The cost associated with trading on the exchange is small. Again, due to the large number of market participants and standardization, the transaction bid-offer spread is relatively low for shorter-dated futures and options contracts. However, even the bid-offer spread of exchange-traded products widens out significantly for longer-dated and less liquid contracts.
3. **Small minimum transaction size.** The minimum size of a Eurodollar futures contract is $1 million. This permits even small investors the ability to transact in exchange-traded products.
4. **Liquidity and execution.** The greatest advantage to using exchange-traded instruments is the high liquidity. The most commonly traded

---

4. Konishi, Atsuo, and Ravi E. Dattatreya (eds.). *The Handbook of Derivative Instruments.* Chicago, IL: Probus, 1991.

futures and options contracts have very large outstanding interest, with tens of thousands of contracts (each contract controlling US$1 million) changing hands each day. An investor looking to liquidate his or her holdings in a quick and efficient manner could probably find no place more efficient than the exchanges. This liquidity cannot be matched by any OTC product such as structured notes. Hence, the bid-ask spread of exchange-traded instruments tends to be considerably smaller than that of structured notes.

5. **Confidentiality.** Exchange trades are performed with a good measure of confidentiality as investors deal through floor brokers. Structured note purchasers have slightly less confidentiality because their identity is known to both the issuer and the underwriter.

6. **Frequent mark-to-market.** Investor positions and profit/losses are settled up daily on exchanges. Thus any gains by investors are rapidly reflected in upfront payments.

As mentioned previously, the CBOE has introduced the Flex option to its trading floor. The Flex option, while offering flexibility, negates several of the above exchange-traded product advantages, namely standardization, low transactions cost, minimum size requirement, and liquidity.

Disadvantages of Exchange-Traded Products

1. **Margin requirement and unknown cash flow outlays.** The investor is required to post additional cash or securities if rates move in such a manner as to cause the established position to go out of the money. A structured note poses no such requirement. This is an important issue because structured note investors do not have unpredictable additional cash requirements after the initial purchase since the maximum possible loss is the principal. On the other hand, investors transacting in exchange-traded products must be always ready to post additional cash margins at any time or face the closing out of their positions by the exchange clearinghouse.

2. **Daily reset.** The daily reset feature of the exchanges can create difficulty for smaller investors. Cash flows and liquidity must be carefully managed so that the investor would always have sufficient liquid assets on hand to post any required margins.

3. **Date inflexibility.** Some investors require cash flow income on pre-determined payment dates. For these investors, the exchange-traded ED futures and options contracts are inflexible in that, in addition to the daily settlement, the standard exchange products have fixed expiration schedules. That inflexibility is also the exchanges' strength, since a standard expiration schedule allows for high liquidity and turnover volume.

4. **View inflexibility.** If the investor wishes to restructure his or her rate views, e.g., he or she now wants to switch out of U.S. rate plays and make plays on Yen rates, he or she would have to close out existing U.S. futures positions and put on new Yen positions. Certain structured note issuers will allow the swap counterparty to restructure the note coupon into another play, provided the issuer is still hedged into its native funding cost.

5. **Credit diversification.** Exchange-based transactions are transacted via brokers and clearing agents. Certain bad trades have been known to have caused the clearing agent to be bankrupted. Although all clearing agents are backed by the exchange's clearinghouse (all U.S. exchanges are either explicitly or implicitly AAA), it must be noted that most of these individual brokers and clearing agents are considerably smaller than some of the larger issuers and underwriters of structured notes. Some nascent and emerging market exchanges would probably be rated substantially below AAA if they were to be rated. Any investor trading and settling through brokers on these exchanges would retain an unknown credit and settlement risk. Structured notes are issued by banks, corporates, and Agencies that vary in rating from AAA to BBB-minus. The investor would thus be able to choose the desired credit and obtain credit diversification.

6. **Non-availability of play.** An investor may have an esoteric view that does not have a traded counterpart on the exchanges. For example, an investor looking for a binary bullish play on Spanish Peseta rates payable in U.S. dollars would be unable to find such an option traded on any exchange. Although some Quanto-type contracts were created in the late 1980s by the American Stock Exchange and briefly traded, the low volume and lack of general interest caused these contracts to die quickly. Structured notes can provide a custom-tailored solution for the investor with non-standard esoteric views.

7. **Tax and accounting.** The tax and accounting treatment of exchange-traded products must be carefully analyzed prior to any transaction. The latest tax rulings from the IRS indicate that unless the exchange transactions are performed as a hedge (and must be fully documented as such), all profit and losses are immediately taxed as capital gains and losses within the current tax year. Thus, an investor trying to replicate a 5-year capped FRN by purchasing a LIBOR FRN and selling exchange-traded Eurodollar puts would obtain gains that would receive capital gains tax treatment since it would be difficult to assert that such a transaction is a hedge. On the other hand, a capped FRN would be able to produce amortized cap proceeds and deliver it to the investor in the form of an enhanced coupon over the 5-year maturity of the note.

   It is extremely difficult to obtain a clear-cut IRS ruling allowing for fully integrated tax and accounting for a combination of a standard underlying security and a derivative. The IRS lost a recent suit against Fannie Mae and has established new guidelines for integrated tax treatment. The essence of the guidelines is that if a good case can be made for the associated derivative being a hedge of the underlying security (and not an outright play), the proceeds from the derivative can, in most likelihood, be amortized and taxed accordingly. However, in another recent ruling, the IRS has apparently ruled against any *leveraged* transactions receiving integrated hedge account treatment.

   The above discussion of the tax implications of exchange-traded products and structured notes points to the necessity of investor research to understand the issues surrounding these products. The investor's task is all the more difficult in the absence of clear-cut IRS regulations and statements.

8. **Dynamic hedging and side effects of market replication.** In addition to performing tax, accounting, regulatory, and legal analysis, an investor interested in using cash and exchange-traded products to replicate structured note plays must be able to perform the necessary dynamic hedging of the outstanding positions. Replicating a structured note-type play requires that the investor take positions in various cash, futures, and options instruments. These instruments have side effects that can cause their prices to vary unexpectedly and function differently than first assumed. An investor must understand

the effects of these "side effects" on the overall portfolio and know how to dynamically hedge these instruments in certain rate situations. For example, a CMT floating rate note can be partially replicated by an investor who shorts the 10-year Treasury note. However, shorting the 10-year Treasury note requires the investor to perform a reverse repurchase transaction to short and then buy back the Treasury note in question.[5] This involves haircut cost and continuously changing repo rates, continuously rolling out of an old issue into the "on-the-run" Treasury issue each time the Treasury Department conducts a 10-year note auction, and continuous adjustments for duration and convexity changes, which cause the price change to mismatch the yield change. These are non-trivial tasks for replicating a relatively simple index.

Finally, it is worth mentioning that the options pricing theory demonstrates that a riskless basket of cash and the underlying security can be used to replicate an option. However, it is obvious that very few investors perform such a task today because of the costs associated with dynamic option replication and the ready availability of options in the market. Similarly, many of the structured notes discussed earlier in this book can be replicated partially in the market. However, the efforts required to implement artificial replication and the availability of structured notes to provide such a rate play preclude the need for performing such replication transactions for many investors.

REPLICABILITY OF STRUCTURED NOTES VIA EXCHANGE AND CASH PRODUCTS

Depending upon the circumstance, exchange-traded products can offer certain advantages over the structured notes. However, many existing structures cannot be fully re-created via exchange-traded instruments. This section discusses how one might use the exchanges to replicate as much of the structured notes described previously as possible.

The structures discussed earlier in this book each have different characteristics that can make them more or less suitable for replication. The issue of replication is discussed in this section, beginning with the structures that are

---

5. Stigum discusses the repo process in Stigum, Marcia, *The Money Market.* Homewood, IL: Dow Jones-Irwin, 1983.

easiest to replicate. Note that the one characteristic of structured notes that cannot be replicated by exchange-traded instruments is that structured note cash flows occur on coupon dates, while replicating via exchange-traded instruments requires daily settlement.

I. Mostly Replicable

The easiest structures to create in the cash market are the floating rate notes based on LIBOR. If the investor is able to overcome the tax, accounting, regulatory, and legal issues as well as use the standard expiration schedule of the exchanges, the plays upon which following structured notes are based can be replicated in the cash, futures, and options markets.

Structure	Cash Market Replication Transaction
Capped FRN*	Short puts on ED futures
Floored FRN*	Long calls on ED futures
Collared FRN*	Short puts and long calls at different strikes on ED futures
Inverse FRN**	Long twice notional amount ED futures
	Long out of money ED puts
Equity bull or bear**	Long or short equity index futures, long equity index call or put options
Commodity bull or bear**	Long or short commodity futures, long commodity call or put options
Currency indexed note**	Long or short forward FX, long forward FX options
Total return bond index**	Long basket of underlying bonds

* Requires the purchase of a LIBOR FRN in addition to the accompanying exchange-traded products.
** Requires the purchase of a fixed rate note in addition to the accompanying exchange-traded products.

For example, an investor who purchases a capped FRN believes that (1) rates will stay low, and (2) current volatility is high. To re-create that play, the investor would purchase a LIBOR FRN and short sell put options on Eurodollar futures. If rates drop, the LIBOR FRN would produce a lower coupon, but the put option that was sold would expire out of the money, resulting in a profit to the investor. That profit would thus enhance the return of the overall portfolio. Similarly, if rates rose, the LIBOR FRN would produce a higher return, which would be offset by the losses from the shorted put option's increase in value.

II. Partially Replicable

Certain structures and plays on interest rates can be partially replicated in the futures and options markets. However, there would be significant and non-negligible residual rate and/or currency risk, which the investor would either have to bear or hedge to the best of his or her ability.

Structure	Partial Replication Cash Market Transaction	Residual Risk
Quanto note	Long (short) interest rate index futures on appropriate non-domestic futures exchange	Contract payoff is in non-U.S. currency; need to currency swap back to US$
CMT, CMS indexed note (no coupon floor)	Short bonds or swaps of appropriate maturity	Dynamic hedging losses, rollover risk, repo cost

For example, the payoff of the CMT note can be partially replicated by an investor purchasing a fixed rate note and shorting Treasury bonds. If Treasury yields rise, the investor would obtain gains from decrease in the price of the shorted Treasury note. If Treasury yields dropped, the investor would lose money from the increase in the price of the shorted Treasury notes. However, the cost of dynamic hedging, rollover, and non-constant repo costs would make this an inexact hedge at best.

III. Unreplicable

Notes with indices and exotic options that do not trade on exchanges cannot be re-created with exchange-traded products. The following are some examples:

Structure	Why Exchange-Traded Products Cannot Provide Such Play
Prime FRN, deleveraged Prime FRN	No Prime futures contracts
SURF (contains CMT floor)	No long-dated (as long as 10 years in maturity) option on Treasury bond futures
Power notes (LIBOR squared)	No LIBOR square futures or options contracts
Index amortization notes, one-way collared notes	No path-dependent LIBOR options contracts
LEAN, binary note, yield curve accrual note	No LIBOR accrual option, no binary accrual option, no yield curve accrual option

For example, the LEAN structure discussed in Chapter 6 provides investors with a coupon that is based on the number of days of the period that LIBOR remains within an accrual range. Since there is no comparable exchange-traded option that could provide this type of payoff, the structure is not reproducible via exchange-traded instruments.

Even though these structures cannot be re-created via exchange-traded products, a highly sophisticated investor would still be able to create the play via the swap market. Off-exchange OTC derivative products such as swaps and swaptions are employed by structurers in creating structured notes. An investor who wishes to re-create a structured note play without purchasing a security can enter into a swap transaction with a counterparty to receive the desired play.

CONCLUSION

This chapter discussed a topic that many have assumed about structured notes: that structured notes are easily replicable via exchange-traded instruments. Some of the first generation structures certainly do fall into this category. However, the discussions of this chapter show that many other structures cannot be so replicated. Even in cases where an investor can mostly replicate a structured note, it may not be advantageous for one to do so due to a variety of reasons such as accounting, tax, legal, and replication costs.

Structured Note Valuation in the Secondary Market

INTRODUCTION

The issue that will be addressed in this chapter is one that is frequently overlooked but whose importance continues to grow with time: the secondary structured note market. The explosive growth in the volume of newly issued structured notes has resulted in an ever-increasing supply of secondary structured notes. How do these seasoned structured notes trade in the secondary market? What issues must the investor be aware of when trying to buy or sell secondary structured notes? What is a fair market price? These issues and others will be addressed in this chapter.

There are two main methods by which a structured note is priced in the secondary market. Notes can be priced on either an asset swap basis, or on a straight basis. Each type of pricing basis, as well as other secondary market issues, will be discussed in this chapter.

ASSET SWAP PRICING

As illustrated in Chapter 8, a structured note is created by embedding forwards and/or optionality in the coupon, principal, or maturity component of a note. Given these embedded derivatives, a swap can be performed on an existing note to strip out the embedded options and convert the structured coupons into a stream of fixed or floating rate based cash flows. This process is known as an asset swap, and any note traded in this manner is known to be priced on an asset swap basis.

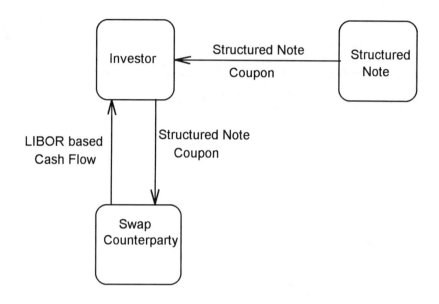

In the above diagram, an investor has just purchased a structured note and retained a swap counterparty to perform the asset swap on the structured note. The role of the swap counterparty is to receive the cash flow of the structured note from the investor and pay a predetermined LIBOR or fixed rate based cash flow back to the investor. The net result is that the investor is swapped out of the complex structured note into a regular fixed or floating rate note. The complication is that the investor is now exposed to the credit-worthiness of the swap counterparty. For that reason, an investor willing to buy a structured note on an asset swapped basis should: (1) obtain a considerably better yield than a comparable non-structured floating rate note of the same issuer; (2) perform a credit analysis on the swap counterparty and find the credit risk acceptable; and (3) have an understanding of the underlying structured note instrument and perform an analysis to assess the risk of swap counterparty default.

Asset swap pricing entails the valuation of the various embedded components of the note. It is a realistic pricing because it shows the investor where the components of the structured note can currently be cashed out in the market and converted into either a fixed or floating rate note. As such, asset swap represents the *break-up value* of the structured note.

The following example will illustrate the methodology of asset swap pricing.

Example 11-1

A secondary collared FRN is being offered by Investor A in the secondary market to a structured note trader. Comparable maturity floating rate notes of the same issuer are currently trading at LIBOR flat. The trader knows of an Investor B who would purchase this note on an asset swap basis at LIBOR + 0.20%. What should be the trader's bid price?

Issuer: AA Bank
Coupon: LIBOR + 0.125% subject to coupon cap and floor
CPN cap: 9.625%
CPN floor: 5.125%
Maturity: 9.5 years

Solution

Step 1. Estimate the costs of disassembling the component pieces.
  The underlying components of the note first must be identified. Since the note has a 5.125% coupon floor, the underlying option is a LIBOR floor with a strike of 5.00% (5.125% coupon floor − 0.125% coupon spread). Likewise, since the note contains a 9.625% coupon cap, the other underlying option is a LIBOR cap struck at 9.50% (9.625% coupon cap − 0.125% coupon spread).

Components: Note contains a 9 1/2-year maturity LIBOR floor at 5.00%
  Note contains a 9 1/2-year maturity LIBOR cap at 9.50%

The note is long the LIBOR floor and short the LIBOR cap. In order to strip the note of these options, the floor that the note is long must be sold, and the cap that the note is short must be purchased in the market. From surveying the market, a 9 1/2-year maturity LIBOR floor at 5% is currently being bid at 415 bps upfront. Similarly, a 9.50% cap for 9 1/2 years is currently being offered at 500 bps upfront.

Step 2. Sum up the components.
  The net amount that is generated from the removal of the embedded options can be calculated by summing up the amount received from the market for the floor (positive) and the amount paid to the market to remove the cap (negative).

Net amount generated = 415 − 500
  = −85 bps upfront

Since the amount generated is negative, removal of the embedded options will not generate any excess cash, but instead will require an inflow of 85 bps in order to remove the cap and floor.

Step 3. Convert the amount required into yield over maturity of note.

The 85 bps can be converted into equivalent yield on a 9 1/2-year maturity note by discounting at the 9 1/2-year swap rate:

−85 bps upfront = −12 bps yield for 9 1/2 years

This yield is the spread that has to be removed from the coupon spread of the collared FRN in order to pay for the removal of the cap and floor.

Step 4. Add the above yield spread to the collared FRN's coupons:

$$\text{Net LIBOR coupon} = \text{LIBOR} + 0.125\% - 0.12\%$$
$$= \text{LIBOR} + 0.005\%$$

This is the actual asset swap yield, or the yield an investor would receive on the stripped note by paying par.

Step 5. Calculate the asset swap bid price given the investor's required yield.

In order to produce an asset-swapped note yielding LIBOR + 0.20%, the bid price would have to be decreased to below par to reflect the present value of the difference between the target spread (0.20%) and the actual asset swap spread (0.005%):

$$\text{Diff} = 0.20\% - 0.005\%$$
$$= 0.195\% \text{ over 9 1/2 years}$$
PV = 140 bps upfront

To produce a note yielding LIBOR + 0.20%, the asset swap bid price should be par minus the PV calculated above, or

$$\text{Asset swap price} = 100.00\% - 1.40\%$$
$$= 98.60\%$$

This is the price at which the note would yield LIBOR + 0.20%. If the structurer were to sell the note to the investor at the same price, no profit would be made. Thus the actual bid price would be lower than the asset swap price to reflect trader profit. Assuming the trader wants to make 10 bps of profit on the transaction, the price at which the trader would purchase this note would be:

Bid price = Asset swap price – Fees

= 98.60% – 0.10%

Bid price = 98.50%

To recap the entire transaction, the secondary structured note trader would purchase the note from Investor A at 98.50%, perform a hedge to sell out the embedded options, and sell the note at 100% to Investor B. Investor B would pass all the cash flow from the collared FRN's coupons to the swap counterparty and in return receive a periodic cash flow of LIBOR + 0.20%.

Asset swap basis pricing allows an investor who may not have an interest rate view to purchase a complicated structured note simply for a yield enhancement over a comparable floating rate note of the same issuer. With the proliferation of structured notes as an investment tool, the supply of secondary structured notes that are available for asset swapping has likewise grown dramatically.

STRAIGHT PRICING

In contrast to the asset swapped note, a note that trades on a straight basis is bought as is, and sold as is. No additional transactions are involved. The secondary note trader would attempt to purchase the note at a price below where it can be sold to another buyer. Although this sounds simple, it requires that the trader have a good knowledge of the market in this particular structure. For example, a trader is asked to put a bid on the following structure:

Issuer: U.S. Agency
Coupon: Prime – 2.50%
Maturity: 4.5 years remaining

In order to bid intelligently, the trader must be familiar with the level at which Agency Prime FRNs of approximately five years in maturity have recently traded, and whether any market conditions have changed dramatically since the last such transaction. The trader also needs to know which investors have bought or sold that particular structure in the past and whether that structure still carries investor interest. In summary, the trader must have a good sense of the current market and players in the particular structure in order to trade intelligently on a straight basis.

Straight pricing rarely emerges an esoteric structure. Even for relatively straightforward structures, there is usually a "get-acquainted" period between the first disclosure of a new structure and when the structure might attain straight pricing. New structures that have large notional amounts (which enhance liquidity) and are publicly disclosed (on sources such as Telerate and Reuters) tend to attain straight pricing quickly because of the broad market exposure that they receive.

Recent structures that have acquired straight pricing in the market include Prime and COFI FRNs, capped, floored, and collared FRNs, SURFs, and IANs.

Straight Pricing with No Interest Rate Movement

Straight pricing of structured notes in the absence of interest rate movement is a straightforward process. The trader must have the following information: the previously traded price, who the prospective buyers are, and how much structural difference exists between the current structure note being traded and the previously traded note. The following example illustrates this pricing process.

Example 11-2

A floating rate note trader has a client who wants to sell a 3-year Prime FRN. The trader knows that a 5-year Prime FRN of the same issuer with a coupon of Prime − 1.80% traded last week in the secondary market at 99.50. Interest rates have remained the same since that last trade. What should be the bid price? (All prices are excluding accrued interest.)

Issuer: Widget Corp.
Maturity: 3 years from settlement
Coupon: Prime − 2.00%

Solution

The following table summarizes the differences between the two structures:

Characteristics	Last Trade	Current Trade
Maturity	5 years	3 years
Coupon	Prime − 1.80%	Prime − 2.00%

In order to observe the effect of the structural differences, the trader needs the following information:

1. What is the effect of two extra years of maturity on the required yield?
2. What is the additional credit spread required for two additional years?

The two pieces of market information that will be required are:

1. Find equivalent LIBOR based rates for the two notes. This will allow the comparison of the two structures on a LIBOR basis since credit spreads can be expressed on a LIBOR basis (but not on a Prime basis).
2. Find the difference between the issuer's 3-year LIBOR based credit spread versus 5-year credit spread.

Step 1. The equivalent LIBOR coupon of the two can be found by examining the appropriate maturity Prime-LIBOR swap. These swap rates are:

3 years: Prime – 2.35% versus LIBOR
5 years: Prime – 2.25% versus LIBOR

The 3-year and 5-year Prime FRNs thus have the following equivalent LIBOR coupons:

3 years: LIBOR + 0.35%
5 years: LIBOR + 0.45%

The yield to the investor of the 5-year note that traded at 99.50 is approximately LIBOR + 0.57% (0.35% LIBOR spread + 0.12% yield equivalent of 50 bps).

Step 2. Widget Corp.'s credit spread differential between 3-year and 5-year maturity is 20 bps. This spread is subtracted from the 5-year yield to produce the anticipated 3-year yield for a par note:

3-year yield = LIBOR + 0.57% – 0.20%
= LIBOR + 0.37%

This is the yield that the 3-year should provide to the investor. Since the coupon on the 3-year Prime FRN is equivalent to LIBOR + 0.35%, the price should be below par to reflect the 2 bps of extra yield, i.e.,

$$PV = 100\% - (\text{PV of 2 bps of yield over 3 years})$$
$$= 100.00\% - 0.05\%$$
$$\approx 99.95\%$$

This is the price of the 3-year note that would bring it to parity with the 5-year Prime FRN's traded price. The trader would thus bid lower than 99.95% to lock in a gain.

Straight Pricing with Interest Rate Changes

A structured note can still be priced on a straight basis even if interest rates have shifted significantly from their levels on the original issue date. In order to account for the change in price due to interest rate movements, the trader has to understand the interest rate and volatility duration characteristics of the note and adjust the price accordingly. Pricing first generation structured notes requires the calculation of duration with respect to the to-maturity Treasury rate in order to calculate the change in value. For more complicated second generation notes, the trader should employ the concept of KTRD discussed earlier to analyze the structured note in question. The value of the note can then be calculated as the change in value from the original trade date as a result of interest rate changes in different portions of the yield curve.

Example 11-3

An investor offers the following CMT-LIBOR differential note for sale. The note was traded at par two days ago. The first coupon of the structure has not been fixed since the note's settlement date must be at least five business days from the initial trade date.

Issuer: U.S. Agency
Maturity: 3.0 years from settlement
Coupon: 10-year CMT minus 3-month LIBOR + 2.00%

In the interim, interest rates have moved the following amount:

Sector of U.S. Treasury Curve	Interest Rate Increase (bps)
0 to 3 year	35 bps
10 to 15 year	50 bps

What should the offer price be?

Solution

The KTRD of CMT-LIBOR differential notes was discussed earlier in Chapter 5 for a slightly different structure. The KTRD of a regular CMT-LIBOR FRN (as opposed to a forward starting CMT-LIBOR note) is as follows:

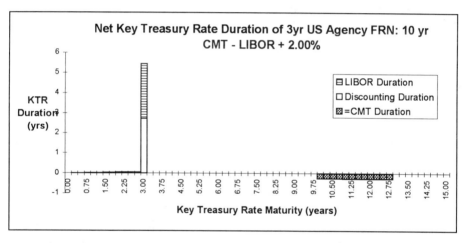

The above graph shows that the maximum positive durational exposure of the note is to the 3-year sector of the Treasury curve. To calculate the change in PV of the note, the interest rate change in each sector must be multiplied by the KTRD of that sector. Due to the definition of duration, the PV change for each Treasury sector is the *negative* of the product of the interest rate change and the KTRD.

Treasury Sector	Interest Rate Movement	KTRD of Treasury Sector	PV Change for Each Sector
0 to 3 year	0.35%	5.8	−1.92%
10 to 15 year	0.50%	−3.1	+1.55%
		Net PV Change:	**−0.37%**

The above durational calculation shows that the value of the note has dropped by 0.37% since trade date. Therefore, relative to the original new issue offer price of 100%, the current *offer* price should be 99.63%. Note that for this example, the CMT-LIBOR differential note has performed well relative to a fixed 3-year note, which would have lost 0.945% (0.35% interest rate rise * 2.7 duration) of value. Since the yield curve has steepened in this scenario, one can see that CMT-LIBOR FRNs do indeed perform well in a steepening yield curve environment.

An important issue to keep in mind is that secondary structured notes typically trade cheap to new issue notes. Thus, the price arrived at in the above calculation needs to be discounted further by a secondary-to-new-issue spread. This secondary-to-new-issue spread includes effects such as the amortized fee, accretion to par, and newness premium (if any).

ISSUER BUYBACK PRICING

Another avenue to liquidity in the secondary market is the willingness of some issuers to purchase back their own structured notes. Unfortunately, some issuers are not overly concerned about maintaining an orderly secondary market for their notes and would simply purchase back outstanding notes on an asset swap basis, creating arbitrage gains for themselves. Other issuers are more receptive to buying back the notes and extinguishing the entire issue at little or no gain to themselves in order to service the investor. Thus, issuer buyback pricing usually fluctuates, depending upon issuer and circumstance, between that of new issue pricing (this is a rare event since few issuers are willing to give up the originally achieved funding level without some compensation) and asset swap pricing. In the issuers' defense, it is customary for the structured note issuers to quickly allocate any funds they received from the initial note issuance and thus may not have any resources or cash to effect a buyback even if they wish to support the secondary market for their notes.

Relative Pricing Levels

The scale of the various secondary pricing schemes shows a consistent level of richness or poorness. In other words, some pricing schemes will be, in most cases, consistently richer or poorer than others. The following graph illustrates the richness or cheapness of each pricing scheme.

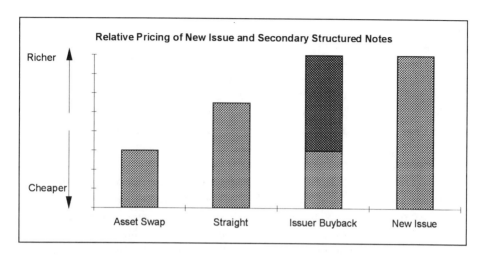

The highest price basis of a structured note is the new issue offer price. This is where a structurer can currently produce a structure on a new issue basis. Because the underwriting fees associated with newly issued notes have yet to be amortized, the new issue offer price is typically higher than any secondary market pricing scheme of the same structured note. The lowest price of a structured note is the asset swap bid price. This is the price at which an investor is willing to purchase a structured note whose structured cash flows have been swapped into a regular LIBOR (or fixed) coupon that generates good yield enhancement over a regular non-structured note of the same issuer. Because it represents the break-up value of the note, the asset swap bid is typically the lowest price given for a structured note. Certain notes can attain a straight, unswapped price that would be between the new issue offer price and the asset swap bid price. Finally, the issuer buyback price has been shown earlier as being typically between the asset swap and new issue basis.

STRAIGHT VERSUS ASSET SWAP PRICING AND SOME RULES OF THUMB

Despite the above discussions of asset swap and straight pricing, the question of identifying the correct price of the note still remains. When asset swap and straight prices differ, which price should be used? The unfortunate answer is that there is no rule that stipulates exactly when a note would be traded on which price basis. Depending on the timing, market reception, perception of the structure, and issuer liquidity (for issuer buyback) the note may be priced at either the asset swap, straight, or issuer buyback price.

The general determination of the note's trading basis is that the more complex a note, the more likely it is to be traded on an asset swap basis. Two rules of thumb generally apply: first, a structured note indexed to U.S. rates involving no more than two indices would usually trade on the straight basis since there is a large market of investors who are familiar with most of the U.S. indices. Secondly, most redemption linked structured notes usually trade on an asset swap basis.

Is there any situation when a note should be traded on an asset swap basis but instead trades differently? Situations in which this occurs do exist. One instance of this deviation occurs when the underwriter is using a portion of the initial structuring profit to maintain a market on the note and to keep the bid-ask spread within reason. When that occurs, the original underwriter is able to bid significantly higher than others and provide better-than-market pricing on the structured notes that it originally underwrote. Thus, it cannot be said that a structured note is blind to its own origins. The purchaser of a structured note is usually able to obtain a better bid-back price from the original structurer than from the rest of the street.

Other factors that can impact the pricing or pricing basis of secondary structured notes will be discussed in the following section.

OTHER SECONDARY PRICING CONSIDERATIONS

Overabundant Supply

The basic economic law of supply and demand shows that an oversupply of any commodity generally results in a lower price. Structured notes are no exception to this rule. An abundant supply of one particular structure in the market generates a definite downward pressure on prices. This occurred in late 1993[1] with the collared FRN. As mentioned in Chapter 5, the supply of new issue collared FRNs created in 1992–93 exceeded $20 billion. When rates continued to drop in 1993, the collared FRNs became more valuable due to their positive duration. However, the price appreciation of the collared FRNs was considerably less than asset swap pricing (or KTRD) would have predicted. As a result, some of the collared FRNs could have been purchased at prices below

---

1. See *Derivatives Week,* Nov. 15, 1993.

asset swap levels, creating good arbitrage opportunities whereby a trader could buy the undervalued notes and sell them on an asset-swapped LIBOR basis.

Issuer Downgrade

The effect of a downgrade of the original issuer of the structured note has a direct impact on the price of a structured note. Take the example of an investor who is interested in purchasing an asset swapped XYZ issued paper at a yield of LIBOR + 0.10%, which is 0.05% higher than currently outstanding XYZ LIBOR FRNs. If XYZ were downgraded, resulting in its outstanding FRNs trading at LIBOR + 0.25%, the asset swap transaction would have to provide the investor with a good yield increment to XYZ's outstanding LIBOR FRN yield in order for the trade to remain attractive. In addition, the swap counterparty performing the asset swap is now performing a swap where it would be receiving the structured coupon from a lesser rated credit. The swap counterparty would thus have to charge to reserve more against the lesser rating. Thus, in addition to the typical spread widening effect of a downgrade, secondary structured note pricing can drop further as a result of the asset swapping complication described above.

Marking-to-Market

As structured notes become an integral component of investors' portfolios, many investors have begun to require periodic mark-to-markets (some require such mark-to-market on a daily basis) of the structured notes in their portfolios. However, the investor should also be aware that mark-to-market pricing may not reflect the bid-offer spread of the note. Most often, mark-to-market levels are based on a mid-market valuation. Mid-market valuation is the mark-to-market convention because the underlying components of the note contain options whose bid-offer spread can widen in an unpredictable manner for different market conditions. Thus, rather than predicting the bid-to-mid spread, most market makers provide a mid-market mark-to-market.

Investors who obtain mark-to-market on secondary structured notes from pricing services should be aware that many such services are currently unable to accurately price these structures and often turn to the original broker-dealers for a daily quote. Thus, investors seeking an independent price quote from these sources should use both an internal mark-to-market as well as direct broker-dealer quotes in order to benchmark these pricing service marks.

Some investors encounter sticker shock when they try to sell their structured note holdings at the mark-to-market price and find that the bid price is significantly different from that level. The cause of this difference is the bid-to-mid market spread since mark-to-market levels are typically mid-market levels. If a note contains a significantly leveraged amount of underlying components, the combination of the bid-to-mid market spread of all the pieces can add up to a significant amount. For example, an Agency structured note with 10 embedded options (each with a bid-to-mid spread of 5 bps) would have a total bid-to-mid spread of 50 bps. Although 50 bps may seem large for an Agency security, this bid-to-mid spread is not exorbitant when viewed in the context of the 10 embedded options.

In order to obtain a more realistic mark-to-market, investors can demand a "bid-side" mark-to-market. Although the dealer may have to make estimations of the bid-to-mid spread, this mark-to-market would lessen the chance of surprise to the investor.

Size Penalty

Investors seeking to diversify holdings by purchasing small pieces of a large structured note deal should be aware of the presence of a secondary market size penalty. This size penalty is akin to the "odd-lot" penalty encountered by equity investors.

The market bid for a small notional amount piece of a secondary structured note is generally weaker than a larger notional amount piece. The definition of *small size* is usually a note whose notional amount is less than $10 million. A good rule of thumb is that secondary notes of sizes smaller than $10 million will produce a bid that is on the order of 0.25% lower than a larger size offering. A more general rule is that the more complicated the structure, the larger this size penalty. Like the presence of the "odd-lot" penalty in the equity market, the presence of a size penalty is an undeniable component of the secondary structured note market, and any structured note investor whose strategy is not of the buy-and-hold variety should be aware of this effect.

From the trader's perspective, the presence of the size penalty is due to two reasons:

1. Many investors refuse to purchase small sized secondary notes on an asset swapped basis. The bookkeeping and management costs asso-

ciated with an asset swap are simply not cost effective for smaller sized deals.
2. Most broker-dealers have difficulty selling these small notional amount pieces and thus end up holding the notes on their own books for an extended period of time. The hedging transactions that are required to maintain the value of these small pieces is often not cost effective for smaller sized notes.

Maturity Penalty

In addition to the size penalty, secondary prices of structured notes can be impaired by the maturity of the underlying note. It has been observed that structured notes whose maturities are longer than five years suffer a maturity penalty, i.e., secondary bid prices are typically lower than would be expected from asset swap levels. There are two reasons for this penalty. First, the great majority of structured note investors prefer maturities of five years and shorter. Longer maturity notes (even those issued by U.S. Agencies) thus are purchased by a much more limited universe of investors and thus suffer more price illiquidity. The second reason for the maturity penalty is that most swap dealers are rated single-A and usually are limited by the end investor to performing shorter-dated asset swaps, i.e., five years or shorter in maturity. Longer maturity structured notes often cannot be sold on an asset swap basis and thus have less access to price liquidity.

CONCLUSION

This chapter illustrates the dilemma of a structured note owner. Some readers might be surprised to discover that, unlike the U.S. Treasury note market, there may not be a well defined pricing methodology for a structured note. A multitude of issues such as availability, market conditions, issuer buyback policies, and other factors combine to determine the basis on which a secondary note is traded.

The most esoteric structures are priced on an asset-swapped basis, while the more generic structures are priced on a straight basis. Since a structured note may contain many different component pieces, even a note that is priced on a break-up value basis can produce a range of prices from different dealers. The investor should be cognizant of the fact that the more complicated the structure, the more transactions are necessary to unravel the structure, and hence the larger bid-ask margin since each transaction carries a transaction cost. In spite of all these secondary market complications, many investors prefer to purchase structured notes because it provides them with the desired play, exposure, and hedge; they view the secondary market complication as an inevitable part of the customization process.

12

Looking Forward

1994 was a pivotal year in the history of the derivative and structured note market. Some form of legislation regarding the regulation of derivatives appeared inevitable. The well-publicized losses of certain institutional and money market investors using derivatives had also contributed to an atmosphere of doubt and uncertainty.

This chapter will discuss some of the more recent regulatory and legislative developments in the structured note market, look forward to some potential future structures, and provide a summation of the topics discussed in this book.

REGULATORY AND LEGISLATIVE ACTION

The explosive growth in the use of structured notes and derivatives is a source of concern for regulators. 1994 saw increased clamor for action as regulators sought to prevent a junk-bond-like debacle. Regulators have focused on the large outstanding notional amount of swaps (over $4 trillion as of 1994) and the systematic dangers of the failure of a large broker creating a domino effect. The other area of concern to regulators is the 2a-7 money market funds, which are regarded by investors as quasi-substitutes for bank deposits. The recent well-publicized losses by money market fund managers which could bring about a fund's net asset value falling below par, i.e., "breaking the buck," provide more impetus for regulators to provide guidance and guidelines.

GAO REPORT OF 1994

The General Accounting Office's report on derivatives (GAO/GDD-94-133) was released in May 1994 after more than two years of study. It made the following recommendations:[1]

To Congress:

1. Bring currently unregulated OTC derivatives activities of securities firms and insurance companies under the purview of one of the currently existing financial regulatory agencies. One possibility is to create an interagency commission under the sponsorship of the SEC to establish principals and standards.
2. Systematically revamp and modernize U.S. financial regulatory system. Periodic hearings should be held on recent developments which could affect the safety, soundness, and stability of the U.S. financial system.

To Financial Regulators:

1. Maintain current information accessible to all regulators.
2. Develop standardized and consistent capital standards for OTC derivatives dealers.
3. Establish internal control requirements for OTC dealers.
4. Perform annual examination of OTC dealers' risk management systems.
5. Work to develop workable regulations on disclosure, netting, and accounting standards.

To FASB:

1. Move quickly to finalize its current draft on disclosure and fair value of derivatives.

---

1. GAO/GDD-94-133. United States General Accounting Office. *Financial Derivatives— Actions Needed to Protect the Financial System,* 1994, pp.123–129.

2. Provide consistent accounting rules for derivative products.
3. Consider adopting a standard market value accounting model for all financial instruments.

To the SEC:

1. Ensure that SEC registrants who use derivatives extensively establish consistent internal controls and risk management systems. Encourage internal audits of these systems.
2. Ensure that FASB quickly adopt comprehensive, consistent accounting rules and disclosure requirements.

SEC

In July 1994, the Securities and Exchange Commission detailed in a letter to managers of money market funds a list of structured notes that the SEC considers inappropriate for 2a-7 money market investors due to the inherent interest rate risk of these notes which would remove the certainty of their being periodically resettable back to par price. The list includes the following structured notes:

1. Capped FRNs
2. COFI FRNs
3. Dual index FRNs (differential notes)
4. CMT FRNs
5. Inverse and leveraged FRNs
6. Multi-step-up callable notes (not discussed in this book)

In addition, the SEC is also in the midst of a major revision of the rules governing 2a-7 money market funds. The main points of revision appear to be aimed at reducing the market risk of 2a-7 accounts. These may include restrictions on the types of instruments that can be purchased and a diversification requirement in stipulating the maximum amount (as a fraction of the overall portfolio) of one issuer's debt that a 2a-7 fund can hold.

OCC

In July of 1994, the Office of the Comptroller of the Currency issued an advisory letter (AL 94-2) to CEOs of U.S. national and community banks warning them about the risks of investing in structured notes. The main thrust of the advisory letter is that banks should be fully aware of the implicit risk of structured notes, and that due to *"the risks involved and the difficulty in assessing these risks, some types of structured securities are inappropriate investments for most national banks."* The letter also implicitly warned that the banks should not be misled into believing by the structured note issuer's high *credit* rating that the structured note's overall risk is minimal.

OTS

Following in the footsteps of the SEC and OCC, the Office of Thrift Supervision issued its own warnings to thrifts about structured notes. In its letter (OTS Thrift Bulletin 65) issued in August, the OTS set out guidelines for thrifts to follow prior to purchasing structured notes:

1. The risks of the structured notes must be understood. Sensitivity and/or simulation analysis to demonstrate the performance of the note under different market conditions is encouraged prior to purchasing a note.
2. The issues of liquidity and pricing of the structured notes in the secondary markets must be known.
3. The structured notes should be consistent with the investment strategy of the thrifts.

The OTS sounded an ominous warning by concluding that a failure to follow the above guidelines would constitute *"an unsafe and unsound practice."*

FEDERAL RESERVE

The Federal Reserve joined the chorus of warnings about structured notes by issuing a letter in August 1994 to bank examiners and supervisors. The letter (SR94-45), titled *Supervisory Policies Relating to Structured Notes*, points out that the inherent risks of structured notes may be inappropriate for certain depository institutions. It urged examiners to assess the ability of the institutions to understand, analyze, and manage the risks of structured notes and perform scenario and simulation analysis. It does point out that, if properly analyzed and managed, "structured notes can be acceptable investments and trading products for banks." However, the Federal Reserve concluded with a similar refrain as the OTS, that a failure of bank management to understand the risks of structured notes can *"constitute an unsafe and unsound practice for banks."*

ACCOUNTING AND DISCLOSURE REQUIREMENTS: FASB

The Financial Accounting Standards Board (FASB) has issued several rules (referred to as the Financial Accounting Standards, or FAS) which are relevant to the structured note market. The two main standards deal with disclosure and accounting.

Investors seeking the latest accounting standards for structured notes and other investment vehicles are directed to Williams's work on general accepted accounting practice.[2] Some of the relevant accounting standards and rules which apply to structured notes and derivatives are summarized below.

FAS 105, 107

FAS 105 and 107 were FASB rules released in 1990 and 1991 dealing with disclosure standards. FAS 105 and 107 were the first two steps in dealing with proper disclosure and measurement of financial instrument risk. Specifically, FAS 105 imposes disclosure standards on off-balance-sheet risk of accounting loss and significant concentration of risk. FAS 107 amended FAS 105 and imposed disclosure standards of fair value of financial instruments. FASB is currently working on the next phase of this work, which will deal with issues of measurement and recognition of financial instruments.

FAS 115

In 1994, the FAS 115 rule on accounting of derivative positions was issued to take effect for fiscal years starting after December 15, 1993. FAS 115 clarified the rules of accounting and reporting for equity and debt securities. Specifically, all such securities are to be classified into one of three investment categories and accounted for accordingly. The classifications and treatments are as follows:

---

2. Williams, Jan R. *1994 GAAP Guide.* New York, NY: Harcourt Brace & Co., 1994.

Classification	Accounting Treatment
Held to maturity (HTM)	Amortized cost
Trading security	Fair value
	Unrealized P/L included in earnings
Available for sale	Fair value
	Unrealized P/L excluded from earnings, reported as separate component of shareholder equity

Source: 1994 GAAP Guide.

Final FASs

In August 1994, the FASB announced that the final step of amending current rules dealing with derivative disclosure requirements will be concluded by October with the release of a final statement, *"Disclosure about Derivative Financial Instruments and Fair Value of Financial Instruments."* As reported by *Swaps Monitor*,[3] the statement will:

1. Require disclosure of options owned.
2. Clarify fair value disclosure and require increasing disclosure information.
3. Require that derivatives be classified as either for trading or other purposes. This appears to be an extension of FAS 115.
4. Require reports of trading losses or gains if the derivative is classified as a trading instrument.
5. Require disclosure of purpose of holding derivatives if derivative is not classified as trading instrument.
6. Require disclosure of nature of transaction being hedged if derivative is classified as a hedging instrument.
7. Encourage disclosure of quantitative information used in risk management.

LEGISLATIVE

Recent action by several Congressional members appears to promise that there will be some measure of government control over the derivatives industry. The well-publicized debacles of unsophisticated municipal retire-

---

3. *Swaps Monitor,* Aug. 29, 1994.

ment fund managers purchasing mortgage IOs (and losing 50% or more of principal) as well as money market funds on the brink of "breaking the buck" have maintained the pressure on Congress to do something to protect the financial community and small investor from a junk-bond-like crisis.

The pendulum of regulation appears to be swinging towards legislation that will restrict derivatives and their uses by investors. The next few years will be instrumental in determining the form of the derivative and structured note market for many years to come. Certain proposals currently before Congress plan to establish a Derivatives Commission in the manner of the SEC that oversees the derivatives market. Regardless of the outcome of these proposals, it is apparent that the form of the derivatives market in five years will be quite different from its current condition.

Even without legislative action, recent losses by structured note investors have resulted in issuers and investors taking it upon themselves to address the issues of risk and appropriateness. Some issuers now require that the broker-dealer sell structured notes to only "sophisticated investors" as defined by Regulation D of the Securities Act of 1933. Investors likewise have begun to monitor risks closer. Many now request periodic (daily, weekly, or monthly) mark-to-market prices to be furnished by either the underwriters or independent pricing agencies. Investors have also begun to proactively request risk assessment from dealers/underwriters of structured notes to fully understand the risks involved before making a purchase. These investor and issuer initiatives should be applauded.

Rating Agencies

The two largest rating agencies (Moody, Standard & Poor) have long been reticent about assigning a top tier rating to a structured note issued by a U.S. Agency because they feared that the AAA rating could be interpreted by investors to refer to the overall risk of the note, which includes the interest rate component of risk. In July 1994, S&P announced[4] that it was reassigning ratings to some 800 mortgage and structured notes issued by U.S. Agencies and other issuers, producing a new rating referring to interest rate risk. The use of this "r" rating will be employed on the following types of notes:

1. Notes whose coupon or principal are linked to non-interest indices such as equity, commodity, and/or currency.

---

4. S&P CreditWire as reported by *Bloomberg Financial Markets,* July 11, 1994.

2. Notes whose maturity is uncertain and linked to certain interest rate conditions.
3. Notes that automatically convert to common stock.
4. Mortgage IO, PO, and residuals (if they contain risks associated with IO or PO).
5. Notes whose redemption is linked to indices. However, principal linkage which can only benefit and not hurt investors would not receive the "r" designation.
6. Leveraged inverse floaters (leverage capped floaters).
7. Notes linked to basket of stock.

Notes which will not receive a designation of "r" are issues which are linked to "commonly used interest rate" such as LIBOR, COFI, T-bill, etc.

STRUCTURAL INNOVATIONS

In spite of the very difficult market circumstances of the second quarter of 1994, structured note market participants continue to innovate and provide solutions that simply cannot be obtained elsewhere. Some of the innovations, both current and future, are outlined below.

New and Potential Indices

As long as there is investor demand for new indices, structured notes will be created around that demand. Much as the original Quanto note arose from investor interest in making non-domestic interest rate plays payable in domestic currency, future indices will be able to provide investors with the required view or hedge. A list (by no means complete) of the indices which could potentially form the basis of the next great structured note success includes:

CPI. This index is of particular interest to corporations and insurance companies which have considerable exposure to the inflation rate. It is a difficult index for structurers to hedge because of the multitude of factors involved.
Long-dated CRB. As of 1994, the CRB index futures trade out to only 1 year, and even those contracts have little liquidity. Longer-dated CRB acts as a proxy for the CPI.
Unemployment. Insurance companies have exposure to this via their payment of unemployment compensation. Corporations also have native exposure to this index.

Credit differential. This is an extension of the bond index note, where an investor would be able to receive the benefit of spread widening or narrowing between two baskets of securities. This would be useful in assisting investors to reallocate assets with great flexibility.

Default. The extension of the credit derivative is the default derivative. Investors will soon be able to purchase notes linked to the default probability of certain companies.

Real estate. This is one area of derivatives that has as yet generated much promise but little payoff. Most real estate linked notes are highly customized structures of small size. However, in the face of stagnant fixed income and equity markets, investors are increasingly looking to alternative investments such as real estate linked notes for gains.

Unique risk basket. Investors who want exposure to unique risks such as the probability of an earthquake occurring in a certain area or a movie performing well at the theaters will be provided such plays via structured notes. The structuring entity will begin to resemble insurance companies such as Lloyds of London by providing these risk hedges or plays.

Trust Structures

Several structurers (Merrill Lynch, Morgan Stanley, and Goldman Sachs) have created trust-based structures which permit investors to purchase, in essence, asset-swapped securities without having to perform a swap with the swap counterparty. A sample trust structure is illustrated in the graph at the top of page 392.

Instead of purchasing a security, the investor purchases a trust certificate that is structured to pay out a desired cash flow from a trust which is collateralized by a structured (or unstructured) note. The swap counterparty performs the swap with the trust to convert the structured cash flow from the underlying security to the desired cash flow of the trust certificate. The trust, if rated by the rating agencies, would generally have the same credit rating as the underlying collateral security.

If the structured note or regular fixed coupon note which is the trust collateral has at least a 70% minimum principal guarantee, the rating agencies will generally grant the trust with the same rating as the underlying security. Investors should understand that if the structuring swap counterparty fails, all that remains would be the trust collateral. Thus, even though the investor would hold a highly rated security if the swap counterparty should

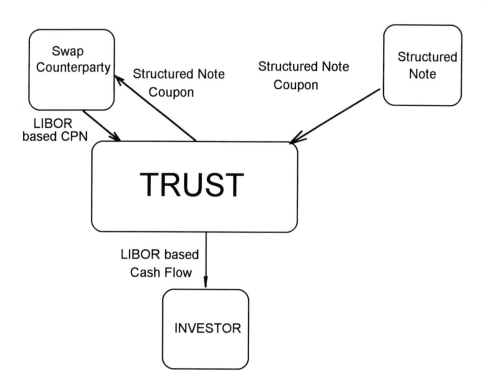

fail, the cash flow characteristics of the collateral security will most likely be far different from the cash flow envisioned by the swap supported trust.

Liquidity

As mentioned previously, the structured note market has grown enormously in both the notional amount of outstanding issues as well as the associated liquidity of such secondary issues. Many securities firms now have full-time asset swap and secondary structured note trading desks dedicated to secondary trading of structured notes.

The newest twist along this theme was unveiled by IBRD (The World Bank) in January 1994. The World Bank created a liquidity facility which obligates a number of dealers to make secondary market prices on all World Bank issued structured notes. The World Bank will also work to restructure a structured note, in essence buying back an outstanding structured note and reissuing a different structured note to the investor. The catch here, of course, is that it is not a zero margin transaction since some profits must be made in order to convince the IBRD and the dealers to continue the process. The investor should thus recognize that issuer buybacks and secondary structuring are not free lunches.

LOOKING FORWARD

Structured notes are extremely powerful financial instruments that have permitted many investors to achieve results which simply cannot be obtained elsewhere. They have changed the face of the fixed income market from one where investors have to select from a rigid menu of products to one in which the investor can purchase a product that is custom-tailored for his or her needs. However, the future growth of structured notes can only be achieved through greater investor understanding of both rewards and risks and it is incumbent upon the derivatives community to inform and educate the investors to the risks of these new instruments.

The stated and oft-repeated goal of this book is to increase investor awareness of the potential risks and benefits of structured notes and to ensure that all parties understand the underlying mechanics that drive the structured note market. The participants in the structured note market must remain ever vigilant against risk due to the prevalence of new and exciting structures that are constantly being generated.

The brief but spectacular growth of the structured note market has engendered much innovation and new ideas. From the flourishing of new and different structures that have sprung up over just the past few years, there is little doubt that this will continue.

SUMMARY

This book attempted to shed some light on a very sophisticated corner of the fixed income market. The basic tools of structured note risk and performance analysis were provided to the readers. The different types of structured notes were then presented and the analytic tools were applied to analyzing the risk and performance of these notes. Other relevant issues such as the secondary market, comparisons to cash and futures, and the structured note creation process were also addressed. Finally, this chapter provided a look at the current condition of the structured note market and what the future might bring.

It is hoped that, after reading this book, the reader is able to come away with an enhanced understanding of the risk and performance analysis methodology which can be applied to the examination of current and future structures. Only by understanding the risks of structured notes can an investor truly take full advantage of the benefits that such structures can bring.

Index

A

Accrual notes, 210

B

Binary accrual note, 219
Black-76 Option Pricing Model, 37–38

C

Capped and floored FRNs
  capped floating rate note
    (CapFRN), 119–128
  definition of, 104
  floored floating rate note (FFRN),
    137–145
  leveraged capped FRN (LCFRN),
    128–137
Capped floating rate note (CapFRN),
  119–128
  analysis of, 121–122
  discussion of, 119–120
  history, 120–121
  interest rate risk, 122, 126
  performance, 122
  volatility risk, 126, 128
CMT-LIBOR differential notes
  analysis of, 195–196
  discussion of, 192, 194
  history, 194–195
  interest rate risk, 196, 201
  performance, 196
  volatility risk, 201–203
Collared floating rate notes (CFRNs)
  analysis of, 146
  definition of, 104
  discussion of, 1145
  history of, 145–146
  interest rate risk, 147, 151
  performance, 146–147
  volatility risk, 151, 153
Commodity linked note (CLN)
  analysis of, 277–280
  commodity index, 276–277
  convenience yield and forward
    commodity prices, 289

discussion of, 275–276
history of, 276
performance/risk with respect to
    spot gold prices, 280–284
performance/risk with respect to
    U.S. interest rate, 284–289
Constant maturity Treasury (CMT)
    and constant maturity swap
    (CMS) FRNs
analysis of, 175
discussion of, 174
history of, 174–175
performance of, 176
risk, 176, 179, 181
Coupon currency indexed note
    (CCIN), 259
Creation and customization of
    structured notes
conceptual phase requirements in,
    298–299
customization factors in, 299–304
example of conceptual/identification
    stages in the, 304–305
example of, of an FRN, 306–309
example of optionality in the,
    311–314
of first generation structures,
    305–314
main steps of, 297–298
obtaining relevant market/issuer
    information for, 305
of second generation structures,
    314–326
summary of the, 326
termsheets in the, 309–311
Cross-category notes
asset allocation with, 257
classifications of, 258
commodity linked note (CLN),
    275–289
currency indexed note (CIN),
    258–275

discussion of, 255
equity linked note (ELN),
    290–292
hedging with, 256
risk analysis, 258
risk capital utilization of, 255–256
summary of, 296
total return index notes (TRIN),
    293–295
Currency indexed note (CIN)
analysis of, 260–263
discussion of, 258–259
duration with respect to U.S.
    interest rate, 267–271
duration with respect to DM
    interest rate, 272–275
FX rate variation, 263–267
history of, 259–260

D

Deleveraged CMT FRN
analysis of, 184–185
discussion of, 181, 183
history of, 183–184
interest rate risk, 185, 188–192
performance, 185
volatility risk, 192
Deleveraged Prime FRN (DPF)
analysis of, 114
history, 113–114
performance of, 115
risk of, 115, 119
Deterministic analysis; *see also*
    Expectation analysis, Forward
    analysis, Historical analysis,
    Simulation analysis, Structured
    notes
definition of, 49
simulation analysis vs., 93–95
summary of deterministic scenario
    analyses, 74–75

types of, used in assessing
structured note risk, 49–50
Duration; *see also* Deterministic
analysis, Simulation analysis,
Structured notes
calculation of, 26–28
discounting rate duration (DRD), 23
KTRD (key Treasury rate
duration), 28–36, 47, 173
misconceptions of structured note,
36–37
non-interest rate index, 41
for notes with optionality
components, 37–38
option adjusted duration (OAD),
93–96
Prime FRN and, 113
review of, 22
of a structured note, 23–24
volatility, 98–99, 101
volatility, and option vega, 39–41
when index rate and discounting
rate are identical, 25–26
when index rate and discounting
rate are not identical, 28–29

E

Equity linked note (ELN)
discussion of, 190
history of, 290
indices, 290–292
Exchange rate mechanism (ERM),
259–260
Exchange-traded products
advantages of, over structured
notes, 359–360
disadvantages of, 360–363
growth of the, market, 355–358
investor criteria for, 358–359
replicability of structured notes via,
363–366

Expectation analysis; *see also*
Deterministic analysis
as an alternative analysis, 59–60
LSE (linear smooth expectation)
analysis, 60
LSE methodology, 60–61
LSE to horizon date, 61–65
LSE to maturity, 61

F

First generation structured notes; *see
also* Structured notes
analysis of, 104–107
capped and floored FRNs,
119–145
capped floating rate note
(CapFRN), 119–128
characteristics of, 103–104
collared floating rate note (CFRN),
145–153
deleveraged Prime floating rate
note (DPF), 113–119
floating rate note (FRN), 107–119
floored floating rate note (FFRN),
137–145
inverse floating rate note (IFRN),
153–161
leveraged capped floating rate note
(LCFRN), 128–137
Prime floating rate note, 108–113
Superfloater, 162–168
summary of, 168, 170
Flex options, 355, 358, 360
Floating rate notes (FRNs)
definition of, 104
deleveraged Prime FRN (DPF),
113–119
history of, 107–108
LIBOR as most popular index for,
107
Prime FRN, 108–113

Floored floating rate note (FFRN)
    analysis of, 138–139
    discussion of, 137
    history of, 137–138
    interest rate risk, 142
    performance, 139
    volatility risk, 142, 145
Forward analysis; *see also*
        Deterministic analysis
    application of, 50
    benchmarking, 57–58
    failure of, 58–59
    to an intermediate horizon date,
        51–54
    to maturity date, 50–51, 55–57
Futures market
    review of, 353–354

H

Historical analysis; *see also*
        Deterministic analysis
    analysis of Prime-LIBOR
        differential note using, 69–74
    discussion of, 65–69
    methodology, 69–74

I

Index amortizing notes
    analysis of 229
    discussion of, 226, 228
    history, 228–229
    interest rate risk, 230–234
    performance, 229–230
    volatility risk, 234, 238
Inverse floating rate notes (IFRNs)
    analysis of, 155, 157
    definition of, 104
    discussion of, 153–154
    history of, 154–155

interest rate risk, 157, 161
performance, 157
volatility risk, 161

K

Key Treasury rate duration (KTRD);
    see Duration

L

Leveraged capped FRN (LCFRN)
    analysis of, 130–131
    discussion of, 128–129
    history, 129–130
    interest rate risk, 134
    performance, 131, 134
    volatility risk, 134, 137
LIBOR differential (Quanto) notes
    analysis, 240–241
    discussion of, 238–239
    history of, 239–240
    interest rate risk, 243, 245
    performance, 241
    volatility risk, 245
LIBOR enhancement accrual note
        (LEAN)
    analysis of, 212, 214
    discussion of, 210–211
    history of, 211–212
    interest rate risk, 214, 217
    performance, 214
    volatility risk, 217, 219
Linear smooth expectation (LSE)
        analysis; *see* Expectation
        analysis

M

Monte Carlo simulation; *see*
    Simulation analysis

O

One-way collared (OWC) note
analysis of, 221–222
discussion of, 220
history of, 221
interest rate risk, 223, 226
performance, 222
volatility risk, 226
Option pricing theory
definition of vega in, 40
Option vega
relationship of volatility duration
and, 39–41
Options market
review of, 353–354
Over-the-counter (OTC) derivatives
market
growth of the, 355–358

P

Performance measurement
comparison to fixed rate note,
44–45
comparison to floating rate note,
45–46
internal rate of return and present
value, 41–43, 47
Portfolio management
active, 331–333, 337–338
asset allocation selection process
summary, 331–332
advantages of indexing and passive
management, 330
considerations in asset selection, 331
determining investment suitability
in, 335
index portfolio selection, 329–330
liquidity, 350
passive, 328–330

priorities of a portfolio manager,
327–328
risk and asset/liability management
(ALM), 333–338
risk measurement, 334–335
risk monitoring, 335–337
risk selection, 332–333
role of structured notes in, 338–350
structured notes for active portfolio
managers, 341–350
structured notes for passive
portfolio managers, 339–341
summary of, 351
Power notes
analysis of, 247–248
discussion of, 247
history of, 247
interest rate risk, 250
performance, 248, 250
volatility risk, 250, 254
Prime FRN
analysis of, 109–110
discussion of, 108
duration and, 113
history of, 109
internal rate of return and, 110, 113
Prime-LIBOR differential notes
analysis of, 204–206
discussion of, 203
history, 203–204
interest rate risk, 206, 209
performance, 206
volatility risk, 209
Principal currency indexed note, 259
Principal exchange rate linked notes
(PERLs), 259

Q

Quanto notes; *see* LIBOR differential
notes

R

Random walk model, 80–81
Range notes, 210
Ratchet floater, 220–226
Risk measurement
  discounting rate determination, 23–24
  duration and, 22–23, 25–38
  index rate determination, 24–25
  structured note, 21–41
  volatility, 39–41

S

Second generation structured notes; *see also* Structured notes
  binary accrual note, 219–220
  accrual notes (range notes), 210
  CMT-LIBOR differential notes, 192–203
  constant maturity Treasury and constant maturity swap FRNs, 174–181
  deleveraged CMT FRN, 181–192
  discussion of, analysis, 173
  exotic options, 209–238
  index amortizing notes, 226–238
  index maturity to reset frequency mismatch, 174–191
  key characteristics of, 171–173
  LIBOR differential (Quanto) notes, 238–245
  LIBOR enhancement accrual note (LEAN), 210–219
  multi-index notes, 192–209
  one-way collared (OWC) note (ratchet or sticky floater), 220–226
  power notes, 247–254
  Prime-LIBOR differential notes, 203–209
  Quanto notes, 173, 238–245

  summary of, 254
  unusual leverage, 245–254
Secondary structured note market
  asset pricing swap, 367–371
  issuer buyback pricing, 376–377
  issuer downgrade price considerations, 379
  marking-to-market price considerations, 379–380
  maturity penalty price considerations, 381
  methods of structured note pricing, 367
  overabundant supply price considerations, 378–379
  size penalty price considerations, 380–381
  straight pricing, 371–372
  straight pricing with interest rate changes, 374–376
  straight pricing with no interest rate movement, 372–374
  straight vs. asset swap pricing, 377–378
  summary of, 381–382
Simulation analysis; *see also* Deterministic analysis, Structured notes
  deterministic analysis vs., 93–95
  discussion of, 77–78
  Monte Carlo, as the preferred technique, 78
  Monte Carlo rate simulation, 79–81
  the random walk model, 80–81
  for a range of expectations, 86–93
  steps to implementing a, 81–86
  summary of, 99, 101
  of two or more indices, 97
  volatility duration, 98–99
  when to use, 78–79
Sticky floater, 220–226

Structured note(s); *see also* Creation and customization of structured notes, Cross-category notes, First generation structured notes, Portfolio management, Second generation structured notes, Secondary structured note market
  accounting and disclosure requirements, 387–388
  analysis of first generation, 103–107
  cash and futures vs., 353–366
  concerns of regulatory agencies regarding, 385–387
  considerations for new investors in, 18–20
  evolution, growth, and issues regarding, 1–5
  examining, risk/return in a deterministic environment, 49–75
  exchange-traded products vs., 359–360
  GAO report of 1994, 384–385
  investors in, 9–14
  issuers of, 5–9
  liquidity, 392–393
  new and potential indices, 390–391
  performance measurement of, 41–47
  rating agencies, 389–390
  regulatory and legislative action, 383–390
  replicability of, via exchange and cash products, 363–366
  risk measurement of, 21–41
  termsheet, 15–18
  trust structures, 391–392
  summary of, 393–394
Superfloaters
  analysis of, 163
  definition of, 104
  discussion of, 162
  history of, 162–163
  interest rate risk, 165, 168
  performance, 165
  volatility risk, 168
SURF note, 181–192

T

Time horizon, 44
Total return index notes (TRIN)
  cross-credit structures, 294
  discussion of, 293–294
  effects of issuer upgrade and downgrade, 294
  sample bond index note, 295

Y

Yield curve accrual note (YCAN), 219–220